Savory Baking

Savory Baking

Recipes for Breakfast, Dinner, and Everything in Between

Erin Jeanne McDowell

Photographs by Mark Weinberg

HARVEST

An Imprint of WILLIAM MORROW

HarperCollins books may be purchased for educational, business, or sales pro-motional use. For information, please email the Special Markets Department at SPsales@harpercollins.com.

FIRST EDITION
Designed by Allison Chi
Photographs by Mark Weinberg
Library of Congress Cataloging-in-Publication Data has been applied for.
ISBN 978-0-358-67140-4
22 23 24 25 26 TC 10 9 8 7 6 5 4 3 2 1

TO MICKEY, MY FAVORITE ADVENTURER..
From: RED WOOD

For Derek, with all
my heart—
Sookie had Jackson,
Rose has Woody,
Julia had Paul,
and I have you.

Welcome to the Office
of the City Clerk
The City of New York

C059

Ceremonies

Please have a seat.

Contents

Before You Dig In . . .

Yes, I have an insatiable sweet tooth. It might be impossible to be this deeply in love with baking and not have one. But a few years back, I started noticing a pattern when it came to my baking style. Whenever I was given the freedom to bake something new, I was turning instead to my trusty—and undeniably passionate—*salt tooth*. I loved surprising friends who come to stay with biscuits and gravy for breakfast. When I wanted to impress a large group of colleagues, I spent an afternoon slow-roasting tomatoes, simmering bacon jam, and laminating Gruyère into rough puff pastry dough to make piles of savory pastries. When my parents came for a visit, I invited my friends and "adopted family" over for a big soiree. I baked three kinds of vegetable galettes, which I served with mounds of vinegary salad served alongside and basked in the glow as everyone dove in around one large crust-crumb–covered table.

I've always wanted to write a book dedicated to savory baking: the cheesy, the crispy, the melty, warm, and doughy. Yummy things to snack on, perfect party bites, and tons of stuff for breakfast, dinner, and everything in between. Savory baking is far from a baking trend—there are beloved savory bakes in just about every corner of the world, and these classics were a huge inspiration and jumping-off point as I built this collection of recipes, one I hope is as varied and exciting as the world of savory baking itself. I've been making and honing some of these recipes since I first started spending time in the kitchen at the age of sixteen, but I've also included new ideas, tips, and tricks that I've learned along the way.

This book is intended to inspire you to think creatively with your own baking. The chapters that follow are filled with dozens of recipes that can be customized in multiple ways for a variety of different results. Take one of the recipes I may have made more than any other, my drop biscuits, which are as delicious served on their own as they are baked atop a potpie filling. That's really what I love most about savory baking: it combines the pleasure and precision of pastry with the freedom and flexibility of cooking. In this book, I provide lots of detailed recipes, but also dozens of variations and idea sparkers meant to encourage you to play around and come up with your own versions to suit your taste buds.

And sweet toothers, never fear—there are plenty of sugary treats scattered throughout these pages. In the name of all that aforementioned creativity, there's a lot of overlap! That same biscuit I mention above? Split it and serve it with whipped cream and strawberries, and it's suddenly shortcake; or crumble atop juicy fruit for a truly perfect cobbler.

There's a sign that hangs right inside my front door to greet guests as they walk in: "Hope You're Hungry." That's what I wish for as you start to dive into these pages. This book shows how I incorporate my love of baking into every meal of the day in my own kitchen. Ring the dinner bell, set the table. *I hope you're hungry.*

CHAPTER 1

Easy and Essential Bakes

QUICKBREADS • MUFFINS • SCONES • BISCUITS • DUTCH BABIES

It seems only right to start this book's baking journey off the same way I did. My first job was after school at a bakery, just a few days a week. I made huge batches of the house scone and muffin mix to take some of the load off the morning baker's early shift. Prep work in professional kitchens means a lot of repetition, and I got a good feel for these baked goods really fast and was soon making boast-worthy versions of my own.

Even after years of baking, the recipes in this chapter are the ones I turn to again and again. Some because they are so easy to make—things like quickbreads, muffins, and Dutch babies. Others use basic baking skills worth knowing back-pocket well—the scones and biscuits. All of them are endlessly adaptable, made with simple techniques you'll want to turn to frequently in your own kitchen. So this chapter is a great place to start your own baking journey. There are a lot of delicious possibilities here.

PREP SCHOOL

How to Prepare Baking Pans

BAKING SHEETS: Usually I just line baking sheets with parchment paper. Some recipes require greasing the pans with nonstick spray, oil, or butter.

SQUARE OR RECTANGULAR BAKING PANS: Lightly grease the base and sides of the pan with nonstick spray. Cut a piece of parchment large enough to line the pan with plenty (2 to 3 inches/5 to 8 cm) of overhang on two opposite sides. Press the paper into the pan, then use scissors to make a small cut in each corner of the paper down to the base of the pan; this will allow the paper to fit flush into the corners. The paper overhang can be used as handles to unmold the baked good. (Alternatively, you can crisscross two pieces of parchment paper in the pan.)

LOAF PANS: Lightly grease the base and sides of the pan with nonstick spray. Some recipes call for lining the pan with parchment paper as described above for square/rectangular pans.

MUFFIN PANS: Lightly grease each cavity with nonstick spray, then lightly spray the top surface of the pan too. Alternatively, line the cavities with muffin liners and lightly spray the top surface of the pan.

CAST-IRON SKILLETS: Grease the base and sides of the skillet evenly with oil, butter, or nonstick spray.

CAKE PANS: Depending on the recipe, the pan may be simply greased (with nonstick spray, oil, or butter), greased and coated lightly with flour, or greased and lined with parchment.

PIE AND TART PANS: Most of these pie and tart recipes do not require any pan preparation, but a few give specific pan prep.

Blending Method

The blending method is the easiest mixing method out there—it's basically just mixing all the ingredients together. The dry ingredients are mixed together first, then the wet ingredients are mixed together, and finally the two are blended together to form an even batter. A whisk or a silicone spatula, or both (depending on the batter), can be used to mix the ingredients. Although these recipes are fairly foolproof, do take care not to overmix batters, which can yield tougher baked goods.

DONENESS INDICATORS

Determining doneness is important, as underbaking can yield wet, gummy interiors and overbaking can result in an overly thick crust and/or make the interior dry. Typically, testing with a skewer works best for items like quickbreads and muffins—if you insert the skewer into the thickest part of the pastry, it should come out clean or with just a few moist crumbs attached. For biscuits and scones, look for the desired level of browning and then press gently in the center: underbaked pastries will feel soft, properly baked interiors will spring back gently when touched.

GET FLEXIBLE

The blending method is one of the most easily adjustable in terms of ingredients—so have fun experimenting and creating new combinations!

ADD INCLUSIONS: Inclusions are super-flexible. You can add anything from chopped fresh ingredients to dry ingredients like nuts and seeds to cheese and even cooked proteins to customize your bakes.

SWAP LIQUIDS: It's fairly easy to vary the liquids in most of these recipes. For example, other dairy products can easily be subbed in recipes that call for buttermilk. If substituting thicker ingredients (like sour cream or yogurt), you may need to add slightly more than when using thinner ones (like milk or buttermilk) to achieve the desired consistency.

SWAP FLOURS: Different flours can be used in many of these recipes without needing to adjust them much (or at all). The general rule when substituting flour is to aim for a flour with a similar protein consistency. All-purpose flour can be replaced with whole wheat pastry flour, spelt flour, or gluten-free all-purpose blends in equal measures. Other flours, such as whole wheat, oat, or rye, can also be used, but for best results, they should be used in conjunction with all-purpose or bread flour. Start with 60 percent all-purpose and 40 percent other flour as a guideline.

Inclusions

Inclusion is just a fancy word for stuff mixed into your baked goods for more flavor and/or texture. You can add them to just about any recipe, but they are most often used for simple batters, like muffins and quickbreads, or doughs. Inclusions can be just about anything. Dry ingredients like nuts, seeds, dried fruit, and herbs can be incorporated fairly easily into most recipes. Fresh ingredients that contain moisture, like fruit, vegetables, cheese, or proteins such as meat and fish may require adjustments to the recipe to ensure the ideal result.

PREP SCHOOL

How to Use Fresh Ingredients as Inclusions

As you flip through the recipes in this chapter, you'll see that sometimes some of the savory ingredients require advance preparation before they are incorporated into a batter or dough. Firmer ingredients, like potatoes, may require cooking before they can be added to the recipe. Here are a few questions you can ask yourself about ingredients to determine whether or not they will require advance preparation:

Will the ingredient be sufficiently cooked in the time the baked good requires?
EXAMPLE: Diced raw potatoes may get enough bake time in a deep-dish pie, which requires a fairly long time in the oven, but even thinly sliced potatoes may not bake sufficiently atop a pizza, which takes much less time. Consider giving your fresh inclusions a brief boil, steam, or roast if they need a head start.

Is the ingredient high in moisture?
EXAMPLE: Ripe summer tomatoes may add so much moisture that they prevent a quiche custard from setting. Cooking or roasting the tomatoes first will reduce the moisture content.

What texture should the inclusion be to achieve the best final result?
EXAMPLE: Pureed squash can be easily incorporated into bread doughs or muffin batters—which means it must be cooked first and then pureed. But for a savory pie filling, you might prefer just-tender chunks of squash and thus can opt to skip precooking.

Cut-In Method

The cut-in method isn't quite as simple as the blending method, but it is just as straightforward. For recipes that use this method, the fat is rubbed or "cut into" the flour—using your hands, a pastry cutter, or a food processor, depending on the recipe.

One of the keys to success with the cut-in method is using very cold butter or other fat (usually cut into cubes) and well-chilled liquids. Cold ingredients ensure the fat will remain as shingled pieces studded throughout the flour, rather than just blending into it (as it would if the fat were at room temperature or melted). Whisk the dry ingredients together well first, then add the cold fat cubes and toss them well to ensure each piece is fully coated in flour. Coating the fat well with flour will "protect" it during the early stages of baking, reducing the risk of the fat melting out of the dough then and ensuring maximum flakiness.

Cut the fat into the flour using one of the methods below until the desired size is reached: large, medium, or fine.

- **WALNUT HALVES (LARGE):** Used for flakier doughs or doughs that call for folding, like that for Buttermilk Biscuits (page 29) or Rough Puff Pastry (page 267).

- **PEAS (MEDIUM):** Used for doughs that are somewhat flaky but less light and airy, producing a more even crumb structure, as for Drop Biscuits (page 31).

- **COARSE CORNMEAL TEXTURE (FINE):** Used for recipes when the fat should be almost fully incorporated into the flour, like the dough for Drop Biscuits (page 31).

USE YOUR HANDS: Usually I prefer mixing by hand, as it allows you to really shingle the fat into large, flat shards that will produce the flakiest results. I use this method for Buttermilk Biscuits (page 29) and even my pie dough (see page 319). Press the cubes of fat between the fingers and thumbs of both hands to flatten them into shards. Drop the pieces of fat into the flour and toss well to keep them coated with flour as you go.

USE A PASTRY CUTTER: This method is ideal for those who have "hot hands" or find that the mixture gets too warm as they add the fat. Work the pastry cutter through the fat and butter, occasionally tossing to recoat the pieces of fat in flour.

USE A FOOD PROCESSOR: The food processor mixes the fat in more finely, in well distributed pearl-like bits. This method is great when a more uniform crumb structure is required, as for Pâte Brisée (page 321). Simply pulse until the desired consistency is reached. Note that this can happen quite quickly, so be careful not to overprocess the dough.

Once the fat has been cut into the flour, stir in any inclusions of your choice (see page 4), then make a well in the center and add the cold liquid. (If using a food processor, you can transfer the flour mixture to a bowl and carefully add the liquid, or add the liquid to the food processor and pulse gently to combine.) Mix until the mixture is evenly hydrated and comes together, again being careful not to overwork the dough. The larger the pieces of fat, the shaggier the dough. The more finely the fat is mixed in, the smoother the dough will be. (Note that it is therefore slightly easier to incorporate inclusions into doughs where the butter or fat is mixed in more thoroughly.)

While recipes vary, doughs made with the cut-in method typically call for chilling after mixing, and sometimes again after shaping, before baking. A cold dough in a hot oven will produce the lightest, flakiest results.

DONENESS INDICATORS

In most cases, look for evenly browned pastries. For many items, you can even gently lift them up to check that the base is browned to your liking as well. A gentle press in the center for thicker pastries, like biscuits, should yield some resistance—they should slightly spring back when you touch the thickest part.

GET FLEXIBLE

Change the shape and/or consistency of the dough: The cut-in method is typically used for flexible, sturdy doughs, such as biscuit dough and pie dough, which can then be manipulated in a lot of different ways. Biscuit doughs, for example, can be mixed enough so that they can be rolled out and cut into shapes or mixed to a softer consistency, using a little more liquid, for a more scone/drop-biscuit–like texture. For a streusel or crumble topping, use less liquid to produce a drier dough.

ADD LAYERS: Firmer doughs, like the rough puff pastry and that for the buttermilk biscuits, can benefit from a sort of quick/rustic *lamination*. This process involves rolling and folding the dough to create more noticeable layers. (For more, see page 7.) I give this method as optional for my favorite biscuit recipe, but truth be told, I always use it.

ADD INCLUSIONS: Thicker, doughier pastries like scones and biscuits are ideal for inclusions. The inclusions should be added after the fat has been cut in, before the liquid is added. This will distribute them more evenly before the batter is hydrated, and also coat them in flour, which will help heavier ingredients stay suspended in the dough. It can be trickier to add inclusions to doughs with a rougher consistency, like that for the buttermilk biscuits, but you can do it by patting the mixed dough out and gently pressing the inclusions into it, then folding it to distribute them (see below).

Egg Wash

An egg wash can help with browning and/or add a glossy sheen to everything from biscuits to croissants. An egg yolk wash promotes browning, while an egg white wash adds shine. Using the whole egg provides both benefits. And egg wash can also be used as a sort of "glue" to help adhere pieces of dough, whether you're applying decorations to the edges of a pie crust or sealing two pieces of dough together for filled or stuffed preparations.

Whole-Egg Wash	56 g / 1 large egg + 15 g / 1 tablespoon water
Egg Yolk Wash	42 g / 2 large egg yolks + 15 g / 1 tablespoon water
Egg White Wash	70 g / 2 large egg whites + 15 g / 1 tablespoon water

Why Fold Flaky Doughs

"Folding" a dough using the process known in classic pastry preparation as *lamination* helps shingle the fat throughout the dough. Then, when it's well chilled, the moisture in the fat produces steam during the bake, creating the beautiful, light, flaky layers that are often associated with pastries made using the cut-in method. But folding dough can be done in a variety of other ways and doesn't have to be nearly as complicated as the traditional lamination technique. When I have the time, for example, I make some extra folds in my Buttermilk Biscuit dough (page 29).

After mixing the dough, chill it well—the folding method works much better when the fat is cold and firm and the dough has had time to relax. Press or roll the dough into a sheet about ½ inch/1 cm thick—the exact size and shape of the dough doesn't really matter, but an even thickness does. Brush any excess flour off the surface of the dough, fold it in half, and then fold it in half again, folding it into quarters.

The folding technique can be done one or more times, depending on the desired result. I typically like 2 folds for my biscuits and extra-flaky pie dough (page 312), and 4 folds for a more laminated effect, as in my rough puff pastry (page 267).

Classic Cornbread

Makes one 8 x 8-inch/20 x 20 cm pan

DIFFICULTY: **EASY**

There are a lot of ways to make a delicious corn-bread. As a corn fanatic, I simply cannot provide just one version, because every one is so special. I usually bake mine in a square pan, but baking it in a skillet produces a crisper crust. Sometimes I leave it plain, other times I baste it with butter toward the end of baking or before serving. Once you've made this classic recipe, try the different variations below in the name of finding your favorite.

I start this ode to cornbread with my tried-and-true original, which allows you to really enjoy the flavor of the cornmeal itself. I do list a bit of brown sugar as optional, as it helps prevent the corn-bread from drying out once sliced. The sweetened variation is lighter, fluffier, and moister, and as great for snacking as it is alongside a meal. My version of traditional cornbread is made with only cornmeal, no flour, and it has a wonderful crumbly texture. If you're like me, you'll find a different one for every mood.

113 g / 4 ounces / 8 tablespoons **unsalted butter, melted**

30 g / 2 tablespoons **neutral oil (such as canola or vegetable)**

56 g / 1 large **egg, at room temperature**

27 g / 2 tablespoons **brown sugar (optional)**

138 g / 1 cup **yellow cornmeal**

120 g / 1 cup **all-purpose flour**

6 g / 1½ teaspoons **baking powder**

4 g / 1 teaspoon **fine sea salt**

230 g / 1 cup **buttermilk, at room temperature**

1. Preheat the oven to 400°F/205°C with a rack in the center. Lightly grease an 8 x 8-inch/ 20 x 20 cm pan with nonstick spray.

2. In a medium bowl, whisk the melted butter and oil together. Add the egg and brown sugar, if using, and whisk well to combine.

3. In another medium bowl, whisk the cornmeal, flour, baking powder, and salt together until well combined. Add half of this mixture to the butter/oil mixture and stir with a spatula to combine. Add half of the buttermilk, mixing to incorporate. Repeat this process, adding the remaining flour and buttermilk and mixing just until the ingredients are uniformly combined.

4. Pour the batter into the prepared pan and spread into an even layer. Bake for 18 to 20 minutes, until the edges are golden brown and a toothpick inserted into the center comes out clean or with just a few moist crumbs clinging to it.

5. Remove from the oven and let cool for at least 15 minutes before slicing to serve warm, or let cool completely before serving.

Variations

SKILLET CORNBREAD **Bake the basic cornbread (or any of the variations below) in a greased 9-inch/23 cm cast-iron skillet for the same amount of time.**

SWEETER CORNBREAD **Use 71 g / ⅓ packed cup light brown sugar and add 63 g / 3 tablespoons honey along with the sugar.**

(CONTINUES)

TRADITIONAL CORNBREAD (GLUTEN-FREE) Omit the all-purpose flour, increase the cornmeal to 276 g / 2 cups, and increase the buttermilk to 287 g / 1¼ cups.

ROASTED PEPPER AND CHEESE CORNBREAD Prepare a hot fire in a grill, preheat the broiler, or turn on a gas burner and roast 120 g / 2 large Hatch chiles or poblano peppers, turning occasionally, until the skin is blackened all over. Transfer to a zip-top plastic bag, seal, and let steam for 10 minutes; this will make it easy to peel away the charred skin. Dice the chiles, discarding the seeds. Fold the chiles and 75 g / ¾ cup shredded cheddar or Monterey Jack cheese into the basic batter. Pour the batter into the baking pan or skillet, scatter with another 50 g / ½ cup shredded cheese, and bake.

Iced Corn Coffee Cake

TO MAKE THE STREUSEL: In a medium bowl, mix 60 g / ½ cup all-purpose flour, 40 g / ½ cup old-fashioned oats, 53 g / ¼ packed cup light brown sugar, 9 g / 1 tablespoon yellow cornmeal, a pinch of fine sea salt, and a pinch of ground cinnamon to combine. Add 56 g / 2 ounces / 4 tablespoons cold unsalted butter, diced, and use your hands to rub the butter into the mixture until it forms moist crumbs. Prepare the batter for the Sweeter Cornbread (page 9), sprinkle the streusel over the top of the batter, and increase the bake time to 28 to 32 minutes. Cool completely.

   TO MAKE THE ICING: In a medium bowl, whisk 113 g / 1 cup powdered sugar with 30 g / 2 tablespoons heavy cream or milk and 2 g / ½ teaspoon vanilla extract. Drizzle the icing over the cooled coffee cake.

Make Ahead and Storage
The cornbread is best within the first 48 hours after it's made. Store leftovers in an airtight container at room temperature for up to 4 days.

Basting Butters

Basting baked goods with butter browns the exterior and can add a ton of flavor. Cornbread, biscuits, and rolls will all get a flavor boost from butter basting, especially if you add another ingredient or two to the butter like fresh herbs, garlic, or honey or maple syrup.

I baste at three different points in the baking process. You can opt to baste just once or twice, or do it three times—it's up to you. Basting multiple times will result in more browning and contribute to the outer texture of the final baked good.

Just Before Baking	Brush the item with butter before placing it in the oven.
Halfway Through Baking	When you rotate your pans, slap a little (more) butter on top of the baked good(s) before closing the oven door.
Just After Baking	Brush the finished baked item with butter when it's fresh from the oven.

BUTTER AND SALT: A brushing of unsalted butter and a sprinkling of flaky salt after baking is one of my favorite ways to finish my Buttermilk Biscuits (page 29).

GARLIC BUTTER: In a medium saucepan, melt 113 g / 4 ounces / 8 tablespoons butter. Add 10 g / 2 cloves garlic, finely grated, and 3 g / 1 teaspoon garlic powder to the butter and heat over low heat, swirling the pan constantly, for 1 minute, or until the butter is fragrant. This is also delicious with the addition of 3 g / 1 teaspoon dried Italian seasoning and/or a pinch of flaky salt.

SPICY BUTTER: Add 15 to 30 g / 1 to 2 tablespoons hot sauce or up to 1 tablespoon red pepper flakes to 113 g / 8 tablespoons melted butter.

HERB BUTTER: Add up to 10 g / ¼ cup chopped fresh herbs to 113 g / 4 ounces / 8 tablespoons melted butter. Some herbs will brown significantly in the oven, so if you're looking for a green/herby look, wait until the bread comes out of the oven to baste it. Personally, I say browning be damned and use herb butters to triple-baste Savory Scones (page 38).

HONEY BUTTER: Whisk 85 g / ¼ cup honey into 113 g / 4 ounces / 8 tablespoons melted butter. This is wonderful on Classic Cornbread (page 9).

MAPLE BUTTER: Whisk 40 g / 2 tablespoons maple syrup into 113 g / 4 ounces / 8 tablespoons melted butter. This is excellent on the Sweet Potato Bread Bowls (page 122).

BROWN SUGAR BUTTER: Add 40 g / 3 tablespoons light or dark brown sugar to 113 g / 4 ounces / 8 tablespoons butter as it melts, stirring until the sugar fully dissolves.

Spicy Zucchini Bread

Makes one 9 x 5-inch/23 x 13 cm loaf

DIFFICULTY: **EASY**

Shredded zucchini keeps this quickbread super-moist. I like it best as a snacking bread, topped with a thin slice of cheese or a smear of hummus. It also makes delicious toast or tea-style sandwiches with veggie cream cheese and some thinly sliced cucumbers. This loaf is for heat lovers; if you like things milder, cut the amount of pepper flakes in half and skip the hot sauce.

BREAD

300 g / 2½ cups all-purpose flour

10 g / 2 teaspoons baking powder

5 g / 1¼ teaspoons fine sea salt

2 g / ½ teaspoon freshly ground black pepper

1 g / 1 teaspoon red pepper flakes

2 g / ¾ teaspoon garlic powder

3 g / 1 tablespoon chopped fresh oregano or thyme

120 g / ½ cup olive oil

115 g / ½ cup whole milk, at room temperature

113 g / 2 large eggs, at room temperature

A few dashes of hot sauce (or 5 g / 1 teaspoon sambal oelek)

300 g / 2 packed cups shredded zucchini (from about 1 large zucchini)

100 g / 1 cup shredded white cheddar, Monterey Jack, Parmesan, mozzarella, or Gouda cheese

OPTIONAL TOPPING

28 g / 1 ounce / 2 tablespoons unsalted butter, melted

25 g / ½ cup panko bread crumbs

12 g / 2 tablespoons finely grated Parmesan cheese

1. Preheat the oven to 375°F/190°C with a rack in the center. Lightly grease a 9 x 5-inch/23 x 13 cm loaf pan with nonstick spray.

2. In a medium bowl, whisk the flour, baking powder, salt, black pepper, red pepper flakes, garlic powder, and oregano or thyme to combine.

3. In a large bowl, whisk the olive oil, milk, eggs, and hot sauce or sambal oelek to combine. Add the dry ingredients and mix with a spatula until thoroughly combined. Gently fold in the zucchini and cheese until fully incorporated. Pour the batter into the prepared loaf pan and spread into an even layer.

4. If making the topping, mix the ingredients together in a small bowl, and sprinkle evenly over the surface of the loaf.

5. Bake until a skewer inserted into the center comes out clean or with just a few moist crumbs clinging to it, 40 to 45 minutes. Cool for 10 minutes in the pan, then unmold onto a cooling rack and let cool completely.

Make Ahead and Storage
This bread keeps well, wrapped tightly, at room temperature for up to 4 days (it's great toasted).

Pine Nut and Salami Quickbread

Makes one 9 x 5-inch/23 x 13 cm loaf

DIFFICULTY: **EASY**

A reliable quickbread recipe is a perfect back-pocket bake. Omit the pine nuts and diced salami, and you've got a perfect base recipe to tweak or dress up however you like. Check out the first two variations below, both inspired by charcuterie board snacking. Depending on the saltiness of the inclusions you add, you may want to adjust the amount of salt in the dough, particularly for the olive and feta version; you may need the lower amount of salt because of the brininess of both inclusions. This bread keeps well for several days, but thin slices can also be toasted for tasty makeshift crackers.

300 g / 2½ cups all-purpose flour

10 g / 2 teaspoons baking powder

4 to 6 g / 1 to 1½ teaspoons fine sea salt (see headnote)

3 g / 1 teaspoon freshly ground black pepper

2 g / 2 teaspoons chopped fresh thyme

45 g / 3 tablespoons vegetable oil

28 g / 1 ounce / 2 tablespoons unsalted butter, melted

113 g / 2 large eggs, at room temperature

383 g / 1¼ cups plain yogurt

113 g / 4 ounces hard salami, finely diced

70 g / ½ cup pine nuts, toasted and cooled

100 g / 1 cup shredded Manchego cheese

1. Preheat the oven to 375°F/190°C with a rack in the center. Lightly grease a 9 x 5-inch/23 x 13 cm loaf pan with nonstick spray.

2. In a medium bowl, whisk the flour, baking powder, salt, pepper, and thyme to combine.

3. In a large bowl, whisk the oil, melted butter, eggs, and yogurt together. Add the dry ingredients and mix with a spatula until the batter comes together.

4. Gently fold in the salami, pine nuts, and cheese until thoroughly incorporated. Spoon the batter into the prepared loaf pan and spread into an even layer.

5. Bake until a skewer inserted into the center of the loaf comes out clean or with just a few moist crumbs clinging to it, 40 to 45 minutes. Cool for 10 minutes in the pan, then unmold onto a cooling rack and let cool completely.

Variations

MARINATED OLIVE AND FETA QUICKBREAD
Omit the salami, pine nuts, and Manchego and fold 225 g / 1¼ cups coarsely chopped pitted brine-cured olives, 175 g / 1¼ cups crumbled feta cheese, 13 g / ⅓ cup chopped fresh parsley, and 6 g / 2 tablespoons minced fresh dill into the batter in step 4.

HAM AND CHEESE QUICKBREAD **Omit the salami, pine nuts, and Manchego and fold 190 g / 1 heaping cup diced ham and 150 g / 1½ cups shredded Gruyère cheese into the batter in step 4. Top the loaf with an additional 25 g / ¼ cup grated cheese before baking. Increase the baking time to 50 to 55 minutes.**

(CONTINUES)

EVERYTHING KALE QUICKBREAD **Before you make the batter, combine 113 g / 4 ounces cream cheese, at room temperature, 56 g / 1 large egg, and 50 g / ½ cup thinly sliced scallions in a medium bowl and mix well. Omit the fresh thyme and stir 9 g / 1 tablespoon white sesame seeds, 9 g / 1 tablespoon black sesame seeds, 9 g / 1 tablespoon poppy seeds, 9 g / 1 tablespoon dried minced garlic, and 9 g / 1 tablespoon dried minced onion into the flour mixture in step 2. Omit the salami, pine nuts, and Manchego and fold 76 g / 1 packed cup shredded kale into the batter in step 4. Pour half of the batter into the pan and spread into an even layer. Dollop the cream cheese mixture on top and gently spread into an even layer, then pour the remaining batter on top. Sprinkle the surface of the loaf generously with Everything Seasoning (page 177). Add 5 to 8 minutes to the bake time.**

Make Ahead and Storage

This bread keeps well, wrapped tightly, at room temperature for up to 4 days (it makes great toast, but be careful, as some inclusions have a tendency to burn).

Muffins Are Just Small Quickbreads

Can you bake one of these quickbread batters as muffins? Totally—just look for the same visual cues for doneness and expect a significantly shorter bake time.

Can you bake most muffin batters as quickbreads? Absolutely, but in most cases, you should reduce the oven temperature by 25 degrees. Many muffin recipes are baked at a somewhat higher temperature to encourage nicely risen/domed muffins, but a loaf could get too dark and overly crusty by the time it bakes through at that higher temperature.

Sweet Corn Spoonbread

Makes 6 to 8 servings
DIFFICULTY: **MEDIUM**

Spoonbread is a light, fluffy cornmeal-based treat. It's not really bread, more like a soufflé, but don't let that intimidate you. It's as delicious at breakfast with fried eggs as it is at dinnertime alongside a pork chop.

71 g / 2½ ounces / 5 tablespoons unsalted butter, at room temperature

460 g / 2 cups whole milk

138 g / 1 cup fine cornmeal

78 g / ⅓ cup heavy cream

226 g / 4 large eggs, separated

25 g / 2 tablespoons granulated sugar

3 g / ¾ teaspoon baking powder

5 g / 1¼ teaspoons fine sea salt

2 g / ½ teaspoon freshly ground black pepper

220 g / 1⅓ cups sweet corn kernels (optional; drained well if canned, thawed if frozen)

16 g / ⅓ cup minced fresh chives (optional)

1. Preheat the oven to 350°F/175°C with a rack in the center. Grease a 9-inch/23 cm ovenproof skillet or a 1½-quart/1.5 L baking dish with 14 g / 1 ounce / 2 tablespoons of the butter.

2. In a medium pot, melt the remaining 42 g / 1½ ounces / 3 tablespoons unsalted butter. Add the milk and bring to a bare simmer over medium heat. Gradually whisk in the cornmeal and cook for 1 to 2 minutes, whisking constantly, until the mixture thickens visibly.

3. Transfer the cornmeal mixture to a large heatproof bowl. Add the heavy cream and mix to combine.

4. Place the egg whites in the bowl of a stand mixer fitted with the whip attachment (or use a medium bowl and a hand mixer) and whip to stiff peaks—the whites should look fluffy and smooth, not clumpy.

5. Whisk the egg yolks into the cornmeal mixture, along with the sugar, baking powder, salt, and pepper. Add about one-quarter of the whipped egg whites, gently folding to incorporate, then add the remaining whites in 2 or 3 additions, folding until thoroughly combined. Overfolding can cause the egg whites to deflate, but don't be timid—if you don't mix it enough, the batter may separate in the oven. Fold in the corn kernels and chives, if using.

6. Pour the batter into the prepared pan and bake until the spoonbread is evenly golden brown and set in the center, 30 to 35 minutes. Let cool for 5 minutes before serving.

Variation

CHEESY GREEN CHILE SPOONBREAD
Omit the optional chives. Add 15 g / 1 medium jalapeño, halved, seeded, and minced, 10 g / 2 cloves garlic, minced, 50 g / 5 large scallions, minced, 150 g / 1 cup diced green chiles (canned or roasted and peeled fresh peppers), and 100 g / 1 cup shredded cheddar or Monterey Jack cheese along with the egg whites in step 5. Top the batter with another 50 g / ½ cup shredded cheese before baking.

Make Ahead and Storage
This spoonbread is best served immediately.

Corn Muffins

Makes 12 muffins

DIFFICULTY: **EASY**

I'm crazy for cornbread (see page 9), but I might love corn muffins even more. These muffins are just sweet enough, with a beautiful buttery flavor. They are not those huge bakery-style muffins, but a perfect homemade muffin size. They can be stuffed with cheese for a savory twist, and the batter can also be baked as a quickbread (see the Variations).

142 g / 5 ounces / 10 tablespoons unsalted butter, melted

45 g / 3 tablespoons neutral oil (such as canola or vegetable)

106 g / ½ packed cup light brown sugar

85 g / ¼ cup honey

56 g / 1 large egg, at room temperature

173 g / 1¼ cups yellow cornmeal

150 g / 1¼ cups all-purpose flour

16 g / 4 teaspoons baking powder

3 g / ½ teaspoon baking soda

6 g / 1½ teaspoons fine sea salt

230 g / 1 cup buttermilk, at room temperature

125 g / ¾ cup corn kernels (optional; drained well if canned, thawed if frozen)

1. Preheat the oven to 400°F/205°C with a rack in the center. Lightly grease the cavities of a muffin pan or line with muffin liners.

2. In a medium bowl, whisk the melted butter and oil together. Add the brown sugar and honey, whisking to combine. Add the egg and whisk well to combine.

3. In another medium bowl, whisk the cornmeal, flour, baking powder, baking soda, and salt until well combined. Add half of this mixture to the butter/oil and mix with a spatula to combine. Add half of the buttermilk, mixing to incorporate. Add the remaining flour mixture and then the remaining buttermilk, mixing just until uniformly combined. Fold in the corn kernels, if using.

4. Divide the batter evenly among the cavities of the prepared pan, filling each one to just under the rim. Bake for 5 minutes, then lower the oven temperature to 375°F/190°C and bake for 18 to 22 minutes more, until the edges of the muffins are golden brown and a toothpick inserted into the center of one comes out clean or with a few moist crumbs clinging to it.

5. Let cool for at least 10 minutes before serving warm, or cool completely and serve at room temperature.

(CONTINUES)

Variations

CHEESE-STUFFED CORN MUFFINS Omit the honey and reduce the brown sugar to 53 g / ¼ packed cup. Scoop about half the batter into the pan, filling each cavity about half full. Press a 1-inch/2.5 cm cube of cheddar cheese into the center of each muffin cup (you'll need about 285 g / 10 ounces cheese total), then use the remaining batter to cover the cheese completely. Bake as directed.

CORN MUFFIN–STYLE QUICKBREAD Lightly grease a 9 x 5-inch/23 x 13 cm loaf pan with nonstick spray. Reduce the baking powder to 12 g / 1 tablespoon. Prepare the batter as directed and pour into the prepared pan. Bake at 375°F/190°C until a toothpick inserted into the center comes out clean, 55 minutes to 1 hour. Cool in the pan for 15 minutes, then unmold onto a wire rack to cool completely.

SWEET-TOOTH BREAK

Add a Glaze

A glaze is a quick and easy way to sweeten up a pastry that's bordering on dessert, like muffins, scones, brioche, or yeasted puff pastry. My basic ratio for glazes is:

140 g / 1¼ cups powdered sugar + 6 to 75 g / ¼ cup to ⅓ cup liquid

The amount of liquid depends on how thick you want the glaze. The lesser amount will make a firmer, spreadable icing; the larger amount will result in a looser, pourable glaze.

The liquid can be just about anything that lends itself to sweet treats! Some of my standbys include:

- Milk, milk substitute, half-and-half, or heavy cream (cream makes a rich glaze that's almost frosting-like).
- Coffee
- Fresh fruit juice
- Fruit puree (see below)
- Other flavorings, such as extracts or liquor, can replace some or all of the liquid

I make my own fruit purees using about 500 g / 3 cups prepared fresh or frozen fruit and 50 g / ¼ cup granulated sugar: Combine in a large saucepan and cook over medium heat, stirring frequently, until the fruit breaks down, 8 to 10 minutes. Use a large fork or potato masher to coarsely mash the fruit, then strain the puree through a sieve. The fruit remaining in the sieve is great mixed into cocktails or used as low-sugar jam.

Florentine Muffins

Makes 12 muffins

DIFFICULTY: **EASY**

Light and fluffy with perfectly domed tops, these are everything a muffin should be. While this particular version is one of my favorites, think of it as a true base muffin batter. You can sub whatever other inclusions (see page 4) you want for the sautéed spinach and cheese. Most of my favorite variations (see below) are inspired by traditional breakfast combinations, like a classic quiche or a Western omelet. (Sautéing any ingredients that are high in moisture before adding them to the batter helps keep the texture of the muffin light and fluffy.) The sugar in the batter is optional, but it helps to keep the muffins soft.

BUTTERY, GARLICKY SPINACH

28 g / 1 ounce / 2 tablespoons unsalted butter

10 g / 2 cloves garlic, minced

180 g / 6 packed cups spinach

BATTER

43 g / 1½ ounces / 3 tablespoons unsalted butter, melted

45 g / 3 tablespoons neutral oil (such as canola or vegetable)

37 g / 3 tablespoons granulated sugar (optional)

113 g / 2 large eggs

270 g / 2¼ cups all-purpose flour

16 g / 2 tablespoons cornmeal

10 g / 2 teaspoons baking powder

2 g / ½ teaspoon fine sea salt

385 g / 1⅔ cups buttermilk

170 g / 1¾ packed cups shredded Gruyère or other Swiss cheese

1. Make the spinach: In a large sauté pan, melt the butter over medium heat. Add the garlic and cook until fragrant, 30 seconds to 1 minute. Add the spinach a few handfuls at a time and cook, stirring, until it's fully wilted, 2 to 3 minutes. Set aside to cool completely.

2. Make the muffins: Preheat the oven to 400°F/205°C with a rack in the center. Lightly grease the cavities of a muffin pan with nonstick spray and spray the top of the pan as well; or use muffin liners and lightly grease both the liners and the top of the pan.

3. In a medium bowl, whisk the melted butter, oil, and sugar, if using, to combine. Add the eggs one at a time, whisking well to fully incorporate each one.

4. In a small bowl, whisk the flour, cornmeal, baking powder, and salt together. Add half of the flour to the butter/oil mixture and mix with a spatula to combine. Add half of the buttermilk and mix to combine. Repeat with the remaining dry ingredients and then the wet ingredients.

5. Gently fold in the cooled spinach mixture and 113 g / 1 cup of the cheese. Using a ¼-cup/#16 scoop, scoop the batter into the prepared pan, filling each cavity just over three-quarters full. Top each muffin with 7 g / 1 tablespoon of the remaining cheese.

6. Bake until a toothpick inserted into the center of a muffin comes out clean, 15 to 18 minutes. Let cool for 10 minutes in the pan, then remove to a wire rack to cool completely.

(CONTINUES)

Variations

LORRAINE MUFFINS Omit the spinach filling and prepare the following mixture: In a medium skillet, cook 226 g / 8 ounces thick-cut bacon, diced, over medium heat until the fat renders and the bacon is very crisp, 4 to 6 minutes. Use a slotted spoon to transfer the bacon to a small bowl. Add 220 g / 1 medium sweet onion, thinly sliced, to the pan and cook until starting to become tender, 4 to 5 minutes. Transfer the onions to the bowl with the bacon and toss to combine. Let cool for at least 15 minutes, then fold into the batter in step 5, along with the Gruyère and 30 g / ⅓ cup grated Parmesan cheese.

WESTERN MUFFINS Replace the Gruyère with cheddar or Monterey Jack. Omit the spinach filling and prepare the following mixture: In a medium sauté pan, melt 28 g / 1 ounce / 2 tablespoons unsalted butter over medium heat. Add 110 g / ½ medium sweet onion, diced, and 113 g / ½ large bell pepper (any color), cored, seeded, and diced, and sauté until starting to become tender, 7 to 8 minutes. Stir in 100 g / ⅔ cup finely diced ham and let cool completely before folding into the batter in step 5, along with the cheese.

SPINACH 2.0 MUFFINS Omit the Gruyère. In step 5, fill each cavity half full with batter, then press a 14 g / ½-ounce cube of feta cheese into the center of each cup. Spoon the remaining batter on top of the cheese.

THREE-CHEESE MUFFINS Omit the spinach filling and prepare the following mixture: In a medium bowl, toss together 113 g / 1 packed cup shredded cheddar cheese, 113 g / 1 cup shredded Monterey Jack cheese, and 45 g / ½ cup shredded Parmesan cheese. Fold 190 g / 1¾ cups of the cheese mixture into the batter in step 5 and top the muffins with the remaining cheese as directed.

WHOLE WHEAT MUFFINS For 100 percent whole wheat muffins, replace the all-purpose flour with an equal quantity of whole wheat pastry flour. Or reduce the all-purpose flour to 210 g / 1¾ cups all-purpose flour and add 60 g / ½ cup whole wheat flour. Add any inclusions you like to these muffins.

Make Ahead and Storage
The muffins are best within the first 48 hours after baking. Store leftovers in an airtight container for up to 4 days.

French Onion Muffins

Makes 12 muffins

DIFFICULTY: MEDIUM

These savory muffins were inspired by the classic gooey-cheese-topped soup. Caramelized onions and herbs flavor the batter, and a cheesy streusel caps them off. If you want to make these truly decadent, add a cube of Gruyère to each muffin before baking to give them a gooey, molten center.

CARAMELIZED ONIONS

28 g / 1 ounce / 2 tablespoons unsalted butter

460 g / 2 medium sweet onions, halved and sliced

2 g / ½ teaspoon kosher salt

Freshly ground black pepper

45 g / 3 tablespoons sherry

7 g / 1½ teaspoons beef bouillon base (such as Better Than Bouillon)

10 g / 2 cloves garlic, minced

TOPPING

60 g / ½ cup all-purpose flour

40 g / ⅓ cup whole wheat flour

Pinch of fine sea salt

85 g / 3 ounces / 6 tablespoons cold unsalted butter, cut into ½-inch / 1 cm cubes

100 g / 1 cup shredded Gruyère cheese

BATTER

43 g / 1½ ounces / 3 tablespoons unsalted butter, melted

45 g / 3 tablespoons neutral oil (such as canola or vegetable)

113 g / 2 large eggs

270 g / 2¼ cups all-purpose flour

10 g / 2 teaspoons baking powder

2 g / ½ teaspoon fine sea salt

2 g / ¾ teaspoon freshly ground black pepper

3 g / 1 tablespoon chopped fresh thyme

230 g / 1 cup buttermilk

78 g / ⅓ cup heavy cream

100 g / 1 packed cup shredded Gruyère cheese

About 180 g / twelve ½-inch / 1 cm cubes Gruyère cheese (optional)

1. Make the caramelized onions: In a large sauté pan, melt the butter over medium heat. Add the onions and cook over medium heat until they begin to soften, 4 to 5 minutes. Season with the salt and pepper, lower the heat, and cook, stirring occasionally, until the onions are deeply caramelized, 30 to 35 minutes.

2. In a small bowl, whisk the sherry and bouillon base to combine. Add the garlic to the onions and cook until fragrant, 30 seconds to 1 minute. Add the sherry mixture and cook, stirring constantly, to deglaze the pan, then continue to cook until the liquid is mostly evaporated. Remove from the heat and let cool.

3. Make the topping: In a medium bowl, stir together the all-purpose flour, whole wheat flour, and salt. Add the butter and rub it into the flour using your hands or a pastry cutter until a crumbly mixture forms. Add the shredded cheese and toss well to combine.

4. Make the muffins: Preheat the oven to 400°F/205°C with a rack in the center. Lightly grease the cavities of a muffin pan with nonstick spray.

5. In a medium bowl, whisk the melted butter and vegetable oil together. Add the eggs one at a time, whisking to fully incorporate each one.

6. In a medium bowl, whisk the flour, baking powder, salt, black pepper, and thyme together. Add half of the flour to the butter/oil mixture and mix with a spatula to combine. Add the buttermilk and mix to combine. Add the remaining dry ingredients, then add the cream, mixing to combine. Gently fold in the cooled onion mixture and the shredded cheese.

7. Using a ¼-cup/#16 scoop, scoop the batter into the prepared pan, filling each cavity just over three-quarters full. If using the cheese cubes, fill each cavity halfway full, press a cube of cheese into the center of the batter, and then spoon the remaining batter over the cheese to cover it. Scatter the topping evenly over the muffins.

8. Bake until a toothpick inserted into the center of a muffin comes out clean, 24 to 30 minutes. Let cool for 10 minutes in the pan, then remove to a wire rack and serve warm.

Make Ahead and Storage
These muffins are best within the first 24 hours after baking. Store leftovers in an airtight container for up to 3 days. To rewarm the muffins, see Rewarming Pastries, page 365.

– FLAVOR BOOSTER –

Onions

Roasted Onions
Makes about 360 g / 1½ cups

I use roasted onions as inclusions in baked goods, as well as for toppings on focaccia or pizza.

Preheat the oven to 400°F/205°C. Grease a baking sheet with olive oil. Cut off both ends of about 650 g / 2 large onions, not peeled, then cut in half from stem to root end. Place the onions cut side down on the baking sheet. Drizzle 15 g / 1 tablespoon extra virgin olive oil over each half and top each with 7 g / ½ tablespoon unsalted butter. Roast until the onions are very tender and browned, 20 to 25 minutes. Let cool until you can handle them, then remove and discard the onion skin and coarsely chop the onions.

Grilled Onions
Makes about 360 g / 1½ cups

Grilled onions take what I love about roasted onions a step further, adding a smoky flavor. Sweet and spring onions are best for grilling.

Prepare a hot fire in a grill and clean and oil the grill grates. (Note: You can also grill onions indoors on a grill pan or cast-iron griddle.) Peel about 650 g / 2 large onions and cut off the ends. Cut the onion into ½-inch-/1 cm thick slices. Brush both sides of the slices with olive oil and place on the hot grill grates. Lower the grill heat (or, if using a charcoal grill, grill the onions over indirect heat) and cook the onions for 25 to 30 minutes, flipping them 3 or 4 times, until grilled and softened. Remove from the heat and let cool slightly, then coarsely chop or slice.

Fried Onions
Makes about 280 g / 2 cups

I prefer to fry onions without any breading, which takes a bit of patience but yields a gorgeously golden, crisp payout. This works great with white or red onions and shallots.

Peel 650 g / 2 large onions (or about 10 large shallots), cut off both ends, and cut in half from stem to root end. Slice very thin (preferably using a mandoline or food processor). Put the onions in a Dutch oven or other large pot and add neutral oil (such as vegetable or canola) until it's level with the surface of the onions. Set over high heat and cook until the onions begin to brown, 5 to 8 minutes. Reduce the heat and continue to fry, stirring frequently, until the onions are evenly golden brown, 20 to 25 minutes. Remove the onions with a slotted spoon and spread in an even layer on paper towels to drain for about 5 minutes. Season with salt and pepper while still warm. The onions can be stored in an airtight container at room temperature for up to 5 days.

Caramelized Onions
Makes about 475 g / 2 cups

Wonderful as an inclusion, as a topping, or blended into a spread.

Peel about 650 g / 2 large onions, cut off both ends, and cut in half from stem to root end. Slice very thin. In a Dutch oven or other large pot, heat 45 g / 3 tablespoons extra virgin olive oil (or 30 g / 1½ tablespoons oil and 15 g / 1 tablespoon unsalted butter) over medium-high heat. Add the onions

Drop Biscuits

Makes 12 biscuits

DIFFICULTY: **EASY**

Say hello to the recipe I've made more often than any other; I am endlessly tweaking and customizing it. The method is flexible too—I usually make the dough in the food processor because that is quick and easy, but I've also whipped them up using just a bowl and my hands while staying in an Airbnb.

The biscuits can be flavored with spices, herbs, or other inclusions like shredded cheese (see the Variations). The cheesy versions are seriously tops—especially when the dough also includes some sort of allium. The garlic Parmesan biscuits are great alongside tomatoey soups. My dad's favorite (the ones made with scallions or chives and cheese) make delicious "buns" for a simple sandwich, with a slice of ham or even just a fat slice of summer tomato. I also love these as a sweet breakfast treat; see Mama's Chocolate Chip Drop Biscuits below.

Egg-wash the biscuits if you want a golden brown, slightly crisper crust. One of my favorite childhood restaurants left them plain, which resulted in some bits that were crispy and some that were softer—it's your choice.

360 g / 3 cups all-purpose flour

39 g / 3 tablespoons brown sugar

15 g / 1 tablespoon baking powder

3 g / ¾ teaspoon fine sea salt

113 g / 4 ounces / 8 tablespoons cold unsalted butter, cut into ½-inch / 1 cm cubes

226 g / 1 cup buttermilk

56 g / 1 large egg

Egg wash (see page 7) for finishing (optional)

1. Preheat the oven to 375°F/190°C with the racks in the upper and lower thirds. Line two baking sheets with parchment paper.

2. In the bowl of a food processor, pulse the flour, brown sugar, baking powder, and salt to combine. Add the butter, breaking up the cubes as you add them to the bowl. Pulse until the butter is almost fully blended into the flour; the mixture should resemble coarse meal.

3. In a liquid measuring cup, whisk the buttermilk and egg to combine. Add to the food processor and pulse until a sticky dough forms.

4. Using a heaping ¼ cup/#16 scoop, scoop the batter onto the prepared baking sheets, staggering the rows and leaving at least 2 inches/5 cm between the biscuits. If desired, egg-wash the biscuits.

5. Bake until the biscuits start to show some browning, 25 to 28 minutes. When you gently press a biscuit in the center, it should spring back slightly.

6. Cool for at least 10 minutes before serving warm, or cool completely and serve at room temperature.

Variations

GARLIC-PARMESAN DROP BISCUITS
Add 170 g / 1½ packed cups shredded Parmesan cheese and 13 g / 1½ tablespoons garlic powder to the dough after you've incorporated the butter. If desired, egg-wash the biscuits and top each with a sprinkling of dehydrated garlic flakes.

(CONTINUES)

31

Make Ahead and Storage
The biscuits are best
immediately after baking.
Store leftovers in an airtight
container for up to 2 days.
To rewarm the biscuits, see
Rewarming Pastries, page 365.

SCALLION OR CHIVE AND CHEESE DROP BISCUITS Add 170 g / 1½ packed cups shredded cheddar, Gouda, or Gruyère cheese and 105 g / 1 cup thinly sliced scallions or minced fresh chives (from about 2 bunches) to the dough after you've incorporated the butter. Egg-wash the biscuits and top each with another 6 g / 1 tablespoon shredded cheese.

Biscuits as Topping

Adding to the flexibility of drop biscuits is the fact that they make an incredible topping. You can scoop the dough onto a filling to partially cover it, but I prefer more of an all-over-crumble situation. Try this instead of a pastry crust on a potpie, or over a filling of roasted veggies to create a savory cobbler. The drop biscuit recipe makes enough dough to cover a 12-inch/30 cm skillet or a 9 x 13-inch/23 x 33 cm baking pan or dish, but the recipe is easily halved for smaller baking vessels.

HOW TO REMIX ANY BRAISE OR STEW AS A COBBLER You'll need about 2 L / 8 to 9 cups of stew, chili, or braise. Pour into the prepared pan or baking dish and spread in an even layer. Drop/dollop the biscuit dough over the surface. If desired, sprinkle up to 150 g / 1½ packed cups shredded cheese over the dough. Bake at 375°F/190°C until the biscuit topping is golden and the filling is hot and bubbling at the edges, 35 to 40 minutes.

SWEET-TOOTH BREAK

Summer Fruit Shortcake

Adding a little more sugar turns the biscuits into sweet shortcakes. Increase the brown sugar to 106 g / ½ packed cup, and garnish the biscuits generously with turbinado sugar after egg-washing them. Toss the fresh fruit of your choice with a little lemon juice and sugar and let it macerate for 10 to 15 minutes. Halve your biscuits, spoon some whipped cream onto the center, pile on a few spoonfuls of the fruit, and dive in!

Green Chile Sausage Gravy

Makes enough to serve 4 generously

If you've made biscuits and gravy before, I love you—and this is one love language I fully believe in sharing. I split the warm biscuits—for a big portion, use 1½ biscuits (3 biscuit halves) per plate, or just use 1 biscuit or even a half, as you like. Ladle the hot gravy over the top, and, if desired, top each serving with a fried or jammy egg (see page 36).

70 g / 2½ ounces / 5 tablespoons unsalted
   butter

454 g / 1 pound ground breakfast sausage

325 g / 1 large sweet onion, minced

15 g / 3 cloves garlic, minced

226 g / 1 cup chicken or beef broth

30 g / ¼ cup all-purpose flour

805 g / 3½ cups whole milk

340 g / 12 ounces canned diced green chiles
   (from three 4-ounce / 113 g cans)

Kosher salt and freshly ground black pepper

10 g / ¼ cup finely chopped fresh chives
   (optional)

10 g / ¼ cup finely chopped fresh parsley
   (optional)

1. In a Dutch oven or other large pot, melt 28 g / 1 ounce / 2 tablespoons of the butter over medium heat. Add the sausage and cook, stirring occasionally, until well browned, 4 to 5 minutes. Add the onion and cook until softened, 3 to 4 minutes. Add the garlic and cook for 1 minute more.

2. Increase the heat to high and stir in the broth, scraping up any browned bits from the bottom of the pot. Cook until the broth has almost entirely evaporated.

3. Reduce the heat to medium and add the remaining 42 g / 1½ ounces / 3 tablespoons butter. When it has melted, sprinkle the flour over the sausage and cook, stirring constantly, for 3 to 4 minutes until the flour has lost its raw taste. Stir in the milk and bring to a simmer, stirring frequently; the mixture will thicken noticeably.

4. Stir in the chiles and season with salt and pepper. Stir in the chives and parsley, if using, and serve.

Green Eggs and Ham Biscuits

Makes 6 biscuits

DIFFICULTY: **HARD**

One of the best compliments I've ever received as a baker was that my work reminded a fan of illustrations from the Dr. Seuss books. I've long taken inspiration from my favorite childhood books, particularly bright, colorful, eye-catching ones like his. Such is the case with these bright-green biscuits, which get their beautiful color from finely chopped herbs. I use my favorite "jammy egg" method—from author and food stylist Susan Spungen—for the eggs. Her technique steams the eggs rather than boiling them, and it works perfectly every time. Skip the ham entirely for a vegetarian version.

JAMMY EGGS

336 g / 6 large cold eggs

BISCUIT

40 g / 1 bunch fresh chives

30 g / about ⅓ bunch fresh dill

40 g / about ½ bunch fresh parsley

300 g / 2½ cups all-purpose flour

12 g / 1 tablespoon granulated sugar

8 g / 2 teaspoons baking powder

4 g / 1 teaspoon fine sea salt

2 g / ½ teaspoon freshly ground black pepper

113 g / 4 ounces / 8 tablespoons cold unsalted butter, cut into ½-inch / 1 cm cubes

135 g / 6 slices deli ham, diced

170 g / ¾ cup cold buttermilk

56 g / 1 large egg

1. Make the eggs: Fill a medium saucepan with ½ inch/1 cm of water and place a steamer basket in it. Bring the water to a boil, then place the eggs in the basket, cover, reduce the heat to low, and steam the eggs for 6½ minutes.

2. While the eggs are steaming, fill a medium bowl with ice water. When the eggs are ready, transfer them to the ice water. Let cool for 5 minutes, then drain and refrigerate for 1 hour (or up to 2 days).

3. Peel the eggs, rinse, and pat dry. Put in a bowl and refrigerate while you make the biscuit dough.

4. Preheat the oven to 400°F/205°C with a rack in the center. Line a baking sheet with parchment paper.

5. Roughly tear the herbs, including the stems, and place in the bowl of a food processor. Pulse until the herbs are finely chopped. Scrape the bowl well, then add the flour, sugar, baking powder, salt, and pepper and pulse until uniformly combined. Add the butter and pulse until the mixture resembles coarse meal—the butter should be in very small pieces.

6. Transfer the mixture to a medium bowl and stir in the diced ham. Make a well in the center and add the buttermilk and egg to the well. Use a small whisk or fork to break up the egg, then mix the batter with a spatula until it's evenly combined and the flour is uniformly hydrated. Turn the dough out and divide it into 6 equal portions (about 110 g / ¾ cup each—or use a #6 scoop).

7. Working with one piece of dough at a time, break off about one-third of each one and form it into a 3-inch/8 cm round on the prepared baking sheet, leaving at least 2 inches/5 cm between the rounds.

8. Place an egg in the center of each circle of dough. One at a time, gently press the remaining pieces of dough over and around the eggs, using your fingers to seal the seam at the base.

9. Bake until the biscuits are lightly browned and spring back slightly when touched in the center, 16 to 19 minutes. Cool for at least 5 minutes before serving warm.

Make Ahead and Storage
These biscuits are best immediately after baking. Store leftovers in an airtight container for up to 24 hours. Leftover biscuits can be rewarmed; see Rewarming Pastries, page 365.

Savory Scones

Makes 15 scones

DIFFICULTY: **EASY**

The summer after my senior year of high school, I had to get up in the middle of the night to head to my new bakery gig: early morning baker. One of my daily tasks was to bake the morning scones. Two days a week, I'd also box up a few fresh baked babes to deliver to some of the local coffee shops; I'd always make a few extra and deliver them to my parents on the way. There was so much joy to be had in bringing them warm breakfast pastries, but the sweetest part was that I had made them, all on my way to being a true baker. Ever since, I've loved to teach folks how easy scones are to make (and what a joy it is to eat freshly baked ones). This base recipe is a perfect place to get started—add any inclusions you like, or try some of my favorites (see the Variations below). You'll notice the sugar in the recipe is optional—it isn't added for sweetness, but rather to extend the shelf life, so you can enjoy your scones for a few days after baking.

360 g / 3 cups all-purpose flour

37 g / 3 tablespoons granulated sugar (optional)

12 g / 1 tablespoon baking powder

3 g / ¾ teaspoon fine sea salt

113 g / 4 ounces / 8 tablespoons cold unsalted butter, cut into ½-inch / 1 cm cubes

240 to 500 g / 1 to 2 cups inclusions (such as shredded or crumbled cheese, finely chopped herbs, minced or diced veggies [see page 4], or cooked meat such as sausage, bacon, or ham—or a combination)

325 g / 1¼ cups cold heavy cream

Egg wash (see page 7) for finishing

1. Preheat the oven to 400°F / 205°C with the racks in the upper and lower thirds. Line two baking sheets with parchment paper.

2. In a large bowl, whisk the flour, sugar, if using, baking powder, and salt to combine. Add the butter and use your hands to break up the cubes, tossing until each one is well coated with flour. Then use your hands or a pastry cutter to cut the butter into the flour until the largest pieces are about the size of peas. Add the inclusions of your choice and stir until evenly incorporated (if desired, you can reserve a small amount of the inclusions to top the scones).

3. Make a well in the center of the flour mixture and add the cream. Mix with your hands or a spatula until the dough comes together; it will look craggy, not smooth.

4. Use a ¼-cup/#16 scoop to scoop the dough into 8 equal mounds on the baking sheet, staggering them on and leaving at least 2 inches/ 5 cm between them. Egg-wash the scones. If you reserved some of the inclusions, garnish the tops of the scones with them.

5. Bake the scones until evenly browned, switching the position of the baking sheets and rotating them halfway through baking, 18 to 22 minutes. Cool for at least 15 minutes and serve warm, or at room temperature.

Variations

FLUFFY CHEESE-CURD SCONES Omit the other inclusions. Crumble 285 g / 10 ounces cheese curds into bite-size pieces. Add to the flour mixture after you've incorporated the butter.

CREAMED LEEK SCONES Before you mix the dough, prepare the following mixture: Trim the dark green portions and bulb ends from about 400 g / 2 medium leeks. Cut the leeks lengthwise in half, wash well, and thinly slice. In a medium pot, melt 28 g / 1 ounce / 2 tablespoons unsalted butter over medium heat. Add the leeks and cook until they wilt, 5 to 6 minutes. Add 313 g / 1 ⅓ cups heavy cream, bring to a simmer, and simmer for 2 minutes. Remove the pot from the heat, transfer the creamed leeks to a storage container, and refrigerate until fully chilled, at least 2 hours. Add this mixture instead of the cream in step 3.

(CONTINUES)

ZA'ATAR CARROT SCONES **Omit the other inclusions, and reduce the salt to 1 g / ¹/₄ teaspoon. Add 142 g / 1 packed cup shredded carrots and 18 g / 2 tablespoons** za'atar to the flour mixture after you've incorporated the butter. Top each scone with a sprinkle of za'atar after egg-washing them.

SWEET-TOOTH BREAK

Iced Lemon Almond Scones

Replace the (optional) granulated sugar with 106 g / ½ packed cup light brown sugar. Add the grated zest of 1 lemon to the sugar before mixing it in with the flour. Use 113 g / 1¹/₄ cups sliced almonds instead of the other inclusions. After egg-washing the scones, sprinkle 6 g / 1 tablespoon toasted sliced almonds on top of each one and sprinkle generously with turbinado sugar. Let the baked scones cool for 30 minutes. While they cool, in a small bowl, whisk together 113 g / 1 cup powdered sugar with 15 g / 1 tablespoon fresh lemon juice and 15 g / 1 tablespoon heavy cream. Drizzle the icing over the scones and sprinkle with more toasted sliced almonds, if desired.

Strawberry Rhubarb (or Blue-barb) Scones

Use 99 g / ½ cup granulated sugar. Use 185 g / 1¹/₂ cups diced rhubarb and 165 g / 1 cup diced strawberries instead of the other inclusions (or replace the strawberries with an equal quantity of blueberries). When I'm feeling fancy, I garnish these with pearl sugar after egg-washing them, but turbinado is good too.

Make Ahead and Storage
The scones are best the same day they're baked. Store leftovers in an airtight container for up to 2 days. To rewarm the scones, see Rewarming Pastries, page 365.

To Shape Triangular Scones
After mixing the dough, refrigerate it for 30 minutes to 1 hour.
Divide the chilled dough into 2 equal portions (about 400 g
each). On a lightly floured surface, pat one piece of dough out
into a circle 6 inches/15 cm wide. Cut into 6 even triangular
pieces and transfer to one of the prepared baking sheets.
Repeat with the remaining portion of dough. Bake for 20 to
24 minutes.

Bacon-and-Eggs Dutch Baby

Makes one 12-inch/30 cm Dutch baby (serves 4 generously)

DIFFICULTY: **EASY**

Dutch babies, or large skillet pancakes, are similar to Yorkshire Pudding (see the Variations). All of these use a liquid pancake-type batter with a higher ratio of eggs and milk to flour than that for classic pancakes, which allows it to become puffy and rise, for a thin, fluffy pancake with crisp outer edges. The batter for this Dutch baby can be flavored with various additions, particularly light-weight, fairly dry ingredients that won't impede its rise. I like to riff with the addition of up to 50 g / ½ cup grated Parmesan cheese, 9 g / 1 tablespoon ground spices, or 13 g / ⅓ cup finely chopped fresh herbs. I top this breakfast-inspired version with fried eggs and bacon, and serve slices with a few generous dashes of hot sauce.

283 g / 5 large eggs

150 g / 1¼ cups all-purpose flour

230 g / 1 cup whole milk

3 g / ½ teaspoon kosher salt

71 g / 2½ ounces / 5 tablespoons unsalted butter

300 g / 6 strips quick candied bacon (page 44), cut roughly into quarters

4 fried, poached, or jammy eggs (see page 45)

Chopped fresh herbs, such as chives, dill, or parsley, for garnish (optional)

Hot sauce for serving (optional)

1. Preheat the oven to 425°F/220°C with a rack in the lower third.

2. In a large bowl, whisk the eggs well to combine. Add the flour, milk, and salt and whisk to incorporate.

3. In a large (12 in/30 cm) ovenproof skillet, preferably cast-iron, melt the butter over medium heat. Pour in the batter, transfer to the oven, and bake until the pancake puffs up around the edges and turns golden brown, 20 to 25 minutes.

4. Serve the Dutch baby topped with or alongside the bacon and eggs, sprinkled with fresh herbs, if using.

Variations

WHOLE WHEAT DUTCH BABY WITH BÉCHAMEL AND MUSHROOMS Reduce the all-purpose flour to 30 g / ¼ cup and add 120 g / 1 cup whole wheat pastry flour along with it in step 1. Instead of bacon and eggs, top or serve with Roasted Mushrooms (page 295) and Béchamel Sauce (page 56).

LARGE YORKSHIRE PUDDING Increase the eggs to 336 g / 6 large, the flour to 300 g / 2½ cups, and the milk to 460 g / 2 cups. Replace the butter with an equal amount of drippings from roasted meat (or bacon drippings) and transfer them (if necessary) to a 9 x 13-inch/23 x 33 cm pan (or similar pan—ideally, the pan you roasted the meat in). Add the batter to the hot pan and bake for 40 to 45 minutes, until deeply browned and very puffed.

Make Ahead and Storage
The Dutch baby is best
immediately after baking.

My Best Bacon

At my house, we almost always cook bacon in the oven—it's usually already on! It produces really evenly cooked bacon, and you can take it to as crisp as you like it.

1. Preheat the oven to 425°F/220°C with a rack in the center. Line a baking sheet with two crisscrossed pieces of aluminum foil, completely covering the base and sides of the pan, with about a 1-inch / 2.5 cm overhang on all sides. Line the slices of bacon up on the baking sheet, almost overlapping (the bacon will shrink as it cooks). I like to add a decent amount of freshly ground black pepper, grinding it evenly over the slices, but that's totally optional (a sprinkling of cayenne is also nice).

2. For quick candied bacon, sprinkle light or dark brown sugar evenly over the bacon—about 13 g / 1 tablespoon per slice. Heavy black pepper is especially good on this sweet version.

3. For just-crisp bacon with a little chew, bake for 14 to 16 minutes. For very crisp bacon, bake for 17 to 19 minutes. Remove the bacon from the pan as soon as you remove it from the oven and transfer to a parchment-lined baking sheet to drain. If you will be chopping it to use in a baking recipe, let cool completely.

Put an Egg on It!

Adding a fried, poached, or "jammy" egg is an alluring and craveable way to finish a variety of savory baked goods.

Crisp-Edged Fried Eggs

Heat a well-seasoned cast-iron or nonstick skillet over medium-high heat. When it's hot, add 15 to 30 g / 1 to 2 tablespoons extra virgin olive oil to the pan for 2 to 4 eggs, swirling it to coat the surface evenly (you may need a bit more if you're cooking more eggs). Crack the eggs directly into the pan, or crack each one into a ramekin and then add to the pan. Reduce the heat to medium and cook until the edges of the whites are crisp and golden and the yolks have reached your desired doneness, 2 to 3 minutes for a runny-jammy yolk. Season with salt and pepper.

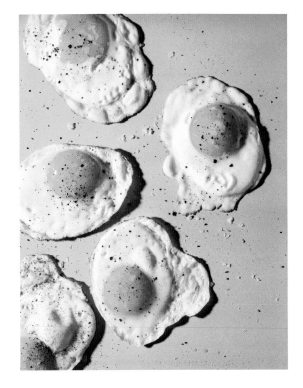

Poached Eggs

Use the freshest eggs possible. Fill a medium or large pot (depending on how many eggs you're poaching) with at least 4 inches/10 cm of water. If desired, add 15 to 30 g / 1 to 2 tablespoons white vinegar to the water (this is optional, but I always do it, as it helps the whites set in the early stages of poaching). Bring it to a boil, then reduce to a gentle but steady simmer.

One at a time, gently crack each egg into a 4-ounce / 120 ml ramekin.

Then, if desired, carefully pour the egg into a fine-mesh strainer—this will allow the thinner part of the white to drain away, leaving the firmer portion behind, then return the egg to the ramekin. Use a slotted spoon to start stirring the water, creating a vortex in the center. Gently drop the egg from the ramekin into the center of the pot—the swirling water will help the egg white more evenly surround the yolk—and cook until the white is fully set, 3 to 3½ minutes, then remove from the water with a slotted spoon and drain on a plate lined with a clean kitchen towel. Let the white of the first egg set slightly before adding the next egg(s), poaching them just a few at a time to prevent overcrowding the pot.

Jammy Eggs

This method makes the perfect jammy egg by steaming the eggs rather than boiling them—it's quick, easy, and reliable, and the eggs always peel easily! For a full description of this method, see page 36.

CHAPTER 2

Stovetop Savories

PANCAKES • WAFFLES • FRITTERS • UNFILLED
DUMPLINGS • GRIDDLED AND FRIED PASTRIES

The recipes in this chapter are made on the stovetop rather than in the oven, but the same part of me that enjoys baking loves making these recipes too. You're still whisking up a batter or kneading together a simple dough. If, say, memories of buttermilk pancakes with syrup are stopping you from picturing this as a savory chapter, think again. Instead, picture some of their savory cousins, eaten all around the world: buckwheat crepes stuffed with ham and cheese, chewy scallion pancakes, tasty fritters of all sorts fried to crisp perfection. There are so many delicious savory avenues these stovetop recipes can take, all the while maintaining their best features: ease of preparation, quick cooking times, loads of flexibility, and flavorful possibilities for every meal of the day.

What's in a Batter's Name?

This chapter's recipes start with simple base batters, but they boast a lot of possibilities. Knowing more about the type of batter you're making can arm you for riffing on it later!

PANCAKES

Classic buttermilk-style pancakes are typically formulated to be softer—often fluffy—than the other items on this list. But there are several different types of pancakes, described below.

CAKEY PANCAKES: The batter for cakey pancakes is formulated to result in a spongier interior texture, like as in classic buttermilk pancakes or the Garlic Parmesan Pancakes on page 57.

THIN PANCAKES: A thinner batter produces thinner pancakes, like the buckwheat crepes on page 51 and the skillet pancake on page 64.

DOUGHY PANCAKES: Some recipes, like the Scallion Pancakes on page 67, start with a dough rather than a batter, which is rolled and shaped before cooking.

VEGETABLE PANCAKES: Sometimes the word *pancake* is used to describe a prepared vegetable mixed with ingredients to bind it—like potato pancakes. That also borders on the definition of fritters. Personally, I use the term *pancake* to describe a thinner item and *fritter* to describe a thicker one.

WAFFLES

Waffle batters are typically formulated to cook up crisper, though some folks believe you can use pancake and waffle batters interchangeably—I stand sort of in the middle on that issue. I wouldn't use my favorite waffle recipe, Yeasted Waffles (page 72) to make pancakes, but some of the batters in this book can be used to create either: see the Garlic Parmesan Pancakes on page 57 and Jalapeño Cornmeal Waffles on page 77.

FRITTERS

Most fritter batters are formulated similarly to pancake batters. The primary difference between the two lies in the proportion of inclusions. For example, the Elote Fritters (page 69) are mostly corn, and the kernels are mixed with just enough batter to bind them.

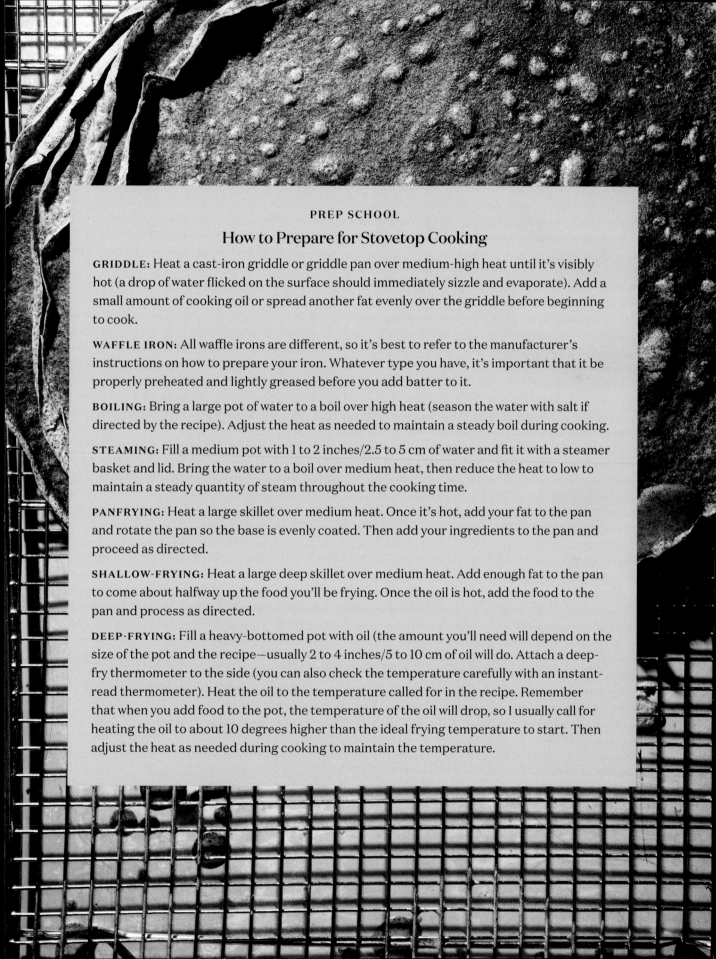

How to Prepare for Stovetop Cooking

GRIDDLE: Heat a cast-iron griddle or griddle pan over medium-high heat until it's visibly hot (a drop of water flicked on the surface should immediately sizzle and evaporate). Add a small amount of cooking oil or spread another fat evenly over the griddle before beginning to cook.

WAFFLE IRON: All waffle irons are different, so it's best to refer to the manufacturer's instructions on how to prepare your iron. Whatever type you have, it's important that it be properly preheated and lightly greased before you add batter to it.

BOILING: Bring a large pot of water to a boil over high heat (season the water with salt if directed by the recipe). Adjust the heat as needed to maintain a steady boil during cooking.

STEAMING: Fill a medium pot with 1 to 2 inches/2.5 to 5 cm of water and fit it with a steamer basket and lid. Bring the water to a boil over medium heat, then reduce the heat to low to maintain a steady quantity of steam throughout the cooking time.

PANFRYING: Heat a large skillet over medium heat. Once it's hot, add your fat to the pan and rotate the pan so the base is evenly coated. Then add your ingredients to the pan and proceed as directed.

SHALLOW-FRYING: Heat a large deep skillet over medium heat. Add enough fat to the pan to come about halfway up the food you'll be frying. Once the oil is hot, add the food to the pan and process as directed.

DEEP-FRYING: Fill a heavy-bottomed pot with oil (the amount you'll need will depend on the size of the pot and the recipe—usually 2 to 4 inches/5 to 10 cm of oil will do. Attach a deep-fry thermometer to the side (you can also check the temperature carefully with an instant-read thermometer). Heat the oil to the temperature called for in the recipe. Remember that when you add food to the pot, the temperature of the oil will drop, so I usually call for heating the oil to about 10 degrees higher than the ideal frying temperature to start. Then adjust the heat as needed during cooking to maintain the temperature.

Get Flexible

Their flexibility is one of my favorite attributes of pancakes, waffles, and fritter batters. If you understand the way the ingredients work together, you can make substitutions based on what you have on hand.

PANCAKES AND WAFFLES

LIQUIDS: As long as you maintain more or less the same level of hydration, you can replace the liquids in pancake and waffle recipes fairly easily. You can use different dairy products—such as yogurt to replace buttermilk, or even a nondairy substitute. Consider the consistency of the ingredient you want to substitute. Replacing a thinner ingredient (e.g., milk) with something thicker (e.g., sour cream) may require you to alter the amounts slightly to maintain the desired consistency of the batter.

FLOURS: Flours are a little trickier to substitute, but don't let that deter you! It's all about the protein content: Flours with a higher protein content, like whole wheat flour, will absorb more liquid and so may require additional adjustments to the recipe to compensate. To avoid problems, you can substitute a higher-protein flour for just part of the flour the recipe calls for (e.g., whole wheat flour for just half of the all-purpose flour called for). Flours with a similar protein content as the type the recipe calls for (like spelt flour, which is a great alternative to all-purpose) can be substituted more easily.

FRITTERS

BINDERS: Fritters can be bound with a variety of different ingredients, from flour to eggs to cornstarch. Fritters made with ingredients with higher moisture levels, like zucchini, may require a higher proportion of binders than other fritters.

COOKING METHODS: Most fritter batters can be either panfried or deep-fried. And, in some cases, you can use a completely different cooking method—like a waffle iron!

Even Browning

GRIDDLING: Maintaining an even temperature is the key to even browning on a griddle. Start with a very hot pan, then adjust the heat as needed. And don't forget the "first pancake rule"—it may turn out a little darker than the others, but it's a great gauge of how to adjust the heat for the rest of cooking.

PANFRYING: For the most even cooking and browning, cook the food over consistent medium heat and flip as needed as it cooks.

SHALLOW-FRYING: Ideally, you want to flip the food only once during shallow-frying. Maintain steady medium heat to prevent overbrowning.

DEEP-FRYING: Flip the food you're cooking as necessary for even browning on both sides. Maintain a frying temperature of between 325 and 350°F/165 and 175°C or as directed by the recipe.

Buckwheat Crepes with Apples, Ham, and Cheese

Makes about 10 crepes

DIFFICULTY: **MEDIUM**

It's difficult for me to pass by a sidewalk cart making crepes with ham and cheese nestled inside. In some neighborhoods in Paris, that very smell wafts through the streets as plentifully as the scent of freshly baked bread. The nutty flavor of buckwheat flour makes a delicious crepe, but when thin slices of ham and cheese are dropped onto the piping-hot crepe, magic is in the air. I like to tuck thin slices of apples in, too. You could also place a fried egg (see page 45) in the center of each crepe, just before serving. Or mix it up and add any fillings that suit your mood!

CREPES

150 g / 1¼ cups buckwheat flour

7 g / 1 tablespoon cornstarch

2 g / ½ teaspoon fine sea salt

290 g / 1¼ cups whole milk, plus more as needed

170 g / 3 large eggs

28 g / 2 tablespoons unsalted butter, melted

FILLING AND FINISHING

75 g / 5 tablespoons Dijon mustard

285 g / 10 ounces thinly sliced ham

226 g / 8 ounces thinly sliced apples (about 2 medium apples)

285 g / 10 ounces Gruyère cheese, shredded

1. Make the batter: In a blender, combine the buckwheat flour, cornstarch, salt, milk, eggs, and melted butter and blend well; the batter will be thin.

2. Transfer the batter to an airtight container and refrigerate for at least 1 hour (and up to 12 hours, or overnight).

3. When you're ready to use it, check the consistency of the batter: It should look similar to how it did when you first blended it, but with longer fridge time, it will become thicker. If necessary, gently whisk in additional milk 30 g / 2 tablespoons at a time to reach that initial thin consistency.

4. Preheat the oven to 350°F/175°C with a rack in the center. Line two baking sheets with parchment paper.

5. Preheat a large (11- to 12-inch/28 to 30 cm) nonstick crepe pan over medium heat. Spray the pan with nonstick spray. Ladle or scoop about 80 g / generous ⅓ cup of batter into the hot pan and immediately tilt and swirl the pan to distribute the batter evenly and create a thin crepe. Cook until the crepe is browned and lacy at the edges, 1 to 2 minutes. Flip the crepe and cook until browned on the other side, about 1 minute more.

6. Gently transfer the crepe to one of the prepared baking sheets. Dollop 7 g / 1½ teaspoons of the mustard across the center of the crepe. Place 28 g / 1 ounce of the ham and 28 g / 1 ounce of the apple slices (i.e., a tenth of the total amount) in the center and top with 28 g / 1 ounce of the cheese.

(CONTINUES)

51

Make Ahead and Storage
The crepe batter can be made up to 12 hours ahead. The filled crepes are best the same day.

7. Fold two opposite sides of the crepe over the filling, then fold the top and bottom over to make a square packet with an opening in the center. Repeat to make more crepes.

8. Once you've filled the first baking sheet with crepes, transfer to the oven to warm the filling through and melt the cheese, 5 to 7 minutes, while you prepare the remaining crepes. Once all the crepes are made, serve immediately.

Perfect Crepes

Check the consistency of the batter and thin it with milk if necessary.

Pour the batter into the hot pan and immediately swirl to evenly coat the base of the pan with a thin layer.

Use a flexible spatula to flip the crepes.

Blintzes with Sweet Peas and Cheese

Makes 8 blintzes

DIFFICULTY: **MEDIUM**

I happen to find blintzes—filled crepes that are lightly browned in butter before serving—to be an especially sweet thing to prepare for friends and family. For years, I was partial to cheese blintzes, topped with some kind of fruit (see Sweet-Tooth Break). Now I also like savory blintzes as a light appetizer or even a side dish. They can be filled with almost anything, like this springy combo of cheese, herbs, and peas. And since crepes can be made ahead and frozen, they are a great way to repurpose leftovers; see Thanksgiving Leftovers Blintzes (below) for an example.

CREPES

280 g / 5 large eggs

290 g / 1¼ cups whole milk

160 g / 1¼ cups all-purpose flour

43 g / 1½ ounces / 3 tablespoons unsalted butter, melted

3 g / ¾ teaspoon fine sea salt

FILLING AND FINISHING

260 g / 2 cups fresh or frozen peas

340 g / 1½ cups whole-milk ricotta cheese

100 g / 1 cup finely grated Parmesan cheese

56 g / 2 ounces cream cheese, at room temperature

56 g / 1 large egg, lightly whisked

20 g / ½ cup chopped fresh parsley

2 g / ½ teaspoon fine sea salt

2 g / ½ teaspoon freshly ground black pepper, plus more for garnish

56 g / 2 ounces / 4 tablespoons unsalted butter

Béchamel Sauce or Cheesy Béchamel Sauce (page 56), warmed, for serving

Chopped fresh chives for garnish (optional)

1. Make the crepes: In a medium bowl, whisk the eggs, milk, and flour to combine. Add the melted butter and salt and whisk until well combined.

2. Heat a medium nonstick pan or crepe pan (about 8 inches/20 cm) over medium heat. Spray lightly with nonstick spray. Ladle or scoop about 70 g / ¼ cup of the batter into the pan, tilting and swirling the pan to cover the base evenly. Cook until the bottom of the crepe is set, 15 to 30 seconds, then gently flip and cook for 30 to 45 seconds more, until the crepe appears set. Remove to a plate and top with a round of parchment paper. Repeat with the remaining batter, making a total of 8 crepes, stacking them on the plate, separated with parchment paper. Set the pan aside.

3. Bring a small pot of water to a simmer over medium-high heat. Add the peas and boil for 1 minute, then drain.

4. Transfer about half of the peas to a medium bowl and mash with a large fork or potato masher until coarsely smashed. Fold in the ricotta, Parmesan, cream cheese, egg, parsley, salt, and pepper, then fold in the remaining peas.

5. To assemble, place a crepe on a clean work surface. Spoon about 55 g / 3 heaping tablespoons of the filling into the center. Fold over

the two opposite sides to encase the filling (as if you're rolling a burrito), then fold up the blintz, aiming to keep it somewhat flat rather than cylindrical.

6. Heat the same pan over medium-high heat. Add 14 g / 1 tablespoon of the butter and melt it, swirling to coat the base of the pan. Working in batches of 2 or 3, add the blintzes to the pan, seam side down, and cook, turning once, until evenly browned, about 2 minutes per side. As they are cooked, transfer the blintzes to a serving platter, and add more butter to the pan as necessary.

7. To serve, spoon the béchamel sauce over the blintzes and garnish with chives, if desired, and freshly ground black pepper.

Variation

THANKSGIVING LEFTOVERS BLINTZES: Fill each crepe with 40 g / 2 tablespoons stuffing and 60 g / 3 tablespoons diced or shredded turkey and top with 15 g / 1 tablespoon cranberry sauce. Serve topped with béchamel sauce or doused with leftover gravy.

SWEET-TOOTH BREAK

Black-and-Blue Blintzes

In a medium bowl, toss 226 g / 8 ounces blackberries and 226 g / 8 ounces blueberries with 30 g / 2 tablespoons fresh lemon juice and 50 g / ¼ cup granulated sugar. Use a potato masher to coarsely mash the fruit, then set aside to macerate while you prepare the blintzes.

In a large bowl, beat the following ingredients together until well combined: 226 g / 8 ounces cream cheese, at room temperature, 226 g / 8 ounces ricotta cheese, at room temperature, 53 g / ¼ packed cup light brown sugar, 56 g / 1 large egg, at room temperature, 5 g / 1 teaspoon vanilla extract, and 2 g / ½ teaspoon fine sea salt. Use this mixture to fill the crepes and proceed as directed. To serve, garnish the blintzes with powdered sugar, if desired, and spoon the fruit mixture over them.

Make Ahead and Storage
The crepes can be made ahead and frozen for up to 3 months. Stack the crepes as directed in step 2, then wrap tightly in plastic wrap. Assembled blintzes are best immediately after they are cooked. Store leftovers in an airtight container in the refrigerator for up to 48 hours.

(CONTINUES)

Béchamel Sauce

Makes about 240 g / 1 cup

In a medium saucepan, bring 230 g / 1 cup whole milk to a bare simmer, then pour into a liquid measuring cup. Melt 28 g / 1 ounce / 2 tablespoons unsalted butter in the same pan over medium heat. Sprinkle 15 g / 2 tablespoons all-purpose flour over the butter and cook, stirring with a silicone spatula or wooden spoon, for 1 to 2 minutes, until the flour has lost its raw taste. Slowly add the warm milk, stirring constantly. Stir in 60 g / ¼ cup heavy cream, bring to a simmer, stirring, and simmer until the sauce thickens, 2 to 3 minutes. Season with salt and white or black pepper and serve warm.

Variations

CHEESY BÉCHAMEL **Add up to 100 g / 1 cup grated cheese to the finished sauce, stirring constantly. Alternatively, stir the cheese into the cooled béchamel sauce; this will thicken it and make it easier to layer/spread in some recipes.**

THICK BÉCHAMEL **For some baking applications, like the Broccoli and Cheese Bierocks (page 217), a thick béchamel works best. Increase the flour to 23 g / 3 tablespoons. Simmer the sauce for 3 to 4 minutes to thicken it.**

Garlic Parmesan Pancakes with Tomato Jam

Makes about 12 pancakes

DIFFICULTY: **EASY**

While I'm more often stuffing my buttermilk babes with blueberries or chocolate chunks, I was inspired by my family to try this savory take. Years ago, when I was searching for tried-and-true family recipes, my grandma Jeanne shared a recipe for tomato jam with me. I probably wrinkled my nose at first, but she explained that sweet, ripe summer tomatoes make a delicious jam. Her mother always made it with sugar and some warm spices, and she often used it to top their pancakes. I love the sweetness of the jam myself, but I especially love it paired with saltier elements. This pancake includes salty Parmesan and one of tomatoes' best accent flavors, garlic—in this case, roasted garlic—and it's the perfect vessel for my inherited jam. The recipe makes more than you'll need for one batch of pancakes, but it keeps in the fridge for up to 1 month, or in the freezer for up to 6 months. To make a lovely meal, serve these pancakes with fried or poached eggs (see page 45).

TOMATO JAM

496 g / 2½ cups chopped ripe tomatoes

248 g / 1¼ cups granulated sugar

3 g / 1½ teaspoons ground cinnamon

2 g / ¾ teaspoon ground cloves

2 g / ¾ teaspoon ground ginger

2 g / ½ teaspoon fine sea salt

PANCAKES

300 g / 2½ cups all-purpose flour

50 g / ½ cup finely grated Parmesan cheese, plus more for finishing

6 g / 1 teaspoon baking powder

3 g / 1 teaspoon garlic powder

2 g / ½ teaspoon fine sea salt

4 g / 1 teaspoon freshly ground black pepper

113 g / ½ cup crème fraîche, sour cream, or plain yogurt

1 head Roasted Garlic (page 159), cloves squeezed out and coarsely mashed with a fork

403 g / 1¾ cups whole milk

56 g / 2 large eggs

9 g / 3 tablespoons finely chopped fresh parsley, plus more for garnish

Unsalted butter for cooking

1. Make the tomato jam: In a medium pot, stir the tomatoes, sugar, cinnamon, cloves, ginger, and salt to combine. Bring to a simmer over medium heat, stirring occasionally, and simmer until the mixture cooks down and thickens to a jam-like consistency, 45 minutes to 1 hour (keep in mind that it will thicken more as it cools).

2. Transfer the jam to a heatproof storage container, let cool to room temperature, and refrigerate until well chilled (if desired, transfer some of the chilled jam to a freezer container for longer-term storage).

3. Make the pancakes: In a large bowl, whisk the flour, Parmesan, baking powder, garlic powder, salt, and pepper to combine.

(CONTINUES)

4. In a medium bowl, whisk the crème fraîche (or sour cream or yogurt), mashed garlic, milk, and eggs until well combined. Add to the dry ingredients and whisk to combine (it's okay if the mixture is a bit lumpy). Fold in the parsley.

5. Heat a large skillet or griddle over medium-heat heat for several minutes. When it is hot, grease it with 14 to 28 g / 1 to 2 tablespoons butter. Working in batches, use a ladle to drop spoonfuls of batter into the hot skillet (or griddle), aiming for pancakes about 4 inches/10 cm in diameter. Reduce the heat to low and cook until the pancakes are evenly golden brown, 2 to 3 minutes. Use a spatula to gently flip the pancakes over and cook for 1 to 3 minutes longer, until fully cooked through and evenly golden brown on the second side. Turn the heat up again as needed before adding each new batch of pancakes.

6. Transfer the pancakes to serving plates, and serve topped with tomato jam, or with the jam alongside. Garnish with chopped parsley and sprinkle with more freshly grated Parmesan.

Variation

PANCAKES MOONLIGHTING AS WAFFLES
Makes 6 to 8 waffles, depending on the size of your waffle maker. **This batter also cooks beautifully in a waffle iron. It works especially well for thinner waffles (like store-bought freezer waffles), which you can cut into quarters for snacks or the base for appetizers.**

Heat your waffle iron as directed, then grease it with nonstick spray. Ladle the batter into the center and close the waffle iron. Cook as directed until the waffle is deeply golden and crisp (usually about 4 to 8 minutes, depending on your waffle iron).

Make Ahead and Storage
The pancakes are best immediately after cooking.

Cooking for a Crowd? How to Keep Stovetop Items Warm

Many of the recipes in this chapter—like pancakes and waffles—are cooked in batches, so how do you keep everything nice and warm until ready to serve?

Preheat the oven to 225°F/110°C with a rack in the center. Place a wire rack on a baking sheet. As you finish each batch, place the food on the rack in a single layer, and tent the pan loosely with foil, if desired. Keep warm in the oven until you're ready to serve.

Hortobágyi Palacsinta (Hungarian Stuffed Crepes)

Makes 12 stuffed crepes

DIFFICULTY: **EASY**

My maternal great-grandmother was Hungarian. My mother describes her cooking with awe, and both of them have passed down a deep love of certain flavors as comfort food to me. These meat-stuffed crepes fit the bill.

To keep the crepes from becoming soggy inside, the meat is drained of the sauce that forms as it cooks. Then this sauce is thickened, spiced with paprika, and finished with sour cream. The crepes are doused in the sauce and finished in the oven. This makes a hearty, rib-sticking meal.

FILLING

30 g / 2 tablespoons extra virgin olive oil

320 g / 1 large sweet onion, minced

115 g / 1 medium green bell pepper, cored, seeded, and minced

570 g / 1¼ pounds ground veal or beef

10 g / 2 cloves garlic, minced

One 795 g / 28-ounce can crushed tomatoes

13 g / 1½ tablespoons hot paprika

Kosher salt and freshly ground black pepper

75 g / ⅓ cup sour cream

10 g / ¼ cup chopped fresh parsley

42 g / 1½ ounces / 3 tablespoons unsalted butter

23 g / 3 tablespoons all-purpose flour

230 g / 1 cup sour cream, plus more for serving

12 crepes (page 54; you'll need to make a double recipe)

Chopped fresh dill for garnish

1. Make the filling: In a large skillet, heat the olive oil over medium heat. Add the onion and bell pepper and cook until tender, 4 to 5 minutes. Add the meat and cook until well browned, 4 to 5 minutes. Stir in the garlic and cook for 1 minute, or until fragrant.

2. Stir in the tomatoes and bring to a simmer. Stir in the paprika, season with salt and pepper, and cook, stirring occasionally, until the mixture thickens slightly, 10 to 12 minutes.

3. Stir in the sour cream and parsley and remove from the heat. Set a sieve over a medium bowl and spoon the meat mixture into the sieve. Press on the meat firmly with a wooden spoon to release as much of the sauce as possible; reserve the sauce.

4. In a medium pot, melt the butter over medium heat. Sprinkle the flour evenly over the butter and stir to combine. Cook for 1 to 2 minutes, until the flour has lost its raw flavor. Slowly add the reserved sauce, whisking well to combine, Reduce the heat to medium-low and cook, stirring constantly, until the sauce thickens somewhat, 2 to 3 minutes. Whisk in the sour cream. Set aside.

5. Preheat the oven to 350°F/175°C with a rack in the center. Lightly grease a 9 x 13-inch/23 x 33 cm baking pan with nonstick spray.

6. Assemble the dish: Spoon a few ladlefuls of the sauce into the prepared pan and tilt the pan to coat the bottom. Place a crepe on a clean work surface. Spoon about 150 g / ½ cup of

the meat mixture into the center, fold over the two opposite sides to encase the filling, and then roll up the crepe; it will be quite fat and full. Place the crepe in the pan, seam side down, then repeat with the remaining crepes and filling. Spoon the remaining sauce over the top of the crepes.

7. Transfer the pan to the oven and bake until the sauce bubbles, 18 to 20 minutes. Serve immediately, topped with more sour cream and dill.

Make Ahead and Storage
The palacsinta are best as soon as they are baked. Store leftovers in an airtight container in the refrigerator for up to 48 hours.

Dill and Chive Blini
with Crème Fraîche and Caviar

Makes about 18 blini

DIFFICULTY: **EASY**

I first saw blini in one of my mom's Martha Stewart cookbooks, and they held a similar level of wonder as the Turkish delight from The Lion, the Witch, and the Wardrobe. *When I discovered, many years later, how easy it is to make blini, I started enlisting them for all kinds of bites. It was a budget entertaining trick of my early dinner parties (they're really just tiny pancakes)—but you could top them with anything, and they always felt effortlessly gussied up. Here I puree fresh herbs into the batter, which gives them a beautiful brightness. If you don't want to serve caviar, these are also delicious topped with balsamic pearls, which look a lot like fish roe but are made from vinegar (see Resources).*

BATTER

175 g / ¾ cup whole milk

10 g / ¼ cup small fresh dill fronds

9 g / 3 tablespoons minced fresh chives

56 g / 1 large egg

14 g / 1 tablespoon unsalted butter, melted

120 g / 1 cup all-purpose flour

3 g / ½ teaspoon baking powder

2 g / ½ teaspoon fine sea salt

FINISHING

115 g / ½ cup crème fraîche or sour cream

Caviar or other roe for serving

Small dill fronds

Snipped fresh chives

1. Combine the milk, dill, and chives and puree with an immersion blender (some small flecks of herbs are okay, but you want a smooth puree). Add the egg and melted butter and blend briefly to combine.

2. In a medium bowl, whisk the flour, baking powder, and salt to combine. Add the milk mixture, whisking, and whisk until evenly incorporated.

3. Heat a griddle or large skillet over medium heat. Grease lightly with nonstick spray. Working in batches, scoop 15 g / 1 tablespoon of the batter for each blini onto the hot pan, leaving at least ½ inch/1 cm between them. Cook until golden brown on the first side, 1 to 2 minutes, then flip and cook until the other side browns, 1 minute more.

4. Transfer the blini to a serving platter. Top each one with 3 g / ½ teaspoon of the crème fraîche and top that with some caviar or roe, a dill frond, and some chives. Serve immediately.

Make Ahead and Storage
The blini are best the same day they are made.

Dutch Skillet Pancake with Gouda

Makes 4 large pancakes

DIFFICULTY: **EASY**

This pancake is thicker than a crepe but much thinner than a fluffy buttermilk pancake. In Amsterdam, I was served one so large that the crisp edges hung off the sides of the plate. It was topped with a few slices of Gouda toward the end of cooking, just before it was put in front of me. The heat carries the aroma of the cheese as it hits the table, and I think this is one of the most craveably savory ways to eat a pancake. It's perfect with a little added brightness, so I serve these with a drizzle of my delicious all-purpose Parsley Sauce (recipe follows).

210 g / 1¾ cups all-purpose flour

12 g / 1 tablespoon granulated sugar

5 g / 1 teaspoon baking powder

3 g / ¾ teaspoon fine sea salt

350 g / 1½ cups whole milk

56 g / 1 large egg

56 g / 2 ounces / 4 tablespoons unsalted butter, melted

About 85 g / 3 ounces Gouda cheese, very thinly sliced (3 or 4 slices per pancake)

Parsley Sauce (recipe follows) for serving

1. In a blender, combine the flour, sugar, baking powder, salt, milk, egg, and melted butter and blend into a thin batter. Cover and let the batter rest for 15 minutes.

2. Heat a large (12-inch/30 cm) nonstick skillet over medium heat. Have ready a lid to cover the pan. Grease the hot pan with nonstick spray.

3. Make the pancakes one at a time: Pour about 160 g / ½ cup batter into the hot pan and immediately tilt and swirl the pan to create a large, thin pancake. Cook until the pancake is browned on the bottom, 1 to 2 minutes. Flip the pancake, top with 3 or 4 slices of Gouda, and cook for 1 minute. Cover the pan and cook until the cheese is just melted, 30 seconds to a minute.

4. Transfer the pancake to a plate and serve immediately, with the parsley sauce. Repeat with the remaining batter and cheese.

Parsley Sauce

Makes 175 g/about ¾ cup

Rustic green sauces made from fresh herbs, like chimichurri, chermoula, and zhoug, are one of my favorite ways to brighten up any meal. This simple sauce is good on everything from empanadas (page 256) to Pizza (page 181).

20 g / ½ packed cup coarsely chopped fresh parsley leaves and stems

30 g / 3 scallions, roughly chopped

5 g / 1 clove garlic

77 g / ⅓ cup extra virgin olive oil

45 g / 3 tablespoons malt vinegar

Kosher salt and freshly ground black pepper

Pinch of ground cumin

1. Combine the parsley, scallions, and garlic in the bowl of a food processor (you can also use a regular blender, or an immersion blender) and pulse until finely chopped. Scrape the bowl and pulse again if necessary. Add the olive oil and vinegar and pulse until thoroughly combined.

2. Transfer the sauce to a serving bowl and season with salt, pepper, and the cumin. The sauce can be made up to 24 hours ahead and refrigerated in an airtight container.

Make Ahead and Storage
The pancake is best immediately after cooking.

Scallion Pancakes

Makes 6 pancakes

DIFFICULTY: MEDIUM

I learned to make Chinese scallion pancakes in culinary school, and I was immediately taken by both the technique and the incredible end result. These pancakes are made with a simple form of lamination to create chewy, tender, flaky layers, which are studded with plenty of thinly sliced scallions. For me, this recipe opened up a whole new world of possibilities. Before I knew about these pancakes, the word "lamination" had seemed like a time-consuming burden, but this method is decidedly unintimidating. The pancakes are traditionally made with oil, which is brushed evenly over the surface of the dough. Since oil has a higher melting point than butter, it is easier to consistently get ideally flaky, tender results. Sometimes I use schmaltz or bacon fat instead, which makes an especially flavorful pancake that is perfect for snacking (no sauce required). These are one of my favorite recipes to make for guests, since I can be cooking them as they arrive, which means the house smells amazing. Best of all, folks can grab them as soon as they are cooked, when they are at their absolute freshest.

300 g / 2½ cups all-purpose flour

3 g / ½ teaspoon kosher salt, plus more for finishing

230 g / 1 cup boiling water, plus more as needed

Neutral oil (such as canola or vegetable), or schmaltz, or bacon fat for brushing

100 g / 10 scallions, thinly sliced

1. In a medium bowl, whisk the flour and salt to combine. Add the boiling water and mix with a wooden spoon (or two chopsticks) until the dough comes together in a ball. If it seems dry, add more hot water 15 g / 1 tablespoon at a time until the dough comes together—it shouldn't be overly sticky.

2. Transfer the dough to a lightly floured surface and knead until very smooth, 4 to 5 minutes. Lightly grease a bowl with nonstick spray. Form the dough into a ball and place in the bowl, turning it a few times to coat. Cover the bowl and let the dough rest at room temperature for 1 hour.

3. Turn the dough out, divide into 6 equal even pieces (about 85 g each), and round each piece into a ball (see page 104); if the dough is at all sticky, add a little flour as needed to help you shape the pieces. Place on a lightly floured work surface, cover with greased plastic wrap, and let rest for 10 minutes.

4. On a lightly floured surface, roll out one piece of dough into a round 8 inches/20 cm wide (about ⅛ in/3 mm thick). Brush the surface of the dough all over with oil (or other fat), then sprinkle with about 17 g / ¼ cup of the scallions. Starting at one side of the circle, roll up the dough into a tight spiraled log. Starting at one end of the log, roll up the dough into a coiled round. Use the palm of your hand to gently press the dough down. Transfer to a clean area of the work surface and cover while you shape the remaining pieces of dough. Let rest at room temperature for 30 minutes (you can also hold the shaped dough in the refrigerator, covered, for up to 8 hours).

5. Working with one piece of dough at a time, on a lightly floured surface, roll out each piece

(CONTINUES)

Make Ahead and Storage
The pancakes can be made through step 4 and held for up to 8 hours in the refrigerator. The cooked pancakes are best immediately after cooking. Rewarm any leftover pancakes in a hot skillet before serving.

into a round 8 inches/20 cm wide. Brush the surface with oil (or other fat).

6. Heat a large skillet over medium-high heat; set a wire rack on a baking sheet nearby. When the pan is hot, brush it fairly generously with oil (or other fat). Add one pancake to the pan, greased side up, and cook, flipping frequently, until deeply golden brown on both sides, 4 to 5 minutes. Transfer to a wire rack and sprinkle with salt. Repeat with the remaining pancakes.

7. Cut the pancakes into wedges and serve immediately.

Making Scallion Pancakes

Roll out the dough into a thin circle, brush all over with oil, and sprinkle with scallions.

Roll up the round into a tight log.

Roll the log into a spiral.

Roll the rested round into a thin pancake.

Elote Fritters

Makes 10 fritters

DIFFICULTY: **EASY**

I am truly, madly, deeply in love with corn. Especially corn on the cob, slathered in butter or—even better—topped with crema, grated Cotija cheese, lime juice, and chili powder: the one, the only, elote, Mexican street corn. It doesn't get much better. Think of these crispy corn beauties as all those big flavors in an easy-to-eat (and dip!) fritter.

Making veggie fritters is a go-to weeknight dinner hack in our house—with a basic ratio of flour and egg, you can fritterize almost any vegetable. Be sure to check out the zucchini and potato version and the Four-Onion Fritters in the Variations below.

FRITTERS

450 g / 3 cups corn kernels (from about 4 ears of corn; or substitute thawed frozen corn or well-drained canned corn)

140 g / 1 bunch scallions, thinly sliced

10 g / ¼ cup chopped fresh cilantro

120 g / 1 cup all-purpose flour

5 g / 1 teaspoon baking powder

4 g / ¾ teaspoon kosher salt

2 g / ¾ teaspoon freshly ground black pepper

113 g / 2 large eggs, whisked

60 g / ¼ cup half-and-half or whole milk

50 g / ½ cup grated Cotija cheese (or queso fresco or feta)

60 g / ¼ cup neutral oil (such as canola or vegetable)

FINISHING

60 g / ¼ cup sour cream

45 g / 3 tablespoons mayonnaise

30 g / 2 tablespoons fresh lime juice

5 g / 1 clove garlic, finely grated

2 g / ¾ teaspoon chili powder

Grated Cotija cheese

Chopped fresh cilantro

Lime wedges for serving

1. Make the fritters: In a medium bowl, toss the corn, scallions, and cilantro together until well combined.

2. In another medium bowl, whisk the flour, baking powder, salt, and pepper to combine. Add the eggs and half-and-half or milk and whisk until well combined. Fold in the corn mixture and Cotija.

3. In a large nonstick skillet, heat the oil over medium heat. When the oil is hot, working in batches, scoop 80 g / heaping-¼-cup mounds of batter into the skillet, without crowding. Use a spatula to gently flatten the fritters and panfry until evenly golden brown on the bottom, 3 to 4 minutes. Flip and cook until golden on the other side, 2 to 3 minutes more. Transfer the fritters to a wire rack.

4. To serve, in a small bowl, whisk the sour cream, mayonnaise, lime juice, garlic, and chili powder together. Spoon a thin layer of this mixture over each fritter and sprinkle with Cotija and cilantro. Serve immediately, with lime wedges.

Variations

FOUR-ONION FRITTERS **In a large skillet, melt 14 g / 1 tablespoon unsalted butter with 15 g / 1 tablespoon extra virgin olive oil**

(CONTINUES)

over medium heat. Add 650 g / 2 large sweet onions, thinly sliced, 650 g / 2 large red onions, thinly sliced, 300 g / 2 large leeks, trimmed and thinly sliced, and 100 g / 4 medium shallots, thinly sliced, and cook until the onions are translucent, 5 to 6 minutes. Reduce the heat to low and continue to cook until the onions are lightly golden brown, 35 to 40 minutes. Stir in 15 g / 3 cloves garlic, minced, remove from the heat, and set aside to cool for 15 minutes.

In a medium bowl, whisk 120 g / 1 cup all-purpose flour, 5 g / 1 teaspoon baking powder, 4 g / 3/4 teaspoon kosher salt, and 2 g / 1/2 teaspoon freshly ground black pepper together. Add 113 g / 2 large eggs and 60 g / 1/4 cup half-and-half or whole milk and whisk well to combine. Fold in the cooled onions. Heat 60 g / 1/4 cup neutral oil (such as canola or vegetable) in a large nonstick skillet over medium heat and cook the fritters as directed above. Season the hot fritters with flaky sea salt and serve with Tomato Jam (page 57) or Parsley Sauce (page 64).

ZUCCHINI AND POTATO FRITTERS Line a colander with two clean kitchen towels (I use flour sack towels). Put 520 g / 3 cups shredded peeled potatoes, 230 g / 1½ cups shredded zucchini, and 220 g / 1 medium sweet onion, thinly sliced, in the lined colander, wrap in the towels to form a tight packet, and squeeze thoroughly to remove excess moisture. Transfer the vegetables to a large bowl and toss with 60 g / 1/2 cup all-purpose flour until evenly combined. Add 56 g / 1 large egg and 35 g / 1 large egg white and toss well to combine. Season with 3/4 teaspoon kosher salt and 2 g / 1/2 teaspoon freshly ground black pepper. Heat 60 g / 1/4 cup neutral oil (such as canola or vegetable) in a large nonstick skillet over medium heat and cook the fritters as directed above. Season the hot fritters with flaky sea salt and serve with sour cream.

Make Ahead and Storage
The fritters are best immediately after cooking. Store leftovers in an airtight container in the refrigerator. Leftovers can be refreshed in a skillet, toaster oven, or air fryer to re-crisp.

Yeasted Waffles

Makes about 12 waffles (depending on your waffle maker)

DIFFICULTY: **EASY**

While I usually opt for a savory breakfast over a sweet one, I am obsessed with the thought of a good waffle. To me, yeasted waffles are the best out there—golden and perfectly crisp outside, fluffy inside. And they can lean savory (see Chicken and Waffles, page 74), though they are, of course, splendid with powdered sugar or syrup. The batter gets whisked up the night before, so all you have to do is roll out of bed and plug in your waffle iron.

360 g / 3 cups all-purpose flour

24 g / 2 tablespoons granulated sugar

3 g / ¾ teaspoon fine sea salt

6 g / 1¾ teaspoons instant dry yeast

345 g / 1½ cups whole milk

118 g / ½ cup heavy cream

70 g / 2½ ounces / 5 tablespoons unsalted butter, melted

170 g / 3 large eggs, at room temperature

1. In a large bowl, whisk the flour, sugar, salt, and yeast to combine. (The batter will increase in volume a bit overnight, so make sure the bowl is large enough to allow it to grow.)

2. In another large bowl (preferably with a spout), whisk the milk, cream, melted butter, and eggs to combine. Gradually pour this mixture into the flour mixture, whisking until thoroughly combined. Cover the bowl with plastic wrap and refrigerate for 10 to 12 hours (no more than 15 hours).

3. The next day, heat your waffle iron until nice and hot. Spray it with nonstick spray. Ladle some of the batter into the waffle iron—the amount you'll use will depend on your iron—and close the iron. Cook as per the manufacturer's instructions until the waffle is golden brown on both sides, usually 3 to 6 minutes. Transfer the waffle to a platter and repeat with the remaining batter.

4. OPTIONAL (BUT WORTH IT!): Place the waffles on a rack on a baking sheet and toast in a 350°F/175°C oven for 5 to 10 minutes (or do this with the waffles as they come out of the iron).

5. Serve immediately.

Make Ahead and Storage
These waffles are best when freshly made, but they do freeze well, wrapped tightly in plastic wrap and stored in a freezer bag, for up to 1 month. Toast in a toaster or toaster oven to refresh.

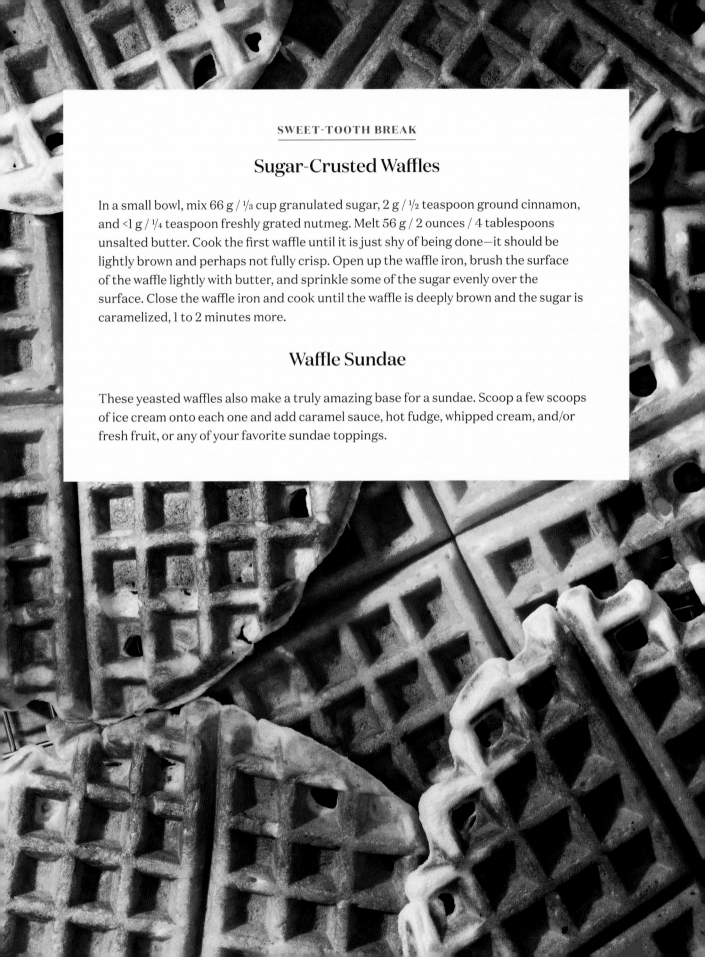

Sugar-Crusted Waffles

In a small bowl, mix 66 g / ⅓ cup granulated sugar, 2 g / ½ teaspoon ground cinnamon, and <1 g / ¼ teaspoon freshly grated nutmeg. Melt 56 g / 2 ounces / 4 tablespoons unsalted butter. Cook the first waffle until it is just shy of being done—it should be lightly brown and perhaps not fully crisp. Open up the waffle iron, brush the surface of the waffle lightly with butter, and sprinkle some of the sugar evenly over the surface. Close the waffle iron and cook until the waffle is deeply brown and the sugar is caramelized, 1 to 2 minutes more.

Waffle Sundae

These yeasted waffles also make a truly amazing base for a sundae. Scoop a few scoops of ice cream onto each one and add caramel sauce, hot fudge, whipped cream, and/or fresh fruit, or any of your favorite sundae toppings.

Chicken and Waffles

Makes 6 servings

My favorite thing to make with my yeasted waffles is some form of chicken and waffles. When I'm eating fried chicken, I almost always prefer bone-in chicken—with one notable exception. My grandma Jeanne used to make me her easy fried chicken when I came visit her—often at my strong request. This usually meant pieces of chicken breast given a traditional Southern fried chicken treatment—an hours-long (or even overnight) soak in buttermilk before being dredged in a thick coating of seasoned flour. The buttermilk brines the chicken during the soak, keeping it super-moist when it's fried. Though these were smaller pieces of chicken, they were thicker than standard "tenders," so you can still appreciate some of the crunchy-exterior-to-juicy-interior ratio of bone-in fried chicken, but with the ease of something that can be done any day of the week, using any quantity of chicken. She used to serve this chicken with crisp twice-baked potatoes, but I use it to make chicken and waffles, a preparation where I've also come to appreciate boneless chicken done right, because the waffles and chicken cut and eat similarly.

906 g / 4 boneless, skinless chicken breasts (thighs work too), cut into 2-inch-/2.5 cm wide strips

690 to 920 g / 3 to 4 cups cold buttermilk

Neutral oil (such as canola or vegetable) for deep-frying

240 g / 2 cups all-purpose flour

21 g / 3 tablespoons cornstarch

2 g / ½ teaspoon baking powder

5 g / 1½ teaspoons smoked paprika

3 g / 1 teaspoon onion powder

3 g / 1 teaspoon freshly ground black pepper

Kosher salt

6 Yeasted Waffles (page 72), freshly made

1. Arrange the chicken pieces in an even layer in a medium dish. Add enough buttermilk so they are completely submerged. Cover and refrigerate for at least 4 hours, or up to 12 hours (or overnight).

2. In a large pot (or a deep fryer), heat 2 to 3 inches/5 to 8 cm of oil over medium heat until it reaches about 375°F/190°C on an instant-read thermometer. Set a cooling rack set over a paper-towel–lined baking sheet.

3. Meanwhile, in a shallow dish, whisk the flour, cornstarch, and baking powder to combine. Whisk in the paprika, onion powder, and black pepper.

4. Remove the chicken from the buttermilk, shaking off the excess (there will still be plenty clinging to the surface), And arrange the chicken out on a baking sheet in a single layer. Season with kosher salt.

5. Working in batches, dredge the chicken pieces in the flour mixture and add to the hot oil, taking care not to overcrowd them. When you add the chicken, the oil temperature will drop—adjust the heat as needed to keep it at around 350°F/175°C. Fry until the strips are deeply golden brown and very crisp, and the chicken is fully cooked, 3 to 4 minutes. Remove from the oil with tongs and transfer to the prepared rack. Season again with kosher salt to taste. Serve immediately, with the yeasted waffles.

Jalapeño Cornmeal Waffles

Makes about 10 waffles (depending on your waffle maker)

DIFFICULTY: **EASY**

These cornmeal waffles are so beautifully crisp that I like to cut them into quarters and dip them in gooey queso. I usually keep them morning-brain-level easy by using pickled jalapeños. But if you've got a little extra time, roast 2 jalapeños over an open flame (or on the grill), turning occasionally, until black and blistered all over. Transfer to a zip-top bag, close tightly, and steam for 15 minutes, then remove the skin, stems, and seeds and chop up to add to the waffles.

No time to make queso? Add 150 g / 1½ cups shredded cheddar to the waffle batter instead, and serve the waffles topped with fried eggs.

35 g / 2½ ounces / 5 tablespoons unsalted butter

10 g / 2 cloves garlic, minced

210 g / 1¾ cups all-purpose flour

175 g / 1¼ cups yellow cornmeal

8 g / 2 teaspoons baking powder

2 g / ½ teaspoon chipotle chile powder

2 g / ½ teaspoon fine sea salt

1 g / ¼ teaspoon freshly ground black pepper

575 g / 2½ cups buttermilk

170 g / 3 large eggs

42 g / 2 tablespoons honey

75 g / ⅓ cup finely minced pickled jalapeños

Mom's Queso (page 78) or Cheddar Beer Sauce (page 78) for dipping

1. In a small saucepan, melt the butter over medium heat. Add the garlic and swirl the pot for 30 seconds to 1 minute, until the garlic is fragrant. Set aside to cool slightly.

2. In a large bowl, whisk the flour, cornmeal, baking powder, chipotle powder, salt, and pepper together.

3. In a medium bowl, whisk the buttermilk, eggs, honey, and reserved garlic butter to combine well. Add to the flour mixture and whisk well to combine. Fold in the jalapeños.

4. Heat your waffle iron until nice and hot. Spray it with nonstick spray. Ladle some of the batter into the waffle iron and close the iron. Cook as per the manufacturer's instructions until the waffle is golden brown on both sides, 3 to 6 minutes, depending on your waffle maker. Transfer the waffle to a platter and repeat with the remaining batter.

5. **OPTIONAL (BUT WORTH IT!):** Place the waffles on a rack on a baking sheet and toast in a 350°F/175°C oven for 5 to 10 minutes (or do this with the waffles as they come out of the iron).

6. Serve immediately.

Make Ahead and Storage
These waffles are best freshly made, but they do freeze well, wrapped tightly in plastic wrap and stored in a freezer bag, for up to 1 month. Toast in a toaster or toaster oven to refresh.

All That Simmers Is Gold

I have strong feelings about queso, and just one recipe will not do. There's a queso below for whatever your cheesy sauce personality is. Serve it with homemade tortillas (pages 209 and 212) or drizzle it over savory waffles and pancakes (pages 57, 67, 72, or 77).

Mom's Queso

In a blender or food processor, combine one 415 g / 14.5-ounce can diced tomatoes, one 113 g / 4-ounce can green chiles, 20 g / 1 jalapeño, halved and seeded, 10 g / 2 cloves garlic, 85 g / ½ red onion, roughly chopped, and 20 g / ½ cup coarsely chopped fresh cilantro (it's okay to use stems too) and puree until fairly smooth; season with fine sea salt and freshly ground black pepper to taste. Transfer to a medium pot and add 340 g / 12 ounces diced Velveeta (yes, I said Velveeta—if you want a sauce made with real cheese, try either of the two below). Heat over medium heat, stirring frequently, until the cheese melts. Serve immediately, or transfer to a Crock-Pot to keep warm.

Cheddar Beer Sauce

Follow the recipe for Cheddar Ale Soup (page 87), but reduce the broth to 345 g / 1½ cups. Serve immediately, or transfer to a Crock-Pot to keep warm. (Note: This will make a lot of sauce, but you can always add more broth to the leftovers to turn them back into a soupier consistency.)

Spicy Fonduta

Pour about 2 inches/5 cm of water into a medium pot and bring to a simmer over medium heat. Reduce the heat to medium-low and set a medium heatproof bowl over the pot. Add 230 g / 1 cup whole milk and 42 g / 3 tablespoons unsalted butter to the bowl and heat, stirring occasionally, until the butter is melted. Reduce the heat to low and very gradually add 145 g / 5 ounces Fontina cheese, shredded, and 145 g / 5 ounces Gouda cheese, shredded (in about 8 additions), stirring until each addition is thoroughly melted before adding more. Stir in 30 g / 2 tablespoons of your favorite hot sauce (or more to taste), 15 g / 1 tablespoon Dijon mustard, and 3 g / 1 teaspoon red pepper flakes. Serve immediately.

Chicken and Dumplings

Makes 6 generous servings

DIFFICULTY: **EASY**

The only thing better than the way your house smells when you're making chicken and dumplings is walking in the door to that smell, knowing someone else has cooked it for you. The perfect chicken and dumplings have a rich, creamy broth loaded with veggies, topped with a layer of plump, fluffy dumplings. If you're looking for the same satisfaction and aroma quotient without any meat, try the Mushrooms and Dumplings in the Variation below.

CHICKEN STEW

1360 g / 3 pounds bone-in, skin-on chicken parts (I usually use a mixture of thighs and breasts)

Kosher salt and freshly ground black pepper

120 g / 1 cup all-purpose flour

24 g / 2 tablespoons extra virgin olive oil

325 g / 1 large sweet onion, diced

220 g / 4 medium carrots, peeled and diced

150 g / 3 stalks celery, diced

170 g / 2 large leeks, white and light green parts only, halved and thinly sliced

20 g / 4 cloves garlic, minced

14 g / 1 tablespoon unsalted butter

1380 g / 6 cups chicken broth

230 g / 1 cup apple cider

2 bay leaves

3 g / 1 tablespoon chopped fresh rosemary

3 g / 1 tablespoon chopped fresh thyme

3 g / 1 tablespoon chopped fresh sage

120 g / ½ cup heavy cream

10 g / ¼ cup chopped fresh parsley

DUMPLINGS

180 g / 1½ cups all-purpose flour

8 g / 1½ teaspoons baking powder

6 g / 1 teaspoon kosher salt

170 g / ¾ cup whole milk

24 g / 1 ounce / 2 tablespoons unsalted butter, melted

1. Pat the chicken dry with paper towels and season all over with salt and pepper. Place 80 g / ⅔ cup of the flour in a shallow bowl and dredge the chicken in it, turning so it's fully coated on both sides.

2. In a large Dutch oven, heat the olive oil over medium heat. Working in batches, add the chicken and cook, turning occasionally, until it is well browned on all sides, 5 to 8 minutes. Remove from the pot and reserve on a plate.

3. Add the onion, carrots, and celery to the pot and cook until the onions start to become translucent, 4 to 5 minutes. Add the leeks and cook until they are wilted and the other vegetables are tender, 4 to 5 minutes. Add the garlic and cook until fragrant, about 1 minute.

4. Add the butter to the pot and melt, stirring to combine it with the fat already in the pot. Sprinkle the remaining 40 g / ⅓ cup flour evenly over the vegetables, then stir to combine. Cook, stirring constantly, for 1 minute. Add the chicken broth and cider and bring to a simmer.

(CONTINUES)

79

5. Return the chicken to the pot and add the bay leaves, rosemary, thyme, and sage. Reduce the heat to low, cover the pot, and simmer until the chicken is just cooked, 25 to 30 minutes. Remove the chicken from the pot and place on a baking sheet to cool slightly. Discard the bay leaves. Set the pot aside.

6. When the chicken has cooled enough to handle, remove and discard the skin. Use forks to gently pull the chicken off the bones (discard the bones), then gently shred or coarsely chop it into bite-size pieces. Return the chicken to the pot, stirring to combine.

7. Make the dumplings: In a medium bowl, whisk the flour, baking powder, and salt to combine. Add the milk and melted butter and mix until a thick, sticky dough forms.

8. Return the pot to the heat and bring the stew to a simmer. Scoop the dough into heaping-tablespoon-size portions (I use a #20/1-tablespoon scoop, but you can just use two spoons) and drop them onto the surface of the stew (you should get about 12 dumplings).

9. Cover the pot and cook until the dumplings are puffy and firm to the touch, 30 to 35 minutes. Remove the lid, and gently stir the cream and parsley into the stew. Season with more salt and pepper, if desired, and serve immediately.

Variation

MUSHROOMS AND DUMPLINGS **Replace the chicken with 1250 g / 2³/₄ pounds mushrooms (any variety, or a combination), cut into bite-size pieces. Substitute an equal amount of mushroom or vegetable broth for the chicken broth and replace the cider with dry white wine. Spread the mushrooms out on two baking sheets and drizzle 30 g / 2 tablespoons extra virgin olive oil over each pan. Roast the mushrooms at 400°F/205°C until tender and lightly browned, 35 to 40 minutes; stir once midway through roasting, spreading the mushrooms back into an even layer before returning them to the oven. Reduce the flour to 40 g / ¹/₃ cup and skip steps 1 and 2. In step 3, start by adding 24 g / 1 ounce / 2 tablespoons unsalted butter to the pot, then proceed as directed. Transfer the mushrooms to the pot, cover, and cook until flavorful, 20 to 25 minutes. Proceed with steps 7 through 9 above.**

Make Ahead and Storage

The chicken stew can be made up to 2 days ahead. Let cool, then transfer to an airtight container and refrigerate until ready to finish the dish; bring the stew to a simmer before adding the dumplings. The final dish is best the same day it's made. Store any leftovers in an airtight container in the refrigerator.

Ode to Boiled Dumplings

I don't think dumplings as a food group get nearly enough love, and, oh, boiled dumplings of all sorts—how I love thee, shall I count the ways? They are simple to make—in some ways, easier and less fussy than their dough cousin, pasta— but they are just as crowd-pleasing. They are easily adaptable, and there are so many varieties to choose from.

Simple boiled dumplings appear in cuisines around the world—the recipes in this book drew inspiration from Jamaica, Austria, Italy, and beyond. I hope I can convince you that delicious dumplings deserve a spot in your regular rotation.

At their simplest, dumplings are made with a starchy ingredient like flour, cornmeal, or potatoes, combined with a liquid and formed into a dough. Some dough recipes also contain enrichments such as eggs or fat. Chemical leaveners, like baking soda or powder, are sometimes used for a lighter texture. Thicker doughs can be shaped by hand. Thinner or softer doughs/batters may require a tool for shaping—like a small cookie scoop to drop rounds of batter into boiling water or a spaetzle maker or a grater. This style of dumplings is typically boiled or poached in simmering water. I recommend fully cooking dumplings separately before adding them to or serving alongside other recipes. And after boiling or poaching, some dumplings are cooked again: sautéed or panfried for a crisp, browned exterior, or added to simmering soups or stews.

Doneness Indicators

Most dumplings sink when they are first added to the pot of boiling water, and rising/floating to the surface is one indicator that they are nearly cooked. However, especially with thicker dumplings, it can be difficult to determine if they are cooked all the way through. As with pasta, I often test doneness by removing one dumpling and tasting it—an undercooked dumpling will be gummy in the center.

Everyday Egg Dumplings

My mom made these dumplings to go with soups or braised meats. Consider adding minced fresh herbs, ground spices, or up to 100 g / 1 cup shredded cheese.

Makes 6 servings

170 g / 3 large eggs

30 g / 2 tablespoons whole milk, plus more if needed

240 g / 2 cups all-purpose flour

6 g / 1 teaspoon kosher salt

2 g / ½ teaspoon freshly ground black pepper

1. In a medium bowl, whisk the eggs and milk to combine. Add the flour, salt, and pepper and mix with a spatula until the mixture forms a thick, sticky dough. If needed, add more milk 15 g / 1 tablespoon at a time until the dough comes together.

2. Scoop the dumplings into simmering soup, broth, or boiling water. (I use a #40/2-tablespoon scoop, but you can just use two spoons.) You can make them bigger or smaller too—just aim to keep the dumplings a similar size (larger dumplings, of course, will take longer to cook).

3. Cover the pot and simmer over medium-low heat until the dumplings are cooked through, 20 to 25 minutes—they should appear puffy on the exterior but be firm to the touch.

Potato

Cornmeal

Everyday Egg

Cheese

Cheese Dumplings

A soft cheese like ricotta or farmer's cheese serves as the base for these chewy dumplings. I've even made them with mascarpone, and they were incredible. Serve these in soups or as a side dish, tossed with melted butter and herbs, or finish them with Pesto (page 96) or tomato sauce (page 155) and enjoy all on their own.

Makes 6 servings

113 g / 2 large eggs

454 g / 1 pound ricotta or farmer's cheese

100 g / 1 cup finely grated Parmesan cheese

3 g / ½ teaspoon kosher salt

2 g / ½ teaspoon freshly ground black pepper

80 g / ⅔ cup all-purpose flour, plus more if needed

1. In a medium bowl, whisk the eggs well. Add the cheeses, salt, and pepper and mix well to combine. Fold in the flour. You should have a thick, sticky dough. If it appears too thin or soft, add more flour, 15 g / 1 tablespoon at a time.

2. Bring a large pot of salted water to a boil. Working in batches to avoid crowding the dumplings, scoop the dumplings into the boiling water (I use a heaping #60/1-tablespoon scoop—or use two spoons). Cook the dumplings for 4 to 5 minutes, until they float on the surface and are firm to the touch. Remove from the water with a spider, or drain in a colander, and use/serve immediately.

Potato Dumplings

I use cold (read: leftover) mashed potatoes when I make these, so they are more similar in style to Polish potato Kopytka than Italian potato gnocchi, which usually use freshly cooked potatoes. These are great in soups, served alongside stews and braises, or tossed in sauce.

Makes 6 servings

56 g / 1 large egg

About 440 g / 2 cups mashed potatoes

25 g / ¼ cup grated Parmesan cheese (optional)

120 g / 1 cup all-purpose flour, plus more as needed

6 g / 1 teaspoon kosher salt

2 g / ½ teaspoon freshly ground black pepper

1. In a medium bowl, whisk the egg well. Add the potatoes, cheese, if using, flour, salt, and pepper and mix until a smooth dough forms; don't overmix. If the dough feels at all sticky, add more flour as needed.

2. Divide the dough into 2 equal pieces (about 320 g each). Roll each piece into a log 1 inch/ 2½ cm thick. Use a bench knife or sharp knife to cut the dough into 1-inch/2.5-cm pieces.

3. Bring a large pot of salted water to a boil. Working in batches to avoid crowding the dumplings, add them to the water and cook for 4 to 5 minutes, until they float to the surface and are firm to the touch. Remove from the water with a spider, or drain in a colander, and use/serve immediately.

Cornmeal Dumplings

You can use yellow or white cornmeal for these dumplings. Sometimes I sprinkle a little more raw cornmeal on top of each one before placing the lid on to cook them. These work perfectly in the Mushrooms and Dumplings recipe (page 61).

Makes 6 servings

113 g / 2 large eggs

45 g / 3 tablespoons whole milk, plus more if needed

24 g / 1 ounce / 2 tablespoons unsalted butter, melted

150 g / 1¼ cups all-purpose flour, plus more if needed

95 g / ⅔ cup cornmeal

5 g / 1 teaspoon baking powder

6 g / 1 teaspoon kosher salt

2 g / ½ teaspoon freshly ground black pepper

1. In a medium bowl, whisk the eggs, milk, and butter to combine. Add the flour, cornmeal, baking powder, salt, and pepper and mix with a spatula until the mixture forms a thick, sticky dough. If the dough seems too wet, add more flour, 7 g / 1 tablespoon at a time; if it's too dry to hold together, add more milk 15 g / 1 tablespoon at a time as necessary.

2. Scoop the dumplings into simmering soup, broth, or boiling water. I use a #40/2-tablespoon scoop, but you can just use two spoons. You can make them bigger or smaller too—just aim to keep the dumplings a similar size (larger dumplings, of course, will take longer to cook).

3. Cover the pot, reduce the heat to medium-low, and cook until the dumplings are cooked through, 18 to 24 minutes—they should appear puffy on the exterior but be firm to the touch.

Poached Fruit Dumplings

Makes 5 servings

I make these dumplings in the summer, usually with apricots or small plums. Serve them with softly whipped cream or ice cream.

90 g / ¾ cup all-purpose flour

160 g / 1⅓ cups fine bread crumbs, divided

26 g / 3 tablespoons cornmeal

26 g / 2 tablespoons light brown sugar

2 g / ½ teaspoon fine sea salt

226 g / 8 ounces cream cheese, cut into pieces, at room temperature

56 g / 1 large egg, at room temperature

About 550 g / 10 medium apricots or small plums

25 g / 10 sugar cubes

24 g / 1 ounce / 2 tablespoons unsalted butter, melted

< 1 g / ¼ teaspoon freshly grated nutmeg

25 g / 2 tablespoons granulated sugar

Powdered sugar and whipped cream for serving

1. In a medium bowl, whisk the flour, 40 g / ⅓ cup of the bread crumbs, the cornmeal, brown sugar, and salt to combine. Add the cream cheese and use a fork, pastry cutter, or your hands to blend it into the mixture until fully incorporated.

2. Make a well in the center of the mixture and add the egg to it. Use a fork or small whisk to beat the egg slightly, then gradually mix in the dry ingredients until

(CONTINUES)

4. Bring a large pot of water to a boil. Meanwhile, in a small bowl, stir the remaining 120 g / 1 cup bread crumbs, the melted butter, and nutmeg together; set aside.

5. Divide the dough into 10 equal pieces (about 45 g each). Dust the work surface lightly with flour, then use your hands to flatten each piece of dough slightly. Carefully wrap each piece of dough around an apricot, pinching the seam well to seal.

6. Reduce the water to a simmer, drop the dumplings into the water, and cook until the fruit is tender and the dough is cooked through, 12 to 15 minutes. At first the dumplings will sink down into the water, but once they're ready, they'll start to float toward the surface.

7. While the dumplings cook, in a small skillet, toast the buttered bread crumbs over medium heat until golden brown, 3 to 4 minutes. Return to the bowl and stir in the granulated sugar.

8. Use a slotted spoon to remove the dumplings from the simmering water, draining them well, and put them on a plate. Gently roll each one in the toasted bread crumb mixture to fully coat.

9. To serve, dust the dumplings generously with powdered sugar and finish with whipped cream.

the dough comes together and is fairly smooth. Turn the dough out, wrap tightly in plastic wrap, and put in the freezer to chill slightly while you prep the fruit.

3. Use a paring knife to cut a small circle in the stem end of each apricot (or plum). Use the handle of a wooden spoon to push the pit out of each one while leaving the fruit whole. The riper the fruit, the easier this is. If it is firm, you may need to use the knife to cut around the pit slightly to remove it. Press a sugar cube into the center of each apricot.

Favorite Soups

Cheddar Ale Soup

Makes 6 servings

85 g / 3 ounces / 6 tablespoons unsalted butter

600 g / 3 medium leeks, white and light green parts only, thinly sliced

300 g / 3 stalks celery, diced

100 g / 1 large carrot, peeled and diced

20 g / 4 cloves garlic, minced

40 g / ¼ cup all-purpose flour

710 ml / 3 cups chicken or vegetable broth

One 355 ml / 12-ounce bottle pale ale or lager

30 g / 2 tablespoons Dijon mustard

454 g / 1 pound cheddar cheese (the sharper, the better), shredded

118 g / ½ cup heavy cream

Kosher salt and freshly ground black pepper

Chopped fresh chives for garnish

1. In a large pot, melt 28 g / 1 ounce / 2 tablespoons of the butter over medium heat. Add the leeks, celery, and carrot and sauté until starting to become tender, 7 to 9 minutes. Add the garlic and sauté until fragrant, about 1 minute.

2. Stir in the remaining butter and let it melt. Sprinkle the flour over the vegetables and cook, stirring, for 2 minutes. Add the broth and beer and bring to a simmer. Reduce the heat to low, cover, and simmer for 15 minutes.

3. Whisk the mustard into the soup. Use an immersion blender, or a food processor to blend the soup until very smooth. Return the soup to the pot if necessary and heat over low heat until hot. Gradually add the cheese and then the cream, stirring constantly until the soup is smooth. Season with salt and pepper. Serve garnished with chives.

Spicy Chicken Noodle Soup

Makes 6 servings

30 g / 2 tablespoons extra virgin olive oil

125 g / 5 shallots, minced

225 g / 3 medium carrots, peeled and minced

300 g / 3 stalks celery, minced

20 g / 4 cloves garlic, minced

A 1-inch/2.5 cm piece peeled ginger, finely grated

15 g / 1 tablespoon sambal oelek, or more to taste

15 g / 1 tablespoon rice wine vinegar

1380 g / 6 cups chicken broth

1 bay leaf

A few sprigs woody herbs (such as thyme, rosemary, and oregano)

290 g / 2 cups diced cooked chicken

10 g / ¼ cup chopped fresh parsley

1 recipe Thick, Chewy Noodles for Soup (page 88)

Thinly sliced scallions and/or jalapeños for garnish

1. In a large pot, heat the olive oil over medium heat. Add the shallots, carrots, and celery and cook until nearly tender, 4 to 5 minutes. Add the garlic and ginger and cook 1 minute.

2. Stir in the sambal oelek, vinegar, and broth, add the bay leaf and herbs, and bring the soup to a simmer. Reduce the heat to low, cover the pot, and simmer for 25 to 30 minutes. Remove the bay leaf and herb stems.

3. Stir the chicken into the soup and heat for 5 minutes. Stir in the parsley. Boil the noodles as directed on page 88. Stir the noodles into the soup. Serve garnished with scallions and/or jalapeños.

Thick, Chewy Noodles for Soup

Makes 435 g / about 1 pound noodles (enough for 6 to 8 servings of soup)

DIFFICULTY: **EASY**

My mom was both a nurse and a very good cook. So when I was sick as a kid, I was taken very good care of—including a regimen of her chicken noodle soup, sometimes complete with homemade noodles. While the real remedy was surely to be found in the broth, the thing I remember are those wonderfully chewy noodles. You can whip up these noodles in less time than it takes for your favorite soup to simmer to flavorful perfection (they are especially good in the Spicy Chicken Soup on page 87). These are also delicious boiled until tender, then sautéed in butter (I top mine with grated Parm and black pepper for the ultimate comfort food snack).

270 g / 2¼ cups all-purpose flour

4 g / 1 teaspoon fine sea salt

113 g / 2 large eggs

45 g / 3 tablespoons water

1. In the bowl of a stand mixer fitted with the dough hook, mix the flour, salt, eggs, and water on low speed until a shaggy dough forms, about 2 minutes. Raise the speed to medium-high and mix until the dough is smooth and elastic, 4 to 5 minutes (see Note). If the dough seems dry, add more water 5 g / 1 teaspoon at a time until it comes together.

2. Turn the dough out, form it into a 1-inch-/ 2.5 cm thick disk, and let rest at room temperature for 30 minutes.

3. On a lightly floured surface, roll out the dough ¼ inch/6 mm thick (even a touch thicker is okay—you want thick and chewy), for a roughly rectangular shape as you work, but the final shape really doesn't matter.

4. Use a pastry wheel to cut the dough into ½-inch-/1 cm wide strips, then cut the strips into 2-inch-/5 cm long pieces. The noodles can be cooked and served immediately. Or spread them on a lightly floured tray, toss with more flour to coat lightly, and let air-dry at room temperature for 15 minutes. Then transfer to an airtight storage container and refrigerate or freeze (see Make Ahead and Storage opposite).

5. To cook the noodles, bring a large pot of salted water to a boil. Add the noodles and cook until they are puffy on the exterior and cooked through, 5 to 6 minutes. Drain well before adding to soups.

Note: You can mix this dough by hand in a bowl. Bring it together into a shaggy dough using a silicone spatula, then turn out onto a floured surface and knead for 7 to 9 minutes, until smooth and elastic.

Flaky Frico

Makes one 8-inch/20 cm frico; serves 6 as an appetizer

DIFFICULTY: **MEDIUM**

My mom and I (and then the rest of my family) first fell in love with Lidia Bastianich while watching her on public television. We also lived close to one of her restaurants (Lidia's Kansas City), where our love for her was further cemented. We always order the frico—a cheese crisp with some kind of filling, often onion and potato. I couldn't help myself from reimagining it as a thin beautiful tart, with the finished frico nestled on a flaky pie crust. I adjust the cooking method so the stuffed frico comes out crisp on one side and a little meltier on the other—which allows it to adhere beautifully to the crust base. It adds another layer of texture to the dish. Lidia serves it with a salad, so I do too.

FRICO

1 recipe All-Buttah Pie Dough (page 319), mixed extra-flaky (see page 312)

226 g / 1 medium russet potato, peeled and diced

15 g / 1 tablespoon extra virgin olive oil

14 g / 1 tablespoon unsalted butter

300 g / 2 large leeks, white and light green parts only, thinly sliced

2 g / ¼ teaspoon kosher salt

2 g / ½ teaspoon freshly ground black pepper

285 g / 10 ounces Montasio cheese, shredded

30 g / 2 tablespoons Dijon mustard

Always Salad (recipe follows)

1. On a lightly floured surface, roll out the dough into a round ¼ inch/6 mm thick. Use a 9-inch/23 cm cake pan (or plate) as a guide to cut a round out of the dough. Use a rolling pin to transfer the dough to a parchment-lined baking sheet.

2. Dock the dough all over with a fork, then loosely cover it with plastic wrap and refrigerate for 30 minutes. Toward the end of chill time, preheat the oven to 400°F/205°C with a rack in the center.

3. Remove the plastic wrap from the dough and place a piece of parchment paper on top of it and another baking sheet on top of that to weight the dough as it bakes. Bake until the round of dough is lightly golden brown, 18 to 20 minutes.

4. Carefully remove the top baking sheet and parchment paper, return the pan to the oven, and bake until the dough is deeply golden brown, 5 to 8 minutes more. Let cool for 5 to 10 minutes on the baking sheet, then transfer to a cutting board or serving platter.

5. Meanwhile, make the filling: Place the potatoes in a small pot and add water to cover by about 1 inch/2.5 cm, bring to a boil over medium heat, and boil until the potatoes are easily pierced with a knife. Drain well and set aside.

6. In a medium (8-inch/20 cm) skillet, preferably nonstick, heat the olive oil and butter over medium heat until the butter melts. Add the leeks and cook until wilted, 3 to 4 minutes. Add the potatoes and cook, tossing occasionally, until very tender, 5 to 7 minutes. Season with the salt and pepper.

7. Transfer the filling to a bowl and set aside. Wipe out the skillet, return to high heat, and heat until a drop of water sizzles and evaporates almost immediately when it hits the

(CONTINUES)

surface. Sprinkle about half of the cheese in an even layer over the base of the pan. Reduce the heat to medium and let the cheese melt for 30 seconds to 1 minute.

8. Spoon the filling over the melted cheese and press it with a spatula into a firmly packed even layer, leaving an ⅛-inch/3 mm border of cheese uncovered all around. Sprinkle the rest of the cheese on top of the filling in an even layer. Cook undisturbed until fat separates out of the cheese and begins to bubble around the edges. Use a flexible spatula (I use a fish spatula) to gently lift the frico and check to see how brown it is on the bottom: It should be deeply brown and very crisp—if it isn't, leave it undisturbed for a few more minutes; it should take 6 to 8 minutes total.

9. Gently slide the spatula under the frico and flip it. (This should be pretty easy, but don't worry if the frico rips, tears, or doesn't flip evenly, just do the best you can and use the back of the spatula to mash it all together again.) Cook on the second side only until the cheese melts and lightly browns (this will ensure that it will still release cleanly in the pan), 3 to 4 minutes. Remove from the heat

10. Spread the mustard evenly over the baked crust. Gently transfer the frico to the crust with the crisp side up. Use the back of the spatula to gently press the frico into the mustard.

11. Cut into wedges and serve immediately, with the salad on top or on the side.

Always Salad
Makes 6 servings

We always have salad ingredients on hand and this salad is our go-to. It's simple, crisp, and tart. I tend to use a higher ratio of acidic ingredients like vinegar and mustard in my salad dressings, which makes them a perfect pairing for rich or buttery baked goods. You can serve the salad as is, or gussy it up with some of the suggestions below.

DRESSING

5 g / 1 clove garlic

Kosher salt

60 g / ¼ cup white wine vinegar

30 g / 2 tablespoons Dijon mustard

15 g / 1 tablespoon mayonnaise

Pinch or two of granulated sugar

2 g / ¾ teaspoon dried oregano

80 g / ⅓ cup extra virgin olive oil

Freshly ground black pepper

SALAD

454 g / 1 pound romaine hearts (about 2), chopped, or 4 heads Little Gem lettuce, leaves separated, small ones left whole, larger ones torn in half

85 g / ½ red onion, thinly sliced

100 g / ½ European (seedless) cucumber, thinly sliced

OPTIONAL ADD-INS

Other vegetables: quartered cherry tomatoes, thinly sliced celery, diced jicama, or cooked beets

Fresh herbs: chopped parsley, small dill fronds, minced chives, and/or torn basil or mint leaves

Cheese: Parmesan shards, fresh mozzarella pearls (perlini), diced provolone, or crumbled goat cheese

Pickled stuff: Diced cornichons, pepperoncini,

dilly beans, giardinara, quick pickled onions (see page 253), or Quick Pickled Chiles (page 180)

1. Peel the garlic clove and smash with the side of a knife. Sprinkle a little salt over it, and use the side of the knife to mash the garlic into a paste.

2. In a medium bowl, whisk the vinegar, mustard, mayonnaise, sugar, and oregano together.

Slowly stream in the olive oil, whisking constantly to create a thick dressing. Season with salt and pepper to taste.

3. Combine all the salad ingredients and any add-in vegetables in a large bowl. Dress the salad to taste and, if using, toss in the fresh herbs, cheese, and/or pickled stuff. Serve immediately.

Go-To Spreads

Pesto

Makes 525 g/2 cups

In a food processor, pulse 170 g / 6 ounces fresh basil leaves, 45 g / ¼ cup almonds, and 15 g / 3 cloves garlic until coarsely chopped. Add the grated zest and juice of 1 lemon and pulse to combine. With the processor running, add 230 g / 1 cup extra virgin olive oil in a slow, steady stream. Add 100 g / 1 cup grated Parmesan and pulse just to combine. Season with salt and pepper to taste.

Sun-Dried Tomato Spread

Makes 375 g/1½ cups

In a food processor, blend 226 g / 8 ounces / 1 packed cup oil-packed sun-dried tomatoes, 113 g / 4 ounces / ½ cup tomato paste, 30 g / 2 tablespoons olive oil (you can use the oil from the jar of tomatoes), 5 g / 1 clove garlic, 2 g / ½ teaspoon dried oregano, and 2 g / ½ teaspoon dried basil and process to a coarse puree. Season with salt and pepper to taste.

Olive Spread

Makes 375 g/1¼ cups

Rinse and pat dry 226 g / 8 ounces pitted olives (any kind you like). Add to a food processor, along with 50 g / 3 tablespoons capers, 10 g / 1 anchovy fillet, 5 g / 1 clove garlic, minced, and 10 g / ¼ cup fresh basil leaves, and pulse until the olives are coarsely chopped. Add 30 g / 2 tablespoons fresh lemon juice and 45 g / 3 tablespoons extra virgin olive oil and blend to a coarse puree. Season with black pepper to taste.

Roasted Garlic Aioli

Makes 125 g/½ cup

In a small bowl, whisk together 42 g / 2 large egg yolks, 15 g / 1 tablespoon fresh lemon juice, and 5 g / 1 teaspoon Dijon mustard. Gradually add 56 g / ½ cup extra virgin olive oil, a few teaspoons at a time, whisking constantly; when all the oil is incorporated, the mixture should be thick and creamy. Squeeze out the cloves from 1 head Roasted Garlic (page 159) and use a fork to smash them into a paste, then blend into the aioli. Season with salt and pepper to taste.

Creamy Mushroom Spread

Makes 800 g/3 cups

In a large sauté pan, melt 56 g / 2 ounces / 4 tablespoons unsalted butter over medium heat. Working in batches if necessary, add 680 g / 1½ pounds mushrooms, coarsely chopped or torn into bite-size pieces, spread out in an even layer, so as to not overcrowd the pan, and cook, stirring occasionally, until well seared on all sides, about 2 to 3 minutes per side. Return all the mushrooms to the pan if necessary, add 150 g / 1 cup minced onion or shallots, and sauté until tender, 3 to 4 minutes. Add 170 g / ¾ cup dry white wine and cook, stirring frequently, until it has almost entirely evaporated. Stir in 60 g / ¼ cup heavy cream and 115 g / ½ cup crumbled goat cheese, season with salt and pepper, and cook over low heat, stirring, until the mixture thickens. Add up to 10 g / ¼ cup chopped fresh herbs, like rosemary, thyme, dill, and/or parsley.

Pickly Peppers

Makes 390 g/1½ cups

In a food processor, pulse 150 g / 1 large red bell pepper, seeds and ribs removed, 170 g / 1 small sweet onion, 25 g / 1 medium Fresno or jalapeño chile, 5 g / 1 peeled clove garlic, 12 g / 1 tablespoon granulated sugar, and 3 g / ½ teaspoon kosher salt until very finely chopped. Transfer to a small pot and add 75 g / ⅓ cup seasoned rice wine vinegar. Bring to a simmer over medium heat and cook for about 2 minutes, until the vegetables are tender-crisp. Let cool, transfer to an airtight container, and refrigerate for at least 2 days, and up to 2 months, before serving.

Pickled Mustard Seeds

Makes 110 g/⅓ cup

In a small pot, combine 113 g / ½ cup apple cider vinegar, 115 g / ½ cup water, 40 g / 3 tablespoons light brown sugar, 5 g / 1 clove garlic, smashed and peeled, 3 g / ½ teaspoon kosher salt, and 2 g / ½ teaspoon freshly ground black pepper and bring to a simmer. Add 35 g / ⅓ cup mustard seeds and stir to combine. Cover the pot, turn the heat to low, and cook, stirring occasionally, until the mustard seeds are plump and soft, 45 to 60 minutes. Let cool, transfer to an airtight container, and refrigerate for up to 3 months.

CHAPTER 3

Breads

LOAVES • ROLLS • DOUGHY SNACKS

When I was in pastry school, students tended to fall into two categories, baking or pastry. The bakers were often up extra early, throwing flour around (and often wearing some evidence of it on their aprons). The pastry chefs were somehow more refined, working with chocolate or cake decorations in near silence. A deep lover of all things doughy, I was a baker through and through; I'm always happiest with my hands and counter covered in flour. I deeply love the rhythm of mixing, shaping, and baking yeasted doughs. In the end, though, that's nothing next to the comfort of eating them and sharing them, still warm from the oven, whenever possible.

One of the things I want to sing from the rooftops about yeasted doughs is that they are so wonderfully flexible. Not only can you adjust the pacing once you understand the bread baking process, you can also manipulate some of these base doughs into a huge variety of incredible recipes.

Enriched Versus Lean Doughs

There are two main categories of yeasted doughs: *enriched* and *lean*. Enriched doughs contain enrichments like butter, eggs, milk, and sugar. Brioche (page 205), monkey bread dough (page 127), and Parker House Rolls (page 117), to name a few, are all enriched doughs. Lean doughs are essentially just flour, water, yeast, and salt. Baby Baguettes (page 119), Ciabattina Rolls (page 110), and Bagels (page 165) are a few examples of lean doughs.

The Incredible Powers of an Incredible Powder

Dry milk powder is an amazing ingredient, particularly when it comes to enriched breads. Milk is used as an enrichment in yeasted breads (along with other ingredients like butter, sugar, and eggs). Like many enrichments, it adds flavor and promotes browning—but its most powerful contribution is a more tender texture and a loftier rise in the final bread. All this for a very small amount of effort: just adding some dry milk along with the other dry ingredients in the recipe. If you don't have dry milk on hand, you can still make any bread recipe in this book that calls for it, but the bread will be slightly denser, and possibly less golden brown than those in the photographs. If you want to add dry milk to a recipe that doesn't call for it, you can add up to 4 percent of the weight of the flour in the recipe as dry milk. My preferred brand of dry milk comes from King Arthur Baking; see Resources.

Why Use Sugar in Savory Bread Recipes?

You'll see that a lot of the yeasted doughs in this book contain sugar, even when they have a decidedly savory flavor profile. Sugar adds a sweet flavor, of course, but it can also be considered an enrichment, and it also helps to keep finished bread moist. That is one reason why homemade breads go stale faster than commercially produced loaves, which often contain sugar as well as preservatives. If you're not crazy about adding sugar to the dough for a savory loaf, you can usually reduce the amount called for, or even eliminate it entirely, without causing major changes in the bread—in the short term. But it will be prone to staling faster, so try to enjoy the bread as quickly as possible after baking.

Understanding Yeast

The primary function of yeast in any recipe is to start the process of fermentation: it feeds on the carbohydrates in the dough and converts them to carbon dioxide and ethanol. Fermentation contributes two wonderful things: structure and flavor. As carbon dioxide gases build up, the dough starts to rise. This continues to happen until it reaches 140°F/60°C, at which point the yeast dies and its activity ceases, *or* until the yeast runs out of food.

There are several types of yeast, including fresh and bread machine yeast, but most of the recipes in this book call for instant dry yeast (you can substitute active dry if that's your jam, though—see below).

INSTANT DRY: I find this kind of yeast the easiest to use because it can be added right to the other dry ingredients in the recipe. The brand of yeast I use, SAF (see Resources), comes in two types: red (multipurpose) and gold (for enriched doughs). Note that while instant yeast can be added directly to the dry ingredients, it dissolves best in liquids at 110°F/45°C or above, so if you are substituting it in a recipe that calls for a lower temperature, it is best to stir the yeast together with the liquid first to encourage it to dissolve (you will see this method specified in a few recipes here).

ACTIVE DRY: Active dry yeast typically must be dissolved in warm liquid to activate it before combining it with the rest of the ingredients in the recipe. It works more slowly than instant yeast, which means it often yields a more flavorful dough.

To substitute active dry yeast for instant in any of the recipes in this book, whisk the yeast with 25 percent of the warm liquid called for in a small bowl to combine. Let sit for 5 minutes before proceeding.

When substituting active dry yeast for instant, you have two alternatives:

- Substitute the same amount of yeast 1:1 by weight or volume but increase the rise time at each stage by 20 to 30 minutes.
- Increase the quantity of yeast by 25 percent (for example, if the recipe calls for 6 g / 2 teaspoons instant yeast, use 8 g / 2½ teaspoons active dry yeast).

Preferments That Are Not Sourdough Starters

I love how popular baking sourdough at home has become. It's a wonderful way to produce easy-to-make loaves that boast artisan quality. It's also a good introduction to preferments. A *preferment* is a dough that is mixed separately and allowed to ferment on its own before adding it to the full bread dough. Sourdough is just one type of preferment—there are many! Unlike sourdough, some preferments are mixed the day before. Others are made just an hour or two before mixing the final dough. The preferments described below require significantly less preparation and maintenance to achieve several of the same positive attributes as a sourdough preferment. While the flavor the preferments below contribute is not as strong as that of a sourdough starter, they do add flavor as well as strength and structure to the final dough.

Poolish

A poolish (the word is of Polish origin) is very liquid and has a high level of hydration, with a ratio of 100 percent flour: 100 percent water: 0.25 percent yeast. Usually a poolish is fermented at room temperature, and therefore it can't have high levels of added yeast, or it could overferment. The ideal fermentation time for poolish is 15 to 18 hours. Poolish will look like a big shaggy ball when just mixed, and then it will transform into a very soupy, liquidy, almost batter-like mixture as it sits.

Biga

A biga (an Italian term) is stiffer than poolish, with a ratio of 100 percent flour: 55 percent water: 0.25 percent yeast. Biga is also typically fermented at room temperature. Ideal fermentation time for biga is 15 to 18 hours. A biga will look very shaggy and not totally put together when it is just mixed, but it will loosen significantly after fermentation, looking more like a bread dough.

Pâte Fermentée

Pâte fermentée (a French term) is sometimes called "pre-fermented dough" because that's what it originally was. Bread bakers would take a portion of the day's bread dough and save it to add it to the next day's dough. But even folks who don't make bread every day can make pâte fermentée. It has a ratio of 100 percent flour: 60 percent water: 1 percent yeast, plus 2 percent salt. Because of the higher proportion of yeast, pâte fermentée doesn't need a long fermentation time—only about 4 to 6 hours at room temperature. But I prefer to make it the day before, ferment it for 4 hours, and then refrigerate it overnight, until I'm ready to use it. Pâte fermentée looks similar to bread dough when it's mixed and loosens slightly as it ferments.

Sponge

A sponge uses a ratio of 100 percent flour: 60 percent water: 1 percent yeast. Compared to other preferments, a sponge has a relatively short fermentation time (therefore, it uses more yeast than other preferments—it needs that to jump-start fermentation). Sponges are generally fermented for 30 minutes to 1½ hours, depending on the recipe (the more yeast in the sponge, the less fermentation time). And, unlike other preferments, a sponge is meant to be used as soon as it's fermented. As soon as there are plenty of bubbles on the surface of the mixture, it's ready to be added to the final dough.

Yeasted Dough Mixing Method

The method used for mixing many yeasted bread doughs is called the "straight dough" method. The straight dough method can be done in a stand mixer fitted with the dough hook, or in a bowl, using a spatula for mixing and then kneading by hand.

To mix a dough using the straight-dough method, start by mixing the dry ingredients together to combine. Add the liquid/wet ingredients (including a preferment, if using).

Mix as the recipe directs. For some recipes, the mixing is minimal. In other recipes, the mixing starts slowly, until the dough comes together, and then increases in intensity until the dough is smooth.

First Rise

Yeast doughs involve multiple stages of rising—or proofing—during which time the dough begins to ferment. The yeast starts a lot of activity, consuming carbohydrates and releasing carbon dioxide gases. The gases created during fermentation cause the dough to puff up (or rise) and help create the final bread's crumb structure.

The first stage of proofing happens after the dough is mixed. The dough is usually transferred to a lightly greased bowl, covered, and allowed to rise as directed in the recipe.

How to Speed Up or Slow Down Rise Times

Two major factors affect a dough rise: ambient temperature of the environment and the amount of yeast. Yeast feeds most rapidly at a temperature of around 95°F/35°C. At typical room temperature, yeast will ferment more slowly, and at cooler temperatures (say in the refrigerator), even more slowly. The quantity of yeast will determine how quickly carbon dioxide gases are produced, causing the bread to rise. Most bread bakers (myself included), prefer to use a relatively smaller amount of yeast and a longer rise time, which contributes to better flavor and structure. However, it is possible to adjust various factors in a recipe, making faster work of a dough that normally requires a long fermentation or turning any recipe into a make-ahead overnight dough (with more flavor to boot).

SLOW IT DOWN

My preferred way to slow rise times is to lower the temperatures of the water and opt for a cooler rising environment. Instead of using warm liquid as a recipe calls for, use room-temperature liquid to mix the dough. After mixing, allow the dough to rise at room temperature, ideally below 75°F/25°C, for the time called for by the recipe. Then transfer the dough to the refrigerator to rise for 8 to 12 hours more. Bring the dough back to room temperature (about 30 minutes) before using.

The other main way to slow rise time is to use less yeast. Less yeast can still produce a similar result, but it will take the yeast more time to feed on the same quantity of present carbohydrates (this is how no-knead recipes with long rise times typically work). If you want to try this method, start by cutting the yeast in the recipe in half—but make sure you have at least 2 g / ½ teaspoon dry yeast per 454 g / 1 pound of flour.

SPEED IT UP

Increasing the temperature of the liquid used in the dough is an easy way to speed up rise times; I recommend liquid no hotter than 130°F/55°C. But my preferred way to speed up rise times is to increase the quantity of yeast. The greater amount of yeast will feed on the available carbs and create carbon dioxide gases faster. You can use up to 20 g / 2 tablespoons dry yeast per 454 g / 1 pound flour.

Dividing the Dough

Many recipes make a large batch of dough that is divided to form loaves, rolls, or stuffed breads. Dividing the dough can be done by eye or, more precisely, by using a scale.

If you want to eyeball it rather than weighing the dough, I suggest halving the dough again and again for the most precise division. Start by gently pressing the dough into an even rectangle or a log—both of these are easy to divide. Use a bench knife (or a sharp knife) to cut the dough in half, cut each half in half again, then cut each quarter in half, and so on until you have the desired number of pieces.

To divide with a scale, weigh the dough, then divide that by the recipe yield to determine the weight of each piece.

Shaping Yeasted Doughs

After the first rise, it's time to shape the dough. Proper shaping isn't just about making a dough look good, it also helps the items bake evenly. Some recipes call for an added step of preshaping the dough. This usually involves shaping the dough into a rough round and letting it rest for a few minutes before the final shaping. When shaping, use flour only as necessary to prevent the dough from sticking while you work—too much flour can actually make the dough harder to shape.

TO SHAPE A ROUND LOAF: Press the dough all over with your fingertips to flatten it slightly. Lift the edges of the dough up and fold them over toward the center, forming a rough round. Use a dough scraper to help you gently flip the dough over so the seams are on the bottom. Place your hands on either side of the dough and begin to round it by moving your hands in a circular motion. The main source of pressure and tightening should be coming from the heels of your hands, and the more you round the dough, the tighter the shape will become.

TO SHAPE AN OBLONG LOAF: Press the dough all over with your fingertips to flatten it slightly. Starting with the portion of dough farthest away from you on the work surface, begin to fold the dough over itself, using your fingertips to press it down firmly as you go. Repeat the folding process two or three times—as you work, the piece of dough will be becoming longer. When there's about 1 to 2 inches/2.5 to 5 cm of unfolded dough left, start using the heel of your hand to secure the dough as you fold it over, finally forming a rough log shape. Starting in the center of the log, roll it under your fingers and the upper part of your palms to elongate it to the desired length. Apply slightly more pressure to the ends of the dough to taper them, if desired.

TO SHAPE ROLLS: Working with one piece at a time, press each piece of dough all over with your fingertips to flatten it slightly. Lift the edges of the dough up and fold them over toward the center, forming a rough round. Use a dough scraper to help you gently flip the dough over so the seams are on the bottom. Cup your hand around the dough and begin to move your hand in a circular motion to round the roll, mostly using the side and heel of your hand to tighten it. Once you get some practice, you can do this with both hands, rounding two rolls at once.

TWIST: On a lightly floured surface, roll out the dough into a rectangle (thickness will vary depending on recipe, but aim for about ¼ inch/ 6 mm thick). Spread/sprinkle the filling(s) evenly over the surface, then roll up the dough into a tight spiral, pinching the seam to seal (some recipes have you start from a longer side of the rectangle when rolling, some start with a shorter side—they will produce slightly different twisted effects). Use a bench knife or a sharp knife to cut

SHAPING A ROUND LOAF

1. Press the dough into a roughly round shape.

2. Fold the dough over onto itself, making a seam in the center.

3. Turn the dough over and use the edges of your hands to lightly round the loaf.

4. Continue until the dough is tightly rounded.

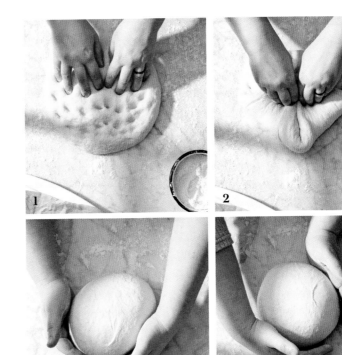

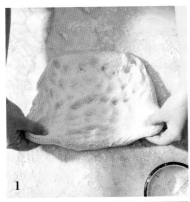

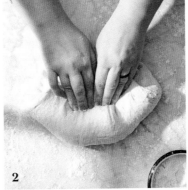

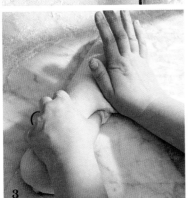

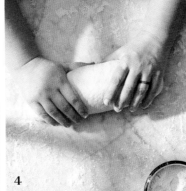

SHAPING AN OBLONG LOAF

1. Press the dough into a roughly rectangular shape.

2. Fold the dough over onto itself a few times.

3. Use the the heel of your hand to press the dough well to seal at the final seam.

4. Use your hands to gently roll the dough to create an oblong loaf.

A Few Words About "Doubled in Size"

If you've ever read a recipe for a yeast-raised dough, you've likely seen this term. My first tip for when a recipe specifies this is to allow the dough to rise in a bowl that's about twice the size of the dough. That way, when the dough reaches the top of the bowl, you'll know it's properly risen. Note that not all doughs will double in size. Some of the recipes in this book, for example, call for allowing the dough to rise until "visibly puffy," which means that it has noticeably expanded.

Enriched doughs are slower to rise than lean doughs. And if a dough has been refrigerated, it may take longer for the yeast to become active after being chilled.

the dough in half down the length of the spiral, showing the layers of filling inside. Twist the two pieces of dough together to make one long twist. Some recipes may have you further twist or manipulate this to create an even stronger effect.

WREATH: Prepare the dough as a twist, transfer to a parchment-lined baking sheet, and form the twist into a round. Pinch the two ends together to seal. If desired, place a heatproof ramekin in the center of the wreath to help it keep a rounded center as the wreath bakes.

SPIRAL: Prepare the dough as a twist, then transfer to a parchment-lined baking sheet and form into a spiral shape. When you reach the end of the dough, tuck it under the loaf. Spirals can also be made without filling/twisting the bread first; this makes beautiful rolls.

Second Rise

The second stage of proofing takes place after the dough is shaped. The dough may be covered during this rise, but some recipes opt to leave it uncovered in order to dry out the surface of the dough, which can make it easier to score. If the dough is covered at this stage, it is important to cover it only loosely so it has room to expand.

Determining Proper Proofing After Shaping

Determining the proper level of rise after shaping is crucial to the quality of the final baked good. Keep in mind that dough will rise faster in a warmer environment than in a cold one.

UNDERPROOFING: If you gently press the surface of underproofed dough, it will quickly spring back. If an underproofed dough is baked, it will have a more dense crumb structure, and the crust may appear ripped or torn.

PROPERLY PROOFED: When the surface of a properly proofed dough is gently pressed, it will only slowly spring back. When baked, properly proofed dough will have an ideal rise and crumb structure, and the crust will look generally smooth.

OVERPROOFED: If you gently press the surface of overproofed dough, it will hold an indentation and not spring back. If an overproofed dough is baked, it may have a wrinkled exterior and/or the loaf may collapse or spread instead of rise high.

STARS OR PINWHEELS:
Use straight or curved lines to create designs like stars and pinwheel shapes.

Ss OR Cs: Continuous curved lines can be more difficult—using the baking pan to rotate the dough as you work can be helpful.

WHEAT STALK OR SMALL LINES: A straight or curved line with more small lines coming out of it will make a wheat stalk effect. Small lines can be used to create elaborate designs.

POUND OR CROSSHATCH:
Cut two lines horizontally and then two vertically.

LINE/LINES: Hold the lame parallel to the surface of the dough and use the blade to start the cuts. Aim to work quickly, which will help keep the cut lines straight.

Scoring

Scoring is done after the final rise, just before the dough is transferred to the oven. Scoring the surface of bread dough, or cutting it with a sharp blade, creates a way for steam to escape as the bread bakes, and it also helps the dough keep its shape. Scoring can be just a single slash or an elaborate decorative pattern. Not all breads require scoring: enriched doughs like brioche (page 205) and monkey bread dough (page 127) usually do not require any kind of scoring. Others, though, such as the Baby Baguettes (page 119), may become misshapen in the oven without score marks to allow the steam to escape in a controlled way. Instead, the steam may burst out the sides of the loaf, creating its own path.

I use a *lame*, a razor blade with an attached handle (see Resources), for the majority of scoring. A sharp knife or even a pair of scissors will also work, though it is harder to get some of the more delicate scoring patterns with these tools. Depending on the score, you want to hold the blade either parallel to the dough's surface or at a 45-degree angle to it. It's important to cut deep enough—a shallow cut won't do the job.

Doneness Indicators

The best way to determine doneness of yeast-raised breads or other baked goods is to check the internal temperature. Insert an instant-read thermometer into the center of the thickest part of the loaf or other baked good to determine the temperature. An internal temperature of between 190 to 215°F/87 to 100°C will usually be ideal. A golden-brown exterior or crust should be treated as a secondary doneness indicator—it's harder to know what's going on inside. If the item is browning too much before the proper internal temperature is reached, tent it with foil for the remainder of baking.

Get Flexible

Yeasted doughs offer a lot of possibilities—you can turn a base dough into many different tasty treats. With that said, yeasted doughs do require careful formulation to ensure a golden crust and perfect interior crumb. If you understand bread ratios, you can reformulate most recipes to include a preferment or allow the dough to rise slowly overnight. Here are a few of my most useful tips for yeasted dough swaps and subs:

USE DOUGH IN DIFFERENT WAYS: Once you've got a dough you love, you've also got a versatile one: I hope that can be one of the biggest take-aways from this chapter. Doughs can be divided into different sizes and shaped in different ways. For example, the dough for making monkey bread (page 127) is incredibly soft and fluffy. That makes it perfect for the Italian Sub Bundt (page 214) too—no need to use another dough. Good dough recipes are true building blocks, allowing you to develop different baked goods of your own.

ADD INCLUSIONS: While there is no hard-and-fast rule here, most inclusions are added to a yeasted dough after its initial rise so as not to impede that first rise. This is most often the case with heavier inclusions like dried fruit, nuts, or cubed cheese. To incorporate inclusion like those, after the initial rise, turn the dough out onto a lightly floured surface and press into an even layer about 1 inch/2.5 cm thick—the exact shape isn't important, but I usually aim for a rectangle. Sprinkle the inclusions evenly over the dough and press them gently into it. Fold the dough over onto itself 4 to 6 times, encasing the ingredients. Return the dough to the bowl it rose in, seam side down, and let rest for 15 minutes before proceeding.

Ciabattina Rolls

Makes 8 rolls

DIFFICULTY: **MEDIUM**

I've eaten more of the beautiful crusty loaves that emerge from the ovens at Wheatfields Bakery in my hometown of Lawrence, Kansas, than any other bread. I'm especially fond of their miniature take on ciabatta, oversized rolls perfect for sandwiches. They have a crisp crust and a light, fluffy interior, the result of a highly hydrated dough, which gains structure during multiple long rests. These can be used to build an epic sandwich—like a BLT, or my mom's salmon sandwiches (see page 115). I've marked this recipe as "Medium" difficulty only because it's a very soft dough and the shaping (although it is easy and minimal) can take some getting used to.

BIGA (PREFERMENT)

210 g / 1¾ cups bread flour

< 1 g / ¼ teaspoon instant dry yeast

226 g / 1 cup room-temperature water (about 75°F/25°C)

DOUGH

420 g / 3½ cups bread flour, plus more for dusting

6 g / 2 teaspoons instant dry yeast

10 g / 2 teaspoons kosher salt

340 g / 1½ cups warm water (about 110°F/45°C)

Biga (above)

Semolina flour or cornmeal for dusting

1. The night before you want to make the bread, mix the biga: In a medium bowl, mix the bread flour, yeast, and water with a spatula until well combined. Cover the bowl with plastic wrap and let sit in a cool place for 12 hours (overnight); if your ambient room temperature is higher than 75°F/45°C, let the dough rise at room temperature for 6 hours, then refrigerate for the remaining 6 hours.

2. When you're ready to make the bread, mix the flour, yeast, and salt together in a large bowl. Add the water and biga and mix with a spatula until the mixture forms a ball. Then continue to mix with the spatula until the dough develops some gluten structure and appears smoother, 4 to 5 minutes. The dough will be very sticky (almost soupy)—never fear, that's how it's supposed to be!

3. Transfer the dough to a greased bowl, cover with plastic wrap, and let proof until doubled in size, about 1 hour.

4. Using greased hands, fold the dough over onto itself (in the bowl) 3 to 5 times. Cover and proof for another 1 hour and 15 minutes, or until the dough is visibly puffy.

5. Set a sifter over a bowl, fill it with a few scoops of bread flour, and sift flour onto your work surface. Turn the dough out onto the floured surface, and sift flour generously over it—be fairly generous (the dough is quite wet). Gently stretch the dough out on the floured work surface, forming a rectangle shape about 9 x 12 inches/23 x 30 cm. Cut the dough into 8 equal squares (about 3 x 4½ inches/8 x 10 cm each).

6. Line two baking sheets with parchment paper, lightly dust the parchment with semolina flour

(CONTINUES)

or cornmeal, and transfer the dough squares to the sheets. As you place each roll on the baking sheet (4 rolls per sheet, staggered), squish it slightly into a smaller square (it's okay if it's somewhat uneven). Use your hands to dust just a little more bread flour over each roll. Cover loosely with a clean kitchen towel and proof the rolls in a warm place until visibly puffy, 45 minutes to 1 hour.

7. Preheat the oven to 450°F/232°C with the racks in the upper and lower thirds. Just before you're ready to bake, fill a 9 x 13-inch/23 x 33 cm baking pan with ice cubes (1 to 2 quarts / 1 to 2 liters). Place this pan on the lower oven rack and place one pan of rolls on the top rack.

8. Bake the rolls for 18 to 22 minutes, until the internal temperature is at least 205°F/96°C and they are evenly golden brown. Remove from the oven and bake the second pan of rolls. You can just leave the baking pan on the lower rack for the second round of baking (it will still provide steam while you bake the second pan) or refill it with a few more scoops of ice cubes before continuing. Cool the rolls for at least 15 minutes before serving.

Make Ahead and Storage
The rolls are best within 24 hours after baking. Store leftover rolls in an airtight container at room temperature for up to 3 days (as they stale, they make great toast or crostini). To freeze the rolls, wrap each one tightly in aluminum foil and freeze in an airtight container for up to 3 months. To refresh, place the foil-wrapped rolls in a cold oven and turn it on to 375°F/190°C; once the preheat buzzer notifies you that the oven is at temperature, leave the rolls in the oven for 4 to 5 minutes more.

The Power of Steam

Steam is a powerful technique when making some types of breads and rolls. The steam promotes an incredibly crisp, well-browned outer crust with that ideal chewy bread texture. Steaming is usually desirable for lean bread doughs, like Ciabattina Rolls (page 110) or Baby Baguettes (page 119). Professional bakeries use special ovens that add steam at the beginning of baking—but at home, I use a pan of ice cubes to create steam in my oven. Here's how:

- Arrange the oven racks in the upper and lower thirds of the oven—you'll be baking the bread on the upper rack. Have ready a 9 x 13-inch/23 x 33 cm or other baking pan or an ovenproof skillet, which will eventually go on the lower rack. When you put the bread in the oven, add at least 900 g / 4 cups and up to 1.5 L / 6 cups ice cubes to the baking pan (more ice will create more steam) and place on the lower oven rack. (If you don't have any ice on hand, pour up to 340 g / 1½ cups cold water into the pan instead.)

I usually bake the bread with the steaming water in the oven the whole time, but for even crustier bread, carefully remove the pan after 15 minutes.

My Best BLT

Makes 1 sandwich

Here's my favorite BLT, some version of which you'll find me eating multiple times a week during peak tomato season (sometimes even without the "B"). Of course, you can multiply this to make as many sandwiches as you like.

1 Ciabattina Roll (page 110) or other crusty roll, split in half (or 2 slices bread, lightly toasted or grilled)

Mayonnaise as needed

¼ avocado, sliced or coarsely mashed

2 or 3 thick slices tomato

5 large fresh basil leaves

2 lettuce leaves of your choice

4 strips quick candied bacon (see page 44)

A few thin slices red onion

Spread mayonnaise on one cut side of the roll (or one slice of bread) and place or spread the avocado on the other side (or other slice of bread). Place the tomatoes on the mayo side and top with the lettuce and basil leaves. Arrange the bacon and red onion on top and place the avocado side of the buns on top to finish the sandwich.

Mama's Salmon Sandwiches

Makes 4 sandwiches

I grew up in Kansas, where good, fresh salmon only landed on our table once in a rare while. My dad traveled for work, and sometimes he'd make his way to Washington State. On those special occasions, he would bring us beautiful fillets of salmon, courtesy of his dry-ice-packed carry-on. These salmon sandwiches are the way my mom chose to celebrate this treat, and they are a lesson in the beauty of simplicity: fresh salmon, vinegary arugula, fat slices of tomato, and a swipe of mayo. On freshly baked bread, they are a true, honest-to-goodness celebration, even if salmon is a fairly everyday affair at your house.

60 g / ¼ cup champagne vinegar
22 g / 1½ tablespoons Dijon mustard
25 g / 1 large or 2 small shallots, minced
170 g / ¾ cup extra virgin olive oil, plus
    1 tablespoon
10 g / ¼ cup finely minced fresh parsley
9 g / 3 tablespoons minced fresh chives
Kosher salt and freshly ground black pepper
Four 142 to 170 g / 5- to 6-ounce salmon fillets
1 medium lemon, halved
4 Ciabattina Rolls (page 110)
Mayonnaise as needed
Tomato slices
100 g / 5 cups arugula

1. In a large bowl, whisk the vinegar, mustard, and shallots together. Slowly drizzle in the olive oil, whisking constantly to make a thick dressing. Add the parsley and chives and season with salt and pepper.

2. Reserve 75 g / ⅓ cup of the dressing and transfer the rest to a gallon zip-top bag. Add the salmon fillets and seal the bag. Rub the dressing into the flesh of the salmon through the bag and refrigerate, turning occasionally to redistribute the marinade, for at least 2 and up to 8 hours.

3. When it's time to cook the salmon, remove it from the marinade, transfer it to a plate, and season with kosher salt and pepper.

TO GRILL THE SALMON: Get your grill nice and hot and oil the grates. Add the salmon, skin side down, and grill, flipping once, to your preferred doneness, 2 to 4 minutes per side (2 per side for rarer, 4 per side for more well done).

TO ROAST THE SALMON: Preheat the oven to 450°F/232°C. Spread 1 tablespoon olive oil over a small baking sheet and place the salmon on it. Roast to your desired doneness, 10 to 14 minutes (10 for a smidge more rare, 14 for more well done).

Remove from the grill or oven and squeeze the lemon over the fish.

4. To assemble the sandwiches, split the rolls in half. Spread mayonnaise on both cut sides of the bread. Place a salmon on each bottom bun and top with a slice of tomato. In a medium bowl, toss the arugula with the reserved dressing. Place a generous handful of arugula on top of each tomato slice, then place the tops of the buns on top to close the sandwiches.

Parker House Rolls

Makes 12 rolls

DIFFICULTY: **MEDIUM**

To me, a Parker House roll is the soft, fluffy dinner roll that dreams are made of. Golden brown on the outside, incredibly soft and fluffy inside, with a decided butteriness (though that doesn't stop me from slathering more butter on the warm rolls when they emerge from the oven). There are two ways to shape these rolls: For the original version, made at the Parker House Hotel in Boston, the rolls were shaped by flattening the dough slightly, brushing it with butter, and folding it, keeping that extra butter trapped inside. But I prefer them shaped as rounded rolls and then basted with butter during and after baking (for more ideas, see Basting Butters, page 11); that way, they rise a bit loftier. Either way, the rolls are perfect all on their own, but there are a number of ways to gussy them up; see the Variations below.

DOUGH

57 g / 2 ounces / 4 tablespoons unsalted butter, plus softened butter for greasing the pan

230 g / 1 cup whole milk

450 g / 3¾ cups all-purpose flour

32 g / ⅓ cup dry milk powder

50 g / ¼ cup granulated sugar

6 g / 2 teaspoons instant dry yeast

5 g / 1 teaspoon kosher salt

56 g / 1 large egg, at room temperature

FINISHING

Egg wash (see page 7)

Coarse or flaky salt (if you use salted butter, skip the salt topping)

113 g / 4 ounces / 8 tablespoons unsalted butter, melted

1. Make the dough: In a medium saucepan, melt the butter over medium heat. Add the milk, swirl the pan a few times to combine, and heat to about 110°F/45°C.

2. Meanwhile, in the bowl of a stand mixer fitted with the dough hook, mix the flour, milk powder, sugar, yeast, and salt on low speed to combine.

3. Add the warm milk mixture and the egg to the flour mixture and mix on low speed for 3 minutes, then increase the speed to medium and mix until the dough is smooth, about 3 minutes more.

4. Transfer the dough to a lightly greased large bowl, cover the bowl with plastic wrap, and let the dough rise in a warm place for 1½ to 2 hours. The dough may not quite double in size, but it should look noticeably puffy.

5. Grease a 9 x 13-inch/23 x 33 cm baking pan fairly generously with butter. Transfer the dough to a lightly floured surface and divide into 12 equal pieces (about 70 g each). Gently round each piece of dough: Cup your hand around the dough in a C shape, using the heel of your hand to help tighten it as you round it. As you shape the rolls, place them in the prepared pan, arranging them in 3 rows of 4.

6. Cover the pan loosely with greased plastic wrap and let the rolls rise in a warm place until noticeably larger and puffy, 45 minutes to 1 hour. Toward the end of the rise time, preheat the oven to 350°F/175°C.

(CONTINUES)

7. Remove the plastic wrap and brush the surface of the rolls with egg wash. If using the salt, sprinkle some over the surface.

8. Bake the rolls for 10 minutes, then remove from the oven and brush generously with melted butter, using about half of the butter. Return the rolls to the oven and bake until deeply golden brown, 15 to 20 minutes more; they should reach an internal temperature of 195°F/90°C.

9. Remove the rolls from the oven and brush them with the remaining butter. Let cool for at least 10 minutes before serving.

Variations

TRADITIONAL FOLDED PARKER HOUSE ROLLS After dividing the rolls into 12 pieces, follow these shaping instructions: Working with one piece of dough at a time, gently flatten the dough into an oblong shape about 4 x 1½ inches/10 x 4 cm. Brush the rolls with about half of the melted butter and fold each piece of dough crosswise in half. Place the rolls in the prepared pan as you shape them, arranging them in 3 rows

of 6. Let rise as directed and brush the rolls with egg wash, if desired. Bake as directed, skipping the mid-bake butter baste. Use the remaining butter to generously brush the rolls when they come out of the oven.

SLIDER ROLLS In step 5, divide the dough into 24 equal pieces (about 35 g each) and round (see page 104) into small rolls. Arrange in the prepared pan (4 rows of 6 rolls each) and cover with greased plastic wrap. Let rise until large and puffy, 30 minutes to 1 hour. Bake for 18 to 24 minutes, until the rolls are deeply golden brown and have an internal temperature of 195°F/90°C.

HONEY OR HERB-BUTTER PARKER HOUSE ROLLS Triple-baste the rolls with Honey Butter or Herb Butter (page 11): just before baking, midway through baking, and when they come out of the oven.

SEEDED PARKER HOUSE ROLLS Top the rolls generously with sesame seeds, poppy seeds, nigella seeds, or Everything Seasoning (page 177) after egg-washing them.

Make Ahead and Storage

The rolls are best within the first 24 hours after baking. Store leftover rolls tightly wrapped at room temperature for up to 4 days, or freeze in an airtight container for up to 3 months. Thaw frozen rolls overnight and refresh using the oven method in Rewarming Pastries, page 365.

Baby Baguettes

Makes 8 rolls

DIFFICULTY: **HARD**

This is a recipe I really hope you will try, even if you don't usually bake bread. If you're intimidated, don't be scared by the word "baguette"—instead, think of these as crunchy sandwich rolls, which they are (delightfully so)! This dough is a great introduction to how the bread-baking process works. It uses a starter, which aids in strength, hydration, and flavor. There's a lot of downtime here, so it's a great little baking project for a weekend. And these rolls freeze beautifully, so you can bake a batch when you have time, then have bakery-level rolls at the ready. Prepare to be impressed with yourself.

STARTER (PREFERMENT)

2 g / ¾ teaspoon instant dry yeast

226 g / 1 cup room-temperature water (about 75°F/25°C)

240 g / 2 cups bread flour

DOUGH

396 g / 1¾ cups warm water (about 110°F/45°C)

1 g / ½ teaspoon instant dry yeast

The starter (above)

660 g / 5½ cups bread flour

10 g / 2 teaspoons kosher salt

1. The night before you want to make the rolls, make the preferment: In a medium bowl, stir the yeast and water together well to combine. Add the flour and mix with a spatula until thoroughly combined and a shaggy dough forms.

2. Cover the bowl and let rise at room temperature for 12 hours (overnight); if your ambient room temperature is higher than 75°F/45°C, let the dough rise at room temperature for 6 hours, then refrigerate for the remaining 6 hours.

3. Make the dough: In the bowl of a stand mixer fitted with the dough hook, mix the water and yeast together with a spatula. Add the starter and stir a few times, then add the bread flour and salt and mix on low speed for 4 minutes until the dough comes together. Raise the speed to medium and mix for 2 minutes more, until the dough is fairly smooth.

4. Transfer the dough to a lightly greased large bowl, cover with plastic wrap, and let rise at room temperature until it nearly doubles in size, about 2 hours.

5. Transfer the dough to a lightly floured surface and divide into 8 equal pieces (about 190 g each). Fold each piece of dough onto itself a few times to make a roughly round shape. Cover the dough rounds and let rest for 10 minutes.

6. Line two baking sheets with parchment paper. Working with one piece of dough at a time, on the lightly floured surface, press the dough all over with your fingertips to flatten it. Starting with the part of dough farthest away from you, fold the dough over onto itself, using your fingertips to press it down firmly as you go. Repeat this process 2 or 3 more times—as you work, the piece of dough will become longer. When there's about ½ inch/1 cm of dough left that hasn't been folded, switch from your fingertips to the heel of your hand to secure the dough as you fold it over, finally

(CONTINUES)

119

forming the dough into a rough log. Starting in the center of the log, roll it under your fingers and upper portion of your palms into a baguette shape about 8 inches/20 cm long, applying slightly more pressure to the ends of the dough to taper them slightly. Gently transfer the baguette to the prepared baking sheets, evenly spacing 4 rolls down the center of each baking sheet. Repeat with the remaining pieces of dough.

7. Loosely cover the baguettes with clean dish towels and let rise until noticeably puffy, 40 minutes to 1 hour; they will not double in size. Toward the end of the rise time, preheat the oven to 450°F/230°C with the racks in the upper and lower thirds; if you have one, put a baking steel or pizza stone on the upper rack.

8. Use a lame (or other tool—see Scoring, page 109) to score the top of the baguettes on one of the baking sheets with 3 diagonal slashes each. (Optional: spritz each baguette with water—the additional moisture on the surface will steam and encourage a crisper crust in the oven.)

9. Fill a 9 x 13-inch/23 x 33 cm baking pan with ice cubes (about 6 cups/1.5 L) and place on the lower oven rack. Transfer the sheet of baguettes you just scored to the top oven rack. Bake for 10 minutes, then carefully remove the pan of steamy water and set it on the back of your stovetop. Continue to bake the baguettes until they are deeply golden brown and the internal temperature in the center is 200°F/93°C, 14 to 18 minutes more. Transfer the baguettes to a wire rack to cool.

10. Score the second pan of baguettes as described above. Return the pan of hot water to the bottom rack, place the baguettes on the top rack, and bake as directed.

11. Let the baguettes cool completely before serving or splitting in half for sandwich rolls.

Make Ahead and Storage

These rolls are best within the first 24 hours after baking. Store leftover rolls in an airtight container at room temperature for up to 3 days (as they stale, they make great toast or crostini). To freeze the rolls, wrap each one tightly in aluminum foil and freeze in an airtight container for up to 3 months. To refresh, place the foil-wrapped rolls in a cold oven and turn it on to 375°F/190°C. When the preheat buzzer notifies you the oven is at temperature, leave the baguettes in the oven for 4 to 5 minutes more.

Sweet Potato Bread Bowls (or Mini Loaves)

Makes 4 bread bowls (or mini loaves)

DIFFICULTY: **MEDIUM**

To make this recipe even easier, I usually use canned sweet potato puree (see the Note if you want to make your own). The canned puree is thinner and has a bit more moisture than mashed sweet potatoes. That extra moisture provides some of the hydration in the recipe, and contributes what potatoes always add to bread doughs: starchiness that makes for an especially beautiful loaf with a soft interior crumb. I also love the color and sweetness the sweet potatoes add. If you use the loaves for bread bowls, be sure to use the bread you scoop out to make croutons (see page 125).

640 g / 5⅓ **cups bread flour, plus more for dusting**

6 g / 2 **teaspoons instant dry yeast**

25 g / 2 **tablespoons granulated sugar**

6 g / 1½ **teaspoons fine sea salt**

28 g / 1 ounce / 2 **tablespoons unsalted butter, at room temperature**

340 g / 1¼ **cups canned sweet potato puree (see Note)**

113 g / ½ **cup warm water (about 110°F/45°C)**

1. In the bowl of a stand mixer fitted with the dough hook, mix the flour, yeast, sugar, and salt on low speed to combine. Add the butter and mix on low speed until the pieces are evenly distributed throughout the mixture. Add the sweet potato puree and water and mix for 3 minutes. Raise the speed to medium and mix for 2 minutes more, or until a smooth dough forms.

2. Transfer the dough to a greased large bowl and cover with plastic wrap (or use a rising bucket and cover with the lid) and let proof until doubled in size, 1 to 1½ hours.

3. Line two baking sheets with parchment paper. Turn the dough out onto a lightly floured surface and divide it into 4 equal pieces (about 290 g each). Working with one piece of dough at a time, fold the dough over onto itself a few times, then use both hands to gently round the dough. Use the sides of your hands to tighten the surface of the dough as you go (see page 104). Transfer the shaped dough to the lined baking sheets, 2 loaves on each sheet.

4. Proof the dough, loosely covered with a clean kitchen towel, until it is noticeably puffy, 1 to 1½ hours.

5. Uncover the dough and let rise for 30 to 45 minutes more, until the dough is slightly puffier. Toward the end of the rise time, preheat the oven to 375°F/190°C with the racks in the upper and lower thirds.

6. Lightly dust the surface of each loaf with flour, then score the dough as desired (see page 109). Bake the loaves for 15 minutes, then switch the positions of the pans, rotating them, and bake for another 20 to 25 minutes, or until the crust is golden brown and the loaves have an internal temperature of 205°F/96°F.

7. Remove the bread from the oven and cool for at least 20 minutes before serving, or cool completely before using the loaves to make bread bowls.

8. You can slice and serve the loaves or use them to create bread bowls: Use a serrated paring knife to cut a round in the top of each loaf. Tear

out the cut portions of the bread—snack on them or turn them into croutons (see page 125).

Note: I usually use Farmer's Market brand sweet potato puree. To make your own puree, peel and dice 300 g / 2 medium sweet potatoes. Place in a medium pot and cover with water by at least 1 inch / 2.5 cm. Bring to a boil over medium heat, then reduce to a simmer and cook until the potatoes are fork-tender, 10 to 12 minutes. Drain the sweet potatoes, transfer to a blender or food processor, and puree with 117 g / ½ cup water. Cool to room temperature before using. The puree can be made up to 5 days ahead and stored in the refrigerator in an airtight container; bring to room temperature before using. Or freeze for up to 6 months.

Make Ahead and Storage
This bread is best the same day it is baked. Loaves can be tightly wrapped and frozen for up to 2 months. Thaw and refresh (see page 112) before serving.

More Bread-Bowl Goodness

Pizza Dough (page 181) as Bread Bowls

Prepare and proof the dough. Divide the proofed dough into 2 equal pieces (about 470 g each) and form into rounds as directed on page 104. Cover loosely with greased plastic wrap and let rise for 1 to 2 hours, until doubled in size. Egg-wash the dough, use a lame or scissors to score the surface with an X, if desired, and bake at 400°F/205°C for 35 to 40 minutes.

Soft Pretzel Dough (page 140) as Bread Bowls

Prepare and proof the dough. Divide the proofed dough into 4 equal pieces (about 260 g each). Form the dough into round loaves as directed on page 104. Cover loosely with greased plastic wrap and let rise for 1 hour, or until doubled in size. Soak and egg-wash, as directed in the Pretzel Bun recipe. Use a lame or scissors to score the surface with an X, if desired. Reduce the baking temperature to 400°F/205°C and bake for 22 to 25 minutes.

Ultimate Garlic Bread Dough (page 156) as Bread Bowls

Prepare and proof the dough. Divide the proofed dough into 2 equal pieces (about 485 g each). Form the dough into round loaves as directed on page 104. Cover loosely with greased plastic wrap and let rise for 1 to 2 hours, until noticeably puffy. Use a lame or scissors to score the surface with an X, if desired. Bake at 425°F/220°C for 30 to 35 minutes.

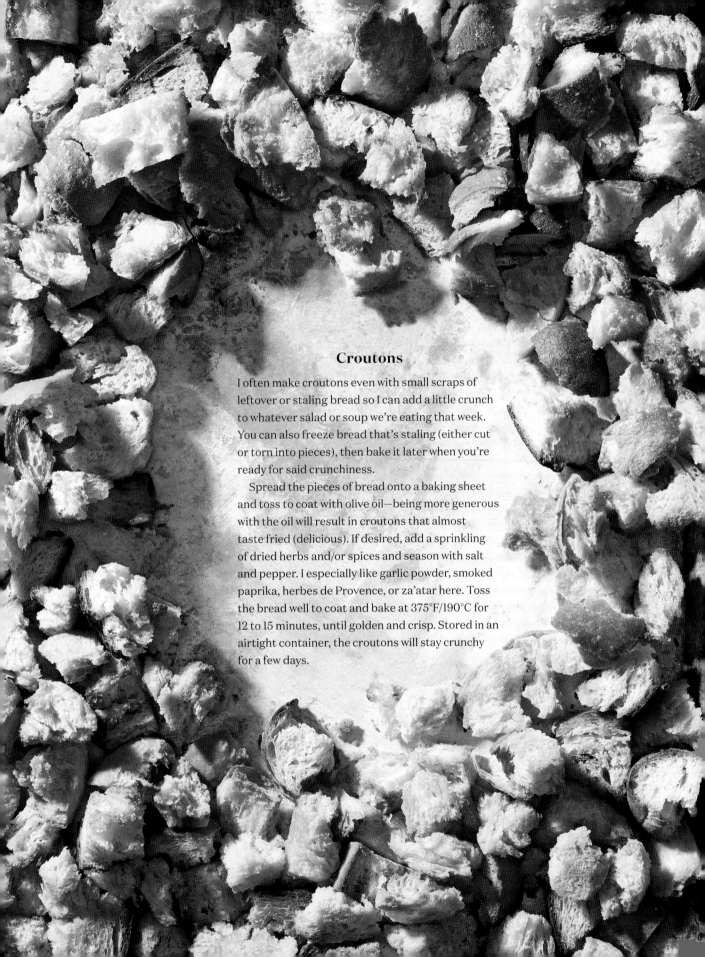

Croutons

I often make croutons even with small scraps of
leftover or staling bread so I can add a little crunch
to whatever salad or soup we're eating that week.
You can also freeze bread that's staling (either cut
or torn into pieces), then bake it later when you're
ready for said crunchiness.

   Spread the pieces of bread onto a baking sheet
and toss to coat with olive oil—being more generous
with the oil will result in croutons that almost
taste fried (delicious). If desired, add a sprinkling
of dried herbs and/or spices and season with salt
and pepper. I especially like garlic powder, smoked
paprika, herbes de Provence, or za'atar here. Toss
the bread well to coat and bake at 375°F/190°C for
12 to 15 minutes, until golden and crisp. Stored in an
airtight container, the croutons will stay crunchy
for a few days.

Sun-Dried Tomato, Goat Cheese, and Walnut Monkey Bread

Makes one 10-inch/25 cm Bundt

DIFFICULTY: **MEDIUM**

Let's talk about monkey bread—a wonderful concept with infinite possibilities. When I say "monkey bread," I mean a party-friendly bread fit for a crowd. Many folks think of it as a sweet icing-topped, cinnamon-sugar pull-apart bread. But there are also many possibilities in the world of savory monkey breads—this version packs a ton of flavor. The dough is stuffed with goat cheese before being dipped in a sun-dried tomato–sesame spread, but the same dough is a wonderful jumping-off point for many other flavors, including roasted garlic and herb, blue cheese and Buffalo dressing, or gooey, melty mozzarella cheese; see the Variations below. And the possibilities don't end with flavor options—there are also a variety of ways to shape pull-apart loaves like this; see the sidebar on page 131. If you've got a sweet tooth, try this dough paired with the Cinnamony, Caramely Biscuit Monkey Bread finishings on page 30 or the Fruity Iced Cream Buns on page 130.

DOUGH

75 g / ⅓ cup water (about 85°F/30°C)

7 g / 2¼ teaspoons instant dry yeast

173 g / ¾ cup whole milk

450 g / 3¾ cups bread flour

28 g / ¼ cup dry milk powder (optional; see page 100)

25 g / 2 tablespoons granulated sugar

6 g / 1½ teaspoons fine sea salt

56 g / 1 large egg

28 g / 1 ounce / 2 tablespoons unsalted butter, melted

30 g / 2 tablespoons sour cream, plain yogurt, or crème fraîche

Neutral oil (such as canola or vegetable) for greasing the bowl

FILLING AND FINISHING

65 g / 1 cup sun-dried tomatoes (well drained if oil-packed)

15 g / 3 cloves garlic, smashed and peeled

145 g / ⅔ cup extra virgin olive oil, plus more if necessary

56 g / 2 ounces / 4 tablespoons unsalted butter, cut into ½-inch/1 cm cubes

Up to 6 g / 2 tablespoons chopped fresh herbs (such as oregano, thyme, or rosemary, or a combination)

45 g / 3 tablespoons tahini

30 g / 2 tablespoons tomato paste

3 g / ½ teaspoon kosher salt

2 g / ½ teaspoon freshly ground black pepper

227 g / 8 ounces goat cheese

60 g / ¼ cup heavy cream

60 g / ½ cup walnuts, finely chopped

18 g / 2 tablespoons sesame seeds

Softened unsalted butter for greasing the pan

1. Pour the water into the bowl of a stand mixer fitted with the dough hook. Sprinkle the yeast over the water and mix with a small spatula to combine. Let sit for 5 minutes.

(CONTINUES)

2. In a small saucepan, heat the milk to about 110°F/45°C over medium-low heat (you can also do this in a liquid measuring cup in the microwave). Remove from the heat.

3. Add the bread flour, dry milk, sugar, and salt to the mixer bowl, then add the warm milk, egg, butter, and sour cream (or yogurt/crème fraîche) and mix on low speed for 4 minutes, or until a soft dough comes together around the dough hook.

4. Scrape the bowl well, then mix on medium speed for about 3 minutes more, until the dough is very smooth.

5. Transfer the dough to a greased medium bowl. Use both hands to gently turn the dough around so it's coated lightly on all sides, then gently tuck it under itself to slightly round it. Cover the bowl with plastic wrap and let the dough rise for 45 minutes to 1 hour, until visibly puffy and almost double in size.

6. Meanwhile, prepare the filling and finishing ingredients: In a small pot, combine the sun-dried tomatoes and smashed garlic cloves, pour the oil over them, and heat this mixture over low heat, stirring and swirling the pot occasionally, until the garlic cloves are very tender and the oil is very fragrant, 10 to 15 minutes.

7. Remove the pot from the heat, add the butter and herbs, and stir until the butter is melted. Cover the pot and let sit for 15 minutes.

8. Add the tahini, tomato paste, salt, and pepper to the sun-dried tomato mixture and puree with an immersion blender until smooth (or transfer the sun-dried tomato mixture to a blender or food processor, add the other ingredients, and puree). If necessary, add an extra glug or two of olive oil; the mixture should resemble a fairly smooth sauce. Transfer to a medium bowl.

9. Crumble the goat cheese into another medium bowl, add the cream, and blend together with a spatula until fairly smooth.

10. When the dough has risen, turn it out onto a lightly floured surface and shape into a square 10 x 10 inches/25 x 25 cm and about ½ inch/ 1 cm thick. Dot the goat cheese mixture over one half of the dough and use your hands to gently press it down to coat that half fairly evenly. Sprinkle the walnuts and sesame seeds evenly over the goat cheese mixture and gently press them into it. Carefully fold the uncovered portion of the dough over the covered portion and pinch the edges gently to seal.

11. Gently roll out the dough to a square 12 x 12 inches/30 x 30 cm. Cut the dough into 1-inch-/2.5 cm wide strips and then cut the strips crosswise to form 1-inch/2.5 cm squares.

12. Generously grease a 10-inch/25 cm Bundt or tube pan with soft butter. Gently dip the dough a few pieces at a time into the sun-dried tomato mixture to coat and transfer to the prepared pan, arranging the pieces in fairly even layers as you go. If any of the filling falls out as you assemble the bread, just add it to the pan with the dipped pieces of dough.

13. Loosely cover the pan and let the dough rise until it comes to about ½ inch/1 cm from the rim of the pan, 1 hour and 15 minutes to 1 hour and 45 minutes. Toward the end of the rise time, preheat the oven to 350°F/175°C with a rack in the center.

14. Place the Bundt pan on a parchment-lined baking sheet and bake until the center of the loaf reaches 200°F/95°C, 35 to 40 minutes.

15. Transfer the pan to a wire rack and let cool for 10 minutes, then use a small offset spatula to gently release the edges of the bread from the sides of the pan and the center tube and unmold onto a serving platter. Serve warm.

Variations

ROASTED GARLIC AND HERB MONKEY
BREAD Omit the filling and finishing
ingredients. Add the cloves from 2 small
heads of Roasted Garlic (page 159), 3 g /
1 tablespoon chopped fresh oregano, 3 g /
1 tablespoon chopped fresh thyme, and
3 g / 1 tablespoon chopped fresh rosemary
to the dough with the other ingredients in
step 3 and mix as directed. Melt 113 g /
4 ounces / 8 tablespoons unsalted butter
and stir in 30 g / 2 tablespoons heavy cream,
6 g / 1½ teaspoons garlic powder, and 3 g /
1 teaspoon freshly ground black pepper.
Skip steps 6 through 10. Shape the dough
as directed in step 11. After cutting the
dough into squares, dip each piece into
the seasoned butter and transfer to the
prepared pan. Let rise and bake as directed.

CARAMELIZED ONION, BALSAMIC, AND
PARMESAN MONKEY BREAD Omit the sour
cream for the dough. Omit the filling and
finishing ingredients. Prepare Caramelized
Onions (page 26) using 460 g / 2 medium
sweet onions. After caramelizing the onions,
stir in 30 g / 2 tablespoons good-quality
balsamic vinegar; let cool. Add the onions to
the dough with the other ingredients in step
3 and mix as directed. Omit the filling and
finishing ingredients. Melt 113 g / 4 ounces /
8 tablespoons unsalted butter and stir in
3 g / 1 teaspoon freshly ground black pepper.
In a small bowl, mix 150 g / 1½ cups finely
grated Parmesan cheese together with 16 g /
2 heaping tablespoons dried minced onion
(not onion powder). Skip steps 6 through 10.
Shape the dough as directed in step 11. After
cutting the dough into squares, dip each
piece into the seasoned butter, then dredge
in the Parmesan mixture. Transfer to the
prepared pan. Let rise and bake as directed.

GOOEY CHEESE-STUFFED MONKEY BREAD
Omit the filling and finishing ingredients.
Add 15 g / 3 cloves garlic, finely minced, to
the dough in step 3. Melt 113 g / 4 ounces /
8 tablespoons unsalted butter; if desired,
stir 2 g / ¾ teaspoon freshly ground black
pepper and 18 g / 2 tablespoons garlic
powder into the melted butter. Cut 395 g /
14 ounces low-moisture mozzarella or brick
cheese into thirty 1-inch / 2.5 cm cubes. After
the dough has risen, divide it into 30 equal
pieces (about 29 g each). Working with one
piece of dough at a time, gently flatten each
piece and place a piece of cheese on top of it.
Wrap the dough around the cheese, gently
pinching the seams to seal. Dip each piece of
dough-wrapped cheese into the butter and
transfer to the prepared pan. Let rise and
bake as directed, increasing the bake time
by up to 8 minutes. Serve with marinara
sauce for dipping, if desired.

BUFFALO-BLUE CHEESE MONKEY BREAD
Omit the filling and finishing ingredients.
Have ready 226 g / 8 ounces blue cheese. In a
small bowl, mix 75 g / ⅓ cup hot sauce, such
as Frank's, 56 g / 2 ounces / 4 tablespoons
unsalted butter, melted, 2 g / ½ teaspoon
garlic powder, and 2 pinches of celery salt.
Shape the dough as directed in step 10,
crumbling the blue cheese over the dough
and pressing it gently into the dough before
folding the uncovered dough over the
covered dough. After cutting the dough into
squares as directed above, dip them into the
Buffalo sauce and transfer the dough to the
prepared pan. Let rise and bake as directed.

PERFECT WHITE SANDWICH BREAD Omit
the filling and finishing ingredients. Prepare
the dough as directed through step 6.

(CONTINUES)

From the dough into a loaf (see page 104), and transfer to a greased 9-inch/23 cm Pullman pan (see Resources) or a regular 9 x 5-inch/23 x 13 cm loaf pan. Cover the pan with greased plastic wrap and let the dough rise until it is about ½ inch/1 cm from the top edge of the pan, about 1 hour. Lightly grease the lid of the Pullman pan, if using, place it on the pan, and transfer to the oven; or, if using a regular loaf pan, just head straight to the oven. Bake the bread at 350°F/175°C with the lid on (if using) for 30 minutes. Remove the lid (if using) and continue to bake the bread until it is well browned and the internal temperature reads 190°F/88°C, 10 to 15 minutes more. Cool for 5 to 10 minutes in the pan, then unmold onto a wire rack to cool completely.

SWEET-TOOTH BREAK

Fruity Iced Cream Buns

Makes 10 buns

After the dough has risen, divide it into 10 equal pieces (about 85 g each). Shape into oblong rolls (see page 104) about 3½ inches/9 cm long, slightly tapering the ends. Transfer the buns to a parchment-lined baking sheet, staggering them to fit. Cover with greased plastic wrap and let rise for 2 to 2 ½ hours, until visibly puffy.

Brush the buns with egg wash (see page 7) and bake at 350°F/190°C until golden brown, 22 to 26 minutes. Cool completely.

Prepare the basic glaze on page 20 using fruit juice or homemade fruit puree—you can use either a thinner or thicker glaze to finish these buns. Whip 315 g / 1⅓ cups heavy cream with 25 g / 2 tablespoons granulated sugar and 5 g / 1 teaspoon vanilla extract to medium peaks. Transfer to a pastry bag fitted with a large star tip. Split the cooled buns and fill with the whipped cream. Spoon the glaze over the buns and serve immediately.

Make Ahead and Storage
The monkey bread is best right after it is baked, served warm.

Four Ways to Shape Monkey and Other Pull-Apart Breads

TRADITIONAL (PULL-APART PIECES): Form the pieces of dough into small rounds as described on page 104. Dip the rounds into the finishings (such as melted butter, or the sun-dried tomato mixture) before placing them in the prepared pan, stacking them as you go.

PULL-APART SHEETS: Roll out the dough ½ inch / 1 cm thick, then cut into squares about the width of your loaf pan. Working with one piece at a time, spread the finishings over the surface to evenly coat, then fold the square in half before placing into the pan, arranging them side by side, with the folded side down.

PULL-APART CIRCLES: Roll out the dough ½ inch/1 cm thick, then cut into circles about the width of your loaf pan. Working with one piece at a time, spread the finishings over the surface to evenly coat, then arrange the rounds tightly side by side in the pan.

TWICE-BAKED: You can make a delicious pull-apart–style dough with a baked loaf of bread. Use a sharp serrated knife to cut a cross-hatch pattern into the loaf (about three-quarters of the way through, so it's

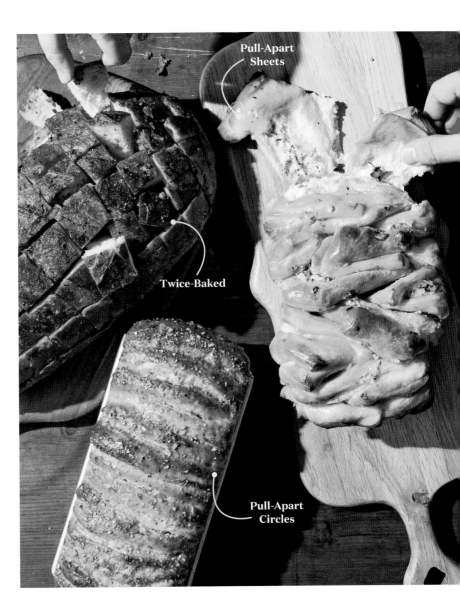

Pull-Apart Sheets

Twice-Baked

Pull-Apart Circles

still attached at the base). Drizzle melted butter and/or stuff the finishings (chopped herbs, cheese, or the sun-dried tomato spread) into the cuts, then wrap the loaf in foil and bake at 350°F/175°C until heated through, 20 to 25 minutes.

English-ish Muffins

Makes 16 muffins

DIFFICULTY: **EASY**

*A few things about these English muffins aren't tra-
ditional, but they are delicious, so hear me out. In
pastry school, my wonderful bread instructor, Eric
Kastel, made his muffins without the round metal
rings many recipes call for. That made the process
easier, no special equipment required. Thus began
my own tweaks to the classic recipe to fit it into my
life and my kitchen so I could have these muffins
more often. The muffins traditionally start with a
soft dough that is cooked either exclusively on a
griddle (or in a skillet) or with some oven time too.
Mine uses a combination of griddle, for that crisp
exterior, and a little bake time, for that interior
with lots of nooks and crannies. I formulated my
recipe to be an overnight dough, so you can bake
fresh muffins in the morning.*

690 g / 5¾ cups bread flour

9 g / 1 tablespoon instant dry yeast

18 g / 1½ tablespoons kosher salt

12 g / 1 tablespoon granulated sugar

454 g / 2 cups water (about 105°F/40°C)

**56 g / 2 ounces / 4 tablespoons unsalted butter,
at room temperature**

Semolina flour or cornmeal for dusting

1. The day before you want to make the English
   muffins, make the dough: In the bowl of a stand
   mixer fitted with the dough hook, combine the
   bread flour, yeast, salt, and sugar and mix on
   low speed for 20 to 30 seconds. Add the water
   and butter and mix for 4 minutes. Scrape the
   bowl and dough hook well, raise the speed to
   medium, and mix for 3 minutes more. The
   dough should be smooth but not overly sticky.

2. Transfer the dough to an oiled large bowl and
   cover with plastic wrap. Let rise at room temperature for 30 minutes, then transfer to the
   refrigerator to proof overnight.

3. The next morning, bring the dough to room
   temperature, 30 to 45 minutes.

4. On a lightly floured surface, roll out the dough
   to a 10 x 10-inch/25 x 25 cm square about ½ in/
   1 cm thick. Use a bench knife, pastry wheel,
   or sharp knife to cut the dough into 4 strips
   2½ inches/6 cm wide, then cut the strips crosswise into 2½-inch/6 cm squares.

5. Sprinkle another part of your work surface
   with semolina or cornmeal and transfer the
   muffins to it, leaving about 1 inch/2.5 cm
   between them. Cover loosely with greased
   plastic wrap or a clean kitchen towel and let
   rise for 30 to 40 minutes, until slightly puffy.

6. Preheat the oven to 475°F/245°C with the
   racks in the upper and lower thirds. Line two
   baking sheets with parchment paper.

7. Uncover the muffins and sprinkle generously with semolina or cornmeal on both
   sides. Heat a griddle or a large cast-iron skillet over medium heat until very hot. Working
   in batches, add the muffins to the hot griddle, without crowding, and cook until golden
   brown on the bottom, 2 to 4 minutes. Flip the
   muffins and cook until golden on the other
   side, 2 to 4 minutes. Transfer the muffins to
   the prepared baking sheets, placing them in
   staggered rows and leaving about 1½ inches/
   4 cm between the rows.

(CONTINUES)

Make Ahead and Storage
The muffins can be stored in an airtight container at room temperature for up to 3 days; toasting them, in a toaster or toaster oven, refreshes them beautifully. They can also be frozen in an airtight container for up to 6 months—split them in half before freezing to help them thaw faster.

8. Transfer the baking sheets to the oven and bake until the muffins are cooked through, 8 to 10 minutes; an instant-read thermometer inserted into the thickest part of a muffin should read 210°F/98°C.

9. Transfer to a wire rack and let cool for 5 to 10 minutes before serving warm, or cool completely.

Small-Batch Oven-Roasted Jam

Makes about 2 pints

When I lived alone in the Hudson Valley some years ago, my number-one hobby was canning and preserving. I knew every farmer and farm stand within a fifty-mile radius of my apartment, and everyone in my life was always getting jam as gifts. When I left for the big city, I had no choice but to partially abandon this hobby because of lack of space. So I'd often opt for the significantly less fussy route of refrigerator or freezer jam—and for much smaller batches. Sometimes I was doing this to capture fruit worthy of preserving at the height of the season, but more often, it was when I had fruit on the counter that was so ripe it was teetering on the edge of spoilage. I call this flexible, easy method roasted or sheet-pan jam. And it requires much less sugar than regular canning recipes to boot.

1.36 kg / 3 pounds fruit of choice (such as stone fruit or berries), peeled if desired and pits/seeds/stems removed as necessary

150 g / ¾ cup granulated sugar

60 g / ¼ cup fresh lemon juice

Pinch or two of fine sea salt

1. Put the fruit on a rimmed baking sheet and toss with the sugar, lemon juice, and salt. Let macerate while you preheat the oven to 375°F/190°C.

2. Transfer the baking sheet to the oven and roast until the fruit is very soft and the juices have thickened a bit (they may start to turn a little darker at the edges of the tray). Timing will depend on the type of fruit—smaller, softer fruits like berries will take 15 to 20 minutes; larger, firmer fruits like stone fruit may take 20 to 30 minutes.

3. When the fruit is very soft and tender, remove it from the oven. While it's still hot, use a potato masher or large fork to mash the fruit well on the baking sheet. Transfer to a jar or other storage container and cool to room temperature, then refrigerate or freeze until ready to use.

Savory Jams and Jellies

The combo of salty and sweet finds no better embodiment than the savory jams or jellies below. I use these for everything from pastries to pizza to pies—and they are also wonderful on a charcuterie platter or other snacking boards too. All these jams can be refrigerated for up to 2 weeks or frozen for up to 1 month.

Bacon Jam

Makes about 1 pint

454 g / 1 pound bacon, finely chopped
About 325 g / 1 large sweet onion, minced
15 g / 3 cloves garlic, minced
140 g / ⅔ packed cup light or dark brown sugar
115 g / ½ cup apple cider
77 g / ⅓ cup apple cider vinegar
Freshly ground black pepper

1. Heat a large pot over medium heat. Add the bacon and cook, stirring often, until the fat renders and the bacon is crisp, 7 to 9 minutes. Remove the bacon with a slotted spoon and drain on a paper towel–lined plate.

2. Drain off all but about 15 g / 1 tablespoon of the bacon fat from the pot. Add the onion and cook until very tender, 7 to 9 minutes. Add the garlic and cook until fragrant, about 1 minute.

3. Return the bacon to the pot and add the brown sugar, cider, and vinegar. Bring the mixture to a simmer and cook, uncovered, stirring frequently, until the liquid has evaporated and the jam has thickened, 8 to 10 minutes. Season with pepper. Transfer to a jar or other storage container, let cool, and refrigerate until ready to use.

Tomato Jam

Makes about 1 pint

495 g / 2½ cups chopped ripe tomatoes
141 g / ⅔ packed cup light brown sugar
30 g / 2 tablespoons balsamic vinegar
2 g / ½ teaspoon fine sea salt
2 g / 1 teaspoon dried oregano

1. Combine all the ingredients in a medium pot, bring to a simmer over medium-low heat, and cook until the tomatoes begin to soften, 5 to 6 minutes.

2. Reduce the heat to low and cook, stirring occasionally, until the mixture reduces and thickens to a jam-like consistency, 35 to 40 minutes. Leave the jam chunky or puree with an immersion blender (or in a regular blender) until smooth, if desired. Transfer to a jar or other storage container, let cool, and refrigerate until ready to use.

Caramelized Onion Jam

Makes about 1 pint

60 g / ¼ cup extra virgin olive oil
About 1300 g / 4 large sweet onions, thinly sliced
115 g / ½ cup balsamic vinegar
140 g / ⅔ packed cup light or dark brown sugar
1 sprig rosemary and 2 sprigs thyme
Kosher salt and freshly ground black pepper

1. In a large pot, heat the oil over medium heat. Add the onions and cook as directed for Caramelized Onions (page 26).

(CONTINUES)

2. Deglaze the pot with the vinegar, stirring well, then stir in the brown sugar, thyme, and rosemary. Bring the mixture to a simmer and cook, uncovered and stirring frequently, until the liquid has evaporated and the jam has thickened, 3 to 4 minutes.

3. Season the jam with salt and pepper and remove the rosemary and thyme sprigs. Transfer to a jar or other storage container, let cool, and refrigerate until ready to use.

Herby Fig Jam

Makes about 1 pint

681 g / 1½ pounds fresh figs, stems removed
About 230 g / 1 medium sweet onion, finely minced
160 g / ¾ packed cup light or dark brown sugar
77 g / ⅓ cup white wine vinegar
1 bay leaf
3 sprigs fresh thyme
2 sprigs fresh rosemary
2 sprigs fresh oregano
Kosher salt and freshly ground black pepper

1. In a large pot, toss the figs, onion, brown sugar, and vinegar together. Add the bay leaf, thyme, rosemary, and oregano and cook over medium heat, stirring frequently, until the figs and onions have broken down and are very tender and the mixture has thickened slightly, 12 to 15 minutes.

2. Remove the bay leaf and herb sprigs. Use a potato masher or immersion blender (or regular blender) to blend the jam until chunky-smooth. Season with salt and pepper. Transfer to a jar or other storage container, let cool, and refrigerate until ready to serve.

Pepper Jelly

Makes about 1 pint

142 g / 5 ounces Fresno chiles (or other fresh chile peppers), stems removed
115 g / ½ cup apple cider vinegar
248 g / 1¼ cups granulated sugar
5 g / 1½ teaspoons powdered pectin
Pinch or two of kosher salt

1. In a blender, combine the chiles and vinegar and puree until smooth.

2. In a medium pot, whisk the sugar, pectin, and salt together. Add the chile/vinegar mixture and bring to a simmer, stirring constantly. Simmer until the mixture thickens, about 10 minutes. Transfer the jelly to a jar or other storage container, let cool, and refrigerate until ready to use.

Dark Rye Bread

Makes one 9 x 5-inch/23 x 13 cm loaf

DIFFICULTY: **EASY**

I love a good rye bread—and this one is my go-to loaf to bake on a lazy winter day. Ideal for sandwiches or toast (slathered in butter), it is also great for croutons. It's a reliably delicious all-purpose bread—and it's incredibly easy to make.

230 g / 1 cup whole milk

113 g / ⅓ cup molasses

7 g / 2¼ teaspoons instant dry yeast

230 g / 1 cup buttermilk

280 g / 2⅓ cups bread flour

160 g / 1½ cups dark rye flour

60 g / ½ cup whole wheat flour

45 g / ⅓ cup cornmeal

10 g / 3 tablespoons unsweetened cocoa powder (preferably black cocoa powder; see Resources)

12 g / 2 teaspoons kosher salt

1. In a medium pot, heat the milk and molasses over medium heat until the mixture reaches about 110°F/45°C on an instant-read thermometer. Transfer to the bowl of a stand mixer, whisk in the yeast, and let sit for about 5 minutes.

2. Attach the bowl to the mixer stand and fit with the dough hook. Add the buttermilk, bread flour, rye flour, wheat flour, cornmeal, cocoa powder, and salt and mix on low speed for 5 minutes, then raise the speed to medium and mix for 8 minutes more, or until the dough is very smooth.

3. Transfer the dough to a lightly greased medium bowl. Cover the bowl with greased plastic wrap and let the dough rise at room temperature for 1 hour to 1 hour and 15 minutes, until nearly doubled in size.

4. Lightly grease a 9 x 5-inch/23 x 13 cm loaf pan with nonstick spray. Transfer the dough to a *very* lightly floured surface—use just enough flour to prevent sticking. Roll the dough into a loaf (see page 104) and transfer to the prepared pan, seam side down.

5. Cover the pan loosely with plastic wrap and let the dough rise until it comes to the rim of the pan, 1 hour to 1 hour and 15 minutes. Toward the end of the rise time, preheat the oven to 375°F/190°C with a rack in the center.

6. Use a lame or sharp knife to score the bread (see page 109). Bake the bread until it's deeply brown and the internal temperature in the center of the loaf is 205°F/96°C, 40 to 45 minutes. Cool the bread in the pan for 15 minutes, then unmold and cool completely on a wire rack before slicing.

Make Ahead and Storage
The bread is best within the first 24 hours after it's baked, but leftovers can be stored tightly wrapped at room temperature for up to 4 days or in the freezer for up to 4 months.

Skillet as Toaster

I have never owned a toaster; when I want toast (which is often), I toast it on the stovetop in a cast-iron skillet. I use thinner slices when I want really crisp, cracker-like bread, and thicker slices when I want a little heartiness, doughiness, and/or chew. Here are some of the ways I make my toast:

DRY: Add the bread to the hot pan and cook over medium-low heat, turning once, until dry and toasty, 1 to 3 minutes. The toast won't get as golden as with the other methods, but it holds up better to saucy toppings and accompaniments, like Béchamel Sauce (page 56) or Creamy Mushroom Spread (page 96).

OLIVE OIL: Gently drizzle both sides of the bread with olive oil (thinner pieces of bread) or gently dip both sides of the slice into oil to fully coat (thicker pieces of bread). Add the bread to the hot pan and cook, turning once, until noticeably charred at the edges, 1 to 3 minutes.

BUTTER: Spread a thin layer of room-temperature butter evenly across both sides of the bread. Add the bread to the hot pan and cook, turning once, until it is evenly golden brown, 1 to 3 minutes.

MAYONNAISE: Spread a thin layer of mayonnaise evenly across both sides of the bread. Add the bread to the hot pan and cook, turning once, until it is evenly golden brown, 1 to 3 minutes.

Mushrooms for Toast

Makes 4 toasts

My husband and I share a love affair with mushrooms—one that has deepened since his growing interest in mycology, the study of fungi. This is one of my favorite ways to prepare mushrooms when we're craving them or he's just harvested a new batch of his home-grown beauties. You can use any kind of mushroom for these toasts—from oysters to cremini to shiitake—or an assortment. I start by frying the slices of bread (see Skillet as Toaster, page 138) in a cast-iron skillet in olive oil until toasted on both sides, then season them with flaky salt and freshly ground black pepper.

About 454 g / 1 pound mushrooms

28 g / 1 ounce / 2 tablespoons unsalted butter

15 g / 1 tablespoon extra virgin olive oil

10 g / 2 cloves garlic, thinly sliced

Kosher salt and freshly ground black pepper

78 g / ⅓ cup heavy cream

2 or 3 sprigs woody herbs, like rosemary or thyme

10 g / ¼ cup chopped fresh parsley

4 thick slices toast fried in olive oil (see page 138)—I use the Ultimate Garlic Bread (page 156), Brioche Loaves (page 208), or Perfect White Sandwich Bread (page 130)

1. Cut the mushrooms into large chunks—keep in mind that they will shrink as they cook, the goal is for them to end up as large-bite size.

2. In a large skillet, heat the butter and olive oil over medium heat. Add the mushrooms and spread them out in an even layer, aiming to give them as much room as possible. Cook, undisturbed, until well browned on the first side before flipping. Flip the mushrooms and continue to cook, flipping often, until they are well browned on all sides and very tender.

3. Add the garlic and cook until fragrant, about 1 minute. Season the mushrooms with salt and pepper, tossing well. Add the cream and herb sprigs, bring the mixture to a simmer, and simmer until the cream thickens to a sauce-like consistency and thickly clings to the mushrooms.

4. Remove the herb sprigs and stir in the parsley. Serve immediately over the fried toast.

139

Soft Pretzels

Makes 12 pretzels, 8 sandwich buns, or 90 pretzel nuggets

DIFFICULTY: **MEDIUM**

Classic pretzels are made with a soak in food-grade lye, which gives them their characteristic chew and deep-brown exterior. But food-grade lye is tricky to use—it can be dangerous if handled improperly. My friend Erin Clarkson, author of the Cloudy Kitchen *blog, finally managed to produce a beautiful pretzel without using lye, and she inspired me to try it too. This combination of two finishes simulates the effect of the lye without the danger: a soak in baking-soda water, which performs a similar reaction as the lye on the surface of the dough, and an egg wash, which helps get the pretzels to the level of brown they deserve. Once you've tried your hand at classic pretzels, there's a ton of fun ways to use this dough. Make pretzel buns for epic sandwiches, pretzel dogs, or nuggets for a perfect party snack. And whatever you do, don't miss the "Stuffed" Pretzels (page 144)—there's something there for every one!*

DOUGH

660 g / 5½ cups bread flour

25 g / 2 tablespoons granulated sugar

9 g / 1 tablespoon instant dry yeast

12 g / 2 teaspoons kosher salt

56 g / 2 ounces / 4 tablespoons unsalted butter, at room temperature

340 g / 1½ cups warm water (about 110°F/45°C)

FINISHING

4.25 kg / 4½ quarts water

160 g / ⅔ cup baking soda

Egg wash (see page 7)

Coarse or flaky salt

1. In the bowl of a stand mixer fitted with the dough hook, combine the flour, sugar, yeast, and salt and mix for 30 seconds to 1 minute on low speed to blend. Add the butter and water and mix for about 3 minutes, until the dough comes together. Raise the speed to medium and mix until the dough is very smooth, about 4 minutes more.

2. Transfer the dough to a greased bowl and cover with plastic wrap. Let rise until noticeably puffy and nearly doubled in size, 1 to 1½ hours.

3. Divide the dough (keep any dough you're not working with covered to prevent drying out):

   FOR PRETZELS: Divide the dough into 12 equal pieces (about 85 g each).

   FOR SANDWICH BUNS: Divide the dough into 8 equal pieces (about 130 g each).

   FOR PRETZEL NUGGETS: Divide the dough into 6 equal pieces (about 175 g each).

4. Shape the dough: Line one baking sheet (if making buns) or two baking sheets (if making pretzels or nuggets) with parchment paper.

   FOR PRETZELS: Working with one piece at a time, press each piece of dough into a slightly oblong shape by pushing it flat with your fingers. Starting at the edge of dough farthest away from you, fold one-third of the dough over onto itself. Press firmly with your fingertips or the heel of your hand to seal the seam. Continue to fold the dough over and press to seal until it has formed a log shape.

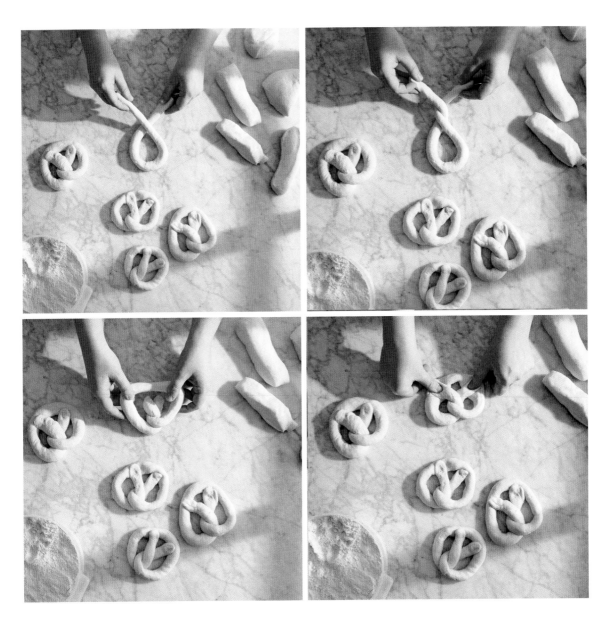

Starting with very light pressure in the center of the dough, roll the dough under your hands on the work surface into a log about 20 inches/50 cm long. Pick up the two ends and twist the strands around each other, then repeat to make a double twist. Lift the rounded part of the dough at the top and bring it down below the two twists. Bring the ends of the twists through the rounded part and press down with your fingers to seal the pretzel. Transfer to the prepared baking sheets, then press the pretzels again to make sure the seams are well sealed.

FOR SANDWICH BUNS: Working with one piece at a time, cup your hand over a piece of dough and roll it in a circular motion on the work surface to form it into a tight round (see page 104). Transfer to the baking sheet.

(CONTINUES)

FOR PRETZEL NUGGETS: Working with one piece at a time, roll each piece of dough into a log about 1 inch in diameter and 9 inches/23 cm long. Cut into 1-inch/2.5 cm pieces and transfer to the prepared baking sheets.

5. Cover the shaped pretzels, buns, or nuggets with greased plastic wrap and let rise until noticeably puffy, 15 to 20 minutes for nuggets, 30 to 45 minutes for pretzels and buns.

6. Make the soaking mixture and boil the pretzels: Bring the water to a simmer in a large pot over medium-high heat. Stir in the baking soda and reduce the heat to low. Working in batches, add the shaped pretzels (or buns or nuggets) to the water and let soak for about 1 minute, using a slotted spoon or spider to gently flip them halfway through. Return the soaked dough to the baking sheet(s), leaving at least ½ inch/1 cm between them.

7. Preheat the oven to 425°F/220°C with racks in the upper and lower thirds.

8. Egg-wash the pretzels and sprinkle with coarse or flaky salt. Bake, rotating the pans halfway through baking if using two sheets, until the pretzels (or buns or nuggets) are deeply golden brown and the interior temperature of the thickest part is at least 195°F/90°C: 12 to 15 minutes for pretzels, 18 to 22 minutes for buns, or 10 to 12 minutes for nuggets. Let cool for at least 10 minutes before serving.

Variations

PRETZEL-WRAPPED HOT DOGS OR SAUSAGES In step 3, divide the dough into 10 pieces (about 105 g each). To shape, work with one piece at a time. Press the piece of dough into a slightly oblong shape by pushing it flat with your fingers. Starting at the edge of dough farthest away from you, fold one third of dough over onto itself. Press firmly with your fingertips or the heel of your hand to seal the seam. Place a hot dog or cooled fully cooked sausage on top of the seal, then fold the remaining dough over the meat, pressing firmly to seal. Transfer to a lined baking sheet, seam side down. Proceed as directed to proof, soak, and egg-wash the dough. Bake for 17 to 20 minutes.

EVERYTHING PRETZELS Shape the dough as for classic pretzels. After brushing them with egg wash, top each one generously with Everything Seasoning (page 177) and bake.

SWEET-TOOTH BREAK

Cinnamon Sugar Pretzels

Shape the dough as for classic pretzels (I still use a little salt, but significantly less). In a medium bowl, mix together 198 g / 1 cup granulated sugar and 13 g / 1½ tablespoons ground cinnamon. After egg-washing the pretzels, lightly sprinkle each one with cinnamon sugar (you'll have plenty left over). Bake for 12 to 15 minutes. While the pretzels bake, melt 170 g / 12 tablespoons unsalted butter. As soon as the pretzels come out of the oven, brush them generously with the melted butter and toss in the cinnamon sugar to coat. Serve warm.

Make Ahead and Storage
Pretzels are best within the first 24 hours after baking. Store
leftover rolls tightly wrapped at room temperature for up to
2 days, or freeze for up to 3 months. Refresh frozen pretzels
using the oven method in Rewarming Pastries (page 365).
After the recommended warming time, remove the foil and
warm for 2 minutes more.

"Stuffed" Pretzels

Makes 8 pretzels

The Apple Pie Bakery Café at my alma mater, the Culinary Institute of America, served delicious "stuffed pretzels." Now I make my own homemade versions of these pretzels. They've become one of my favorite ways to use leftovers—everything from taco filling to pizza toppings to roasted vegetables to curry.

Shape the dough as for sandwich buns, but after you shape each round, punch the dough down to flatten it and make it larger. Proof, soak, egg-wash, and salt the dough rounds as directed in steps 5 through 7, then transfer to parchment-lined baking sheets, leaving at least 2 inches/ 5 cm between them. If the center of the pretzels seem too puffy at this stage, use the greased base of a ¼-cup measuring cup to press the centers down and make room for the filling. Pile about 2 to 4 tablespoons of your favorite topping in the center and top each pretzel with about 25 g / ¼ packed cup shredded cheese of your choice. Bake until the pretzels are deeply golden brown and the cheese has melted and browned, 22 to 25 minutes.

Variations

THE ROOMMATE SPECIAL In a medium bowl, toss 175 g / 1 cup cooked black beans, 75 g / ½ cup corn kernels, 40 g / 4 large scallions, thinly sliced, 5 g / 1 clove garlic, minced, 15 to 30 g / 1 to 2 tablespoons fresh lime juice, 26 g / 2 tablespoons minced pickled jalapeño, and 9 g / 3 tablespoons chopped fresh cilantro. Season with salt and pepper. Divide the filling evenly among the shaped pretzels and top each with 25 g / ¼ packed cup shredded Monterey Jack cheese.

CARAMELIZED ONION PRETZELS Spread 10 g / 2 teaspoons whole-grain mustard over the center of each pretzel, then top with 36 g / 3 tablespoons Caramelized Onions (page 26) and 25 g / ¼ cup packed shredded Gruyère cheese.

CHILI CHEESE PRETZELS Spoon 70 g / 3 tablespoons cooled chili into the center of each pretzel. Bake as directed, then top each pretzel with 14 g / 1 slice American cheese as soon as they come out of the oven. If the cheese doesn't melt sufficiently, return to the oven for a minute or two. Serve immediately.

SWEET-TOOTH BREAK

PB S'mores Pretzels

Spread 18 g / 1 tablespoon peanut butter over the center of each pretzel, then place 28 g / 1 ounce dark or milk chocolate, coarsely chopped, on top. Cut 40 g / 4 jumbo marshmallows in half, and place on top. Finish each one with 7 g / 1 tablespoon coarse graham cracker crumbs.

Smoked Salmon Breakfast Buns

Makes 12 buns

DIFFICULTY: **MEDIUM**

*Morning people are breakfast people. I am unde-
niably both, and cooking breakfast is almost more
enjoyable for me than eating it. As one of the early
risers in my family, I often bake up a treat we can
enjoy as everyone starts gathering in the early
part of the day on a holiday or another celebration.
Swirly breakfast rolls—the kind that are golden on
the outside, soft and fluffy inside, and boast some
kind of flavorful filling—are a favorite, and when
they are served fresh and warm, everyone gobbles
them up in no time.*

*This dough is formulated to allow the shaped
buns an overnight rise, so they will be ready and
waiting for your breakfast come morning. The
slower rise in the refrigerator also gives it more
flavor. I dreamed up all kinds of fillings to make a
savory version of those swirly breakfast rolls. This
smoked salmon version was inspired by a dip my
mom regularly makes for company, layering hot-
smoked salmon with cream cheese, onions, capers,
and dill. All of the variations below were created
with celebratory, crowd-pleasing fare in mind.*

DOUGH

600 g / 5 cups bread flour

36 g / 3 tablespoons granulated sugar

6 g / 2 teaspoons instant dry yeast

5 g / 1¼ teaspoons fine sea salt

**230 g / 1 cup warm whole milk (about
110°F/45°C)**

168 g / 3 large eggs, at room temperature

**56 g / 2 ounces / 4 tablespoons unsalted butter,
at room temperature**

21 g / 1 tablespoon honey

FILLING

**226 g / 8 ounces cream cheese, at room
temperature**

**140 g / 5 ounces Gournay cheese (such as
Boursin, or see page 150 for recipe)**

75 g / ¾ cup finely grated Parmesan cheese

10 g / 2 cloves garlic, minced

30 g / 3 large scallions, thinly sliced

**170 g / 6 ounces hot-smoked salmon, coarsely
crumbled**

25 g / 3 tablespoons finely chopped capers

6 g / 2 tablespoons chopped fresh dill

1 g / 1 teaspoon grated lemon zest

**14 g / 1 tablespoon soft unsalted butter for
greasing the pan**

FINISHING

Egg wash (see page 7)

Everything Seasoning (page 177)

**28 g / 1 ounce / 2 tablespoons unsalted butter,
melted (optional)**

1. The day before you want to bake the buns,
   make the dough: In the bowl of a stand mixer
   fitted with the dough hook, mix the flour,
   sugar, yeast, and salt on low speed to combine.
   Add the milk, eggs, butter, and honey and mix
   for 4 minutes. Scrape the bowl well. Raise the
   speed to medium and mix for 3 minutes more,
   or until the dough is smooth.

2. Transfer the dough to a lightly greased large
   bowl and cover with plastic wrap. Let rise until

(CONTINUES)

the dough nearly doubles in size, 45 minutes to 1 hour 15 minutes.

3. While the dough rises, make the filling: In the bowl of a stand mixer fitted with the paddle attachment, whip the cream cheese, Gournay cheese, and Parmesan cheese together until light and fluffy, 2 to 3 minutes. Add the garlic, scallions, salmon, capers, dill, and lemon zest and mix well to combine. Cover and set aside.

4. Punch down the dough and transfer it to a lightly floured work surface. Form it into a rough rectangle with your hands, then use a rolling pin to roll it out into a rectangle about 12 x 24 inches/30 x 60 cm and ½ inch/1 cm thick.

5. Dollop the cheese filling evenly over the surface of the dough and use a small offset spatula to gently spread it into an even layer. Starting from one of the longer sides, roll the dough up into a tight spiral. Using kitchen twine, unflavored dental floss, or a sharp serrated knife, cut it into 12 equal pieces.

6. Grease a 9 x 13-inch/23 x 33 cm baking pan with the soft butter. Arrange the rolls cut side up in the pan in 3 rows of 4. Spray the surface of the rolls with nonstick spray and cover with plastic wrap.

7. Let the rolls rise at room temperature for 30 minutes, then refrigerate for 10 to 12 hours.

8. In the morning, bring the rolls to room temperature, 30 to 45 minutes. Preheat the oven to 325°F/160°C with a rack in the center.

9. Egg-wash the rolls and sprinkle generously with everything seasoning. Bake for 55 to 65 minutes, until rolls are lightly brown; they should have an internal temp of 190°F/90°C. If using the melted butter, brush it over the rolls when you pull them out of the oven.

Variations

ROAST BEEF AND CHEESE BUNS Replace the Everything Seasoning with sesame seeds. Replace the filling with the following mixture: In the bowl of a stand mixer fitted with the paddle attachment, whip 226 g / 8 ounces room-temperature cream cheese until fluffy, 2 to 3 minutes. Add 226 g / 8 ounces shredded cheddar cheese, 15 g / 1 tablespoon prepared horseradish, and 2 g / ¾ teaspoon freshly ground black pepper and mix to combine. Use this filling to assemble the rolls (step 5), then layer the roast beef evenly it, overlapping the meat as necessary, before rolling up the dough. To really take these up a notch, baste them mid-bake and then when they come out of the oven with Garlic Butter (page 11).

BUFFALO CHICKEN BUNS Eliminate the salmon, capers, dill, and lemon zest in the filling and add 120 g / 1 cup finely minced celery to it. In a medium bowl, toss 226 g / 8 ounces shredded cooked chicken with 28 g / 2 tablespoons unsalted butter, melted, and 60 g / ¼ cup Buffalo-style hot sauce. After spreading the filling over the dough in step 5, arrange the sauced chicken in an even layer on top, then crumble 85 g / 3 ounces blue cheese over it before rolling up the dough. Omit the Everything Seasoning and just egg-wash the surface.

Make Ahead and Storage
The buns are best the same day they are baked. Store any leftover buns in an airtight container and refresh (see page 112) before serving.

Overnight Cinnamon Buns

Replace the filling with the following mixture: In a medium bowl, whisk 106 g / ½ packed cup light or dark brown sugar, 40 g / ⅓ cup all-purpose flour, 50 g / ¼ cup granulated sugar, 9 g / 1 tablespoon ground cinnamon, 2 g / ½ teaspoon fine sea salt, and a few gratings of nutmeg together. Add 140 g / 10 tablespoons unsalted butter, melted, and mix to combine. Crumble/pat this mixture over the surface of the dough in an even layer in step 5 before rolling it up into a spiral. Bake for 45 to 50 minutes and let cool for 15 minutes before serving. If you like, top the buns with a thick glaze (see page 20) made with heavy cream. Serve warm.

Homemade Gournay-Style Cheese

Makes 370 g/about 1¾ cups

Gournay cheeses are soft, spreadable cream cheeses boasting flavors from ingredients like alliums and herbs. This was one of my mom's secret ingredients. She would stir a little into pasta for a boost of creaminess, or spread some on a platter and top with crisp bacon and caramelized onions for an easy dip. I like to use it in baking applications because it's beautifully spreadable—and the flavor is very adaptable; see the suggestions below.

226 g / 8 ounces cream cheese, at room temp
120 g / ½ cup heavy cream
25 g / ¼ cup finely grated Parmesan cheese
2 g / ½ teaspoon garlic powder
Kosher salt and freshly ground black pepper

In the bowl of a stand mixer fitted with the whisk attachment (or in a medium bowl, using a hand mixer or whisk), whip the cream cheese until fluffy, 2 to 3 minutes. Add the cream and whip until well combined. Scrape the bowl well, add the Parmesan and garlic powder, and mix well to incorporate. Season with salt and pepper to taste. Refrigerate, covered tightly, until ready to use or serve (up to 5 days).

Other Flavorings

- Squeeze the cloves from 1 head Roasted Garlic (page 159), mash, and stir into the cheese.
- Stir up to 6 g / 2 teaspoons dried herbs or 9 g / 3 tablespoons chopped fresh herbs (dill, parsley, rosemary, thyme, basil, or chives, or a combination) into the cheese.
- Stir 28 g / ¼ cup finely minced scallions into the cheese.
- Stir in up to 4 g / 2 tablespoons grated citrus zest.
- In a small pan, melt 14 g / 1 tablespoon unsalted butter. Add 3 tablespoons finely minced shallots, spring onions, or sweet onions and cook until tender, about 2 minutes. Let cool before stirring into the cheese.

Pizza Babka

Makes one 9 x 5-inch/23 x 13 cm loaf

DIFFICULTY: **HARD**

To know babka is to deeply, deeply love it. If you don't already know, babka is a cake-like yeasted bread that usually has a spiraled sweet filling inside, like chocolate or cinnamon spread, and a tasty crumb topping. It's ripe for savory riffing, as in this crowd-pleasing pizza inspired combination or any of the variations below. Or try your own creative version—maybe using the Sun-Dried Tomato or Olive Spread on page 96.

DOUGH

390 g / 3¼ cups all-purpose flour

21 g / 3 tablespoons nonfat dry milk

37 g / 3 tablespoons granulated sugar
   (optional; see page 100)

4 g / 1½ teaspoons garlic powder

3 g / 1 teaspoon Italian herb seasoning

5 g / 1½ teaspoons instant dry yeast

5 g / 1¼ teaspoons fine sea salt

77 g / ⅓ cup warm whole milk (about
   110°F/45°C)

170 g / 3 large eggs, at room temperature

113 g / 4 ounces / 8 tablespoons unsalted
   butter, at room temperature, plus more for
   greasing the pan

FILLING AND FINISHING

200 g / ¾ cup Thick Tomato Sauce (page 155)

10 g / 2 cloves garlic, minced

85g / 3 ounces sliced pepperoni

170 g / 6 ounces mozzarella cheese, shredded

56 g / 2 ounces finely grated Parmesan cheese,
   plus more for finishing

Egg wash (see page 7)

28 g / 1 ounce / 2 tablespoons unsalted butter
   (or Garlic Butter, page 11), melted

15 g / 1 tablespoon heavy cream

1. The day before you want to bake the bread, make the dough: In the bowl of a stand mixer fitted with the dough hook, mix the flour, dry milk, sugar, garlic powder, herb seasoning, yeast, and salt and mix on low speed until evenly combined, about 30 seconds. Add the warm milk and eggs and mix until the dough comes together and is fairly smooth, about 3 minutes. Raise the speed to medium and mix for 1 minute.

2. Set a timer for 7 minutes and, with the mixer running, gradually add the butter, 14 g / 1 tablespoon at a time, making sure each addition is fully incorporated before adding the next. Once it's all incorporated, continue to mix for the time remaining; the dough should be smooth, but it may be a bit sticky.

3. Transfer the dough to a greased large bowl and cover the bowl with plastic wrap. Let the dough rise at room temperature until visibly puffy, 45 minutes to 1 hour.

4. Punch down the dough, cover the bowl again, and transfer to the refrigerator to rise for 10 to 12 hours (overnight).

5. Grease a 9 x 5-inch/23 x 13 cm loaf pan with butter. Remove the dough from the refrigerator and transfer to a lightly floured surface. Use your fingertips to flatten the dough slightly, aiming for an approximately square shape.

(CONTINUES)

Creamy
Mushroom and
Goat Cheese
Babka

Pesto
Babka

Pizza
Babka

6. Use a rolling pin to roll out the dough into an 8 x 15-inch/20 x 38 cm rectangle. Spoon about three-quarters (about 150 g) of the tomato sauce over the center of the dough, then spread in an even layer, leaving the outer ½ in/1 cm edge uncovered. Sprinkle the garlic evenly over the sauce. Arrange the pepperoni evenly over the sauce, leaving a little space between the slices. Dollop the remaining sauce over the pepperoni and gently spread it out (this will help the cheese stick a bit better, but there's no need to fuss over it). Sprinkle the mozzarella and Parmesan evenly on top.

7. Starting with one of the longer sides, roll the dough up into a tight spiral and pinch the seam firmly to seal. Use a bench knife or a sharp knife to cut the dough lengthwise in half, exposing the layers of filling inside. Twist the 2 pieces of dough together to make one long twist. Then twist it together once or twice more and transfer to the prepared pan. Cover with greased plastic wrap and let the dough rise until visibly puffy (it may not double in size, but it should look soft and puffed), about 1 hour and 15 minutes to 1 hour and 45 minutes. Toward the end of the rise time, preheat the oven to 350°F/190°C with a rack in the center.

8. Place the loaf pan on a baking sheet and brush egg wash over the doughy portions. Transfer to the oven and bake the loaf for 35 minutes, or until it starts to become lightly brown.

9. In a small bowl, stir the melted butter and cream together. Remove the bread from the oven and baste it all over with the butter mixture. Sprinkle finely grated Parmesan over the top, return the loaf to the oven, and bake for 40 to 45 minutes more; the internal tempera-ture of the thickest part of the bread should be at least 200°F/93°C.

10. Cool the babka for at least 15 minutes before serving, warm or at room temperature.

Note: Wondering why you see sugar as an optional ingredient in this savory dough? See page 100.

Variations

PESTO BABKA **Replace the tomato sauce with 180 g / ¾ cup Pesto (page 96). Omit the pepperoni and mozzarella and increase the Parmesan to 85 g / 3 ounces.**

CREAMY MUSHROOM AND GOAT CHEESE BABKA **Replace the tomato sauce with 260 g / 1 cup Creamy Mushroom Spread (page 96). Omit the pepperoni. Replace the mozzarella with 142 g / 5 ounces goat cheese, crumbled.**

VEGGIE CREAM CHEESE BABKA **Omit the tomato sauce, pepperoni, mozzarella, and Parmesan. For the veggie cream cheese, in a medium bowl, mix together 226 g / 8 ounces cream cheese, at room temperature, 75 g / ½ cup finely minced celery, 70 g / ½ packed cup finely minced carrots, 40 g / 4 scallions, minced, 3 g / 1 teaspoon onion powder, and 2 g / ½ teaspoon garlic powder. In step 5, dollop and spread 235 g / 1 cup of the cream cheese mixture over the dough and roll up the dough as directed. In step 9, sprinkle sesame seeds, poppy seeds, or Everything Seasoning (page 177) over the loaf instead of the Parmesan.**

(CONTINUES)

Make Ahead and Storage
The babka is best the same day it is baked. Store leftovers tightly wrapped at room temperature.

Tomato Sauces

I adore all things tomato, and things tossed in, dunked in, or drowned in tomato sauce are go-to comfort food. These three sauces are the ones I make the most often. One is super-garlicky, one is spicy and creamy, and one is quite thick, making it suitable for a variety of baking applications. If I have one, I toss a Parmesan rind in with the crushed tomatoes to simmer with the sauce. These recipes will make more sauce than you'll need for many of the baking recipes in this book that call for them, but they all keep well in an airtight container in the refrigerator for up to 5 days or in the freezer for up to 2 months. If you'd like an ultrasmooth sauce, puree the finished sauce with an immersion blender or in the food processor. **All of these sauces yield 1 L / 4 cups.**

Roasted Garlic Tomato Sauce

In a large pot, heat 30 g / 2 tablespoons extra virgin olive oil over medium heat. Add 325 g / 1 large sweet onion, minced, and cook for 4 to 5 minutes, until the onions begin to soften. Add 10 g / 2 cloves garlic, minced, and cook for 1 minute. Add one 795 g / 28-ounce can crushed tomatoes, then squeeze in the cloves from 1 head Roasted Garlic (page 159) and bring to a simmer. Stir in 3 g / 1 teaspoon dried oregano and simmer for 20 to 25 minutes. Season with kosher salt and freshly ground black pepper.

Spicy Creamy Tomato Sauce

In a large pot, melt 43 g / 1½ ounces / 3 tablespoons unsalted butter over medium heat. Add 325 g / 1 large sweet onion, minced, and cook for 4 to 5 minutes. Add 15 g / 3 cloves garlic, minced, and 10 g / 2 teaspoons crushed Calabrian chile (see Resources), or more to taste, and cook for 1 minute. Add one 795 g / 28-ounce can crushed tomatoes and bring to a simmer. Stir in 3 g / 1 teaspoon dried oregano, and simmer for 20 to 25 minutes. Stir in 60 g / ¼ cup heavy cream and cook, stirring frequently, for 2 minutes. Season with kosher salt and freshly ground black pepper.

Thick Tomato Sauce

In a large pot, heat 30 g / 2 tablespoons extra virgin olive oil over medium heat. Add 325 g / 1 large sweet onion, minced, and cook for 4 to 5 minutes. Add 15 g / 3 cloves garlic, minced, and cook for 1 minute. Stir in one 170 g / 6-ounce can tomato paste and cook, stirring constantly, for 1 minute. Add one 795 g / 28-ounce can crushed tomatoes and bring to a simmer. Stir in 3 g / 1 teaspoon dried oregano and simmer, stirring frequently, until thickened, 30 to 35 minutes. Season with kosher salt and freshly ground black pepper.

Ultimate Garlic Bread

Makes one 16-inch-/41 cm long loaf
DIFFICULTY: **MEDIUM**

I come from a garlic-loving family. My parents grow their own, and they can grow enough to keep themselves in fragrant cloves for the year in a single season. That deep, garlic-loving nature is so deep in my bones, I set out to create the ultimate garlic bread—and I don't take the "U" word lightly! So I put roasted garlic in the dough itself and then use the loaf to make garlic bread. The bread is also crazy delicious on its own or made into bread bowls (see page 124). You can also turn any favorite plain loaf into garlic bread.

DOUGH

1 large or 2 small heads Roasted Garlic (page 159)

60 g / ¼ cup extra virgin olive oil

540 g / 4½ cups all-purpose flour

3 g / 1 teaspoon garlic powder

5 g / 1¼ teaspoons fine sea salt

2 g / ¾ teaspoon freshly ground black pepper

4 g / 1½ teaspoons instant dry yeast

345 g / 1½ cups warm water (about 110°F/45°C)

GARLIC BREAD

56 g / 2 ounces / 4 tablespoons unsalted butter

20 g / 4 large cloves garlic, grated

2 g / ½ teaspoon fine sea salt

30 g / 2 tablespoons extra virgin olive oil

1 large clove garlic, smashed and peeled (optional)

Flaky salt and freshly ground black pepper

50 g / ½ packed cup freshly grated Parmesan cheese (optional)

1. Make the dough: Squeeze the garlic cloves into a small bowl and use a fork to mash them into a paste. Add the olive oil and mash the garlic into the oil, then whisk until the mixture is fairly well combined.

2. In a large bowl, whisk the flour, garlic powder, salt, and pepper, along with the garlic/olive oil mixture. Add the yeast, and stir to combine, then add the water. Use a spatula to mix the dough until it is fairly well combined and comes together, about 4 minutes. Scrape the sides and bottom of the bowl well and mix again.

3. Cover the bowl with greased plastic wrap and let the dough rise at room temperature for 2 to 3 hours, until visibly bubbly on the surface. (If your ambient room temperature is higher than 75°F/25°C, let the dough rise at room temperature for 30 minutes, or until bubbly, then refrigerate for the remaining rise time to allow the dough to gain more flavor from a slower rise.)

4. Turn the dough out onto a lightly floured surface. Gently fold the edges of dough over onto it a few times to make a roughly round shape. Turn the dough over, cover with a clean towel, and let rest for 10 minutes.

5. Line a baking sheet with parchment paper. Gently press the dough all over with your fingertips to flatten it, adding flour as needed to the work surface to prevent sticking. Starting with the part of the dough farthest away from you, start to fold the dough over onto itself, using your fingertips to press it down

(CONTINUES)

156

firmly as you go. Repeat this process 2 or 3 more times—as you work, the piece of dough will become longer. When there's about 1 to 2 inches/2.5 to 5 cm of dough left unfolded, switch from your fingertips to the heel of your hand to secure the dough as you fold it over, finally forming a rough log shape.

6. Starting in the center of the log, roll it under your fingers and upper portions of your palms into a loaf about 16 inches/41 cm long (do not taper the ends).

7. Gently transfer the loaf to the prepared baking sheet, placing it on a diagonal from one corner to the opposite corner. Loosely cover the loaf with a clean dish towel and let rise until noticeably puffy, about 45 minutes to 1 hour 30 minutes (it will not double in size).

8. Meanwhile, toward the end of the rise time, preheat the oven to 450°F/230°C with racks in the upper and lower thirds; if you have a baking steel or pizza stone, place it on the upper rack. Place a baking dish, cake pan, or oven-proof skillet on the lower rack. Bring a kettle (or a medium pot) of water to a boil.

9. Use a lame (or other tool—see Scoring, page 109) to score the top of the loaf. Transfer the loaf to the upper oven rack. Fill the baking dish (or pan or skillet) about one-third full with boiling water. Bake the loaf until deeply golden, 40 to 45 minutes—it should have an internal temperature in the center of at least 200°F/93°C. If desired, slide the loaf directly onto the baking steel or pizza stone for the last 5 minutes of baking.

10. Remove the loaf from the oven and let cool for at least 20 minutes. Reduce the oven temperature to 375°F/190°C and remove the baking dish of water. (You can also cool the loaf completely and make the garlic bread the next day, if desired.)

11. While the loaf cools, make the garlic butter: In a small saucepan, melt the butter over medium heat. Meanwhile, on a cutting board, use the side of a heavy knife to mash the minced garlic with the salt to form a paste. Transfer to a small bowl, add the oil, and use a fork to mash the paste into the oil.

12. Add the garlic oil to the butter and cook, stirring constantly, until fragrant, about 30 seconds. Remove the pan from the heat, cover, and set aside.

13. When the bread has cooled slightly, use a serrated knife to cut the loaf horizontally almost in half, leaving one of the longer sides attached, and open it up like a book. Place a large piece of aluminum foil on the baking sheet you baked the bread on and place the bread cut side up on the foil. If desired, rub the smashed garlic clove over the cut sides of the bread. Use a pastry brush to slather the butter-garlic mixture over both cut sides of the bread. Sprinkle with flaky salt and pepper. If using the Parmesan cheese, sprinkle it over the bottom half of the bread. Close the loaf back up, pressing it firmly together, and wrap it tightly in foil.

14. Bake the bread for 17 to 20 minutes, until it is very fragrant, toasty, and heated through Remove from the oven and unwrap the bread, and when it's cool enough to handle, slice and serve warm.

Make Ahead and Storage
The loaf is best eaten within 24 hours of baking, but you can store it overnight before turning it into garlic bread. The garlic bread should be served as soon as it is made.

Garlic

I am garlic's number-one fan—and when you love something this much, you find lots of ways to maximize all that garlicky goodness. Here are a few of the ways that I use garlic to boost the flavor of my bakes.

Roasted Garlic

You can do this with as many heads as you want. Cut off the top of the head to expose the cloves and discard. Cut a piece of aluminum foil large enough to encase the head(s) and place the garlic in the center, cut side up. Drizzle a generous glug of olive oil over the head(s) and roast in a 400°F/205°C oven until the cloves are tender and caramelized, 35 to 45 minutes. To use, let cool until easy to handle, and squeeze the roasted garlic out of the skins.

Crispy Fried Garlic (and Garlic-Infused Oil)

Separate 1 head of garlic into cloves, peel them, and cut into thin even slices. Heat a small skillet over medium heat and add enough extra virgin olive oil to cover the base of the pan. Add the garlic slices, spread in an even layer, and cook, stirring and flipping the garlic occasionally, until evenly golden brown, 2 to 3 minutes. Remove from the pan using a slotted spoon and drain on paper towels. The fried garlic can be stored in an airtight container for up to 5 days; the garlic-infused oil can be refrigerated for up to 3 weeks.

Fried Garlic Powder

I learned about this secret ingredient from Mandy Lee, author of the wonderful blog *Lady and Pups*. Drain and cool fried garlic slices (above), then grind them in a mortar and pestle to a coarse powder. Store refrigerated for up to 1 month. I sprinkle this over pretty much everything.

159

Seeded Burger (or Hot Dog) Buns

Makes 12 round or 15 long buns

DIFFICULTY: **MEDIUM**

This reliable recipe has seen me through many a summer cookout, and more than a few beach barbecues. The easy, lightly enriched dough made with mashed potatoes makes for soft, beautifully golden buns that are firm enough to stand up to a hefty portion of fillings and toppings. They can be shaped as round burger buns or oblong hot dog buns. I sprinkle these with seeds for an extra crunchy, toasty exterior, but you can leave them plain, if you prefer.

540 g / 4½ cups bread flour

66 g / ⅓ cup granulated sugar

7 g / 2¼ teaspoons fine sea salt

9 g / 1 tablespoon instant dry yeast

226 g / 1 cup warm water (about 110°F/45°C)

162 g / ¾ cup prepared mashed potatoes (leftovers are fine)

85 g / 3 ounces / 6 tablespoons unsalted butter, at room temperature

113 g / 2 large eggs, at room temperature

42 g / 2 tablespoons honey

Egg wash (see page 7) for finishing

Sesame, poppy, caraway, or nigella seeds or Everything Seasoning (page 177) for finishing

56 g / 2 ounces / 4 tablespoons unsalted butter (or basting butter, see page 11), melted (optional)

1. In the bowl of a stand mixer fitted with the dough hook, mix the flour, sugar, salt, and yeast together on low speed. Add the water, mashed potatoes, butter, eggs, and honey and mix for about 2 minutes, until the dough starts to come together. Raise the speed to medium and mix for 3 minutes more.

2. Transfer the dough to a greased large bowl, cover tightly with plastic wrap, and let rise until doubled in size, 1½ to 2 hours.

3. Shape the rolls: Line two baking sheets with parchment paper. Turn the dough out onto a lightly floured work surface.

   TO SHAPE HAMBURGER BUNS: Divide the dough into 12 equal pieces (about 100 g each). Working with one piece of dough at a time, press the dough a few times with your fingertips to flatten it slightly, then fold it over onto itself several times, without elongating it. Shape the dough into round rolls (see page 104) and transfer to the prepared baking sheets, leaving 2 inches/5 cm between them.

   TO MAKE HOT DOG BUNS: Divide the dough into 15 equal pieces (about 80 g each). Working with one piece of dough at a time, press the dough a few times with your fingertips to flatten it slightly, then fold it over onto itself several times to create a log shape. Roll the dough into an oblong roll (see page 104) and slightly taper the ends. Use a bench knife or the back of a paring knife to press a line firmly down the center of each roll, pressing three-quarters of the way into the dough (this will make it easier to split them after baking). Transfer the buns to the prepared baking sheets, leaving about 2 inches/5 cm between them.

4. Cover the buns with greased plastic wrap and let rise until visibly puffy, 1 hour and 15 minute to 1 hour and 45 minutes. Toward the end of the rise time, preheat the oven to 350°F/175°C with the racks in the upper and lower thirds.

5. Egg-wash the buns and sprinkle generously with seeds (or everything topping).

6. Transfer to the oven and bake for 12 to 15 minutes, until the buns start to turn golden brown. If using the melted butter, remove the pans from the oven, brush with the melted butter, and return to the oven, switching the positions of the pans and rotating them; or just rotate the pans, if skipping the butter. Bake for 14 to 18 minutes more, until the buns are deeply golden brown; the buns should have an internal temperature of at least 200°F/93°C. Cool completely before halving the burger buns with a serrated knife, or cutting a slit down the center of each hot dog bun, to serve.

Make Ahead and Storage
The buns are best within 2 days of baking. Store leftovers in an airtight container at room temperature, or wrap tightly and freeze for up to 2 months. Thaw and refresh (see page 112) before serving.

Pickly Pepper Bialys

Makes 12 bialys

DIFFICULTY: **MEDIUM**

I had my first bialy on a sidewalk outside Penn Station, and I was hooked. A bialy has an enviable chew, like its cousin the bagel. But unlike bagels, bialys are not boiled before baking, so they have a crustier exterior. Perhaps most important, they contain a flavorful filling. One of the most common versions features caramelized onions—feel free to make a batch (see page 26) and sub them for the peppers here. Cheese isn't a traditional bialy topping, but it adds a salty punch and a bit of golden-brown crispness; your choice.

SPONGE (PREFERMENT)

200 g / 1⅔ cups bread flour

< 1 g / ¼ teaspoon instant dry yeast

226 g / 1 cup room-temperature water (about 75°F/25°C)

DOUGH

540 g / 4½ cups bread flour

2 g / ½ teaspoon instant dry yeast

6 g / 1½ teaspoons fine sea salt

200 g / ¾ cup plus 2 tablespoons warm water (about 110°F/45°C)

Sponge (above)

FILLING AND FINISHING

390 g / 1½ cups Pickly Peppers (page 97)

100 g / 1 packed cup shredded white cheddar cheese (optional)

1. Make the sponge: In a medium bowl, stir the flour and yeast to combine. Make a well in the center of the flour, add the water, and mix with a spatula until thoroughly combined.

2. Cover the bowl with plastic wrap and let sit at room temperature for about 1 hour. There should be lots of small bubbles on the surface when it's ready.

3. Make the dough: In the bowl of a stand mixer fitted with the dough hook, combine the flour, yeast, and salt and mix together on low speed. Add the water and sponge and mix for 2 minutes. Scrape the bowl well, raise the speed to medium, and mix for 7 minutes—the dough should be very smooth.

4. Transfer the dough to a greased large bowl, cover with plastic wrap, and let rise until nearly doubled in size, 1 to 1½ hours.

5. Turn the dough out onto a lightly floured surface and divide it into 12 equal pieces (about 90 g each). Round each piece into a roll (see page 104), place the rolls on a lightly floured surface, cover with plastic wrap, and let rest for 15 minutes.

6. Line two baking sheets with parchment paper. Working with one piece of dough at a time, gently stretch each piece into an oval shape and place on one of the prepared baking sheets (6 per sheet). Use your fingers to gently press the dough, starting in the center and working outward, to elongate the oval slightly and make a cavity in the center for the filling. The edges of the dough should be thicker, kind of like pizza.

7. Cover the bialys with greased plastic wrap and let rise for 30 minutes. Toward the end of the rise time, preheat the oven to 475°F/245°C with the racks in the upper and lower thirds.

8. Remove the plastic wrap from the baking sheets and spoon about 30 g / 2 scant table-spoons peppers into the center of each bialy. If using, top each with about 12 g / 2 tablespoons cheese.

9. Transfer to the oven and bake until the bialys are golden around the base and edges, 16 to 20 minutes. Cool for at least 15 minutes before serving.

Make Ahead and Storage
The bialys are best the day they are made, but leftovers can be stored in an airtight container for 1 to 2 days. Toast to refresh them.

Bagels

Makes 10 bagels

DIFFICULTY: **MEDIUM**

When I was a pastry student, the bakery on campus made bagels, but only on certain days of the week. A few friends and I had a standing breakfast date each week we called "Bagel Day." Those mornings are one of the things I miss most from my college days, and some kind of breakfast—preferably fresh baked bagels—is usually on the docket whenever those friends and I get together nowadays. Even if you aren't baking for a crowd, making homemade bagels is a pleasure—enjoy some fresh, then freeze the rest to toast in the days that follow.

SPONGE (PREFERMENT)

< 1 g / ¼ **teaspoon instant dry yeast**

226 g / 1 **cup room-temperature water (about 75°F/25°C)**

200 g / 1⅔ **cups bread flour**

DOUGH

540 g / 4½ **cups bread flour**

2 g / ½ **teaspoon instant dry yeast**

7 g / 1¾ **teaspoon fine sea salt**

200 g / ¾ **cup plus 2 tablespoons warm water (about 110°F/45°C)**

Sponge (above)

FINISHING

2.26 kg / 10 **cups water**

30 g / 2 **tablespoons barley malt syrup (see Resources)**

3 g / ½ **teaspoon baking soda**

Sesame or poppy seeds, Everything Seasoning (page 177), or flaky salt

1. Make the sponge: In a medium bowl, stir the yeast and water to combine. Add the flour and mix with a spatula or wooden spoon until well combined.

2. Cover the bowl with plastic wrap and let sit at room temperature for 1 hour. There should be lots of small bubbles on the surface when the sponge is ready.

3. Make the dough: In the bowl of a stand mixer fitted with the dough hook, combine the flour, yeast, and salt and mix together on low speed. Add the water and sponge and mix for 2 minutes. Scrape the bowl well, raise the speed to medium, and mix for 7 minutes—the dough should be very smooth.

4. Transfer the dough to a greased large bowl, cover with plastic wrap, and let rise until nearly doubled in size, 1 to 1½ hours.

5. Turn the dough out onto a lightly floured surface and divide into 10 equal pieces (about 115 g each). Round each piece into a roll (see page 104). Place the rolls on a lightly floured surface and cover with plastic wrap. Let rest for 15 minutes.

6. Line two baking sheets with parchment paper. Working with one piece of dough at a time, use your fingers to stipple the dough to flatten it slightly. Starting with the part of the dough farthest away from you, start to fold the dough over onto itself, using your fingertips to press it down firmly as you go. Repeat this process 2 or 3 more times—as you work, the piece of dough will become longer. When there's 1 to

(CONTINUES)

2 inches/2.5 to 5 cm of dough left unfolded, switch from your fingertips to the heel of your hand to secure the dough as you fold it over, forming a rough log shape. Starting with very light pressure at the center of the log, roll the dough under your hands to elongate the log to about 12 inches/30 cm long.

7. Have a small bowl of cool water ready. Use your fingers to lightly moisten one end of one of the dough logs, then place the other end on it, overlapping it slightly, to create a circle of dough. Insert your fingers in the hole in the center and roll the dough under your hands to seal the seam and even out the dough. Transfer the shaped bagel to one of the parchment-lined baking sheets and keep covered with a clean kitchen towel while you shape the remaining bagels.

8. Let the bagels rise at room temperature for 30 minutes. Toward the end of the rise time, preheat the oven to 425°F/205°C with the racks in the upper and lower thirds.

9. In a medium pot, bring the water to a simmer over medium heat. Add the malt syrup and baking soda and stir to combine. Keep the mixture at a simmer while you cook the bagels. Gently drop the bagels into the water a few at a time and cook, flipping them once with a slotted spoon, for about 20 to 30 seconds per side. Then use the spoon to transfer the bagels to a wire rack to drain.

10. You can sprinkle the topping over the boiled bagels, or you can put the topping on a plate and use the slotted spoon to transfer the bagels to the plate to coat them with the topping. Return the bagels to the parchment-lined baking sheets, staggering them to allow plenty of room between them.

11. Transfer the baking sheets to the oven and bake until the bagels are deeply golden brown, 20 to 25 minutes. Cool for at least 10 minutes before serving.

Variations

MINI BAGELS *Makes 20 minis* In step 5, divide the dough into 20 pieces (about 60 g each). Instead of rolling them into strands, round into rolls (see page 104). Use your thumb to poke a hole in the center of each one, then gently stretch the dough to form the bagel shape. After boiling them, arrange 10 minis on each baking sheet and bake for 12 to 15 minutes.

PIZZA BAGELS Cut 10 Mini Bagels horizontally in half and place cut side up on a parchment-lined baking sheet. Brush the cut sides of the bagels lightly with olive oil, letting it seep into the bagels. Spoon 5 g / 1 teaspoon Thick Tomato Sauce (page 155) onto each bagel and spread evenly with the back of the measuring spoon. Sprinkle some finely diced pepperoni on top of the tomato sauce, then sprinkle some finely diced low-moisture mozzarella on top. Bake at 400°F/205°C until the cheese is melted and the bagels are toasted, 10 to 12 minutes.

Make Ahead and Storage
The bagels are best the same day they are baked, but leftovers can be stored in an airtight container at room temperature; they can be refreshed by toasting. The bagels also freeze well, in airtight containers, for up to 2 months.

How to Shape Bagels

BAGELS

Form a long strand with one piece of dough and bring the ends together, overlapping the ends, to form a circle.

Insert your fingers in the hole in the center and rub the seam against the work surface to seal it.

MINI BAGELS

Form the dough into rounds, then poke a hole in the center of each one with your thumb.

Stretch this opening to form the bagel.

Flakiest Cheese Biscuits

Makes 12 biscuits
DIFFICULTY: **MEDIUM**

These were inspired by Hungarian pogácsa—a yeast-raised dough that goes through a quick lamination to create light, flaky layers. The tenderness is similar to that of an American-style buttermilk biscuit, with a lovely crisp exterior and a beautiful lightly yeasty, very cheesy flavor.

600 g / 5 cups all-purpose flour

9 g / 1 tablespoon instant dry yeast

12 g / 1 tablespoon granulated sugar (optional)

3 g / ¾ teaspoon fine sea salt

282 g / 10 ounces unsalted butter
(56 g / 2 ounces / 4 tablespoons cold butter, cut into ½-inch/1 cm cubes, and 226 g / 8 ounces butter at room temperature)

454 g / 2 cups sour cream, plus more as needed

200 g / 2 packed cups shredded cheese (such as cheddar, Gruyère, or Gouda)

Egg wash (see page 7) for finishing

1. In a large bowl, whisk the flour, yeast, sugar (if using), and salt to combine. Add 56 g / 2 ounces / 4 tablespoons of the cold butter and use your hands to break up the cubes, tossing until well coated with flour. Use your hands or a pastry cutter to cut the butter into the flour until it's fully incorporated and the mixture looks like coarse meal. Make a well in the center of the flour and add the sour cream. Mix with your hands or a spatula until the dough comes together; it will look craggy, not smooth. If the dough appears dry, add cool water 15 g / 1 tablespoon at a time until it comes together.

2. Turn the dough out, wrap in plastic wrap, and refrigerate for at least 30 minutes (and up to overnight).

3. On a lightly floured surface, roll out the dough to a rectangle about 10 x 12 inches/25 x 30 cm and ½ inch/1 cm thick. Brush away excess flour with a pastry brush. Dot the remaining 226 g / 8 ounces butter over the surface of the dough and gently spread in an even layer. Fold the dough in quarters.

4. Wrap the dough in plastic wrap and refrigerate for 30 minutes.

5. On a lightly floured surface, roll out the dough again to a rectangle about 10 x 12 inches/25 x 30 cm and ½ inch/1 cm thick. Sprinkle about one-third of the cheese over it and fold the dough into quarters. Wrap and refrigerate for 30 minutes to relax the dough.

6. Repeat this process twice more, using the remaining cheese. Refrigerate the dough for at least 1 hour (and up to overnight).

7. When ready to bake the biscuits, preheat the oven to 375°F/190°C with a rack in the center. Line a baking sheet with parchment paper.

8. On a lightly floured surface, roll out the dough to a rectangle about 9 x 10 inches/23 to 25 cm and ¾ inch/2 cm thick. Use a 3-inch /8 cm round cutter to cut out biscuits and transfer them to the prepared baking sheet, leaving at least 2 inches/5 cm between them and staggering the rows. The dough scraps can be pressed together and rerolled 1 or 2 more times to make more biscuits.

9. Egg-wash the biscuits and bake until deeply golden brown, 30 to 34 minutes. Cool for at least 10 minutes before serving warm, or cool completely and serve at room temperature.

Make Ahead and Storage
These biscuits are best within the first 24 hours after baking.
Store leftovers in an airtight container at room temperature.
To rewarm, use the oven method described in Rewarming
Pastries (page 365).

CHAPTER 4

Flatbreads, Pizzas, and Stuffed Breads

TOPPED • FILLED • STUFFED

When you love good bread, you have an appreciation for the fresh stuff. One of my favorite parts of being a bread baker was my incredible haul—sometimes still steaming when I pulled it from my bag back at home. At the end of my bread-baking gig, I began living alone for the first time—no roomies or significant others. The entire refrigerator real estate was *all mine*. But I was often baking only for myself. Enter flatbreads, some of which became staples in my menu rotation.

If you too love fresh bread but also appreciate ease, you may return to the recipes in this chapter the same way I found myself making them over and over again when I first lived on my own. You can make the dough ahead of time, letting it rise slowly in the fridge, sometimes even for days before it needs to be used (and the flavor of the baked goods will only get better!). This flexibility also means you can use just what you need and save the rest of the dough for later—meaning fresh bread goodness every time, instead of toasted leftovers. By adding toppings, like the sliced tomatoes or onions on the Weeknight Focaccia (page 192), or fillings, like that for the herby, cheesy klobásník (page 203), I turned some of these favorite doughs into snacks, or even full meals. And now that I'm regularly cooking for a crowd, I can attest that these recipes are even more loved.

Shaping Flatbreads

One of the best things about flatbreads is how simple they are to shape. Keeping a few general guidelines in mind can make the process even simpler. Some flatbreads are relatively thick, with a chewier crumb (like the naan on page 185), others are much thinner and flatter (like tortillas), and still others are somewhere in between (like pita bread). Since it's common to work in batches with flatbreads, be sure to keep any pieces you aren't working with covered so they don't dry out.

ROLLING

Rolling out both thicker and thinner doughs rather than shaping them by hand helps to ensure a more even thickness so that the flatbread will cook evenly. A good example is pita bread: starting with an even thickness before baking gives it the best chance of puffing up just right in the oven and creating the pocket. Roll doughs on a lightly floured surface, using only as much flour as is needed.

PRESSING

Some thinner doughs, like the Corn Tortillas on page 209, are pressed to ensure an even thickness. Place the dough between two pieces of parchment or wax paper to prevent sticking and make it easier to handle after pressing. You can use a special press (often made of a heavy material like cast iron) or the bottom of a heavy skillet to apply pressure to the dough.

HAND-SHAPING

Hand-shaping can be used for lots of different styles of flatbreads and stuffed breads. And while many flatbread recipes celebrate a rustic shape, it's important to maintain a fairly even thickness so the bread will cook evenly. Some stickier doughs require that you use floured hands and/or a floured work surface—I also sometimes use wet or oiled hands to hand-shape dough.

SHAPING A ROUND: Form the dough into a round (see page 104). Cover and let rest for 10 to 15 minutes (or as the recipe directs). Then use your fingertips to press out the dough to flatten it to an approximately even thickness that is slightly thicker than the final thickness you want, aiming to maintain a round shape. Finally, gently stretch the dough with your hands to the desired thickness or continue to press it with your fingers to flatten it further, rotating the dough a few times as you work to help you maintain the even thickness.

SHAPING AN OBLONG: Form the dough into a round (see page 104). Cover and let rest for 10 to 15 minutes (or as the recipe directs). Then use your fingertips to press out the dough to flatten it to a roughly oblong shape that is slightly thicker than the final thickness you want. Finally, gently stretch the dough with your hands to the desired thickness and size, pulling it gently to encourage it into an oblong shape.

SHAPING A SQUARE OR RECTANGLE: Form the dough into a rough square. Cover and let rest for 10 to 15 minutes (or as the recipe directs). Then use your fingertips to flatten the dough into a roughly square or rectangular shape that is slightly thicker than the final thickness; use a bench knife and your hands to help keep the edges squared off. Gently pull the edges of the dough if necessary into straighter sides. Use a rolling pin to roll the dough to an even thickness of the desired dimensions, using the bench knife to keep the edges squared.

SHAPING A ROUND

SHAPING AN OBLONG

  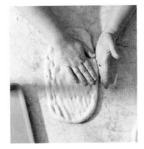 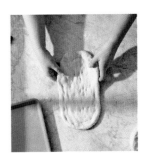

SHAPING A RECTANGLE

  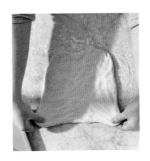 

PREP SCHOOL

Cooking Techniques for Flatbreads, Stuffed Breads, and Pizzas

Flatbreads are cooked in a variety of ways, not just baked. Grilling, griddling, frying, or steaming can produce a variety of delicious filled breads and flatbreads.

Some general tips to keep in mind: Shorter cooking times leave breads softer, while longer cooking times can make them crisp and toasty. Higher cooking temperatures will yield more deeply browned items, while lower cooking temperatures will leave them blonder.

BAKING: Stuffed breads like the Spicy Cheese Brat Klobásník (page 203) and flatbreads can be baked on baking sheets or other ovenproof pans. Sometimes a baking steel (see Resources) or pizza stone is used to help maintain higher oven temperatures and promote crisp bottom crusts and even baking. The baking pan can be placed on it, or the item can be baked directly on it.

GRILLING: A grill offers a beautiful high-heat environment for breads and flatbreads, and it can add a beautiful char and/or markings to the bread. For more on grilling bread techniques, see page 176.

HIGH-HEAT (PIZZA/BREAD) OVENS: High-heat ovens, such as wood-fired or gas pizza ovens, are ideal here because they can fairly easily simulate many of the cooking environments that are typically used for certain flatbreads, including clay ovens, tandoors, and more. I use a portable propane-powered oven (see Resources) for everything from calzones to naan to pita.

GRIDDLING/HOT PAN: One of the simplest ways to cook flatbreads and some stuffed breads is to griddle it or cook it in a hot pan, such as a cast-iron skillet or a comal, commonly used for tortillas and other masa recipes. Be sure to preheat the pan and get it plenty hot before adding the dough to it. Only grease the pan if the recipe specifies—very often the dough is added straight to the ungreased griddle or pan.

DEEP-FRYING: Flatbreads and stuffed breads are usually deep-fried in at least 2 inches / 5 cm of neutral oil. I generally heat my oil to around 350°F/175°C before adding the dough, in batches to avoid crowding. Monitor the oil temperature with a thermometer, adjusting the heat as necessary to maintain the desired temperature for even cooking and browning.

STEAMING: My first steamed bread was a revelation—so soft, so fluffy, so utterly craveable. You can use any kind of steamer pot (such as those with metal steamer inserts), but I prefer a bamboo steamer set over a pot or wok that holds it snugly. Fill the pot with 1 to 2 inches/2.5 to 5 cm of water (it should not touch the steamer racks or inserts). Bring to a boil, then carefully place the steamer on top to cook the bread.

How to Re-Create a Professional Bakery Oven

When I worked as a bread baker, we used huge deck-style ovens. We baked the loaves directly on the oven decks, using huge manual loaders to fill them and peels to get them out of the oven. A peel is a large wooden paddle with a handle. Often the end of the paddle is beveled for a thinner edge, making it easy to slide it under breads.

At home, I re-create a deck oven by using a baking steel or pizza stone, which helps achieve similarly crisp crusts on everything from pizzas to flatbreads to big, beautiful loaves. If you don't have a peel, line the back of a baking sheet with parchment paper. Place your shaped dough on the paper and use the upturned baking sheet to help you slide the parchment onto the baking steel or pizza stone.

Filling and Sealing Stuffed Breads and Pastries

Properly filling and sealing stuffed breads and pastries is really the hardest part of the process. If you've been burned by over- or under-stuffed baked goods or exploding fillings, read on!

THE SWEET SPOT—FILLING JUST RIGHT

I call this a sweet spot for a reason. Too little filling produces skimpy, overly doughy baked goods, but using too much can prevent the filling from remaining inside the dough as it bakes and distort the shape of the baked item. Take a little extra care when forming the first one, noticing just how much filling you're using and how easy or difficult it is to seal and finish the bread or pastry. If you have problems with the first one, try using a little less filling for the rest of them.

SEALING WITH EGG WASH OR WATER

Not all recipes call for it, but a brushing of egg wash (see page 7) or water can encourage a beautiful seal on stuffed breads and pastries. For stuffed breads, I most often just use water, applying a bit with my finger as needed. However, an egg wash is even more effective—it will also promote browning and add a little shine anywhere it's visible on the exterior of the dough.

ENCASE THE FILLING TIGHTLY TO PREVENT AIR POCKETS

When encasing a filling, it's important to wrap the dough tightly against it to prevent air pockets. Air pockets will not only leave a gap in the center of the stuffed baked good, they also weaken the structure, meaning the item could collapse or be more prone to springing a leak.

DON'T USE TOO MUCH FLOUR

While flour will prevent the dough from sticking to your work surface/tools/hands, too much flour will prevent the dough from sticking to itself and making a nice seal. Brush away excess flour from both sides of the dough before adding the filling and sealing the dough.

CRIMPS

While it is not necessary for all stuffed doughs, crimping the dough is not merely decorative. Pressing the edges of the dough together with your fingertips or the tines of a fork, or other tool, helps them adhere more fully and can be another important step in preventing the filling from leaking out in the oven.

Why I Love the Grill for Bread

One of my earliest bakery jobs was in a bake-shop where we had access to incredible ovens, perfect for baking beautiful loaves. While I am happy with my home oven, it lacks pretty much all of the features those professional ones had, including the ability to produce some seriously high heat. The grill, on the other hand, is all about high heat, which makes it one of the best oven substitutes for getting gorgeously crisp crusts at home. Here's some general tips to get you ready for grill-baking:

- Always preheat the grill. Light it, put the lid on, and allow it to heat up to as high as it goes.
- Use a grill brush or a crumpled-up ball of aluminum foil to clean the grill grates well once the grill is hot. Then close the lid and let heat for at least 5 minutes longer.
- Oil the grates just before using by dipping a paper towel into oil and using tongs to apply the oil to the grates.
- Once you add your item to be grill-baked, monitor the temperature to keep it close to the temperature called for in your recipe. If you want to try a recipe not formulated for the grill, or you're unsure about the temperature, aim for between 400 and 500°F/205 and 260°C. For large loaves, take the internal temperature to be sure your bread is baked all the way through

Here are three ways I use the grill for breads:

Right on the Grates

My love affair with the grill started with stretching some leftover pizza dough, slathering it with olive oil, and placing it right onto the hot grates. The grill produced an incredibly soft, pillowy flatbread with a hint of smokiness and some lovely char. You can cook a lot of different breads directly on the grates, but I frequently use this technique for pizza and flatbreads.

On a Baking Steel or Pizza Stone

A baking steel or pizza stone provides a wonderful surface for baking loaves or flatbreads on the grill, helping to maintain a consistent heat and promoting a crispy crust. All of these are made to withstand high heat, like the temperature your grill can reach.

In a Dutch Oven or Cast-Iron Skillet

You can use these heavy-bottomed pots or pans on the grill in the same way you use them to promote crisp crusts in the oven. Be sure your pot sits comfortably and level on your grill grates before using this method.

Seasonings

I enjoy mixing up my own seasoning blends when I'm making a particular recipe, but there are some of these I like so much that I keep jars of them in my spice cabinet. Feel free to double or triple these recipes, if you'd like to do the same. Store in jars or other airtight containers.

Everything Seasoning

Mix 15 g / 2 tablespoons white sesame seeds, 15 g / 2 tablespoons black sesame seeds, 12 g / 2 tablespoons poppy seeds, 20 g / 2 tablespoons dried garlic flakes, 20 g / 2 tablespoons dried minced onion, and 10 g / 2 teaspoons kosher salt to combine.

Nigella Everything Seasoning

Replace the black sesame seeds in the Everything Seasoning with 12 g / 2 tablespoons nigella seeds.

Italian Herb Seasoning

Mix 18 g / 2 tablespoons dried oregano, 9 g / 1 tablespoon dried thyme, 19 g / 1 tablespoon dried rosemary, 6 g / 2 teaspoons dried marjoram, and 6 g / 2 teaspoons dried sage to combine.

Smoky Spice

Mix 14 g / 1½ tablespoons smoked paprika, 9 g / 1 tablespoon sweet paprika, 6 g / 2 teaspoons chipotle chile powder, 6 g / 2 teaspoons ground cumin, 6 g / 2 teaspoons freshly ground black pepper, and 6 g / 2 teaspoons onion powder to combine.

Cumin Salt and Pepper

In a small skillet, toast 9 g / 1 tablespoon cumin seeds until fragrant, 30 seconds to 1 minute. Use a mortar and pestle or spice grinder to grind the seeds, then rub into 45 g / 3 tablespoons kosher salt with your hands. Stir in 6 g / 2 teaspoons freshly ground black pepper.

Flavored Salt

You can use the technique for Cumin Salt to add other freshly ground whole spices to salt. Or rub ingredients that don't require toasting, like grated citrus zest, ground spices, or dried lavender, into the salt.

Lahmacun with Chiles

Makes 6 lahmacun

DIFFICULTY: **MEDIUM**

After college, I traveled to Eastern Europe with a boyfriend. On a particularly harried day of travel, we missed our transport and suffered a mid-sidewalk suitcase explosion, and I was bordering on a meltdown. He thought I was hangry, so he ran down the street to a food cart and brought me back a folded paper plate that held a beautifully crisp, charred flat dough with a thin layer of meat on top. He squeezed a lemon half over it and handed the plate to me. I hated to admit he was right, but my problems were soon forgotten, and I was enthusiastically chatting with the food cart operator as he generously showed me how to stretch and roll the dough. My relationship with that boyfriend fizzled after that trip, but lahmacun has been a part of my dinner rotation ever since.

DOUGH

240 g / 2 cups bread flour

5 g / 1 teaspoon sugar

4 g / 1 teaspoon fine sea salt

3 g / 1 teaspoon instant dry yeast

151 g / ⅔ cup warm water (about 110°F/45°C)

15 g / 1 tablespoon extra virgin olive oil

FILLING

75 g / 1 Roma (plum) tomato, chopped

85 g / ½ small red onion

10 g / 2 cloves garlic

20 g / ½ packed cup fresh parsley leaves

15 g / 1 tablespoon sambal oelek or sriracha

4 g / 1 teaspoon fine sea salt

3 g / 1 teaspoon freshly ground black pepper

170 g / 6 ounces ground lamb or beef

FINISHING

1 large lemon, cut into 6 wedges

Chopped fresh parsley

Thinly sliced fresh chiles or Quick Pickled Chiles (recipe follows; optional)

Ground sumac

1. Make the dough: In the bowl of a stand mixer fitted with the dough hook, mix the flour, sugar, salt, and yeast on low speed to combine, about 30 seconds. Add the water and olive oil and mix until the dough comes together, about 4 minutes. Raise the speed to medium and mix for 5 minutes more, or until the dough is very smooth.

2. Turn the dough out and form it into a ball. Transfer to a lightly greased large bowl, cover, and let rise until nearly doubled in size, 1 hour to 1 hour and 15 minutes.

3. Turn the dough out onto a lightly floured surface. Divide into 6 equal pieces (about 70 g each). Gently round each piece (see page 172), transferring them to another lightly floured part of the work surface. Cover and let rest for 15 to 20 minutes.

4. Preheat the oven to 500°F/260°C with an oven rack in the center; put a baking steel or pizza stone on the rack if you have one. Cut 6 squares of parchment paper about 12 x 12 inches/ 30 x 30 cm.

5. Make the filling: In a food processor or blender, combine the tomatoes, onion, garlic, parsley, sambal oelek or sriracha, salt, and pepper and

(CONTINUES)

pulse until smooth. Transfer to a medium bowl and add the ground meat. Mix well to combine.

6. Flour both sides of one piece of dough and place it in the center of a parchment square. Roll the dough out as thin as possible without tearing—use more flour as needed during rolling—aiming for an elongated oval about 10 inches/25 cm long and 6 inches/15 cm wide. Spread a thin layer of the filling evenly over the dough, leaving about ½ inch/1 cm clear all around the edges. Traditionally this layer is very thin, just barely covering the surface.

7. Use the parchment paper to slide the topped dough onto the steel or stone, or place on a baking sheet. Bake for 5 to 7 minutes, until the dough is very crisp and the meat is fully cooked. Transfer to a serving plate.

8. Repeat with the remaining dough and filling. Serve with the lemon wedges, generously garnished with parsley, chiles, and sumac.

Note: This flavorful dough can also be cooked all on its own. Roll it out as directed in step 6, dock it a few times with the tines of a fork, and brush generously with olive oil. Add a sprinkling of flaky salt, sesame seeds, or spices, if you like. Bake until it begins to brown and the edges are crisp, 4 to 5 minutes.

Quick Pickled Chiles

Pickled chiles of some sort are a common find in my fridge. Drain the chiles and pat them dry to use in baked goods, or add them as a finishing touch to any number of baked goods or other dishes.

Slice 60 g / 3 medium or 5 small jalapeño, Fresno, serrano, habanero, or other fresh chile peppers very thin and place in a small glass jar or other heatproof airtight container. In a small saucepan, combine 115 g / ½ cup seasoned rice vinegar, 5 g / 1 clove garlic, smashed and peeled, 12 g / 1 tablespoon granulated sugar, and 3 g / ½ teaspoon kosher salt, bring to a boil, and cook, stirring, until the sugar and salt have dissolved. Pour the vinegar over the chiles. Cover and shake the jar a few times to settle the chiles into an even layer.

Let cool, then store in the refrigerator for up to 3 weeks.

Make Ahead and Storage
The lahmacun is best served immediately after baking. Store leftovers in an airtight container in the refrigerator for up to 1 day. You can lightly re-crisp the crust after refrigerating on a griddle or in a large cast-iron skillet.

Pizza

Makes 4 round pizzas or 1 large pan pizza

DIFFICULTY: **EASY**

I have multiple pizza personalities—which is to say, I've met very few pizzas I don't like, and I make pizza any number of ways, depending on my mood. Sometimes I decide I want pizza for dinner that night. Other times, I like to let the dough hang out in the fridge, slowly rising, which gives it more flavor—as well as being ready to go whenever I am. See the note below for instructions on making the dough up to 48 hours in advance. Either way, this recipe is here for all your pizza needs.

DOUGH

480 g / 4 cups all-purpose flour

82 g / ½ cup semolina flour

12 g / 1 tablespoon granulated sugar (optional)

5 g / 1¼ teaspoons fine sea salt

3 g / 1 teaspoon instant dry yeast

340 g / 1½ cups warm water (about 110°F/45°C)

30 g / 2 tablespoons extra virgin olive oil, plus more for greasing the bowl

FINISHING

Extra virgin olive oil

Semolina flour or cornmeal

Sauce of choice, such as tomato (see page 155) or Béchamel (page 56)

Topping(s) of choice (see page 84)

Grated or shredded cheese(s) of choice

1. Mix the dough:

   TO MIX THE DOUGH BY HAND: In a large bowl, whisk the all-purpose flour, semolina flour, sugar, if using, salt, and yeast to combine. Add the water and olive oil and mix with a spatula until a smooth dough forms, about 3 minutes.

   TO MIX THE DOUGH IN A STAND MIXER: In the bowl of a stand mixer fitted with the dough hook, mix the all-purpose flour, semolina flour, sugar, if using, salt, and yeast on low speed to combine, about 30 seconds. Add the water and olive oil and mix until a smooth dough forms, about 2 minutes.

2. Drizzle a glug of olive oil into a large bowl and use your hands to fully coat the inside of the bowl. Use your oiled hands to transfer the dough to the bowl, turning it over a few times to round it slightly and coat it in oil. Cover the dough and let rise at room temperature until nearly doubled in size, 1 to 1½ hours.

3. Divide and preshape the dough:

   FOR ROUND PIZZAS: Turn the dough out onto a lightly floured work surface. Divide into 4 equal pieces (about 240 g each). Round each piece slightly (see page 104) and transfer to another lightly floured part of the work surface. Cover and rest for 15 minutes.

   FOR A PAN PIZZA: Generously grease a 13 x 18-inch/33 x 46 cm baking sheet with olive oil. Turn the dough out onto the baking sheet and use your fingertips to stipple the dough into a rough rectangle with a fairly even thickness; it likely won't reach the edges of the pan yet. Drizzle oil over the surface of the dough and let rest for 15 minutes.

(CONTINUES)

4. Shape the dough:

FOR ROUND PIZZAS: Use your hands to gently stretch each portion of dough into a round about 12 inches/30 cm wide. Work gently and gradually to stretch the dough—the edges should be thicker than the center, but take care not to tear the center.

FOR THE PAN PIZZA: Use your fingertips to stipple the dough again—it should easily reach almost to the edges of the pan as you work it into a fairly even layer.

5. Finish and bake the pizza:

FOR ROUND PIZZAS: Preheat the oven to 500°F/260°C with the racks in the upper and lower thirds; if you have one, place a baking steel or pizza stone on the lower rack; if you don't have either one, bake the pizza on a lightly greased baking sheet. Sprinkle a pizza peel generously with semolina or cornmeal.

Just before baking, gently transfer one round of the dough to the pizza peel (or to the greased baking sheet). Immediately apply a thin layer of sauce, your desired toppings, and cheese. Use the peel to slide the pizza onto the steel or stone (or transfer baking sheet to the oven). Bake until the dough is deeply browned at the edges and the cheese is melted, 8 to 10 minutes. Once the crust is set and crisp, if more browning is desired for the topping (or if the bottom or edges of the crust are getting overly dark/crisp), use the peel to slide the pizza onto the rack above it (or transfer the baking sheet to the upper rack) for the remainder of baking.

FOR THE PAN PIZZA: Preheat the oven to 425°F/220°C with a rack in the center. Apply a thin layer of sauce, your desired toppings, and cheese to the dough. Transfer the pan to the oven, onto the steel or stone, if using, and bake until the dough is golden at the edges, 20 to 25 minutes.

Note: To make the pizza dough ahead, reduce the yeast to 2 g / ½ teaspoon. Cover the bowl and let the dough rise at room temperature for 4 to 6 hours, until visibly puffy, then refrigerate for up to 2 days. (If your ambient room temperature is higher than 75°F/45°C, let the dough rise at room temperature for 2 hours, until visibly puffy, then refrigerate for the remaining rising time.)

Pizza Dough: Anything Is Possible

Pizza-Joint Rolls

Makes 8 large or 16 small rolls

1. Turn the risen dough out onto a lightly floured work surface. Divide it into 4 equal pieces (about 250 g each).

2. Working with one piece of dough at a time, use your fingers to gently stipple and stretch the dough into a rectangle about 8 x 16 inches/ 20 x 40 cm and ½ inch/1 cm thick. Cut the dough lengthwise in half. Spread a thin layer of sauce on each piece of dough and arrange the toppings and cheese on top in an even layer.

   FOR LARGE ROLLS: Starting from one of the short ends, roll up each piece of dough into a tight spiral. Transfer the rolls to a parchment-lined baking sheet, seam side down, and brush with olive oil or Garlic Butter (page 11). If desired, sprinkle Parmesan cheese over the top of the rolls.

   FOR SMALL ROLLS: Assemble large rolls as directed above, then cut each one crosswise in half to expose the swirled filling. Place the rolls cut side up on a parchment-lined baking sheet.

3. Cover the rolls and let rise for 20 to 30 minutes. Bake the rolls at 400°F/205°C until they are deeply golden, 25 to 30 minutes for large rolls, 20 to 25 minutes for small ones. Serve warm.

Cheesy Breadsticks

Makes about 16 breadsticks

1. Grease a baking sheet generously with olive oil and place the risen dough on it. Use your fingers to stipple the dough out into a large

rectangle about ½ in/1 cm thick. Cover and let rest for 15 minutes, then stipple the dough again until about 10 x 15 inches/25 x 38 cm.

2. In a small saucepan, melt 56 g / 2 ounces / 4 tablespoons unsalted butter, then stir in 6 g / 2 teaspoons garlic powder, 3 g / 1 teaspoon Italian herb seasoning, a few pinches of salt, and lots of pepper. Brush the butter all over the surface of the dough. Top with 226 g / 8 ounces shredded low-moisture mozzarella cheese and a generous sprinkling of freshly grated Parmesan cheese.

3. Bake at 425°F/225°C until the dough is golden at the edges and the cheese is melted and browned, 15 to 20 minutes. Cool for 5 minutes, then slice into 1-inch-/2.5 cm wide strips and serve warm.

Roasted Garlic Naan

Makes 10 naan

DIFFICULTY: **EASY**

When I was a teenager, I went to theater camp every summer (jazz hands!). On our dinner break each night, we would head to nearby Mass Street to grab a bite. One night, I saw one of my closest friends, Andrew, beelining toward the local bakery, so I joined him. I was surprised to see that he ordered only two large rolls for his dinner. He revealed it was part of a larger master plan—he would eat as cheaply as he could for most of the week, so he could put the rest of his dinner money toward a feast at his favorite Indian restaurant on Friday. That became a bit of a tradition between us, and after hunting down the best bargains in town for four days in a row, we'd eat like kings and queens at the restaurant, where we always ordered extra garlic naan. Light and fluffy, naan is made for dipping and dunking in flavorful sauces or chutneys. Nowadays I make my version with a generous spread of roasted garlic on top—and it, too, is worth waiting all week for. If you want to make it even more weeknight friendly, consider the overnight version below.

DOUGH

440 g / 3⅔ cups all-purpose flour

6 g / 2 teaspoons instant dry yeast

6 g / 1½ teaspoons fine sea salt

200 g / ¾ cup warm water (about 110°F/45°C)

113 g / ½ cup whole-milk Greek yogurt, at room temperature

43 g / 2 ounces / 4 tablespoons ghee or unsalted butter, melted

FINISHING

1 head Roasted Garlic (page 159)

56 g / 1.5 ounces / 3 tablespoons ghee or unsalted butter, at room temperature

Flaky salt

Chopped fresh cilantro

1. Make the dough: In the bowl of a stand mixer fitted with the dough hook, mix the flour, yeast, and salt on low speed to combine, 15 to 30 seconds. Add the water, yogurt, and ghee or butter and mix until the dough comes together, about 4 minutes. Raise the speed to medium and mix for 3 minutes more.

2. Transfer the dough to a lightly greased bowl, cover with plastic wrap, and let rise until nearly doubled in size, 1 hour to 1 hour 15 minutes.

3. Turn the dough out onto a lightly floured surface and divide into 10 equal pieces (about 80 g each). Gently round each piece of dough (see page 104) and transfer to another lightly floured part of the workspace. Cover and let rest for 15 minutes.

4. Heat a large cast-iron skillet or griddle over medium heat until very hot. While the pan heats, squeeze the roasted garlic cloves out of their skins and into a small bowl and use a fork to mash them. Add the butter or ghee and mash to a paste. Have a pastry brush ready.

5. Roll one piece of dough out on a lightly floured surface to a round about 8 inches/20 cm wide. Immediately add the naan to the hot skillet and cook for 2 to 3 minutes, until the dough puffs up—it may form large bubbles/blisters, which will deeply brown. The rest of the dough

(CONTINUES)

may not brown, but it should become matte across the surface. Flip the naan and cook on the other side, 1 to 2 minutes more.

6. Transfer the naan to a serving platter and immediately brush generously on both sides with roasted garlic butter, making sure some of the bits of garlic transfer to the surface of the bread. Sprinkle with flaky salt and cilantro. Cover the naan loosely with a clean kitchen towel to keep warm.

7. Shape and cook the rest of the breads. Serve warm.

Variation

OVERNIGHT NAAN **Let the dough rise, covered, at room temperature for 30 minutes, then refrigerate for 8 to 12 hours (overnight). The next day, bring the dough to room temperature, 45 minutes, before dividing it and proceeding as directed.**

Make Ahead and Storage
The naan can be prepared ahead through step 3 and frozen; wrap each round tightly in plastic wrap and freeze in an airtight container for up to 2 months. Thaw overnight in the refrigerator before shaping and cooking. The naan is best the same day it's made. Store leftovers in an airtight container at room temperature for up to 2 days.

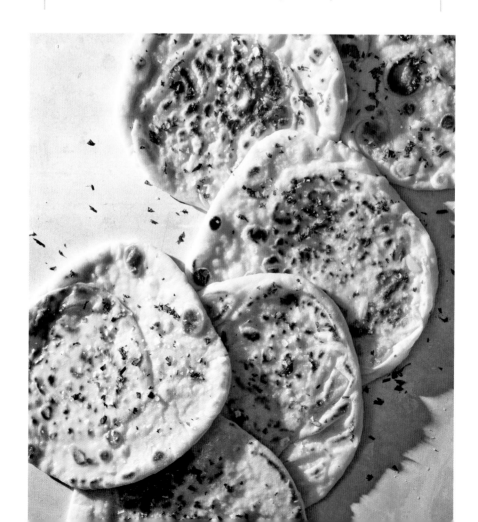

FINISHING (SEE NOTE)

45 g / 3 tablespoons extra virgin olive oil, plus more for pan

30 g / 2 tablespoons warm water

6 g / 1 teaspoon kosher salt

Flaky salt

1. Twelve to 48 hours before you want to bake the focaccia, make the dough: In a large bowl, stir the flour, salt, and yeast together. Add the water, olive oil, and honey and mix until thoroughly combined, 1 to 2 minutes. The dough will be very wet and sticky. Cover the bowl and let rise at room temperature for 30 minutes.

2. Using a dough scraper or damp hands, gently reach under the dough, folding the bottom portion of it over onto the top. Repeat this process 4 to 5 times, working your way around the bowl. Cover the bowl and refrigerate for at least 12 hours, and up to 48 hours.

3. When ready to make the focaccia, bring the dough to room temperature for 30 minutes.

4. Grease your baking pan generously with olive oil. Add the dough to the pan and gently turn it over so both sides are lightly oiled. Cover the pan and let the dough rise until it nearly doubles in size and almost fills the pan, 30 minutes to 1 hour.

5. Use your fingertips to gently stipple the dough (see page 195)—this will even out the thickness of the dough, spread it out over the base of the pan, and add texture to the surface. Cover and let rest while you preheat the oven.

6. Preheat the oven to 450°F/235°C with a rack in the center.

7. In a medium bowl, using a pastry brush, vigorously mix together the olive oil, water, and salt until the salt is dissolved and the mixture is emulsified and thick. Brush the surface of the dough generously with the oil mixture—it will pool in the dimples. Sprinkle the dough with flaky salt.

8. Transfer to the oven and bake until the focaccia is deeply golden brown:

    9-IN/23 CM ROUND: 24 to 28 minutes

    9 X 9-INCH/23 X 23 CM SQUARE: 25 to 30 minutes

    9 X 13-INCH/23 X 33 CM RECTANGLE: 28 to 32 minutes

    13 X 18-IN/33 X 46 CM SHEET: 30 to 34 minutes

    Cool the focaccia in the pan for 5 minutes, then unmold onto a wire rack. Serve warm, or cool to room temperature.

Note: Depending on the size of the focaccia you make, you may not need all of the finishing mixture. You can save any extra, covered, at room temperature for a future bake.

Variations

ONION AND HERB FOCACCIA **After brushing the focaccia with the oil mixture in step 7, arrange about 325 g / 1 sweet or red onion, thinly sliced, on top and finish with a generous sprinkling of fresh thyme and rosemary leaves and bake as directed.**

SQUASH BLOSSOM FOCACCIA **Omit the flaky salt for finishing. In a medium bowl, toss up to 140 g / 10 squash blossoms with a glug of extra virgin olive oil. Arrange the squash blossoms over the focaccia before baking. Grate a thin layer of Parmesan cheese over the top, covering the squash blossoms. Bake as directed.**

FRESH TOMATO FOCACCIA **After brushing the focaccia with the oil mixture in step 7,** arrange about 330 g / 1 large tomato, thinly sliced, on the top of the dough before sprinkling with the flaky salt and some pepper. Bake as directed. Sprinkle up to 6 g / 2 tablespoons chopped fresh herbs, such as basil, oregano, dill, parsley, or mint, over the top of the baked focaccia.

CACIO E PEPE FOCACCIA Omit the flaky salt for finishing. After brushing the focaccia with the oil mixture in step 7, grate a thin layer of Parmesan cheese all over the top of the bread, generously grind black pepper evenly over it, and bake as directed.

SWEET PEPPER AND ONION FOCACCIA
After brushing the focaccia with the oil mixture in step 7, arrange about 165 g / ½ thinly sliced red onion and 226 / 8 ounces thinly sliced mini sweet peppers (or pepper of choice) on top. Finish with chopped rosemary or oregano, and a sprinkling of freshly ground black pepper.

> **Make Ahead and Storage**
> Focaccia is best the same day it's baked, but it will keep at room temperature, tightly wrapped, for up to 3 days.

How to Stipple

Stippling means pressing a dough with your fingertips to create a dimpled effect on the surface. Press straight down with your fingertips, applying more or less pressure, depending on the desired effect.

In some recipes, stippling is done in the early stages of shaping the bread to help deflate it before shaping.

Stippling can also be part of the shaping. I do it in the early stages of shaping doughs like pizza and khachapuri. It helps to even the thickness and to start to create the rough shape I want, before some gentle stretching.

Stippling can also be a final step in the shaping process, as for focaccia, where it adds a beautiful texture to the surface, perfect for capturing oil and seasonings in the resulting nooks and crannies.

Pita Bread

Makes 8 pitas

DIFFICULTY: **EASY**

Making homemade pita is incredibly satisfying—and much easier than you might expect, and much quicker! I use a little bit of whole wheat flour for a more flavorful bread. When properly made, the pita will naturally form a pocket in the center, which makes it great for stuffing with meat or veggies for a simple sandwich. Or serve it alongside just about anything—it will be delicious whatever you dip or dunk it in.

360 g / 3 cups all-purpose flour

40 g / ⅓ cup whole wheat flour

10 g / 1 tablespoon instant dry yeast

6 g / 1½ teaspoons fine sea salt

280 g / 1¼ cups warm water (about 110°F/45°C)

30 g / 2 tablespoons extra virgin olive oil, plus more for the bowl

1. In the bowl of stand mixer fitted with the dough hook, mix the all-purpose flour, whole wheat flour, yeast, and salt on low speed to combine. Add the water and olive oil and mix for about 3 minutes, until the dough comes together. Raise the speed to medium and mix for 2 minutes more, or until the dough is very smooth. (The dough can also be mixed by hand in a large bowl with a rubber spatula, then turned out and kneaded by hand for 5 to 7 minutes.)

2. Lightly oil a medium bowl with olive oil. Add the dough to the bowl and gently turn it over onto itself a few times to round it and lightly coat it with oil. Cover the bowl and let the dough rise until nearly doubled in size, 1 to 1½ hours.

3. Preheat the oven to 500°F/260°C with a rack in the center; if you have a baking steel or pizza stone, place it on the rack—if you don't have either, see Note. After the oven has come to temperature, allow the steel or stone (if using), to preheat for 30 minutes longer.

4. Cut out eight 8-inch/20 cm parchment circles. Turn the dough out onto a lightly floured surface and divide into 8 equal pieces (about 90 g each). Gently round each piece (see page 104) and transfer them to another a lightly floured part of the work surface. Cover with a clean kitchen towel and let rest for 15 minutes.

5. Work with one piece of dough at a time, keeping the dough you are not working on covered. On a lightly floured surface, roll out one piece of dough to a round between 6 and 7 inches/15 and 18 cm wide and about ¼ inch/6 mm thick, trying to maintain an even thickness to ensure the pita puffs properly. Transfer the dough to one of the parchment circles and cover loosely with plastic wrap.

6. Bake as many pitas as easily fit on the steel or stone at a time (2 to 4), sliding the parchment circles right onto the steel or stone. Bake for 2 to 3 minutes, until visibly puffed in the center; the pitas may brown slightly. Remove the pitas from the oven and wrap tightly in a clean kitchen towel to steam them and keep them soft and warm. Serve warm.

Note: If you don't have a baking steel or pizza stone, place a large cast-iron skillet in the oven when you turn it on. Bake the pitas one at a time in the skillet.

Compound-Butter Paratha

Makes 10 paratha

DIFFICULTY: **MEDIUM**

I love buttery paratha, an easy-to-make unleavened Indian flatbread. The dough is rolled out, brushed with ghee, and folded and rolled to create a beautiful layered effect. The outside is charred and crisp, and the interior is shattery and flaky, good for serving alongside just about anything saucy. I like using melted compound butter rather than ghee to assemble the paratha, such as Garlic Chive Butter (page 200), to add another layer of flavor.

520 g / 4⅓ cups all-purpose flour

8 g / 2 teaspoons fine sea salt

56 g / ¼ cup neutral oil (such as canola or vegetable)

285 g / 1¼ cups warm water (about 80°F/25°C)

285 g / 10 ounces 1 cup plus 2 tablespoons Garlic Chive Butter or another compound butter (page 200) or Ghee (page 200)

1. In a large bowl, whisk the flour and salt together. Drizzle the oil over the flour and use your fingers to rub the two together until well combined. Make a well in the center of the flour mixture and add the water to it. Mix with your hands or a spatula until the dough comes together and is thoroughly combined.

2. Turn the dough out onto a clean work surface and knead until it forms a fairly smooth ball, 4 to 5 minutes (it may still be a bit sticky, but you shouldn't need to use any additional flour). Form the dough into a disk and wrap tightly in plastic wrap. Refrigerate for at least 1 hour (and up to 48 hours).

3. Line a baking sheet with parchment paper. Melt the compound butter or ghee and have a pastry brush ready. Turn the dough out onto a clean work surface and divide into 10 equal pieces (about 85 g each), then cover loosely with plastic wrap or a clean kitchen towel.

4. On a lightly floured work surface, roll out one piece of dough to a very thin rough round, ⅛ inch/3 mm or thinner (it will probably be about 5 inches/12 cm wide, but the exact size and shape don't matter—thickness is more important).

5. Brush the surface of the dough all over with some of the melted butter (or ghee). Fold about 1 inch/2.5 cm of the left and right sides of the dough over toward the center. Repeat this process 2 or 3 more times, until the two edges meet in the center. Fold the dough over itself along the center seam, then roll it up into a tight spiral. Transfer the dough to the prepared baking sheet and use the palm of your hand to gently flatten it. Cover the dough and repeat with the remaining dough.

6. When all the dough has been shaped, transfer the baking sheet to the refrigerator and let rest for 2 hours (and up to 12 hours or overnight).

7. Shape and cook the paratha: Roll out one piece of dough on a lightly floured surface to a round about 7 inches/18 cm wide and ⅛ in/3 mm thick. Place the round on a sheet of parchment, and place another sheet of parchment on top. Repeat with the remaining dough.

8. Heat a large cast-iron skillet or griddle over medium heat until very hot. Brush both sides

of a paratha with compound butter, add to the pan, and cook until the bottom is evenly brown and flaky, 2 to 4 minutes. Flip and cook until golden on the other side, 2 to 3 minutes more.

Transfer the paratha to a clean kitchen towel and wrap in the towel to keep warm. Repeat with the remaining breads and serve warm.

Make Ahead and Storage
Paratha is best the same day it is made. Store leftovers in an airtight container at room temperature.

— FLAVOR BOOSTER —

Butter

Ghee

Makes about 285 g / 10 ounces

Ghee is butter that has been clarified to remove the milk solids. Sometimes I flavor it by adding dried whole spices, smashed garlic cloves, sliced ginger, or saffron threads after the butter has melted.

In a medium pot, melt 340 g / 12 ounces unsalted butter over medium heat. Reduce the heat to medium-low and let the butter simmer slowly until the milk solids separate out, 3 to 5 minutes. Use a small spoon to skim off and discard the foam from the surface, then slowly pour the clear butter through a small strainer into a glass jar—pour slowly and stop when you get to the bottom of the pot, leaving the milk solids in the pot. Let cool, cover, and refrigerate for up to 6 months.

Brown Butter

Makes about 285 g / 10 ounces

Brown butter is butter that is cooked until the milk solids separate out and become toasty and flavorful.

In a medium pot, melt 340 g / 12 ounces unsalted butter over medium heat. Reduce the heat to low and cook, swirling the pot occasionally, until the milk solids separate out and drop to the bottom of the pot, 3 to 5 minutes. Then continue to cook, swirling the pot frequently, until the milk solids begin to turn brown and the butter smells toasty, 3 to 5 minutes more. Transfer to a jar or other container, cover, and refrigerate for up to 1 week.

Compound Butters

Makes 226 to 285 g / 8 to 10 ounces

Compound butters are made by adding other flavorful ingredients to softened butter.

In a food processor or blender, pulse 226 g / 8 ounces room-temperature unsalted butter with any of the flavorings below until smooth. Transfer the butter to a piece of plastic wrap and form it into a log about 2 inches/5 cm wide. Wrap tightly in the plastic wrap and refrigerate for up to 1 week or freeze, well wrapped, for up to 1 month.

GARLIC-DILL: Mash 4 cloves raw garlic or Roasted Garlic (page 159) with the side of a heavy knife and combine with 25 g / ½ packed cup fresh dill leaves.

GARLIC CHIVE: Mash 4 cloves raw garlic or Roasted Garlic (page 159) with the side of a heavy knife combine with 30 g / ¾ cup minced fresh chives.

LEMON PEPPER: Combine the grated zest of 1 lemon and 6 g / 2 heaping teaspoons coarsely ground black pepper or 3 g / 1 teaspoon red pepper flakes.

SUN-DRIED TOMATO: Dice enough oil-packed sun-dried tomatoes to make 60 g / ½ packed cup.

CHIPOTLE: Combine 40 g / 2 canned chipotle peppers in adobo sauce, finely chopped, and 21 g / 3 tablespoons dried minced onions.

TURMERIC: Melt 56 g / 2 ounces / 4 tablespoons of the butter and whisk 14 g / 1½ tablespoons ground turmeric into it. Cook, swirling constantly, for 1 to 2 minutes, until fragrant. Let cool to room temperature, then add to the remaining butter and blend until smooth.

Spicy Cheese Brat Klobásník and Kolaches

Makes 10 pastries

DIFFICULTY: **MEDIUM**

Klobásník and kolaches are both made with a stuffed soft, golden yeast-raised dough, originally of Czech origin. Savory klobásník, popular in Texas, are oblong, sausage-filled pastries. Classic Czech kolache (see the Variations) often contain sweet fillings, but I also love them with all things meaty, cheesy, salty, and savory.

DOUGH

175 g / ¾ cup whole milk

480 g / 4 cups all-purpose flour

66 g / ⅓ cup granulated sugar

14 g / 2 tablespoons nonfat dry milk powder (optional, but recommended; see page 100)

10 g / 1 tablespoon instant dry yeast

6 g / 1½ teaspoons fine sea salt

113 g / 2 large eggs, at room temperature

113 g / 4 ounces / 8 tablespoons unsalted butter, melted and cooled slightly

FILLING AND FINISHING

About 250 g / 10 cheese-stuffed brats or other sausage links of your choice

20 g / 1 medium jalapeño, thinly sliced

125 g / 1¼ packed cups shredded sharp cheddar cheese

Egg wash (see page 7)

1. In a small saucepan, heat the milk over medium-low heat until it reaches about 110°F/45°C. Remove from the heat.

2. In the bowl of a stand mixer fitted with the dough hook, mix the flour, sugar, dry milk, if using, yeast, and salt on low speed to combine. Add the warm milk, eggs, and butter and mix for 4 minutes. Raise the speed to medium and mix until the dough is smooth, about 2 minutes more.

3. Transfer the dough to a lightly greased large bowl, cover with plastic wrap, and let rise until the dough is visibly puffy, 1 hour to 1 hour 15 minutes.

4. While the dough rises, cook the sausages until well browned and cooked through. Cool completely, then use a paring knife to cut a lengthwise slit about halfway into each sausage. Arrange 3 to 4 slices of jalapeño inside each sausage.

5. Divide the dough into 10 even pieces (about 95 g each). Gently round each piece of dough (see page 104) and place on a lightly floured work surface. Cover with a clean kitchen towel and let rest for 15 minutes.

6. Line a baking sheet with parchment paper. Working with one piece of dough at a time, gently press and stretch the dough with your fingers (or use a rolling pin) to flatten it into a rectangle about 3 x 4 inches/8 x 10 cm. Place a sausage on one of the shorter ends of the dough, sprinkle 7 g / 1 tablespoon of the shredded cheese on top of the sausage, and roll the dough up around the sausage. Repeat with the remaining dough and sausages.

7. Transfer the pastries, seam side down, to the prepared baking sheet, staggering the rows so there is space between them. Cover with greased plastic wrap and let rise for 30 minutes. Toward the end of the rise time, pre-

(CONTINUES)

203

heat the oven to 350°F/175°C with a rack in the center.

8. Uncover the pastries and egg-wash the surface. Sprinkle the remaining cheese on top of the pastries. Bake until evenly golden brown, 20 to 25 minutes.

9. Let the pastries cool for 5 to 10 minutes before serving warm.

Variations

KOLACHES **Prepare the dough as directed through step 5 above and let rest. Use your fingers to firmly press each round down, starting in the center to make it thinner than the edges of the dough, and then continue to press firmly until the dough widens to a round about 4 inches/10 cm across. Transfer the rounds to a parchment-lined baking sheet, staggering the rows to leave space between them. Lightly spray the bottom of a ramekin or ¹/₂-cup measure with nonstick spray and gently press it into the center of each round of dough to create a deep indentation. Cover the rounds with greased plastic wrap and let rise for 30 minutes, then press each again with the greased ramekin or measuring cup to deepen the indentation before filling with one of the fillings below. Egg-wash the edges, fill the center, and bake as directed for sausage rolls.**

LASAGNA KOLACHES **In a medium skillet, heat 30 g / 2 tablespoons extra virgin olive oil over medium heat. Crumble 226 g / 8 ounces Italian sausage into the pan and** cook until well browned. Drain off all but 15 g / 1 tablespoon of the fat from the pan, then stir in 15 g / 3 cloves garlic, minced, and remove from the heat. Stir in 145 g / ¹/₂ cup Thick Tomato Sauce (page 155) and cool to room temperature.

Shape the dough as for kolaches, transfer to a parchment-lined baking sheet, and let rise as directed. Egg-wash the edges of the rounds. Spoon 30 g / 2 heaping tablespoons of the filling into the center of each kolache, then top with 15 g / 1 heaping tablespoon whole-milk ricotta cheese. Sprinkle a pinch of Italian herb seasoning over each one, then top each with a ¹/₄-inch- / 6 mm thick round of fresh mozzarella cheese. Bake for 24 to 28 minutes, until the cheese is gooey.

MARINATED TOMATO, OLIVE, AND FETA KOLACHES **In a medium bowl, mash 226 g / 8 ounces crumbled feta cheese with 30 g / 2 tablespoons extra virgin olive oil, 6 g / 2 tablespoons chopped fresh dill, 6 g / 2 tablespoons chopped fresh parsley, 1 g / ¹/₂ teaspoon dried oregano, the grated zest and juice of 1 lemon, and a few pinches of red pepper flakes. Season with salt to taste (it won't need much) and lots of pepper. Coarsely chop 80 g / ³/₄ cup pitted olives of your choice and add to the feta mixture. Fold in 250 g / 1¹/₄ cups diced tomatoes. Shape the dough as for kolache, transfer to a parchment-lined baking sheet, and let rise as directed. Egg-wash the edges of the rounds and divide the feta mixture among them, filling the centers. Bake as directed for sausage rolls.**

Make Ahead and Storage
The pastries are best the same day they are baked. Store leftovers tightly wrapped in the refrigerator and warm to refresh (see page 365) before serving.

Brioche Buns with Crème Fraîche and Gruyère

Makes 16 buns

DIFFICULTY: **MEDIUM**

I like to think that baking has "mother doughs" the same way classic French cooking has "mother sauces." Soft, pillowy brioche certainly would be one, and it's a must-have recipe for your own baking repertoire. It bakes up deeply golden brown and is dreamily buttery but strong enough to stand up to inclusions, toppings, or fillings, like those in the Variations below. I make these buns year-round, subbing in different fillings depending on what's in season. Ring in fall with butternut squash and rosemary, or celebrate summer with tomato, corn, and burrata.

DOUGH

630 g / 5¼ cups **bread flour**

99 g / ½ cup granulated **sugar**

12 g / 1 tablespoon fine sea **salt**

10 g / 1 tablespoon instant dry **yeast**

285 g / 5 large **eggs**, at room temperature

230 g / 1 cup warm whole **milk**, heated to about 110°F/45°C

397 g / 14 ounces unsalted **butter**, at room temperature

FILLING AND FINISHING

Egg wash (see page 7)

226 g / 8 ounces very cold **crème fraîche**

190 g / 1¼ cups finely chopped cooked **bacon** (about 7 ounces; optional)

225 g / 2¼ cups shredded **Gruyère cheese** (about 8 ounces)

1. The day before you want to make the buns, make the dough: In the bowl of a stand mixer fitted with the dough hook, mix the flour, sugar, salt, and yeast on low speed to combine, 15 to 30 seconds. Add the eggs and milk and mix until the dough comes together around the hook, 4 minutes; it will be sticky.

2. Scrape the bowl and dough hook well, then increase the speed to medium and mix for 1 minute. With the mixer running, add the butter about 12 g / 1 tablespoon at a time, making sure each addition is incorporated before adding the next—this whole process should take about 6 to 7 minutes; scrape the bowl a few times as you add the butter to help keep the dough homogenous. Once all the butter is incorporated, mix on medium speed for 1 minute more.

3. Transfer the dough to a lightly greased large bowl, turn it a few times in the bowl to lightly coat, and form it into a rough ball. Cover the bowl with plastic wrap and let the dough rise at room temperature for 30 minutes, then refrigerate for 8 to 12 hours (overnight).

4. Line a baking sheet with parchment. Turn the dough out and divide it into 16 equal pieces (about 100 g each). Shape each dough into a round (see page 104), and place on the prepared sheet. Cover with greased plastic wrap and refrigerate for 15 minutes.

5. Line an additional baking sheet with parchment paper (you'll also use the baking sheet

(CONTINUES)

the dough is chilling on again, lined with a fresh sheet of parchment paper). On a lightly floured surface, roll out one piece of dough into an oval about 4 inches/10 cm long and ½ inch/1 cm thick. Transfer to one of the baking sheets and repeat with the remaining dough, arranging the buns on the baking sheets in staggered rows, 8 buns per sheet.

6. Use the handle of a wooden spoon to make a valley down the center of each piece of dough, pressing firmly, to give the buns their characteristic shape. Cover with greased plastic wrap and let rise until the brioche is visibly puffy, 1 to 1½ hours. Toward the end of the rise time, preheat the oven to 350°F/175°C with the racks in the upper and lower thirds.

7. Uncover the brioche and egg-wash the surface of each bun evenly. Spoon 15 g / 1 tablespoon crème fraîche onto the center of each bun. If using, divide the bacon evenly among the buns. Top each one with 14 g / 2 heaping tablespoons of the shredded Gruyère.

8. Bake the buns until deeply golden brown, 35 to 38 minutes. Cool for at least 5 minutes before serving warm, or let cool completely.

Variations

BUTTERNUT SQUASH AND ROSEMARY BRIOCHE BUNS Omit the optional bacon. In a medium bowl, toss 390 g / 3 cups finely diced butternut squash with 30 g / 2 tablespoons extra virgin olive oil. Add 4 g / 1½ tablespoons chopped fresh rosemary, season with salt and pepper, and toss again. Spread the mixture evenly in a 9 x 13-inch/23 x 30 cm baking pan and roast at 400°F/205°C until the squash is tender and browning, 20 to 25 minutes. In step 7, spoon the roasted butternut squash on top of the crème fraîche, dividing it evenly among the buns, then sprinkle the Gruyère on top.

CARAMELIZED ONION, CABBAGE, CARAWAY, AND PARSLEY BRIOCHE BUNS Omit the optional bacon. In a large skillet, heat 24 g / 2 tablespoons unsalted butter with 15 g / 1 tablespoon extra virgin olive oil over medium heat until the butter melts. Add 330 g / 3 cups shredded cabbage and cook, tossing frequently, until it begins to wilt, 5 to 10 minutes. Cover the pan and cook over medium-low heat, stirring occasionally, until the cabbage is very tender, 30 to 35 minutes. Stir 160 g / ½ cup Caramelized Onions (page 26) and 9 g / 1 tablespoon caraway seeds into the cabbage and cook until fragrant, 2 to 3 minutes. Let cool to room temperature, then stir in 20 g / ½ cup chopped fresh parsley. In step 7, spoon the cabbage mixture on top of the crème fraîche, dividing it evenly among the buns, then sprinkle the Gruyère on top.

ASPARAGUS, PEAS, MINT, AND RICOTTA BRIOCHE BUNS Omit the optional bacon and the Gruyère. Bring a medium pot of salted water to a boil, and fill a medium bowl with ice water. Add 226 g / 8 ounces asparagus, diced, to the boiling water and blanch for 1 minute, then stir in 150 g / 1 cup peas and cook for 15 seconds more. Use a slotted spoon to transfer the asparagus and peas to the ice water to stop the cooking and chill (or drain them in a colander and add to the ice water), then drain and pat dry. In a medium bowl, toss the vegetables with 28 g / 2 tablespoons melted unsalted butter and 25 g / ¼ cup finely grated Parmesan. In step 7, spoon the asparagus/pea mixture on top of the crème fraîche, dividing it evenly among the buns, and spoon 30 g / 2 tablespoons ricotta over the top of each one. After baking, garnish the buns with chopped fresh mint.

(CONTINUES)

TOMATO, CORN, BASIL, AND BURRATA BRIOCHE BUNS **Omit the optional bacon and the Gruyère. In a medium skillet, melt 28 g / 2 tablespoons unsalted butter over medium heat. Add 210 g / 1¼ cups corn kernels and cook until the corn is starting to brown, 8 to 10 minutes. Stir in 280 g / 1½ cups roasted cherry tomatoes (page 331) and season with salt and pepper. In step 7, spoon the corn/tomato mixture on top of the crème fraîche, dividing it evenly among the buns. After baking, cool the buns for 10 minutes, then top each one with a spoonful of burrata, garnish generously with chopped fresh basil, and serve.**

BRIOCHE LOAVES **Lightly grease two 8 x 4-inch/20 x 10 cm loaf pans with nonstick spray. In step 4, divide the dough into 2 equal pieces (about 830 g each). Shape each piece into an 8-inch-/20 cm long log (see page 104) and place seam side down in the prepared pans. Cover with greased plastic wrap, and let rise until the dough comes to ½ inch/1 cm above the tops of the pans, 1½ to 2½ hours. Egg-wash the surface of each loaf and bake at 375°F/190°C until the loaves are deeply golden brown and reach an internal temperature of 200°F/95°C in the center, 30 to 35 minutes. Cool in the pans for 10 minutes, then unmold onto a wire rack to cool completely. These loaves freeze beautifully, well wrapped, for up to 3 months.**

Make Ahead and Storage

The dough—or half of the dough, if you like—can be frozen at step 3, before rising, for up to 1 month. Thaw overnight in the refrigerator, then proceed to let rise and shape as directed. Once baked, the pastries are best the same day.

If Brioche Were Focaccia

Although brioche is usually made as sandwich loaves or individual buns, I sometimes bake the dough on a baking sheet. With the wide surface area, it becomes beautifully, evenly golden brown, and it has a slightly thicker, chewier crust. Like focaccia, it makes the perfect canvas for a variety of tasty toppings; you can add just about any of the suggestions on pages 206–8 when giving this method a go.

Prepare the dough through step 3. Grease an 18 x 13-inch/46 x 30 cm baking sheet with 28 g / 2 tablespoons softened unsalted butter. On a lightly floured surface, roll out the dough into a ½-inch-/1 cm thick rectangle about the size of the baking sheet. Use the rolling pin to gently roll up the dough and unfurl it onto the baking sheet, then gently press into an even layer. Cover with greased plastic wrap and let rise for 30 minutes.

Egg-wash (see page 7) the brioche before baking. If using, add any toppings to the surface. Bake for 32 to 36 minutes, until the bread is evenly golden brown. Cool for at least 15 minutes before slicing and serving warm, or let cool completely before serving.

Corn Tortillas

Makes about 18 tortillas

DIFFICULTY: **EASY**

A trip with my dad to Santa Barbara led me to a truly life-changing tortilla experience. We waited in a long line at La Super-Rica Taqueria and watched—our noses almost pressed against the windows—as a woman deftly pressed and cooked tortillas by the dozens. By the time we made it to the front of the line, we were starving and so excited that we ordered one of everything on the menu. The meal was filled with some of the best things I've ever tasted, and it inspired me to learn how to make my own tortillas.

310 g / 2½ cups masa harina, plus more if needed

2 g / ½ teaspoon fine sea salt

45 g / 1½ ounces / 3 tablespoons butter, lard, or beef tallow, melted, or neutral oil

340 g / 1½ cups warm water (about 110°F/45°C)

1. In a large bowl, stir the masa harina and salt together. Drizzle the melted butter or oil over the masa and mix with your hands until it's evenly distributed. Add the water, mixing with a dough scraper or a spatula until the dough is smooth and uniform—it should be nice and pliable, not sticky. If it appears dry or crumbly, add more water 5 g / 1 teaspoon at a time to bring it together. If it appears too wet, add more masa a little at a time.

2. Turn the dough out, wrap tightly in plastic wrap, and let rest at room temperature for at least 1 hour (and up to 8 hours).

3. When you're ready to make the tortillas, cut 20 squares of parchment or wax paper (about 5 inches/13 cm across). Line a basket, plate, or tortilla warmer with a clean kitchen towel. Heat a large skillet or griddle, preferably cast-iron, or a comal, over medium heat.

4. Working in batches, tear off portions of dough about the size of a golf ball (35 to 40 g each). Place each ball between two pieces of the parchment or wax paper and flatten, ideally in a tortilla press; if you don't have a press, use a skillet to flatten the balls on a cutting board. As you shape them, stack the tortillas, with the parchment/wax paper separating them, and keep the stack covered with plastic wrap.

5. As you continue to press the tortillas, you can start cooking the first ones in the hot skillet (or on the griddle). Cook the tortillas, turning once, until they begin to blister and brown on both sides, 45 seconds to 1 minute per side. Place the cooked tortillas in the basket and wrap them while you press and cook the remaining tortillas (this is an important part of the process—the tortillas steam inside the towel and become even more wondrous). Serve immediately.

Make Ahead and Storage
The tortillas are best freshly made, but cooked tortillas can be tightly wrapped (separated with parchment/wax paper) and refrigerated for up to 3 days, or frozen for up to 4 months. Thaw at room temperature and refresh the tortillas in a hot skillet.

Flirting with Tacos (Braised Pork Tacos)

Makes 18 tacos

I met my husband at a roller rink. We became fast friends—the kind of friends who got a lot of questioning looks from other folks we knew. You know the look—that "Why aren't you guys together?" sort of look. Several years of being buddies passed before we admitted our feelings for each other—with words, that is. If he'd been paying more attention, he might have figured it out when I brought two carefully assembled tacos to him at the rink one night: homemade corn tortillas filled with slow-cooked spicy pork and topped with piles of pickled onions and cilantro. This recipe is still a hit in our house, many years (and a wedding ring) later.

1.36 kg / 3 pounds boneless pork shoulder, cut into 1-inch/2.5 cm cubes
Kosher salt and freshly ground black pepper
Neutral oil (such as canola or vegetable) for cooking the pork
340 g / 2 small red onions, diced
9 g / 1 tablespoon ground cumin
6 g / 2 teaspoons chili powder
4 g / 1½ teaspoons ground coriander
4 g / 1½ teaspoons chipotle chile powder
30 g / 6 cloves garlic, minced
40 g / 2 jalapeños, minced
One 795 g / 28-ounce can crushed tomatoes
565 g / 2½ cups beef broth
60 g / ¼ cup fresh lime juice

18 Corn Tortillas (page 209)

FOR SERVING (OPTIONAL)

Quick pickled onions (page 253)
Chopped fresh cilantro
Sour cream
Lime wedges for serving

1. Pat the meat dry with paper towels. In a large bowl, season the pork cubes with salt and pepper and toss well.

2. Heat a large Dutch oven over medium heat. Drizzle in enough oil to evenly cover the base of the pot. Working in batches, add the meat to the pot and sear on all sides until well browned. Remove each batch of meat as it is done and reserve in a bowl while you cook the next batch, adding a little more oil only if needed.

3. Add the onions, cumin, chili powder, coriander, and chile powder to the pot, stir well, and cook until the onions are translucent, 4 to 5 minutes. Add the garlic and jalapeños and cook until fragrant, about 1 minute. Add the tomatoes and broth, then return the meat to the pot and bring the mixture to a simmer over medium heat. Reduce the heat to low, cover the pot, and simmer until the meat is tender, about 2 hours. Remove the lid and continue to simmer, stirring occasionally, until the meat is falling-apart tender and the sauce has thickened and reduced, 40 minutes to 1 hour more.

4. Stir in the lime juice and season the braise with salt and pepper. If desired, use two forks or a hand mixer to shred the meat; I prefer to leave it in tender chunks.

5. Use tongs to fill the tortillas with the pork. Top with pickled onions, cilantro, and sour cream, if desired—and serve with lime wedges.

Flour Tortillas

Makes 12 tortillas

DIFFICULTY: **EASY**

I made my first-ever flour tortillas with butter, but since then, I've come to favor lard or beef tallow instead. I could honestly eat them all on their own, fresh, warm, and toasty, but they make fabulous quesadillas (see page 213). Try playing around with the Variations below, using vegetable juice to make spinach or carrot tortillas. And the XL size is perfect for wraps, burritos, and the Enchilada Pie on page 263.

360 g / 3 cups all-purpose flour, plus more if needed

3 g / ¾ teaspoon fine sea salt

113 g / ½ cup lard or beef tallow or 113 g / 4 ounces / 8 tablespoons unsalted butter, melted

170 g / ¾ cup room-temperature water (about 75°F/25°C)

1. In a large bowl, stir the flour and salt together. Drizzle the melted lard, tallow, or butter over the masa and stir with your hands or a fork until it's evenly distributed. Add the water to the bowl in a slow, steady stream, mixing with a spatula until the dough is smooth and uniform—it should be nice and pliable, not sticky. If it appears dry or crumbly, add more water 5 g / 1 teaspoon at a time to bring it together. If it appears too wet, add more flour 7 g / 1 tablespoon at a time as needed.

2. Turn the dough out and knead it until very smooth, 2 to 3 minutes. Wrap the dough tightly in plastic wrap and let rest at room temperature for 30 minutes.

3. Unwrap the dough and divide it into 12 equal pieces (about 50 g each). Gently round the dough (see page 104). Cover the dough with a towel and let rest for 15 minutes.

4. When you're ready to start making the tortillas line a basket, plate, or tortilla warmer with a clean kitchen towel. Heat a large skillet or griddle, preferably cast-iron, or a comal over medium heat until hot.

5. On a lightly floured surface, working with one piece of the dough at a time, roll out each piece into a round, rotating it frequently, about 7 inches/18 cm wide; transfer to a lightly floured work surface.

6. Meanwhile, as you continue to roll the tortillas, you can start to cook the first ones in the hot skillet (or on the griddle). Cook the tortillas, turning once, until they begin to blister and brown on both sides, 45 seconds to 1 minute per side. Place the cooked tortillas in the lined basket and wrap overhang over them as you continue to roll and cook the remaining tortillas (this is an important part of the process—the tortillas steam inside the towel and become even more wondrous).

7. When all the tortillas are cooked, serve immediately (or see the storing instructions).

Variations

XL FLOUR TORTILLAS **In step 3, divide the dough into 6 equal pieces (about 100 g each). In step 5, roll out the dough to 10 inches/ 25 cm wide.**

SPINACH TORTILLAS **Using an electric juicer or high-speed blender, process 113 g / 4 ounces raw spinach until liquid. If using** a blender, strain the liquid, discarding any fibrous solids. You should have about 125 g / ⅔ cup. Add warm water as necessary until you have 170 g / ¾ cup, then use this instead of the water to make the dough.

CARROT TORTILLAS Using an electric juicer or high-speed blender, process 275 g / 5 medium carrots, peeled, until liquid. If using a blender, strain the liquid, discarding any fibrous solids. You should have about 190 g / ¾ cup; if necessary, add warm water.

Make Ahead and Storage
The tortillas are best freshly made, but they can be tightly wrapped (stacked and separated with parchment or wax paper) and refrigerated for up to 3 days, or frozen for up to 4 months. Thaw at room temperature and refresh the tortillas by warming them in a hot skillet, just as you cooked them.

Avocado and Grilled Onion Quesadillas

I grew up in a semi-rural area, about thirty minutes from the nearest major city, but when I was thirteen, we moved into town. Suddenly I could walk everywhere—and before long, my favorite activity was taking myself out for lunch. One of my regular stops was a little restaurant on the main drag, La Parilla. Teenage me loved their chubby quesadilla Suiza, which was stuffed with Swiss cheese, avocado slices, and large chunks of grilled onion.

Use two regular flour tortillas or one XL tortilla. Slice up an avocado and squeeze lime juice generously over the slices. Heat a large skillet over medium heat, drop in a bit of unsalted butter, and melt it. Lay one small tortilla or the large tortilla in the skillet and reduce the heat to low. Top the tortilla with shredded cheese of your choice, a few slices of avocado, and a handful of Grilled Onions (page 26), then pile a bit more cheese on top. If using small tortillas, top with the second one and cook until the cheese begins to melt, then flip and cook on the other side, pressing gently with a spatula to flatten. If using a large tortilla, cook over low heat until the cheese melts a bit, then fold the tortilla in half and press with a spatula gently to flatten it before flipping. When the cheese is melted and the tortilla is crisp and toasty, remove the quesadilla from the pan and cut in half if using the large tortilla or into quarters if using the smaller ones to serve.

Italian Sub Bundt

Makes one 10-inch/25 cm sandwich; serves 6 to 8

DIFFICULTY: **EASY**

Bundt pans are an effortless way to make a cake or loaf of bread look like a million bucks. This recipe uses my Biscuit Monkey Bread dough (page 30) for a Bundt-shaped loaf. The dough bakes up crisp on the outside, and fluffy on the inside—perfect for cutting in half and filling with your favorite sub fillings. This is my Bundt version of an Italian sub, but you could build it as a turkey, roast beef, or club sandwich—whatever you crave. Slice the Bundt sandwich into wedges just before serving.

28 g / 2 tablespoons unsalted butter, at room temperature

Sesame seeds for sprinkling

1 recipe Biscuit Monkey Bread dough (page 30), prepared through step 5

30 g / 2 tablespoons extra virgin olive oil

15 g / 1 tablespoon red wine vinegar

3 g / 1 teaspoon dried Italian seasoning

Freshly ground black pepper

70 g / ⅓ cup mayonnaise

60 g / ¼ cup Dijon or whole-grain mustard

Pickly Peppers (page 97) as desired (optional)

170 g / 6 ounces deli sliced pepperoni

170 / 6 ounces deli sliced salami

170 g / 6 ounces deli sliced ham

170 g / 6 ounces deli sliced turkey

170 g / 6 ounces deli sliced provolone

60 g / 1 heaping cup shredded romaine or iceberg lettuce

80 to 160 g / 1 to 2 tomatoes, thinly sliced

170 g / 1 small red onion, thinly sliced

1. Grease a 10-cup/2.36 L Bundt pan generously with the butter. Sprinkle sesame seeds lightly over the base and sides, turning the pan as necessary.

2. Turn the dough out onto a lightly floured surface. Using your hands, gently press the dough to flatten it, aiming for a round shape, until the dough is roughly the diameter of the Bundt pan. Use your fingers to make a hole in the center of the dough for the center tube, then slide the dough into the pan. Use your fingertips to firmly press the dough into an even layer.

3. Cover the pan with greased plastic wrap and let rise until the dough is within ½ inch/1 cm of the top of the pan, 45 minutes to 1 hour and 15 minutes. Toward the end of the rise time, preheat the oven to 350°F/175°C with a rack in the center.

4. When the dough has risen, place the Bundt pan on a baking sheet and transfer to the oven. Bake until the bread reaches 200°F/95°C in the center, 35 to 40 minutes. Let cool for 10 minutes, then use a small offset spatula to gently release the edges of the bread from the pan and the center tube and unmold onto a wire rack to cool completely.

5. Use a serrated knife to halve the Bundt horizontally. Place the bottom half on a cutting board or serving platter and use your fingers to pull out most of the doughy center portion of the dough (you can use this bread to make Croutons, page 125, or for bread crumbs). I don't remove any dough from the top half, but if you like a less bready sandwich, you can.

6. In a small jar, combine the olive oil, vinegar, and Italian seasoning and shake together. Season with salt and pepper. Drizzle this mixture over the cut side of the top half of the loaf.

7. In a small bowl, stir the mayonnaise and mustard together. Spread this mixture on the bottom half of the bread. If using, top with a layer of pickly peppers. Then stack the meats and cheese onto the bread. Top with the lettuce, tomato slices, and onion slices and then the top of the bread.

8. Use a serrated knife to cut the sandwich into wedges just before serving (if desired, use toothpicks/skewers to secure the wedges for easier serving).

Make Ahead and Storage
The bread is best the same day it's baked, but it can be tightly wrapped and stored at room temperature for up to 24 hours before serving. The sandwich is best within a few hours after it's assembled.

Broccoli and Cheese Bierocks or Runzas

Makes 9 bierocks or runzas

DIFFICULTY: **MEDIUM**

These two pastries are essentially the same thing, though they go by different names. Originating from the Russian pirozhki, they are both made with soft doughs and a savory filling, such as ground beef and cabbage. The first is the bierock, which is popular in the United States in areas with large Russian and German populations, including Mennonite communities, and are usually referred to by that name in those areas. The term "runza" has origins in German, but the recipe known by this name today hails from Nebraska, and there's even a chain of restaurants named for it in the Midwest (not gonna lie—huge fan). Both bierocks and runzas can be made in a variety of shapes: round, triangle, half-moon, square, or rectangular. I consider them to be the same thing, but I usually use the name bierock for a round or crescent pastry and runza when referring to a rectangular pastry (more sub sandwich–shaped). Whatever you call them, think of them as like a very satisfying, yeast-risen version of an all-in-one sandwich. I've been known to "runza" leftovers like chicken vindaloo, beef stew, or veggie chili. Do as I do and turn your own leftovers into a filling, or see the Variations for ideas. Or try my sweet version for dessert!

DOUGH

290 g / 1¼ cups whole milk

600 g / 5 cups all-purpose flour

50 g / ¼ cup granulated sugar

10 g / 1 tablespoon instant dry yeast

6 g / 1½ teaspoons fine sea salt

56 g / 1 large egg, at room temperature

21 g / 1 large egg yolk, at room temperature

45 g / 1½ ounces / 3 tablespoons unsalted butter, at room temperature

FILLING AND FINISHING

270 g / 3 packed cups bite-size chopped broccoli

120 g / ½ cup Thick Béchamel (page 56)

200 g / 2 cups shredded sharp cheddar cheese (about 7 ounces)

Kosher salt and freshly ground black pepper

45 g / 3 tablespoons Dijon mustard

Egg wash (see page 7)

1. Make the dough: In a medium saucepan, heat the milk over medium-low heat until it reaches about 110°F/45°C. Remove from the heat.

2. In the bowl of a stand mixer fitted with the dough hook, mix the flour, sugar, yeast, and salt on low speed to combine. Add the warm milk, egg, egg yolk, and butter and mix for 4 minutes. Raise the speed to medium and mix until the dough is smooth, about 2 minutes more.

3. Transfer the dough to a lightly greased large bowl, cover with plastic wrap, and let rise until visibly puffy, 45 minutes to 1 hour and 15 minutes.

4. While the dough rises, blanch the broccoli: Bring a medium pot of salted water to a boil and prepare an ice bath in a medium bowl. Add the broccoli to the boiling water and cook for 1 minute. Drain in a colander, or use a slotted spoon to remove the broccoli from the boiling water, and transfer to the ice bath to stop the cooking.

(CONTINUES)

5. When the broccoli is well chilled, use the slotted spoon to transfer it to a medium bowl, draining it well as you lift it from the water. Add the béchamel and cheese and toss well to combine. Season with salt and pepper.

6. Turn the dough out and divide it into 9 equal pieces (about 120 g each). Gently round each piece of dough (see page 104) and place on a lightly floured work surface. Cover with a clean kitchen towel and rest for 15 minutes.

7. Shape and fill the dough: Line two baking sheets with parchment paper.

TO SHAPE THE DOUGH AS ROUND BIEROCKS: Working with one piece of the dough at a time, gently press each piece with your fingers to flatten it into a round about 6 inches/15 cm wide (or use a rolling pin, if you prefer). Spoon 5 g / 1 teaspoon of the mustard onto the center of the dough and use the back of the spoon to spread it evenly over the center. Scoop about 70 g / heaping ¼ cup of the filling onto the center of the dough. Fold the edges of the dough gently around the filling, pinching firmly to seal: Take care to seal the edges well—apply a little water to the dough with your finger to help seal it if necessary (you don't want them to leak in the oven). Turn the dough over, so the seam is on the bottom, and gently round the dough (see page 104). As you shape them, transfer the bierocks to the baking sheets, staggering the rows so there is space between them. Then use the palm of your hand to gently flatten each pastry.

TO SHAPE THE DOUGH AS RECTANGULAR RUNZAS: Working with one piece of dough at a time, gently press and stretch each piece with your fingers to flatten it into a rectangle about 4 x 5 inches/10 x 13 cm (use a rolling pin, if you prefer). Scoop about 70 g / heaping ¼ cup of the filling onto the center of the dough and shape it into a log. Bring the two longer

sides of the dough over toward each other, to encase the filling, and pinch the seam in the center firmly to seal. Do the same with the two shorter sides, fully enclosing the filling and pinching the dough well to seal the seam. Pinch the ends of the rectangle firmly to seal. As you shape them, transfer the runzas to the baking sheets, staggering the rows so there is space between them. Then use the palm of your hand to gently flatten each pastry.

8. Cover the shaped pastries with greased plastic wrap and let rise for 45 minutes to 1 hour, until the dough is lightly puffy. Toward the end of the rise time, preheat the oven to 350°F/175°C with the racks in the upper and lower thirds.

9. Uncover the pastries, and egg-wash the surface evenly. Bake until the pastries are evenly golden brown, 25 to 30 minutes.

10. Let the pastries cool for 5 to 10 minutes before serving warm.

Variations

CHEESEBURGER RUNZAS Omit the broccoli, mustard, and béchamel sauce and make the following filling: In a large skillet, heat 15 g / 1 tablespoon extra virgin olive oil and 14 g / 1 tablespoon unsalted butter over medium heat until the butter melts. Add 295 g / 2½ packed cups shredded cabbage and cook, stirring frequently, until it wilts, about 10 minutes. Add 325 g / 1 large sweet onion, thinly sliced, and cook until the vegetables are very tender, 8 to 10 minutes. Transfer the mixture to a medium bowl. Heat another 15 g / 1 tablespoon extra virgin olive oil in the same pan and add 340 g / 12 ounces ground beef, along with 9 g / 1 tablespoon onion powder, 15 g / 1 tablespoon Worcestershire sauce, 3 g / 1 teaspoon garlic powder, 3 g / 1 teaspoon smoked paprika, and salt and pepper to taste. Cook until the beef is evenly browned, 4 to 5 minutes, then add it to the bowl with the cabbage and cool for 10 minutes.

Fold the shredded cheddar cheese into the mixture. Shape and fill the dough as runzas, as in step 8, and let rise. Egg-wash and bake as directed.

VEGGIE CHILI RUNZAS Omit the broccoli, mustard, and béchamel sauce and use 500 g / 2 cups of your favorite veggie chili for the filling. Fold the cheese into the chili, if desired, or leave it out. Shape and fill the dough as runzas, as in step 8, and let rise. Egg-wash and bake as directed. This also works well with any thick stew or braise, vegetarian or not.

QUESO FUNDIDO BIEROCKS Omit the broccoli, béchamel sauce, and cheddar cheese (and salt and pepper) and make the following filling: Heat a large skillet over medium heat until hot. Crumble in 454 g / 16 ounces Mexican ground chorizo and cook until well browned, 4 to 5 minutes. Remove from the heat and cool completely, Then stir in 140 g / 1 bunch scallions, thinly sliced, and 3 cloves garlic, minced.

Finely dice 454 g / 16 ounces queso Oaxaca (or fresh mozzarella). Shape and fill the dough as bierocks, as in step 7, scooping 50 g / heaping ¼ cup of the cheese onto the center of each piece of dough and then dividing the chorizo mixture among them, spooning the meat mixture and any oil over the cheese. Let rise, egg-wash, and bake as directed.

SWEET-TOOTH BREAK

Caramel Apple Bierocks

You can also use any precooked fruit pie filling you like to make sweet bierocks. Omit the broccoli, béchamel sauce, and cheese (and salt and pepper) and make the following filling: In a medium pot, melt 14 g / 1 tablespoon unsalted butter over medium heat. Add 340 g / 12 ounces Cosmic Crisp, Honeycrisp, or Gala apples, cored and finely diced, and cook, stirring frequently, until the apples are well coated in the butter, about 1 minute.

Meanwhile, in a medium bowl, mix 70 g / ⅓ packed cup dark brown sugar, 4 g / 1½ teaspoons ground cinnamon, 1 g / ¼ teaspoon freshly grated nutmeg, and 2 g / ½ teaspoon fine sea salt to combine. Sprinkle this mixture over the apples and cook, stirring frequently, until the apples soften, 5 to 6 minutes. In a small bowl, whisk 24 g / 2 tablespoons granulated sugar and 14 g / 2 tablespoons all-purpose flour to combine and sprinkle over the apples. Cook, stirring constantly, until the juices thicken and fat bubbles break the surface, 3 to 5 minutes. Cool completely. Shape and fill the dough as bierocks, as in step 8. Let rise, egg-wash, and bake as directed.

CHAPTER 5

Pastries

BAKERY-LEVEL TREATS TO MAKE AT HOME

This chapter is filled with all the things I was most excited to learn about when I went to pastry school. The word "pastry" can be hugely overarching, and these recipes include a variety of my favorites from that category. In the pages that follow, you can learn to stretch a delicate strudel dough, perfectly proof a croissant, and nail a beautiful lofty soufflé. I often bake these treats when I want to impress, but I don't want you to be intimidated! While some of the recipes require time and a bit of patience, they can be incredibly satisfying. They are wonderful baking projects that are totally achievable at home—and be prepared for oohs and ahhs when you do so.

A Pep Talk

There are three doughs in this chapter I especially want folks to try. The first two, phyllo and strudel, are both paper-thin and perhaps dauntingly delicate, but I promise you, they are nothing to fear. The third dough is yeasted puff pastry, which relies on the classic technique known as *lamination* to produce the dough that brings us croissants, Danish, and more. I enjoy making these doughs at home, and I think you will too—especially because I tried to formulate my recipes to be as comprehensive and easy to understand as possible.

Shaping Filled Pastries

When you've got a dough and a filling, there are a lot of possibilities. Here are a few of my favorite filled pastry shapes, used in the recipes in this chapter. For all of them, you start by rolling out the dough according to the instructions in the recipe. Some recipes call for using a small amount of water, egg wash (page 7), or Egg White Wash

(page 7) to help seal the pastries. Even if a recipe doesn't specify doing this, you still can! Use your judgment, and add a little water or wash if the seal doesn't seem solid.

HALF-MOONS: Half-moons start by cutting rounds from rolled-out dough. The filling is spooned into the center and then the dough is folded in half, so the edges meet and the dough fully encases the filling.

UPRIGHT HALF-MOONS: For a different look, you can shape half-moons so that the seams face upward—this allows both sides to brown more evenly during baking.

TRIANGLES: Triangles—the classic turnover shape—start by cutting squares from the rolled-out dough. The filling is spooned into the center and then the dough is folded diagonally in half to make the triangle shape and encase the filling.

UPRIGHT TRIANGLES: Just like upright half-moons, you can make upright triangles. Start with a square cut out of the rolled-out dough. Spoon filling into the center, then bring all of the corners inward toward the center to encase the filling, making a pyramid-like shape.

SQUARES AND RECTANGLES: For these, start by cutting squares or rectangles from the rolled-out dough, then spoon the filling into the center and then fold the dough in half (fold rectangles crosswise in half) so that the edges line up and the filling is fully encased.

CIGARS AND RINGS: To make cigars, start by cutting rectangles out of the rolled-out dough. Spoon the filling onto one long side of the rectangle and roll the dough up around the filling to encase it. The cigars can be baked as is, or formed into ring shapes.

Overnight Proofing—Wake Up to Perfect Pastries

Yeasted puff pastry is a proofing triple whammy. Obtaining a proper proof is important for all yeasted doughs, to ensure that they achieve the ideal interior crumb structure. Proofing also takes longer with enriched doughs, and yeasted puff is about as enriched as it gets. In pastry school, we used a special proof box. We would load it at night, when the box would be cold—as cold as a refrigerator or, sometimes, a freezer. Overnight, the temperature in the box would be based on a particular schedule, so that the pastries would be proofed perfectly when we were ready to bake them the next morning. While I haven't had access to a beautiful proof box in years, I've hacked the method in my home kitchen.

After shaping pastries and placing them on your prepared baking sheets, cover the pans loosely with greased plastic wrap (loose is important, so as not to impede their rise).

Refrigerate the pastries for up to 10 hours. During this time, they will start to slowly rise. They may even reach the perfect proof in the fridge. If not, after you remove them in the morning, let them continue to rise at room temperature until proofed.

Note: The instructions for croissants (see page 239) include information on freezing shaped pastries. If you have opted to freeze your shaped pastries and want to use this overnight proofing method, place the frozen pastries on a parchment-lined baking sheet as directed above. Allow the pastries to thaw fully in the refrigerator (8 to 12 hours) before following the steps above.

Phyllo Dough

Makes 820 g/about 1¾ pounds

DIFFICULTY: **HARD**

Phyllo dough may not be currently filed under your "to-bake" list, but like most things, it's far better made from scratch. I am in awe of the professional phyllo makers of the world who can toss, stretch, and roll dough impressively thin with incredible ease. But this recipe doesn't require a master level of technique, especially not when you scale down the most intimidating factor—the size. Using smaller pieces of dough makes it easier to roll out the phyllo perfectly thin, even in a home kitchen.

The key to mixing phyllo is time, long enough to allow strong gluten strands to form that make the dough very strong and capable of being rolled very thin. This type of mixing is called intense mixing. Melted butter or oil is usually brushed over each piece of dough to help the dough crisp up evenly and adhere to the other pieces when stacked. I sometimes use flavored butters—like the Basting Butters on page 11 to make shattery, flaky crusts that work well for pies, tarts, and pastry preparations galore.

Making phyllo dough is a great baking project for a weekend afternoon. And you can store the sheets of the dough in the freezer, ready to bake with whenever!

510 g / 4¼ cups bread flour

4 g / 1 teaspoon fine sea salt

60 g / ¼ cup extra virgin olive oil

230 g / 1 cup water

15 g / 1 tablespoon white vinegar

Cornstarch for rolling

1. In the bowl of a stand mixer fitted with the dough hook, mix the flour and salt on low speed to combine, about 15 seconds. Add the olive oil and mix until the mixture has a mealy consistency. Mix in the water and vinegar, then continue to mix on low speed until the dough forms a ball around the dough hook, about 2 minutes. Raise the speed to medium and mix for 6 minutes. The dough should be smooth and not at all sticky.

2. Turn the dough out and divide into 8 equal pieces (about 100 g each). Wrap each piece tightly in plastic wrap and let rest at room temperature for 30 minutes.

3. Place a small sifter over a bowl and fill with cornstarch—you'll use this to sift over the dough and surface as you work. Lay a sheet of parchment paper next to your work surface. On the lightly cornstarched surface, start to roll out the dough. The point is to get the dough as thin as possible, so I rotate it frequently to help prevent it from sticking and dust both sides of the dough with cornstarch occasionally. When the dough is so thin that you can see the work surface through it, dust both sides well with cornstarch and gently transfer it the parchment paper, laying it flat on the paper, and cover with plastic wrap.

4. Repeat the process to roll out the remaining pieces, dusting each rolled out piece well on both sides with cornstarch and stacking them on top of each other (the cornstarch should

prevent the sheets of dough from sticking to one another, but if you're nervous, layer parchment paper between the pieces of dough); be sure to re-cover the stack each time you add a new sheet.

5. The dough is ready to use, or it can be stored. To store, remove the plastic wrap from the top of the dough stack, and place a piece of parchment paper on top. Gently roll up the dough in the paper into a log and tightly wrap in plastic wrap. Refrigerate or freeze; see Make Ahead and Storage.

Make Ahead and Storage
The dough can be refrigerated for up to 5 days or frozen for up to 1 month, rolled up and tightly wrapped in plastic wrap as directed in step 5.

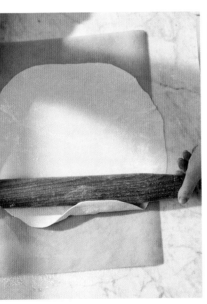 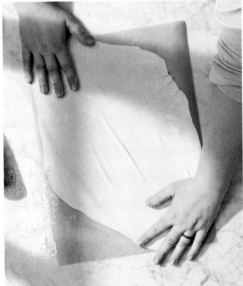 

Root Vegetable Pastilla

Makes one 9-inch/23 cm pie

DIFFICULTY: **HARD**

Pastilla is a delicious pie hailing from northern Africa, where it is made with warqa, or brick pastry. Paper-thin warqa is similar to my homemade phyllo, and that is what I use in this recipe. This vegetarian filling is heavily inspired by North African flavors, but veers a bit from a classic pastilla filling, which often features a meat or seafood base. Although this hearty pie is perfect for any time of year, it's especially good during cooler weather. It's undeniably impressive when you bring the tall pie to the table (it's great for dinner parties). This recipe is marked "Hard" because of the homemade phyllo crust, but if you want to use store-bought dough, it's actually a very easy one. The pastilla is a great way to pack a lot of vegetables into a single, sliceable beauty.

FILLING

115 g / ½ cup dry sherry or white wine

45 g / ⅓ cup dried apricots

50 g / ⅓ cup dried currants

454 g / 1 pound parsnips, peeled and chopped

340 g / 12 ounces carrots, peeled and chopped

340 g / 12 ounces celeriac, peeled and chopped

325 g / 1 large red onion, chopped

50 g / 5 scallions, chopped

70 g / ½ cup pine nuts

10 g / 2 cloves garlic

30 g / 2 tablespoons extra virgin olive oil

30 g / 2 tablespoons tomato paste

460 g / 2 cups chicken or vegetable broth

4 g / 1¼ teaspoons ras el hanout
  (see Resources)

2 g / ¾ teaspoon smoked paprika

Kosher salt and freshly ground black pepper

30 g / ¾ cup chopped fresh cilantro

Grated zest and juice of 1 lemon

PASTILLA

8 sheets Phyllo Dough (page 224)

113 g / 4 ounces / 8 tablespoons unsalted
  butter, melted

Egg wash (see page 7) for finishing

Flaky salt and freshly ground black pepper

1. Make the filling: In a small saucepan, bring the sherry (or wine) to a simmer. Place the dried fruits in a small heatproof bowl and pour the hot sherry over them. Let sit for 10 minutes.

2. Combine the parsnips, carrots, celeriac, onion, and scallions in the bowl of a food processor and pulse until coarsely chopped. Add the soaked fruits and sherry, pine nuts, and garlic and pulse until everything is finely chopped.

3. In a large pot, heat the olive oil over medium heat. Add the tomato paste and cook for 30 seconds, then add the broth and bring to a simmer. Stir in the ras el hanout and smoked paprika. Stir in the root vegetable mixture and cook, stirring frequently, until the broth has been almost entirely absorbed, 12 to 15 minutes.

4. Season the filling with salt and pepper and fold in the cilantro, lemon zest, and lemon juice. Transfer to a heatproof bowl and cool completely.

5. Make the pastilla: Preheat the oven to 375°F/190°C with a rack in the center. Grease

(CONTINUES)

a 9-inch/23 cm springform pan with nonstick spray and place on a baking sheet.

6. Lay out one piece of phyllo on a clean work surface; keep the remaining phyllo covered as you work so it won't dry out. Brush the phyllo all over with melted butter, then gently lay another piece on top, placing it slightly askew so that the edges of the sheets do not line up. Brush all over with butter and repeat the process until you've created a stack of 5 phyllo sheets. Brush the surface of the top sheet all over with butter.

7. Gently transfer the stack, centered as best you can, into the prepared springform pan, pressing it against the base and up the sides of the pan. Spoon the filling into the crust and spread in an even layer.

8. Transfer the pastilla to the oven and bake until the phyllo is deeply and evenly golden brown and very crisp, 1 hour to 1 hour and 15 minutes. If the top of the crust or the edges brown too quickly, tent the pastilla with foil for the remainder of bake time.

9. Let the pastilla rest in the pan for 5 minutes, then gently release the ring and serve warm, or let cool to room temperature.

Make Ahead and Storage
The filling can be made up to 3 days ahead and refrigerated in an airtight container until ready to use. The assembled pastilla can be tightly wrapped and refrigerated for up to 12 hours before baking.

Flavorful Finishes

Sweet baked goods are often finished with a sprinkling of sugar. While I like the sweetness it provides, it's really more about the textural gains for me—a caramelized crunch, a shattery, sugary crust that gives way to a flakier butter crust underneath. Savory stuff deserves the same consideration, and I have a few toppers I enlist to finish them with a little flair.

SEEDS OR SPICE BLENDS: Many savory baked items can be finished with sesame seeds, caraway seeds, or nigella seeds; onion, garlic, or shallot flakes; or seed/spice blends like Everything Seasoning (page 177). Other spices and dried herbs may be prone to burning during longer bake times, so choose your finisher carefully.

COARSE OR FLAKY SALT AND/OR FRESHLY GROUND BLACK PEPPER: These add a boost of flavor and a little texture too.

FINELY GRATED CHEESE: Firm cheeses that brown and crisp well make excellent pie crust finishers. A scant layer will provide a lightly salty contrast, while a hefty layer will be like a full-on cheese cracker combined with the crust.

Strudel Dough Handling and Shaping Tips

I was shocked to discover how truly easy strudel dough is to work with. Since it goes through an intense mixing time, it actually *wants* to stretch—it's literally made for it, and there's nothing to fear. My biggest piece of advice for strudel? Don't stress if the dough rips or tears. This will usually only happen when the dough is really thin, and once you roll up the strudel, you likely won't be able to see any evidence of the tear. See the tips below for more guidance.

- I stretch strudel dough out on my 2 x 4-foot/60 x 120 cm kitchen island, and I have excess dough when I do this, after trimming. A kitchen table or card table will also work well—any setup where you can get all the way around the dough to stretch it evenly in every direction. You may have more or less excess dough depending on the size of your work surface.

- I cover the work surface with a linen or oilcloth tablecloth, which helps give you a surface that's easy to shift and move as needed as you work. The dough will cling to the tablecloth but not stick to it, making it easier to manipulate the dough and stretch it as thin as possible. If the tablecloth has a pattern, it can serve as an indicator of when your dough has stretched thin enough—if you can clearly see the pattern through the dough, it's ready.

- Lightly oil your hands when stretching the dough. Start by stretching the dough a little like a pizza, though trying to keep it rectangular as you go. Once the dough is no longer easy to handle with your hands, lay it down on the covered table, and begin to stretch with the backs of your hands (see the recipe on page 230 for more details).

- When shaping the dough, exact dimensions aren't important—you can fill it and roll it at any size—but the thickness is. It should be very thin, thin enough to see through. If the dough is too thick (even ⅛ in/3 mm is too thick), it will be tough and unpleasant to eat.

- Save any excess dough. Knead it into a ball, let it rest for at least 4 hours, and re-stretch it to make another strudel.

- The final strudel will vary in length depending on the size you stretch the dough to. I usually place the strudel diagonally across the baking sheet, but you can also shape it into a U or S shape if necessary.

Kale and Leek Strudel

Makes 1 large strudel

DIFFICULTY: **MEDIUM**

When we lost both my maternal grandparents within about a year, my mom spent a long time looking through their collection of old photos. My oldest brother, a photographer, lovingly restored some of the older images, bringing to life images of, among others, my toweringly tall grandpa Mac in his woodworking shop and my tiny great-grandma Nagy, wearing a smocky sort of apron, next to a large table covered in strudel dough—juicy cherries spread over the surface of the paper-thin strudel dough. My mom told me that while she had watched her grandma make strudel many times, she was never able to get a full recipe. I worked on my dough recipe for a long time afterward, as well as many sweet and savory variations on strudel, including this creamy kale and leek–filled beauty.

Along the way, I discovered that strudel is one of those impressive creations that's actually a lot easier than you may think. The intense mixing creates an extremely elastic gluten structure. After a nice long rest, the stretching is so fun, and much less scary than it may seem. Strudel has become one of my favorite things to bake, and I think it's a perfect baking project to tackle (especially with a friend or family member) during a long winter.

DOUGH (MAKES 875 G/ABOUT 2 POUNDS)

480 g / 4 cups bread flour

3 g / ¾ teaspoon fine sea salt

288 g / 1¼ cups warm water (about 110°F/45°C)

85 g / 4 large egg yolks

15 g / 1 tablespoon neutral oil (such as canola or vegetable), plus more for greasing the bowl

7 g / 1½ teaspoons white vinegar

FILLING

45 g / 1½ ounces / 3 tablespoons unsalted butter

150 g / 1 large leek, white and light green parts only, split lengthwise and thinly sliced

20 g / 4 cloves garlic, minced

About 290 g / 2 bunches lacinato kale or 1 large bunch curly kale, torn into bite-size pieces

6 g / 1 teaspoon kosher salt

2 g / ½ teaspoon freshly ground black pepper

170 g / 6 ounces cream cheese, at room temperature

115 g / ½ cup sour cream

226 g / 1⅓ cups walnuts, toasted

50 g / ½ cup finely grated Parmesan cheese

10 g / ¼ cup minced fresh chives

ASSEMBLY

113 g / 4 ounces / 8 tablespoons unsalted butter, melted

80 g / ⅔ cup fine bread crumbs

3 g / 1 teaspoon garlic powder or Fried Garlic Powder (page 159; optional)

2 g / ½ teaspoon freshly ground black pepper

Freshly grated Parmesan cheese for sprinkling

1. Make the dough: In the bowl of a stand mixer fitted with the dough hook, mix the flour and salt on low speed to combine, about 15 seconds.

2. In a large liquid measuring cup, whisk the water, egg yolks, oil, and vinegar to combine. Add to the mixer bowl and mix on low speed

(CONTINUES)

until the dough starts to come together, about 1 minute. Then continue to mix on low speed for about 10 minutes longer. The dough should have formed a ball around the dough hook and appear relatively smooth. It should be just slightly tacky, not sticky, but not dry—if it seems dry, add more water 15 g / 1 tablespoon at a time, mixing for 1 minute before checking the consistency again.

3. Raise the mixer speed to medium and mix for about 10 minutes longer, until the dough is very light in color and smooth. Lightly oil a medium bowl, place the dough in it, and turn the dough over a few times to coat it lightly with oil. Cover the bowl with plastic wrap and refrigerate overnight.

4. The next day, make the filling: In a large skillet, melt the butter over medium heat. Add the leeks and cook until tender, 3 to 4 minutes. Add the garlic and cook until fragrant, about 1 minute. Add the kale a few handfuls at a time, cooking until each addition wilts a bit before adding more. Once it's all been added, continue to cook until the kale is fully wilted, 6 to 8 minutes. Season with the salt and pepper.

5. Transfer the mixture to a food processor, add the cream cheese, sour cream, walnuts, Parmesan, and chives, and process until a fairly smooth mixture forms.

6. Prepare the bread crumbs: In a medium skillet, melt 28 g / 1 ounce / 2 tablespoons of the butter over medium heat. Add the bread crumbs, garlic powder, if using, and pepper and toast, stirring constantly, until the crumbs are golden brown and fragrant, 2 to 3 minutes. Transfer to a bowl.

7. Assemble the strudel: Cover a large work surface with a tablecloth—oilcloth or linen work especially well. A folding card table, kitchen table, island, or any surface you can walk all the way around works best and makes stretching easier).

8. Remove the dough from the refrigerator and lightly oil your hands. The dough should feel lightly tacky but not sticky, and it should stretch easily. Start by stretching the dough a little like a pizza, trying to keep it rectangular as you work. Once the dough is no longer easy to handle, lay it down on the covered table.

9. Use the backs of your hands (closed fists if you have long nails) to stretch the dough: Put your hands under the dough at one corner and gently work them outward, toward the edge of the table. Continue to do this bit by bit, working around the dough, to slowly stretch it out. The goal is to get it so thin you can see through it (if your tablecloth has a pattern, that can be a good guideline). Don't be alarmed if the dough tears (you'll be rolling it up, and the tears will ultimately be hidden inside), but the dough is very strong, so you should be able to stretch it without major tearing. Once the dough is stretched to the edges of the table, use your fingers to stretch it gently at the edges to make sure they aren't too thick.

10. Drizzle the dough with about three-quarters of the remaining melted butter (brushing it on could tear the dough, so be gentle if you attempt that). Sprinkle the surface with the toasted bread crumbs. Dollop the filling all over the surface, then gently spread it into a fairly even layer (it doesn't need to be perfect).

11. Starting from one of the shorter sides, gently pick up the dough and roll it up into a tight spiral. Use the tablecloth to help you—the less you handle the dough, the less likely you are to rip it.

12. Use scissors to cut any excess dough away at the ends of the strudel. Lift up the rolled strudel and place it diagonally on a baking sheet,

seam side down; if it's too long to fit in the pan, you can form it into an S or U shape.

13. Preheat the oven to 400°F/205°C with a rack in the center.

14. Brush the strudel with the remaining melted butter and sprinkle with Parmesan. Bake until the strudel is deeply golden brown, 35 to 40 minutes; rotate the pan halfway through the bake time for more even browning.

15. Remove the strudel from the oven and let cool for at least 15 minutes before slicing and serving.

Variations

SPINACH AND GOAT CHEESE STRUDEL

Replace the kale with 567 g / 20 ounces spinach leaves. Replace the cream cheese with an equal amount of goat cheese, the walnuts with raw almonds, and the chives with basil. Assemble and bake as directed.

SWEET-TOOTH BREAK

Apple Butter–Pecan Strudel

Prepare the strudel dough and let rest overnight, as directed. Make the candied pecans: In a medium bowl, whisk 21 g / 1 large egg white, 15 g / 1 tablespoon heavy cream, and 2 g / ½ teaspoon vanilla extract to combine. Add 2 cups (250 g) raw pecan halves and toss until evenly coated, then spread in an even layer on a parchment-lined baking sheet. In a small bowl, mix 53 g / ¼ packed cup dark brown sugar, 50 g / ¼ cup granulated sugar, 3 g / 1 teaspoon ground cinnamon, and 3 g / ¾ teaspoon fine sea salt to combine. Sprinkle this over the pecans and toss to coat. Bake in a 300°F/150°C oven for 12 minutes, then stir the pecans well, spread back into an even layer, and bake for 12 minutes more. Continue this process, stirring and tossing the pecans every 12 minutes, for about 48 minutes total. The sugar will crystallize and make a firm crust on the exterior of the pecans. Cool completely, then coarsely chop.

To assemble the strudel, stretch the dough as directed in steps 7 through 9. Melt 85 g / 3 ounces / 6 tablespoons unsalted butter and drizzle about half of it over the stretched dough. Sprinkle half of the pecans over the dough, then dollop 480 g / 2 cups apple butter over the surface. Sprinkle the remaining pecans on top. Roll and trim as directed in steps 11 and 12. Brush the strudel with the remaining butter, sprinkle with turbinado sugar, and bake as directed, for 44 to 48 minutes.

Lamination

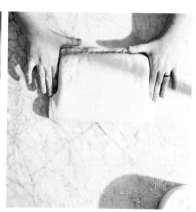

Lamination is a baking technique that produces incredibly flaky, layered pastries. In this method, butter is formed into a block and "locked" inside the dough. The dough is rolled out and undergoes a series of folds, or "turns," which require chilling in between to relax the dough and keep things at the ideal temperature. When the dough hits the oven heat, the moisture in the butter quickly evaporates, creating steam, which pushes the dough up to create the beautiful, delicate layers. The key is to keep the dough chilled but still pliable as you work with it for the most even layers. Before each step, the dough is rolled out into a rectangle about ½ inch/1 cm thick, and it often requires chilling and more rest before continuing. Alternating what are called 3- and 4-folds for a total of four times will create the ideal number of layers.

STEP 1: **Perform a 4-fold: Place the rectangle of dough so that one of the longer sides of is facing you. Fold the left side three-quarters of the way over the dough, then fold the right side one quarter of the way over the dough so it meets the left edge (like an open book with an off-center spine). Then fold the larger side over the smaller side (essentially folding the dough in half). Wrap the dough and refrigerate for 15 to 30 minutes.**

  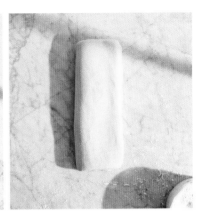

STEP 2: Perform a 3-fold: Place the dough so that one of the longer sides of the rectangle is facing you. Fold the left side one-third of the way over the dough. Do the same with the right side, so it is resting on top of the rest of the dough (like the way you'd fold a piece of paper to fit into a business envelope). Wrap and refrigerate for 15 to 30 minutes.

STEP 3: Complete another 4-fold, then wrap the dough and refrigerate for 15 to 30 minutes.

STEP 4: Complete another 3-fold, wrap the dough, and refrigerate for 8 to 12 hours.

SHAPING: After the dough has rested, it can be divided, rolled, and shaped. For more on shaping pastries made with laminated dough, see page 246.

Note: You can use simpler forms of lamination in other recipes that still offer a hugely flaky payoff. For example, I use simple folds in my Buttermilk Biscuits (page 29) and All-Buttah Pie Dough (page 319) to create flakier doughs. For more, see page 7.

Yeasted Puff Pastry Dough

Makes about 3 ⅔ pounds/1.66 kg

DIFFICULTY: HARD

Yeasted puff pastry is used to make croissants and Danish, among other treats. Puff pastry can feel intimidating (especially compared to its simpler cousin, Rough Puff Pastry (page 267), and it is a long process, but wonderfully worthwhile. The dough gains its signature layers through the process called lamination (see page 234). Be sure to allow the dough enough time to rest and relax at each stage, as this both makes it easier to roll and ensures that the dough and the butter inside it are at the ideal temperature: chilled but pliable. This combination ensures easy handling, even layering, and the coveted honeycomb interior. After you've mastered the classic dough, try using a flavorful compound butter to make your butter block (see the Variations). In addition to the Ham and Cheese Croissants (page 238) and Creamed Spinach Danish (page 243) or French Onion Danish (page 243), you can use this dough in other creative ways—see, for example, Croissant Breakfast Pie (page 241), which uses it for a deliciously decadent piecrust.

DOUGH

383 g / 1⅔ cups whole milk

570 g / 4¾ cups bread flour

66 g / ⅓ cup granulated sugar

6 g / 1½ teaspoons fine sea salt

7 g / 2¼ teaspoons instant dry yeast

70 g / 2½ ounces / 5 tablespoons unsalted butter, at room temperature

BUTTER BLOCK

454 g / 1 pound unsalted butter, at room temperature

80 g / ⅔ cup bread flour

1. Make the dough: In a medium saucepan, heat the milk over medium heat to about 85°F/30°C.

2. Meanwhile, in the bowl of a stand mixer fitted with the dough hook, mix the flour, sugar, salt, yeast, and butter on low speed until the butter is broken up, 1 to 2 minutes.

3. Add the warm milk to the flour mixture and mix on low speed for 3 minutes, then beat on medium-high speed for 3 more minutes, until the dough is fairly smooth. Transfer the dough to a lightly greased large bowl, cover the bowl with plastic wrap, and let rise in the refrigerator for 10 to 12 hours (overnight).

4. When you're ready to laminate the dough, make the butter block: In a medium bowl, using a wooden spoon, or in the bowl of a stand mixer, using the paddle attachment, mix the butter and flour together until well combined.

5. Lay a 12 x 15-inch/30 x 38 cm sheet of parchment on your work surface, with one of the shorter sides closest to you. Dollop the butter mixture on the lower half of the parchment and use a small offset spatula to spread it into a rectangle 6 x 9 inches/15 x 23 cm and about ½ in/1 cm thick. Use the blade of the spatula to help keep the edges as squared-off as possible. Fold the top half of the parchment over the butter block so it's completely encased. Place on a baking sheet and transfer to the refrigerator to chill until firm but still pliable (about 65 to 70°F/18 to 21°C).

6. On a lightly floured surface, roll out the chilled dough to a rectangle about 10 x 12-inches/ 25 x 30 cm. If necessary, turn the dough so that one of the shorter sides is facing you. Peel the

paper back from the top of the butter block, leaving it on the paper so you can use it to help you to guide it onto the dough, and position the butter block on the dough so there is about a ½-inch/1 cm margin around the base and right and left sides of the block. Gently fold the dough down over the butter block, fully encasing it. Firmly pinch the edges of the dough around the butter block to seal, then fold the excess dough underneath itself to create a package of dough about 6 x 10 inches/ 15 x 25 cm. If the dough or butter feels at all soft or sticky, refrigerate it for 10 to 30 minutes before continuing. Otherwise, proceed with the first fold.

7. On a lightly floured surface, roll out the dough to a rectangle about 13 x 18 inches/33 x 45 cm and about ½ inch/1 cm thick. If you're having a hard time rolling out the dough, it may be too cold—let it soften at room temperature for a few minutes before proceeding. Or, if the dough is squishy or soft, refrigerate it briefly before proceeding.

8. Perform the first fold (a 4-fold): Position the dough so that one of the longer sides is facing you. Fold the left side about three-quarters of the way over the dough. Fold the right side one quarter of the way over the dough so it meets the left edge. The dough will now look somewhat like an open book with an off-center spine. Fold the larger half over the smaller half. Cover the dough with plastic wrap and refrigerate for 15 to 30 minutes.

9. Perform the second fold (a 3-fold): On the lightly floured surface, roll out the dough to about 13 x 18 inches/33 x 45 cm. Position the dough so that one of the longer sides is facing you. Fold the left side one-third of the way over the dough. Then fold the right side one-third of the way so that it is resting on the rest of the dough (like the way you'd fold a piece of paper to fit into a business envelope). Cover the dough with plastic wrap and refrigerate for 15 to 30 minutes.

10. Perform the third fold: Repeat steps 7 and 8.

11. Perform the final fold: Repeat step 9. Cover the dough tightly with plastic wrap and refrigerate for 8 to 12 hours before using.

Variation

CHIVE-COMPOUND BUTTER YEASTED PUFF PASTRY Prepare the butter block in the food processor: Start by processing 170 g / 6 ounces (about 1 large or 2 medium bunches) chives until coarsely chopped. Add the butter and process until the mixture is well combined and fairly smooth, scraping the bowl a few times as needed. Increase the flour to 120 g / 1 cup, add it to the food processor, and mix to combine before proceeding as directed. The chive butter block may be softer at room temperature than a regular butter block and firmer when well chilled because it is slightly higher in moisture—take care to maintain the correct working temperature, or the dough may be more difficult to work with.

Make Ahead and Storage
The puff pastry should be used after the recommended chill/ rest time. (Shaped yeasted puff pastry items, like croissants, can be frozen.)

Ham and Cheese Croissants

Makes 10 croissants

DIFFICULTY: **HARD**

Croissants may feel like an impossible baking project, but while making them is time-consuming, it's an incredibly rewarding experience. Classic croissants are cut into a triangle shape, but filled croissants like these are easier, cut as rectangles and rolled into fat log shapes. My major piece of advice for croissants is that they will probably take longer to rise than you think. If you rush the proofing, you won't have the coveted "honeycomb" texture inside the croissants. Allow plenty of time, and remember, the cooler the room, the longer rising will take!

One of the best things about this recipe is that you can freeze the croissants after shaping. Frozen croissants thaw and start to slowly rise in the refrigerator overnight—meaning you can put in all that prep work in one weekend, then benefit with freshly baked pastries for mornings to come!

1 recipe Yeasted Puff Pastry Dough (page 236), chilled overnight as directed

120 g / ½ cup whole-grain mustard

About 90 g / 10 slices deli ham

140 g / 5 ounces Gruyère cheese, thinly sliced

Egg wash (see page 7) for finishing

Sesame seeds for sprinkling

1. Divide the dough into 2 equal pieces (about 830 g each) and wrap and refrigerate one piece.

2. On a lightly floured surface, roll out the other piece of dough into a rectangle 8 x 20 inches/20 x 50 cm. Use a pastry wheel to cut the dough crosswise into 5 equal rectangles (each 4 inches/10 cm wide). One at a time, gently stretch each piece of dough to elongate it slightly.

3. Line two baking sheets with parchment paper. Spread 15 g / 1 tablespoon of the mustard in an even layer over the dough and place a slice of ham and 14 g / ½ ounce of the cheese on top. Roll up the dough into a fat log. Repeat with the remaining rectangles of dough.

4. Transfer the croissants, seam side down, to one of the prepared baking sheets, leaving at least 3 inches/8 cm between them. (If you're freezing the croissants for later, you can place them closer together, with just about a ¼ inch/6 cm between them.) Press them down gently to flatten the seams against the baking sheet.

5. Repeat with the remaining dough and filling. (To freeze the croissants, cover the tray and put in the freezer until the croissants are fully frozen, then transfer to zip-top freezer bags or plastic storage containers and freeze for up to 2 months.)

6. Cover the croissants loosely with greased plastic wrap and let rise until nearly doubled in size. The time this will take can vary dramatically, from as little as 2 hours in a warm environment to up to 6 hours (or more) if it's colder. To see if the dough is properly proofed, gently press a finger into the surface of a croissant: It should leave an imprint that slowly starts to spring back. If it won't hold an imprint, it needs more time. Toward the end of the rise

(CONTINUES)

238

Make Ahead and Storage
The croissants can be shaped ahead and frozen before
baking (see step 5). To bake frozen croissants, arrange
them on a parchment-lined baking sheet with at least
2 inches/5 cm between them. Cover loosely with greased
plastic wrap and let thaw in the refrigerator overnight
(8 to 12 hours). When the croissants are fully thawed, allow
to rise as directed in step 6 and bake as directed. The baked
croissants are best the same day they are made. Store
leftovers in an airtight container at room temperature.

time, preheat the oven to 375°F/190°C with the racks in the upper and lower thirds.

7. Brush the croissants all over with egg wash and sprinkle with sesame seeds. Bake until evenly golden brown, 28 to 32 minutes; they should have an internal temperature of at least 200°F/95°C in the thickest part. If the croissants start to brown too much before they reach the desired internal temperature, tent them with foil and/or lower the oven temperature to 350°F/175°C. Let cool for at least 5 minutes before serving.

Variations

MINI CLASSIC CROISSANTS Use ½ recipe Yeasted Puff Pastry Dough and divide it into 2 equal pieces (about 415 g each); wrap and refrigerate one while you work with the other. On a lightly floured surface, roll out the dough into a rectangle 5 x 20 inches/ 13 x 50 cm. Use a knife or a pastry wheel to cut the rectangle of dough crosswise into 8 triangles, each with a 1¾-inch-/4.5 cm wide base. Working with one triangle at a time, gently stretch it to elongate it, then roll up into a crescent shape, starting from the wider end. Place the shaped croissants seam side down on a parchment-lined baking sheet, leaving 1½ inches/5 cm between them. Repeat with the second piece of dough. Cover loosely with greased plastic wrap and let rise until noticeably puffy, 1 to 2 hours. Egg-wash the croissants and bake at 375°F/190°C for 25 to 30 minutes, until they are deeply golden brown and have an internal temperature of at least 200°F/95°C in the thickest part.

240

Croissant Breakfast Pie

Makes one 9-inch/23 cm pie

DIFFICULTY: **HARD**

I love a bacon, egg, and cheese sandwich on a flaky croissant so much that I wanted to pie-ify it. For this recipe, yeasted puff pastry is baked into a shattery, buttery crust. All the components of the sandwich are transformed into a creamy custard filling, and more of the dough is formed into tiny croissant puffs to garnish the pie. If you want to do something even fancier, roll out and cut the scrap dough into triangles and shape and bake as mini croissants (see page 240), then use them to decorate the top of the pie after baking or serve separately.

½ **recipe Yeasted Puff Pastry Dough (page 236), chilled overnight as directed**

125 g / 1¼ **cups shredded Gruyère cheese**

570 g / 10 **large eggs**

345 g / 1½ **cups whole milk**

6 g / 1 **teaspoon kosher salt**

2 g / ½ **teaspoon freshly ground black pepper**

80 g / 1 **cup diced cooked bacon (about 10 strips)**

50 g / 5 **scallions, thinly sliced**

Egg wash (see page 7) for finishing

1. Make the crust: Divide the dough into 2 equal pieces (about 415 g each); wrap one piece in plastic wrap and refrigerate.

2. On a lightly floured surface, roll out the other piece of dough ¼ inch/6 mm thick. Use the rolling pin to gently transfer it to a 12-inch/30 cm cast-iron or other ovenproof skillet, unfurling it into the center. Gently press the crust over the base and sides of the skillet. Use scissors to trim the excess dough to about a ½-inch/1 cm overhang (save the dough scraps to make

the croissant toppers or mini croissants), then tuck the overhang under itself all the way around the edges.

3. Cover the dough loosely with lightly greased plastic wrap and refrigerate for 2 hours. Toward the end of the chill time, preheat the oven to 375°F/190°C with the racks in the upper and lower thirds.

4. Cut a piece of parchment paper a little larger than the skillet and place it over the dough. Fill with pie weights to come to the top edge of the crust.

5. Transfer the crust to the lower oven rack and bake until it is starting to brown and set, 22 to 26 minutes. Remove the paper and pie weights and use a fork or the tip of a paring knife to poke holes all over the crust, then return to the oven and bake for 8 to 10 minutes more, until lightly golden brown. Remove from the oven, sprinkle the cheese evenly over the base of the crust, and cool to room temperature.

6. Meanwhile, make the croissant toppers: On a lightly floured surface, roll out the second piece of dough to ¼ inch/6 mm thick. Use a pastry wheel to cut the dough into 1-inch-/2.5 cm wide strips, then cut the strips crosswise into 1-inch/2.5 cm squares. Transfer the squares to a parchment-lined baking sheet (it's okay if some are touching) and let rise until visibly puffy, 45 minutes to 1 hour.

7. Assemble and bake the pie: In a large bowl, whisk the eggs, milk, salt, and pepper to combine. Spread the bacon and scallions in an even layer in the cooled crust, then pour the egg

(CONTINUES)

241

mixture on top. Transfer the pie to the lower oven rack and bake until the crust is deeply golden brown and the custard is set around the edges but still slightly jiggly in the center, 35 to 40 minutes. Let cool for about 15 minutes.

8. Meanwhile, egg-wash the croissant toppers and transfer the pan to the upper oven rack. Bake until deeply golden brown, 15 to 18 minutes.

9. Break up the croissant toppers to separate any pieces that are stuck together, and pile them on top of the warm pie. Slice and serve warm.

Note: Instead of forming the toppers as squares, you can skip step 6 and shape the scrap dough into Mini Classic Croissants (page 240); see the headnote.

Make Ahead and Storage
The pie is best the same day it's baked.

Creamed Spinach Danish

Makes 9 Danish

DIFFICULTY: **HARD**

This recipe was inspired by my friend Evan. We baked our way through pastry school together, a time marked by a plethora of warm, flaky pastries around just about every corner, and it bonded us for life. Fast-forward to adulthood after many months of not seeing each other, when we sat down at a diner one morning for breakfast. She ordered a fairly standard breakfast, but with a side of creamed spinach. Unfortunately, the diner didn't have creamed spinach, but a craving was born, and I was inspired to create a crave-worthy breakfast pastry filled with creamy spinach with that morning in mind.

These are a beautiful savory Danish boasting a rich veggie filling atop layers of flaky, buttery pastry. If you like, use a full batch of the pastry and try one of the Variations below. Depending on the shape you make the Danish, you may have a little extra filling, but it's delicious on toast—run it under the broiler until it bubbles and browns!

FILLING

42 g / 1½ ounces / 3 tablespoons unsalted butter

170 g / 6 ounces fresh spinach (or frozen, thawed and squeezed well)

110 g / ½ medium sweet onion, minced

10 g / 2 cloves garlic, minced

7 g / 1 tablespoon all-purpose flour

58 g / ¼ cup whole milk

60 g / ¼ cup heavy cream

56 g / 2 ounces cream cheese, at room temperature

Kosher salt and freshly ground white or black pepper

Dash of freshly grated nutmeg

DANISH

½ recipe Yeasted Puff Pastry Dough (page 236), chilled overnight as directed

Egg wash (see page 7) for finishing

Finely grated Parmesan cheese for sprinkling

1. Prepare the filling: In a large skillet, melt 14 g / 1 tablespoon of the butter over medium-low heat. Add the spinach in batches, letting each batch wilt before adding more, then cook until all the spinach is fully wilted, 3 to 4 minutes (if using frozen spinach, cook just until well coated with butter, 30 seconds to 1 minute). Transfer the spinach to a bowl and set aside.

2. Add the remaining 28 g / 1 ounce / 2 tablespoons butter to the pan and let it melt. Add the onion and cook until tender, 4 to 5 minutes. Add the garlic and cook until fragrant, about 1 minute.

3. Sprinkle the flour evenly over the onions and stir until well combined, then cook, stirring constantly, for 1 minute. Gradually add the milk and cream, whisking well to combine. Bring the mixture to a simmer, whisking occasionally, until the mixture thickens. Stir in the spinach until well combined and remove from the heat.

4. Cut the cream cheese into pieces and stir into the spinach mixture until fully combined. Season to taste with salt, pepper, and the nutmeg. Set aside to cool completely.

(CONTINUES)

French Onion
Danish (page 245)

Creamed
Spinach Danish

5. On a lightly floured surface, roll out the dough into a square slightly largely than 12 x 12 inches/30 x 30 cm. Use a pastry wheel to trim the excess dough to make an even 12-inch/30 cm square. Cut the dough into 9 squares: First cut it into three 4-inch-/10 cm wide strips, then cut the strips crosswise into 4-inch/10 cm squares.

6. Shape the Danish as desired (see page 246) and transfer to two parchment-lined baking sheets, staggering the pastries so they are evenly spaced. Cover loosely with a kitchen towel or greased plastic wrap and let rise until nearly doubled in size. The time this will take can vary, from as little as 1 hour in a warm environment to up to 4 hours or more if it's colder. To see if the dough is properly proofed, gently press a finger into the surface: It should leave an imprint that slowly starts to spring back. Toward the end of the rise time, preheat the oven to 375°F/190°C with the racks in the upper and lower thirds.

7. Fill and bake the Danish: Fill each piece of dough with about 30 g / 2 tablespoons of the spinach filling. Brush the exposed dough all over with egg wash and sprinkle with Parmesan. Bake the Danish until evenly golden brown, 25 to 30 minutes; they should have an internal temperature of at least 200°F/95°C in the thickest part. If the Danish start to brown too much, tent them with foil and/or lower the bake temperature to 350°F/175°C. Cool for at least 5 minutes before serving.

Variation

FRENCH ONION DANISH **Omit the spinach filling. Make a batch of Caramelized Onions (page 26), increasing the amount of onions to 920 g / 4 large sweet onions. In step 7, fill each Danish with 40 g / 2 heaping tablespoons of the onion filling and top with 25 g / ¼ cup shredded Gruyère cheese (you can keep the Parmesan for an extra-cheesy finish). Bake as directed.**

SWEET-TOOTH BREAK

Lemon Cheesecake Danish

Omit the spinach filling and prepare the following mixture: In the bowl of a stand mixer fitted with the paddle attachment, mix 226 g / 7 ounces cream cheese, 56 g / ½ cup powdered sugar, and the grated zest of 1 lemon until light and fluffy. Add 21 g / 1 large egg yolk and 5 g / 1 teaspoon vanilla extract and mix well. In step 7, scoop 40 g / 2 heaping tablespoons of this filling into the center of each Danish. Top each one with 15 g / 1 tablespoon coarse graham cracker crumbs. Bake as directed.

Make Ahead and Storage
The Danish can be assembled ahead and frozen as directed for Ham and Cheese Croissants (page 238). The baked Danish are best the same day they are made.

Shaping Danish

There are lots of ways to shape Danish, but here are four of my favorites for when I want to make sure there's plenty of filling tucked inside.

Classic Turnovers

Scoop the filling toward one corner of each square, then fold the dough in half to form a triangle. Crimp with your fingers or the tines of a fork to seal.

Simple Squares

Use a 3-inch/8 cm round cookie cutter to lightly score the center portion of each square of dough and then scoop the filling on the center portion. The pastry on the outside will rise higher than the centers.

Fancy Squares

Cut ½-inch-/1 cm wide strips of dough from scrap pieces. Prepare simple squares as above and use the strips to form a "wall" on the outside edges of each one—egg-wash the edges of the squares before adding the walls so they will adhere. The walls will rise even higher.

Fancy-Pants Twists

Use a paring knife or pastry wheel to make 4 cuts in each square of dough (see photo). Gently fold one of the cut portions over to the other side of the dough and press firmly, or use egg wash (see page 7) to help the dough adhere. Repeat all around. Scoop the filling into the centers.

Sour Cream and Onion Knishes

Makes 9 knishes
DIFFICULTY: **MEDIUM**

On my mom's first trip to New York City, she had her sights set on a warm, fresh knish. I've since hunted down some of the best in the city and try to pick up some for her whenever she visits. My homemade version is, admittedly, not your bubbe's knish, but my mom has certified it. And be sure to try the Twice-Baked Potato Knish variation below, inspired by one of her recipes.

DOUGH

400 g / 3⅓ cups all-purpose flour

75 g / ⅓ cup vegetable oil

80 g / ⅓ cup room-temperature water (about 75°F/25°C)

56 g / 2 ounces / 4 tablespoons unsalted butter, melted

113 g / 2 large eggs, at room temperature

21 g / 1 large egg yolk, at room temperature

7 g / 1¼ teaspoons baking powder

1 g / ½ teaspoon fine sea salt

FILLING

454 g / 1 pound russet potatoes, peeled and diced

70 g / 2½ ounces / 5 tablespoons unsalted butter, at room temperature

110 g / ½ medium sweet onion, minced

56 g / 2 ounces cream cheese, at room temperature

115 g / ½ cup sour cream

20 g / ½ cup minced fresh chives

10 g / 2 teaspoons malt vinegar

5 g / 1¼ teaspoons fine sea salt

2 g / ½ teaspoon freshly ground black pepper

Egg wash (see page 7) for finishing

1. Make the dough: In the bowl of a stand mixer fitted with the paddle attachment, mix the flour, oil, water, melted butter, eggs, egg yolk, baking powder, and salt at medium speed until combined and fairly smooth, about 3 minutes.

2. Turn the dough out, shape it into a square about 1 inch / 2.5 cm thick, and wrap tightly in plastic wrap. Refrigerate for at least 2 hours (and up to 24 hours) before using.

3. Make the filling: Place the potatoes in a medium pot, cover with water by at least 1 inch/2.5 cm, and bring to a boil over medium-high heat, then reduce the heat to medium-low and simmer until the potatoes are fork-tender, 15 to 18 minutes. Drain well and transfer to a medium bowl.

4. In a medium skillet, melt the butter over medium heat. Add the onions and cook until lightly golden, 5 to 6 minutes. Remove from the heat.

5. Use a potato masher or large fork to coarsely mash the potatoes. Add the onions, along with the cream cheese, and mix well to combine. Fold in the sour cream, chives, and vinegar and season with salt and pepper. Cool to room temperature.

6. Preheat the oven to 400°F/205°C with a rack in the center. Line a baking sheet with parchment paper.

7. Divide the dough into 9 equal pieces (about 80 g each) and roll each piece into a ball.

(CONTINUES)

8. Working with one piece of dough at a time, use your hands to pat it out and flatten into a 4-inch/10 cm round, about ¼ inch/6 mm thick. Scoop 100 g / heaping ¼ cup of the filling into the center of the round. Pinch the edges of the dough to make them even thinner and gently pull them up to cover the sides of the filling. The look will be pretty rustic, and the top of the filling will be exposed. Place the assembled knishes on the prepared pan, staggering the rows to evenly space them.

9. Brush the dough with egg wash and bake the knishes until the dough is deeply golden brown, 24 to 28 minutes. Serve warm.

Variations

TWICE-BAKED POTATO KNISHES **Omit the chives and malt vinegar. Use only 28 g / 1 ounce / 2 tablespoons of the butter to cook the onions and save the rest for topping the knishes. After filling them, divide the remaining 45 g / 3 tablespoons butter among them, placing 1 teaspoon of butter on the center of each portion of filling. Bake as directed above. When the knishes come out of the oven, sprinkle with sweet paprika.**

GOOEY CHEESE-STUFFED KNISHES **Cut off the rind of 255 g / 9 ounces Taleggio cheese and cut the cheese into 9 fat cubes. When filling the knishes, use a scant 80 g / ¼ cup of the potato mixture to fill each one, then press a cheese cube into the center. Top with the remaining filling (20 g / 2 tablespoons each) to encase the cheese. Bake as directed and serve warm.**

Make Ahead and Storage
The dough and filling can be prepared up to 24 hours ahead and stored, wrapped well, in the refrigerator. The knishes are best the same day they are baked. Store leftovers in an airtight container at room temperature.

Fried Piroshki

Makes 18 piroshki

DIFFICULTY: MEDIUM

The name of this pastry can mean a lot of different things, depending on where you are and who is making them. Russian piroshki are always some sort of dough with a yummy filling packed inside. While there are many baked versions out there, I really like the fried ones, filled with meat, as here, or braised cabbage (see the Variation). And for a sweet piroshki, try the blueberry variation.

DOUGH

570 g / 4¾ cups all-purpose flour

12 g / 1 tablespoon granulated sugar

6 g / 2 teaspoons instant dry yeast

6 g / 1½ teaspoons fine sea salt

290 g / 1¼ cups warm water (about 110°F/45°C)

115 g / ½ cup whole milk, warmed to about 110°F/45°C

15 g / 1 tablespoon neutral oil (such as canola or vegetable)

FILLING

14 g / 1 tablespoon unsalted butter

170 g / 1 medium white onion, finely minced

15 g / 3 cloves garlic, minced

454 g / 1 pound ground beef

5 g / 1 teaspoon Worcestershire sauce

5 g / 1¼ teaspoons kosher salt

2 g / ¾ teaspoon freshly ground black pepper

2 g / ½ teaspoon sweet paprika

9 g / 3 tablespoons chopped fresh dill

Neutral oil (such as canola or vegetable) for deep-frying

Flaky or kosher salt (optional)

Sour cream for serving

1. Make the dough: In the bowl of an electric mixer fitted with the dough hook, mix the flour, sugar, yeast, and salt on low speed to combine, about 15 seconds. Add the water, milk, and oil and mix until the dough comes together around the dough hook, about 3 minutes. Raise speed to medium and mix for 2 minutes more; the dough should be fairly smooth.

2. Transfer the dough to a lightly greased large bowl, cover with plastic wrap, and let rise until nearly doubled in size, 1 hour and 15 minutes to 1 hour and 45 minutes.

3. Meanwhile, make the filling: In a medium skillet, melt the butter over medium heat. Add the onion and cook until translucent, 4 to 5 minutes. Add the garlic and cook until fragrant, about 1 minute. Transfer to a heatproof bowl and cool to room temperature.

4. Add the ground beef, Worcestershire, salt, pepper, paprika, and dill to the cooled onion mixture and mix well. Divide the filling into 18 equal portions (about 35 g each) and roll into balls. Place the balls on a parchment-lined baking sheet or plate, cover, and refrigerate until ready to assemble the piroshki.

5. When the dough has risen, turn it out and divide it into 18 equal pieces (about 55 g each). Round each piece of dough (see page 104), cover, and let rest for 10 to 15 minutes.

6. On a lightly floured surface, roll out one piece of dough to a round about 5 inches/13 cm in diameter. Place a portion of filling in the center, use your finger to apply cool water to half

250

of the dough's edge, and fold the dough over to make a half-moon shape; press the edges firmly to seal. Repeat with the remaining dough and filling. Then gently press the piroshki down to flatten them, ideally making them an even thickness all over.

7. Pour 2 to 3 inches/5 to 8 cm of oil into a heavy-bottomed pot. Attach a deep-fry thermometer to the side of the pot, and heat the oil over medium heat to around 350°F/175°C

(or check the temperature carefully with an instant-read thermometer). I fry these at around 325°F/165°C, but it's best to heat the oil to hotter than you need to start, as the temperature will drop once you add food to it. Set a wire rack over a baking sheet to drain the fried piroshki.

8. Working in batches to avoid crowding, add the piroshki to the hot oil and fry, turning once,

(CONTINUES)

until they are evenly golden brown and the filling is cooked through, 3 to 4 minutes per side; adjust the heat as necessary to maintain a temperature of around 325°F/165°C. (The internal temperature of the piroshki should read 160°F/70°C.) Transfer the piroshki to the prepared rack to drain. Cool for at least 5 minutes before serving warm, with sour cream.

Variation

BRAISED CABBAGE PIROSHKI Omit the filling and prepare the following mixture: In a large skillet, melt 28 g / 2 tablespoons unsalted butter over medium heat. Add 325 g / 1 large white onion, minced, and cook until starting to become tender, about 3 minutes. Add 475 g / 5 cups shredded cabbage and cook until it wilts slightly, 2 to 3 minutes. Add 15 g / 1 tablespoon whole-grain mustard (or Pickled Mustard Seeds, page 97), 115 g / ½ cup light-bodied beer, hard cider, or apple cider, and 15 g / 1 tablespoon apple cider vinegar. Cover the pan and cook, stirring occasionally, until the cabbage is tender, 5 to 7 minutes. Remove the lid and cook for another 4 to 5 minutes, stirring frequently, to evaporate the excess moisture. Season with salt and pepper. Cool completely. (The filling can be made up to 2 days ahead and refrigerated in an airtight container.) Fill the piroshki as directed in step 6, using about 70 g / packed ¼ cup for each one, and fry as directed.

Blueberry Piroshki

In a medium pot, combine 510 g / 3 cups fresh or well-drained thawed frozen blueberries with 50 g / ¼ cup sugar and cook over medium-low heat, stirring frequently, until the berries soften and break down, 6 to 8 minutes. In a small bowl, whisk 99 g / ½ cup sugar with 35 g / 5 tablespoons cornstarch and a pinch of fine sea salt. Add this mixture to the softened berries, mix well, and cook over low heat, stirring constantly, until the mixture thickens and fat bubbles break the surface. Remove from the heat and stir in 14 g / 1 tablespoon unsalted butter and 5 g / 1 teaspoon vanilla extract. Cool completely. (The filling can be made up to 2 days ahead and refrigerated in an airtight container.) Fill the piroshki as directed in step 6, using 40 g / 2 heaping tablespoons for each one, and fry as directed.

Make Ahead and Storage
The assembled piroshki, covered with greased plastic wrap, can be refrigerated for up to 4 hours before frying. The piroshki are best served the same day they are fried.

— FLAVOR BOOSTER —

Quick Pickles

I'm a lifelong pickle fan. I love that hit of acid, especially paired with anything rich. While I certainly fancy a good canning project, I usually make refrigerator-style quick pickles for cooking or garnishing at home.

Pack the prepared vegetables tightly into a 1-pint/475 ml canning jar. I usually use 2 parts seasoned rice vinegar to 1 part water. Start with the smaller amount of water given below, and add more boiling water if necessary to fully submerge your vegetables. In a medium saucepan, bring 230 g / 1 cup seasoned rice vinegar and 115 to 170 g / ½ to ¾ cup water to a simmer over medium heat; you can add flavoring ingredients like smashed garlic cloves, thinly sliced chiles, or dried spices here. Then pour the brine over the vegetables in the jar. If you want to substitute another vinegar, add a few tablespoons sugar and a few pinches of salt to the liquid before bringing it to a boil.

Cucumbers	About 170 g / 1 European (seedless) cucumber, thinly sliced; sometimes I add 170 g / 1 small red onion, thinly sliced
Carrots	About 190 g / 5 medium carrots, peeled and sliced into ¼-inch-/ 6 mm thick coins
Radishes	About 300 g / 2 bunches radishes, trimmed and quartered or sliced into ¼-inch-/6 mm thick coins
Shredded Carrots and Daikon	Grate 115 g / 3 medium carrots and 170 g / ½ medium daikon radish and toss to combine
Celery	About 200 g / 4 stalks celery, sliced ¼ inch/6 mm thick
Onions	440 g / 2 medium onions, halved lengthwise and thinly sliced

Bánh Patê Sô (or Pâté Chaud)

Makes 12 pastries

DIFFICULTY: **MEDIUM**

These delicious meat-filled pies, made of a simple pork filling, scented with onion and garlic and kept juicy with plenty of mushrooms, are one of the pastries born from the French colonial occupation of Vietnam. The filling is wrapped in flaky rough puff pastry for a killer combo that's both portable and always a crowd-pleaser.

FILLING

14 g / 1 tablespoon unsalted butter

15 g / 1 tablespoon olive oil

170 g / 1 medium sweet onion, minced

140 g / 5 ounces mushrooms (any kind), trimmed and finely minced

10 g / 2 cloves garlic, minced

226 g / 8 ounces ground pork

14 g / 2 teaspoons honey

7 g / 1¼ teaspoons kosher salt

2 g / ½ teaspoon freshly ground black pepper

6 g / 2 teaspoons cornstarch

1 recipe Rough Puff Pastry Dough (page 267), divided into 2 equal pieces and chilled as directed

Egg wash (see page 7) for finishing

1. Make the filling: In a medium skillet, melt the butter over medium heat, then add the olive oil. Add the onion and mushrooms and cook until they are tender and most of the liquid they release has evaporated, 5 to 6 minutes. Add the garlic and cook until fragrant, about 1 minute. Transfer the mixture to a heatproof bowl and cool to room temperature.

2. Add the pork, honey, salt, pepper, and cornstarch to the cooled mushroom mixture and mix well.

3. On a lightly floured surface, roll out one piece of the puff pastry into a rectangle about 9 x 12 inches/23 x 30 cm and ¼ inch/6 mm thick. Use a pastry wheel or bench knife to cut the dough into 12 equal pieces: Cut it lengthwise into three 3-inch-/8 cm wide strips, then cut the strips crosswise into 4 squares each.

4. Arrange the squares in staggered rows on a parchment-lined baking sheet. Place about 40 g / 2 heaping tablespoons of the filling in the center of each piece (sometimes I take the extra care to form the meat mixture into a square to fill the pastry more evenly). Cover the pan loosely with plastic wrap and refrigerate while you roll out the second piece of dough.

5. Roll out and cut the second piece of dough to make 12 more squares, as directed in step 3. Remove the sheet of pastries from the refrigerator, uncover, and brush the edges of each one lightly with cool water. Place a second square of dough on top of each one and press the edges firmly to seal. Crimp the edges with a fork. If the dough feels soft or sticky, refrigerate for 30 minutes before proceeding.

6. Preheat the oven to 375°F/190°C with a rack in the center.

7. Egg-wash the surface of the pastries and cut a small X in the top of each one, using the tip of a paring knife, to serve as a vent. Transfer the pastries to the oven and bake until deeply golden brown, 38 to 45 minutes. Cool for at least 5 minutes before serving warm, or cool completely and serve at room temperature.

Make Ahead and Storage
The pastries are best the
same day they are baked.

Crispy Shredded Chicken Empanadas

Makes 15 empanadas

DIFFICULTY: **MEDIUM**

When folks come to visit me in in New Jersey, there are a few must-eats in my neighborhood I always make sure they try. There are the grilled onion–topped sliders at White Manna, the Cuban sandwiches at La Pola, and then there are the empanadas. There are so many good empanadas in my neighborhood, but as with anything fried, it's hard to beat the freshest of fresh, the crispest of crisp: homemade. This version, filled to the brim with juicy shredded chicken, was inspired by some of my favorite local fried empanadas. The shredded chicken recipe is a go-to in my kitchen, and it can be doubled/tripled/quadrupled to use for meals throughout the week, if you like.

CHICKEN

15 g / 1 tablespoon neutral oil (such as canola)

795 g / 1¾ pounds boneless, skinless chicken thighs

Kosher salt and freshly ground black pepper

14 g / 1 tablespoon unsalted butter

220 g / 1 medium sweet onion, thinly sliced

15 g / 3 cloves garlic, minced

6 g / 2 teaspoons ground chili powder

5 g / 1½ teaspoons ground cumin

3 g / 1 teaspoon onion powder

2 g / ½ teaspoon ground coriander

575 g / 2½ cups chicken broth, plus more if needed

DOUGH

420 g / 3½ cups all-purpose flour

4 g / 1 teaspoon fine sea salt

90 g / 6 tablespoons cold lard or vegetable shortening

175 g / ¾ cup ice water

Neutral oil (such as canola or vegetable), for deep-frying

1. Prepare the filling: In a large pot, heat the oil over medium-high heat. Season the chicken thighs with salt and pepper, add to the hot oil, and sear, turning once, until browned on both sides, 3 to 4 minutes per side. Remove the chicken from the pot and set aside.

2. Add the butter to the pot, reduce the heat to medium-low, and let it melt. Add the onion and cook until translucent, 4 to 5 minutes. Add the garlic, chile powder, cumin, onion powder, and coriander, season with salt and pepper, and stir well.

3. Return the chicken to the pot, in a single layer, add the broth, and bring to a simmer. Cover the pot, reduce the heat to low, and simmer until the chicken is very tender—it should fall apart when tested with a fork—1 to 1½ hours. Add more broth to the pot as needed if it gets low.

4. With a slotted spoon, remove the chicken and onions from the pot and set aside to cool slightly (reserve any extra broth for another use). When the chicken is cool enough to handle, shred with two forks (or with an electric hand mixer, which makes quick, easy work of shredding it). Transfer the chicken and onion mixture to a bowl, cover, and refrigerate until ready to assemble the empanadas.

(CONTINUES)

5. Make the dough: In the bowl of a food processor, pulse the flour and salt to combine, 5 to 10 seconds. Add the lard or shortening and pulse until the mixture resembles coarse meal. (You can also do this in a bowl with a pastry blender.) Add the water and pulse until the dough comes together around the processor blade. If the dough appears dry, add more water 5 g / 1 teaspoon at a time until it comes together.

6. Remove the dough from the food processor, form into a disk about 1 inch/2.5 cm thick, and wrap tightly in plastic wrap. Refrigerate for at least 1 hour. (The dough can be made ahead and refrigerated for as long as overnight.)

7. Turn the dough out and divide into 15 equal pieces (about 45 g / 2 heaping tablespoons each). Shape each piece of dough into a ball, setting them aside on the work surface, then cover loosely with plastic wrap and let rest for 15 minutes.

8. Roll one piece of dough into a 1/8-inch-/3 mm thick round (about 5 1/2 inches/14 cm wide). Scoop about 60 g / 1/4 cup filling into the center and fold the dough over to make a half-moon shape and encase the filling. If necessary, use your fingertip to moisten the edges with a little water. Crimp the edges firmly with a fork to seal. Repeat with the remaining dough and filling.

9. Line a baking sheet with paper towels and set a wire rack on top. Pour 2 to 3 inches/5 to 8 cm of oil into a large heavy-bottomed pot or deep fryer. Attach a deep-fry thermometer to the pot and heat the oil over medium heat to around 360°F/180°C (or check the temperature carefully with an instant-read thermometer). I usually fry these at around 350°F/175°C, but it's best to heat the oil to hotter than you need to start, as the temperature will drop when you add food to it.

10. Working in batches to avoid crowding, fry the empanadas until deeply golden brown on both sides, 4 to 6 minutes total; adjust the heat as needed while you fry. Remove the empanadas from the oil and transfer to the rack to drain. Serve warm.

Variation

QUESO EMPANADAS **Omit the chicken filling and prepare the following mixture: In a medium skillet, melt 14 g / 1 tablespoon unsalted butter over medium heat. Add 220 g / 1 medium white onion, minced, and cook until tender, 4 to 5 minutes. Add 15 g / 3 cloves garlic, minced, and cook for 1 minute more. Remove from the heat and cool to room temperature, then toss with 570 g / 1 1/4 pounds Oaxaca cheese, shredded, and 70 g / 1/3 cup finely minced pickled jalapeños. Use about 55 g / 1/4 packed cup of this filling for each empanada.**

Make Ahead and Storage
The chicken filling can be made up to 4 days ahead and refrigerated (or frozen for up to 3 months). The empanadas can be assembled up to 12 hours ahead. Store on a parchment-lined baking sheet, tightly wrapped in plastic wrap, in the refrigerator until ready to fry. Once fried, the empanadas are best served immediately.

Skillet Cheese Soufflé

Makes 8 servings
DIFFICULTY: **MEDIUM**

A lot of people hear the word "soufflé" and assume the recipe will be difficult. I would love to permanently remove that notion from the baking zeitgeist. The only tricky part of making a soufflé is whipping the egg whites. The air trapped inside the egg whites serves as the only leavening for the soufflé as it bakes, giving it its signature light and airy texture. This recipe falls into the category of dinner-party–worthy side dishes. Or try it "Moonlighting as Pie," as in the Variation below—this lofty, cheesy beauty is right at home in a flaky golden crust.

85 g / 3 ounces / 6 tablespoons unsalted butter, at room temperature

100 g / 1 cup finely grated Parmesan cheese

306 g / 1⅓ cups whole milk

118 g / ½ cup heavy cream

30 g / ¼ cup all-purpose flour

2 g / ½ teaspoon fine sea salt

2 g / ½ teaspoon freshly ground black pepper

1 g / ¼ teaspoon cayenne pepper, or more to taste

<1 g / ¼ teaspoon freshly grated nutmeg

340 g / 6 large eggs, separated

1 g / ¼ teaspoon cream of tartar

285 g / 10 ounces firm cheese, such as Gruyère, cheddar, Comté, Fontina, or Gouda, shredded

1. Generously grease a 9-inch/23 cm ovenproof skillet with 28 g / 1 ounce / 2 tablespoons of the butter. Add the Parmesan cheese and tilt and shake the pan until it has an even all-over coating of cheese.

2. In a medium saucepan, heat the milk and cream to just under a simmer. Remove from the heat.

3. In a medium saucepan, melt the remaining 56 g / 2 ounces / 4 tablespoons butter over medium heat. Sprinkle the flour evenly over the butter, stirring to combine, and cook, stirring constantly, for 1 minute. Reduce the heat to low and, whisking constantly, stream the warm milk/cream mixture into the pan. Raise the heat to medium-low and cook, whisking constantly, until the mixture simmers (fat bubbles should break the surface). Simmer, stirring constantly, for 1 minute. Remove from the heat and season the sauce with the salt, pepper, cayenne, and nutmeg.

4. Transfer the mixture to a large heatproof bowl and cool for 10 to 15 minutes (it should still be warm, but not hot).

5. Preheat the oven to 400°F/205°C with a rack in the center.

6. In the bowl of a stand mixer fitted with the whip attachment, combine the egg whites and cream of tartar and whip on medium-low speed until foamy, then raise the speed to high and whip to medium peaks, 4 to 5 minutes (see page 260).

7. Whisk the egg yolks into the warm sauce until well combined. Gently fold in 226 g / 8 ounces of the cheese. Add about one quarter of the egg whites and mix to incorporate—you can mix a little more vigorously here because you're tempering the mixture by lighten-

(CONTINUES)

ing the texture, which will make it easier to incorporate the rest of the egg whites. Add the remaining egg whites in 2 or 3 additions, folding just until evenly incorporated.

8. Pour the batter into the prepared pan. Scatter the remaining 56 g / 2 ounces cheese evenly over the surface. Transfer to the oven and bake until the soufflé is very puffy, golden brown, and just set, 30 to 35 minutes. (Try not to open the oven door during this time.)

9. Remove the soufflé from the oven and serve immediately (it will begin to deflate almost instantly, but it is insanely light and delicious as long as it's warm).

Variations

SOUFFLÉ MOONLIGHTING AS PIE Reduce the butter to 56 g / 2 ounces / 4 tablespoons and omit the Parmesan. Instead of coating the skillet with butter and cheese, line it with All-Buttah Pie Dough (page 319) or Pâte Brisée (page 321). Trim the excess dough, tuck the edges under as directed on page 314, and crimp as desired. Refrigerate while you prepare the soufflé batter.

Pour the batter into the prepared crust and bake for 35 to 40 minutes, until the crust is deeply golden brown and the soufflé is just set. For an even crispier crust, parbake the piecrust first (see page 315).

Make Ahead and Storage
The soufflé is best immediately after baking.

Tips for Whipping Egg Whites Without Sugar

When properly whipped, egg whites are capable of aerating to up to eight times their original volume. In dessert recipes, egg whites are often whipped with sugar. The granules of sugar help to aerate the whites, and as the sugar is gradually incorporated, it helps them whip to a beautiful, glossy meringue. In savory recipes where egg whites are whipped without sugar, following the steps below will help you achieve the loftiest results:

1. Start whipping the egg whites on medium-low speed to break them up before you crank up the speed. Whisk on medium-low for about 1 minute; if you're using an acidic ingredient, like cream of tartar, add it here.

2. Gradually raise the speed to high and continue to whip until you achieve the desired peaks. Watch the whites carefully as they whip—it's easier to overwhip the whites without additions like sugar. Overwhipped whites will look dry and clumpy.

3. Once you reach the ideal volume, gradually reduce the mixer speed, mixing for about 30 seconds on medium speed before stopping. The whipped whites are now ready to use.

Club-Sandwich Napoleons

Makes 4 servings

DIFFICULTY: **EASY**

A club sandwich has three slices of bread, and these individual Napoleons have three layers of puff pastry each. Loaded with the traditional club fillings—turkey, bacon, and ham, plus a few of my favorite sandwich additions (tomato jam and avocado)—this is a simple but unusual savory pastry to serve for brunch or lunch. I top the Napoleons with a pile of lightly dressed arugula. I should probably say it's a fork-and-knife situation, but let's get real—I have definitely picked one of these up and taken lovely, flaky bites.

1 recipe Golden Cheese Rough Puff Pastry (page 268), chilled as directed

170 g / ½ cup Tomato Jam (page 135)

60 g / ¼ cup mayonnaise

113 g / 4 ounces thinly sliced deli turkey

30 g / 2 tablespoons fresh lemon juice

150 g / 1 ripe avocado, halved, pitted, peeled, and thinly sliced

113 g / 4 ounces thinly sliced deli ham

About 75 g / 6 strips bacon, cooked and cut in half

50 g / 2½ cups baby arugula

15 g / 1 tablespoon extra virgin olive oil

Kosher salt and freshly ground black pepper

1. Preheat the oven to 400°F/205°C with the racks in the upper and lower thirds. Line two baking sheets with parchment paper. Have ready two additional pieces of parchment paper (the size of the baking sheets) and two more baking sheets.

2. On a lightly floured surface, roll out the dough into a large rectangle about ¼ inch/ 6 mm thick, aiming for slightly larger than 15 x 20 inches/38 x 50 cm. Use a pastry wheel, bench knife, or sharp knife to cut the dough lengthwise into three 5-inch-/13 cm wide strips, then cut each strip to create 5 x 5-inch/13 x 13 cm squares, for a total of 12 squares. Arrange them on the lined baking sheets, staggering them to fit 6 on each one. Place another piece of parchment on top of the dough on each baking sheet and place a second baking sheet on top (this will serve as a weight to keep the pastry flat while it bakes).

3. Transfer the pans to the oven and bake for 20 minutes. Remove the top baking sheets and parchment, return the pans to the oven, and bake until the pastry is well browned, 12 to 15 minutes more. Cool completely before assembling the Napoleons.

4. In a small bowl, stir the tomato jam and mayonnaise together. (If desired, use an immersion blender to blend the mixture until it's smooth.) Spread 15 g / 1 tablespoon of this mixture evenly on top of each piece of pastry.

5. To assemble the Napoleons, you'll use 3 pieces of pastry for each one: Place a piece of pastry on a plate or serving platter, sauce side up. Arrange one quarter of the turkey on top of the sauce. Drizzle 15 g / 1 tablespoon lemon juice over the avocado slices, then arrange one quarter of the avocado slices in an even layer on top of the turkey. Top with another piece of pastry, sauce side up. Press down gently to mash the avocado a little (it will adhere better to the pastry this way). Arrange one quarter of the ham on top of the pastry and top with

1½ strips of bacon. Place the final piece of pastry sauce side down on top of the bacon and press gently to adhere slightly. Repeat with the remaining pastry squares and filling.

6. To serve, in a medium bowl, toss the arugula with the olive oil and the remaining 15 g / 1 tablespoon lemon juice until well coated. Season with salt and pepper. Top each Napoleon with some of the salad and serve immediately.

Make Ahead and Storage
The pastry squares can be made up to 24 hours ahead and held in an airtight container. The Napoleons are best shortly after they are assembled.

CHAPTER 6

Snacks, Bites, and Appetizers

STUFF TO SERVE FOR PARTIES • GET TOGETHERS • HOOTENANNIES

My family doesn't necessarily throw parties—they just have "get-togethers." But since I come from a large family, it's fairly easy to confuse them for all-out parties. Whatever your reasons for having guests over, the recipes in this chapter are the perfect snacks, small bites, or appetizers for fueling the festivities. My number-one party rule? Give people choices! I like to have a bunch of different shapes, textures, and flavors, mixing and matching until there's enough variety. This chapter has plenty of recipes to get you started, as well as tons of ideas to inspire you to customize your own.

Small or Bite-Size Shapes

For me, part of the fun of small bites is finding the perfect shape for the base dough, and there are many options. You can use these different shapes in lots of different ways, and they can also serve as a jumping-off point for building your own party snacks. For any of these shapes, the dough should be rolled out ¼ inch/6 mm thick.

Cups or Boats

For these shapes, pan(s) like muffin tins or oval ramekins are lined with dough. The shapes can be baked with filling inside or blind-baked and then filled afterward.

Spirals, Palmiers, and Elephant Ears

For these shapes, puff pastry dough is rolled thin and rolled up into a log. The log is then sliced to form the spiral or elephant ear/palmier shapes. Spirals will bake up as rounds, while elephant ears/palmiers are closer to heart-shaped.

Free-Form Rounds or Squares

Basic rounds or squares of dough can be used for many types of appetizers. The size you choose is often determined by what you want to fill or top them with—such as scoops of roasted veggies; slices of onion, pepper, or tomatoes; or spoonfuls of something like Bacon Jam (page 135). Whatever size you cut the dough, you can use a smaller cookie cutter of the same shape to press a slight indentation into the center of the dough. This will guide you as to where to put your filling and will also cause the outer portion of the pastry to rise up nicely around it when it is baked.

Pinwheels

This shape is made with squares of dough. A pastry wheel is used to make cuts into each piece of dough running from the corners to about halfway to the center. After each cut, that piece of dough is folded inward toward the center and pressed firmly against the bottom dough to seal.

Diamonds

For these, squares of dough are cut and folded to form diamond shapes with raised exterior walls and room for filling in the center. This is a more rustic version of the Danish shape where strips of dough form the walls on the edges of the pastry (see Shaping Danish, page 246).

Flowers / Scalloped Edges

This shape starts with circles of dough that are topped with strips of scrap dough to form "walls" around the outsides. The filling is placed in the center, and then the back of a paring knife is used to pleat the dough all around the edge to make petals / scalloped edges.

Crescent

For this shape, triangles of dough are rolled up to form crescents. (For more on this technique, see Sesame Rugelach, page 278.)

Rough Puff Pastry

Makes 1⅓ pounds/605 grams

DIFFICULTY: **MEDIUM**

The only thing I love more than making puff pastry is teaching folks how to make it. The classic full-puff is definitely possible at home (check out the recipe for Yeasted Puff Pastry Dough on page 236), but my "rough puff pastry" is almost as light, flaky, and delicious as the traditional version, with much less stress and effort. Traditional puff pastry is made using the process called lamination, where a block of butter is locked into the dough and then incorporated using a series of folds to create flaky layers (for more on classic lamination methods, see page 234). This method is much simpler. It starts out more like making pie dough, but each butter cube is flattened into a large shard. Then, after the water has been added and the dough has chilled, it is folded. As the folded dough is rolled out, the butter inside forms thin sheets, layered throughout the dough. Then, when the sheets of fat hit the heat of the oven, the moisture turns to steam to create the light, flaky layers you know and adore. This dough is incredibly versatile. It's especially great for free-form pies and mini pies.

302 g / 2½ cups all-purpose flour

2 g / ½ teaspoon fine sea salt

226 g / 8 ounces cold unsalted butter, cut into ¾-inch / 2 cm cubes

75 g / ⅓ cup ice water, plus more as needed

1. In a medium bowl, stir the flour and salt together. Add the cubed butter, tossing until each piece is well coated. Cut the butter into the flour by pressing the pieces between your fingers, flattening them into big shards. As you work, continue to toss the butter with the flour, recoating the shingled pieces; the goal here is to only flatten each piece of butter once, leaving the pieces very large (they will get smaller/more dispersed through the process of folding).

2. Make a well in the center of the flour mixture and add the water. Toss to start incorporating the water, then use your fingers to break up any larger clumps to distribute the moisture. Continue to mix, adding more water 15 g / 1 tablespoon at a time as needed, until the dough comes together. It should hold together fairly easily and not appear dry. It will look quite rough, not smooth, and it shouldn't be sticky.

3. Turn the dough out and form it into a disk. Wrap tightly in plastic wrap and refrigerate for at least 30 minutes. (*The dough can be refrigerated at this point for up to 24 hours.*)

4. On a lightly floured surface, roll out the dough about ½ inch/13 mm thick—the exact size/shape of the dough doesn't matter here, just the thickness. Dust away any excess flour with a pastry brush and fold the dough in half. Fold the halved dough in half again (the dough will probably be sort of a square shape). Wrap tightly in plastic wrap and chill for 15 to 30 minutes, until firm.

5. Repeat step 4 a total of three times, rolling out the dough, folding it, and chilling it before continuing with the next round. If you work quickly, you can sometimes perform two rounds of folds back to back, but if the dough is soft or sticky, don't rush it—chill the dough after each fold.

(CONTINUES)

6. Once the final fold is completed, tuck the edges of the dough under to help form the dough into a rounded shape, wrap it again, and chill for at least 1 hour (and up to 2 days) before using.

Note: This dough is best baked at 400°F/205°C, but it can be used in any recipe that calls for puff pastry.

Variations

CACIO E PEPE ROUGH PUFF PASTRY **Add 226 g / 8 ounces Pecorino Romano cheese, grated, and 14 g / 1½ tablespoons freshly ground black pepper after you cut in the butter in step 1.**

GOLDEN CHEESE ROUGH PUFF PASTRY **Add 226 g / 8 ounces firm or semi-firm cheese, such as white cheddar, Gruyère, Manchego, or Parmesan, shredded, after you cut in the butter in step 1.**

Make Ahead and Storage
The tightly wrapped disk of dough can be refrigerated for up to 24 hours. The final dough can be refrigerated, wrapped tightly in plastic wrap, for up to 2 days; wrapped in plastic wrap and then aluminum foil, it can be frozen for up to 3 months. Thaw overnight in the fridge before using.

When and Why to Dock

Puff pastry is meant to puff up, but, as I always like to point out, the baker controls where this happens. If you're using rough puff pastry to line a pan, or you're looking for a thin-crust presentation, you can prick or poke small holes in the dough, or dock the dough, to allow steam to escape and to help prevent it from puffing as it bakes. Docked dough will be thinner and crisper when baked than undocked dough, which will bake up light and fluffy inside (and crisp outside). You can also dock just a portion of the dough so that it doesn't rise higher—for example, when you want to create an outer wall of pastry and a flatter center surface for the filling, just dock the center portion.

Stuff on Puff!

Looking for something to make for a party? Try this: Put some stuff on puff. There's not much that doesn't work on a crispy, flaky, buttery puff pastry bed. Roll out some puff pastry, cut it into bite-size shapes, and put something on top of it before tossing it in the oven, and you've got yourself a guaranteed crowd-pleaser. Or blind-bake the puff and then add a filling or topping (such as the shrimp salad on page 282). Use your creativity. Looking for some guidance to start? See the Brie Bites (page 289), Jalapeño Pastry Poppers (page 283), or Stuffed Mushroom Puffs (page 293).

Spicy Cheese Crackers

Makes about 100 crackers

DIFFICULTY: **MEDIUM**

This recipe was inspired by the crispy, spicy, cheesy crackers served at Bemelmans Bar in the Carlyle Hotel in New York City. I adore the murals on the walls by Ludwig Bemelmans, the beloved children's author, including my childhood favorite, Madeline herself. The experience of sitting there is an absolutely dreamy one. The dark piano-bar ambience makes me want to stay for hours—not to mention the incredibly addictive crackers they serve with the cocktails. My version incorporates a few changes: I add some whole wheat flour for nuttiness, use two kinds of cheese, and amplify the spicy notes and smokiness with a bit of smoked paprika. These allow me to have a sophisticated cocktail hour at home, where the drinks are far cheaper and the ambience is still pretty wonderful.

120 g / 1 cup all-purpose flour

60 g / ½ cup whole wheat flour

2 g / ½ teaspoon fine sea salt

2 g / ½ teaspoon freshly ground black pepper

2 g / ½ teaspoon smoked paprika

1 to 2 g / ¼ to ½ teaspoon cayenne pepper (more if you like spicy)

113 g / 4 ounces / 8 tablespoons cold unsalted butter, cut into ½-inch / 1 cm cubes

50 g / ½ cup finely grated Parmesan cheese

125 g / 1 packed cup grated sharp white cheddar cheese

115 g / ½ cup whole milk

30 g / 2 tablespoons cold water

1. In a medium bowl, whisk the all-purpose flour, whole wheat flour, salt, black pepper, smoked paprika, and cayenne to combine. Add the butter and toss well, separating the cubes and ensuring they are evenly coated in flour. Cut the butter into the flour using your hands or a pastry cutter until it's about the size of walnut halves. Stir in the Parmesan and cheddar cheese.

2. Make a well in the center of the flour mixture and add the milk and water. Toss the mixture with your hands to start to distribute the moisture, then gently knead the dough until it comes together.

3. Turn the dough out, form it into a square about 1 inch/2.5 cm thick, and wrap tightly in plastic wrap. Refrigerate for at least 1 hour (and up to 24 hours).

4. On a lightly floured surface, roll out the dough into a square about ½ inch/1 cm thick. Don't worry about the exact dimensions of the dough, just try to keep it roughly square shaped and focus on the thickness. Fold the dough into quarters. If it feels warm or sticky at all, wrap it tightly and chill for 30 minutes.

5. Repeat step 4, rolling out the dough and performing another fold. Wrap the dough tightly and chill for at least 1 hour (and up to 24 hours)

6. Preheat the oven to 400°F/205°C with the racks in the upper and lower thirds. Line two baking sheets with parchment paper.

7. On a lightly floured surface, roll out the dough into a rectangle about ¼ inch/6 cm thick; don't worry about the exact dimensions of the dough, just try to keep it roughly rectangular in shape and focus more on the thickness. Use a pastry wheel to cut the dough

(CONTINUES)

269

lengthwise into 1-inch-/2.5 cm wide strips, then cut the strips crosswise into 1-inch/2.5 cm squares. (Pieces that aren't quite squares can still be baked, or you can press the dough back together and re-roll into a rectangle one or two more times.)

8. Transfer the squares to the prepared baking sheets. They won't spread, so they can be quite close together—within ¼ inch/6 mm of each other. Dock the center of each square with the tines of a fork.

9. Bake until the crackers are deeply, evenly golden brown, 15 to 18 minutes. Cool completely on the baking sheets.

Variations

CHEESE STRAWS *Makes 24* Prepare the dough as directed. To shape the straws, on a lightly floured surface, roll out the dough to a 16 x 12-inch/41 x 30 cm rectangle. Cut the dough crosswise in half, to form two 8 x 12-inch/20 x 30 cm rectangles. Brush one of the squares all over with egg wash (see page 7), then place the other piece of dough on top and press down gently all over to adhere. With one of the longer sides of the dough facing you, cut it into ½-inch-/1 cm wide strips (you should get 24). Transfer the strips to two parchment-lined baking sheets.

Use a pastry wheel or sharp paring knife to cut each strip almost in half lengthwise, leaving the top ¼ inch/6 mm as a solid piece.

Use your thumb to press that portion of the dough firmly against the baking sheet, then twist the two skinny pieces of the dough together. Pinch them together at the other end and use your thumb to press that end firmly against the baking sheet. Refrigerate for 30 minutes to 1 hour. Bake the straws at 375°F/190°C for 22 to 25 minutes, until golden brown. Cool completely on the baking sheet (these are also delicious served warm, but they are a bit more flaky-fragile).

Make Ahead and Storage
The crackers (or straws) are best within the first 48 hours, but they will keep for up to 4 days in an airtight container at room temperature. If they become soggy, they can be refreshed on a parchment-lined baking sheet, tented with foil, at 350°F/190°C for 4 to 6 minutes.

Parmesan Sablés

Makes about 40 sablés

DIFFICULTY: **EASY**

Sablés are buttery shortbread cookies, typically sweet. They've gone salty in this Parmesan twist, which maintains the same short, sandy texture of the original and makes a perfect snack with cocktails. Since the dough can be made ahead of time, these are as easy as they are delicious—a go-to recipe that you may become known for!

240 g / 2 cups all-purpose flour

3 g / 1 teaspoon fresh rosemary needles or oregano leaves

3 g / ¾ teaspoon fine sea salt

2 g / ½ teaspoon freshly ground black pepper

170 g / 6 ounces / 12 tablespoons cold unsalted butter, cut into ½-inch/1 cm cubes

150 g / 1½ packed cups finely grated Parmesan cheese

42 g / 2 large egg yolks

15 g / 1 tablespoon whole milk

Egg White Wash (page 7) for finishing

1. In the bowl of a food processor, pulse the flour, herbs, salt, and pepper to combine, 15 to 30 seconds. Add the butter and Parmesan and pulse until the butter is thoroughly incorporated and the mixture resembles coarse meal. Add the egg yolks and milk and pulse just until the dough comes together.

2. Lay a piece of parchment paper about the size of a baking sheet (12 x 18 inches/30 x 46 cm) on your work surface. Turn the dough out onto the parchment and form it into a rough log along one of the longer sides of the paper. Use the paper and a bench knife to help form the dough into a smooth log about 1½ inches/

4 cm in diameter. Unwrap the log and see how it looks—repeat the process if needed—and then wrap it in the parchment. Transfer the dough to the refrigerator and chill overnight, or freeze for 20 to 30 minutes.

3. Preheat the oven to 350°F/175°C with the racks in the upper and lower thirds. Line two baking sheets with parchment paper.

4. Unwrap the chilled dough log and roll it under your palms a few times to even out the shape. Use a sharp knife to cut the dough into ¼-inch-/6 mm thick slices and transfer the slices to the prepared baking sheets—stagger the rows, leaving ½ inch/1 cm between them.

5. Bake the sablés, rotating the sheets from front to back and top to bottom at the halfway mark, until the surface appears set and they are evenly golden brown around the edges, 15 to 18 minutes. Cool completely on the baking sheets.

SWEET-TOOTH BREAK

Salted Butter–Vanilla Bean Sablés

Omit the herbs, black pepper, and Parmesan cheese. Reduce the salt to 2 g / ½ teaspoon and use salted butter. Add the seeds scraped from a split vanilla bean and 106 g / ½ packed cup light brown sugar to the food processor along with the flour. Proceed as directed.

Make Ahead and Storage
The dough can be made
through step 2, wrapped
tightly in plastic wrap, and
stored in the refrigerator
for up to 3 days or in the
freezer for up to 1 month.
Thaw frozen dough in the
refrigerator overnight
before slicing and baking.

Parmiers (Parmesan Palmiers)

Makes 24 palmiers

DIFFICULTY: **MEDIUM**

Sweet, caramelized palmiers are one of the first pastries I fell in love with. Taken in a savory direction by replacing the sugar with Parmesan, as here, they are wonderful party fare—the kind of thing my family would snack on all day long. They are a good baking project for all skill levels, because even if you're just beginning to tackle the process of lamination, or folding the dough, my Rough Puff Pastry (page 267) makes easy work of it. The palmiers are full of delicious layers thanks to the folded heart or elephant ear shape.

75 g / ¾ cup finely grated Parmesan cheese

2 g / ½ teaspoon freshly ground black pepper

1 recipe Golden Cheese Rough Puff Pastry (page 268), made with 226 g / 8 ounces grated Parmesan cheese and chilled as directed

1. Preheat the oven to 400°F/205°C with the racks in the upper and lower thirds. Line two baking sheets with parchment paper.

2. In a small bowl, whisk the Parmesan and black pepper together.

3. Shape the palmiers: Cut the chilled dough in half; wrap one piece and refrigerate it. On a lightly floured surface, roll out the other piece of dough into a rectangle about 8 x 12 inches/20 x 30 cm. Sprinkle about 25 g / ¼ cup of the Parmesan and pepper mixture over your work surface and place the dough on top of it. Sprinkle the top of the dough with 20 g / 3 tablespoons of the Parmesan mixture. Roll out the dough to a rectangle slightly larger than 9 x 13 inches/23 x 33 cm, then use a pastry wheel to trim the edges to make a clean 9 x 13-inch/23 x 33 cm rectangle.

4. Fold the two long sides of the rectangle over to meet in the center of the dough. Then fold the dough in half along the seam where they meet, forming a flattened log.

5. Use a sharp knife to cut the dough into ½-inch-/1 cm wide slices. Transfer to the prepared baking sheets, arranging them in staggered rows and leaving at least 1½ inches/ 4 cm between them. Sprinkle the remaining Parmesan mixture over the palmiers.

6. Place another piece of parchment paper on top of each sheet of palmiers and place another baking sheet on top of each sheet (this will help them keep their shape as they bake). Transfer to the oven and bake for 12 to 15 minutes, until the palmiers are lightly golden.

7. Remove the pans from the oven, remove the top pan and parchment sheet from each, and gently flip the palmiers over. Return to the oven and bake for 12 to 15 minutes more, until deeply golden brown and very crisp. Transfer the pans to wire racks to cool.

Make Ahead and Storage
The baked parmiers are best the same day they are made. Store leftovers in an airtight container at room temperature.

Garlic Thumbprints with Tomato Jam

Makes 32 savory cookies

DIFFICULTY: **EASY**

Who doesn't love thumbprints, easy, buttery cookies with a center pool of jam. But take that cookie to a savory place, and it becomes a completely different kind of delicious. This version, loaded with sweet roasted garlic and plenty of cheese, is paired with my tomato jam, a recipe inherited from my great-grandma.

226 g / 8 ounces unsalted butter, at room temperature

1 head Roasted Garlic (page 159)

56 g / 1 large egg, at room temperature

100 g / 1 packed cup grated Asiago cheese

50 g / ½ packed cup finely grated Parmesan cheese

9 g / 1 tablespoon chopped fresh oregano or 2 g / ¾ teaspoon dried oregano

Pinch or two of red pepper flakes

200 g / 1⅔ cups all-purpose flour

140 g / 1 cup fine yellow cornmeal, plus more if needed

14 g / 1½ tablespoons garlic powder

2 g / ½ teaspoon fine sea salt

255 g / ¾ cup Tomato Jam (page 135)

1. Preheat the oven to 350°F/175°C with the racks in the upper and lower thirds. Line two baking sheets with parchment paper.

2. In the bowl of a stand mixer fitted with the paddle attachment, cream the butter on medium speed until light and fluffy, 3 to 4 minutes. Add the roasted garlic and mix until well combined, about 1 minute. Add the egg and mix until thoroughly incorporated. Scrape the bowl well, then add the Asiago, Parmesan, oregano, and pepper flakes and mix on low speed to combine. Add the flour, cornmeal, garlic powder, and salt and mix on low speed until the mixture becomes a smooth scoopable dough.

3. Scoop heaping tablespoons of the dough onto the prepared baking sheets in staggered rows, leaving at least 2 inches/5 cm between them. Use your hands to roll the dough into balls, returning them to the baking sheet; if necessary, roll the balls lightly in cornmeal to prevent the dough from sticking to your hands as you work.

4. Use your thumb to make a deep well in the center of each cookie, without going all the way down to the baking sheet. Spoon about 8 g / heaping 1 teaspoon tomato jam into the center of each cookie.

5. Transfer the baking sheets to the oven and bake until the cookies are golden brown around the edges, 20 to 22 minutes. Cool completely on the baking sheets.

Make Ahead and Storage
The cookies can be stored for up to 3 days in an airtight container at room temperature.

276

Sesame Rugelach

Makes 16 rugelach

DIFFICULTY: **MEDIUM**

These unexpected savory cookies are flaky in texture and complex in flavor. They are delicious all on their own (and they make a delicious and unusual addition to holiday cookie tins), but they are also wonderful as part of a grazing board or for parties.

DOUGH

120 g / 1 cup all-purpose flour

23 g / 3 tablespoons whole wheat flour

27 g / 3 tablespoons white or black sesame seeds

3 g / ¾ teaspoon fine sea salt

3 g / 1 teaspoon chopped fresh thyme or 1 g / ½ teaspoon dried thyme

2 g / ½ teaspoon ground cumin

2 g / ½ teaspoon ground sumac

Pinch or two of red pepper flakes (optional)

113 g / 4 ounces / 8 tablespoons cold unsalted butter, cut into ½-inch / 1 cm cubes

113 g / 4 ounces cold cream cheese, cut into ½-inch / 1 cm cubes

30 g / 2 tablespoons sour cream

FILLING

100 g / ¼ cup tahini

85 g / ½ cup cooked or canned chickpeas, drained and patted dry

15 g / 1 tablespoon fresh lemon juice

10 g / ¼ packed cup torn fresh parsley leaves and stems

2 g / ½ teaspoon fine sea salt

Freshly ground black pepper

60 g / ½ cup finely chopped walnuts

FINISHING

White or black sesame seeds

Egg wash (see page 7)

Flaky salt

1. Make the dough: In the bowl of a food processor, pulse the all-purpose flour, whole wheat flour, sesame seeds, salt, thyme, cumin, sumac, and pepper flakes, if using, to combine, 10 to 15 seconds.

2. Add the butter and cream cheese and pulse a few times until the cubes have become fairly small. Add the sour cream and pulse until the dough comes together into a ball around the processor blade.

3. Turn the dough out and form it into a 1-inch-/2.5 cm thick disk. Wrap tightly in plastic wrap and refrigerate until well chilled, at least 2 hours (and up to 24 hours).

4. Make the filling: Wipe out the food processor bowl well, then add the tahini, chickpeas, lemon juice, parsley, and salt and process until very smooth. Transfer to an airtight container and refrigerate until ready to assemble the rugelach (up to 2 days).

5. Line a baking sheet with parchment paper. On a lightly floured surface, roll out the dough into a round about 7 inches/18 cm wide. Brush away any excess flour from another part of the work surface, then sprinkle sesame seeds generously over the work surface. Place the dough on top and sprinkle more sesame seeds evenly over the dough. Then roll the dough out (this will press the sesame seeds into the dough)

into a round about 12 inches/30 cm wide and ⅛ in/3 mm thick.

6. Spread the prepared filling evenly over the dough, leaving the outer ½ inch/1 cm uncovered. Sprinkle the filling with black pepper to taste (I'm fairly generous), then sprinkle the walnuts evenly over it.

7. Using a pastry wheel, cut the dough into 16 equal pieces: First cut the round into quarters, then cut each quarter into 4 equal pieces. Starting at the bottom of the triangle, roll each piece of dough up into a crescent shape.

8. Transfer the rugelach to the prepared baking sheet, seam side down, staggering the rows of

cookies so there's at least ½ inch/1 cm between them. As you transfer them, gently curve the ends of each rugelach toward each other to emphasize the crescent shape.

9. Transfer the baking sheet to the refrigerator and chill for 30 minutes to 1 hour. Toward the end of chill time, preheat the oven to 350°F/175°C with a rack in the center.

10. Egg-wash the surface of the rugelach. Sprinkle with flaky salt, and with more sesame seeds, if desired. Bake until deeply golden brown, 32 to 40 minutes. Cool completely on the baking sheet.

Chile-Crunch Gougères

Makes about 40 bite-size gougères

DIFFICULTY: **MEDIUM**

Gougères are a go-to party snack in my house, whether it's with a crowd of friends or a two-person pajama party. Spicy chile crisp adds flavor and texture to the pâte à choux base, and the topping echoes the crispy ingredients inside. I make these with bread flour, which results in crunchier gougères, but if you don't have it, all-purpose flour will work well in its place.

115 g / ½ cup water

115 g / ½ cup whole milk

56 g / 2 ounces / 4 tablespoons unsalted butter

45 g / 3 tablespoons well-stirred chile crisp (see Resources)

4 g / 1 teaspoon fine sea salt

180 g / 1½ cups bread flour (see headnote)

226 g / 4 large eggs, plus up to 2 more eggs if necessary

150 g / 1½ packed cups shredded Gruyère cheese

FINISHING

Egg wash (see page 7)

Dried garlic flakes

Dried shallot or onion flakes

Red pepper flakes or other crushed dried chile peppers

1. In a medium pot, bring the water, milk, butter, chile crisp, and salt to a boil over medium heat. Add the flour to the boiling liquid all at once, stirring constantly with a silicone spatula or wooden spoon. Reduce the heat to low and cook, stirring constantly, until the mixture becomes a slightly sticky paste; it should form a ball around the spatula/spoon as you stir, and a visible film of starch should form on the bottom of the pan—this should take 2 to 3 minutes. Once you see the film, transfer the mixture to the bowl of a stand mixer fitted with the paddle attachment.

2. Whisk the 4 eggs together in a large liquid measuring cup. With the mixer running on medium speed, add the eggs in a slow, steady stream and continue mixing until fully incorporated, 4 to 6 minutes.

3. Test the consistency of the pâte à choux batter by dipping the paddle into it and lifting it up. The batter should form a V shape that eventually breaks away from the batter still in the bowl. If the dough is too stiff or pulls away too quickly, whisk another egg and add it in a slow, steady stream to loosen the consistency; repeat with some or all of the remaining egg if necessary. Remove the bowl from the stand and fold in the cheese until evenly incorporated.

4. Line two baking sheets with parchment paper. Transfer the batter to a pastry bag—you can fit the bag with a large round tip (about ½ inch/1 cm), or just cut an opening in the end of a disposable pastry bag with sharp scissors. Hold the pastry bag straight up above one of the baking sheets and pipe 1½-inch/3 cm mounds of batter onto the parchment, spacing them at least 1½ inches/3 cm apart and staggering the rows as you go. As each mound nears the correct size, release the pressure on the bag and use a quick flick of the wrist to

(CONTINUES)

help break the connection between the dough and the pastry tip.

5. Use a fingertip dipped in cool water to smooth the tops of the mounds, if desired. Let the puffs sit at room temperature for 15 to 30 minutes.

6. Preheat the oven to 400°F/205°C with the racks in the upper and lower thirds.

7. Brush the puffs with egg wash and bake until lightly golden brown, 20 minutes. Remove the pans from the oven and, one at a time, brush each puff with egg wash and sprinkle with garlic, shallot, and red pepper flakes. Return to the oven and bake for 3 to 4 minutes more, until very golden brown and crisp.

8. Remove the puffs from the oven and immediately use a paring knife to poke a small vent into the side of each one to allow steam to escape (this will help keep them crisp). Serve warm, or let cool completely.

Variations

LARGE GOUGÈRES In step 4, pipe the batter into 2½-inch/6 cm mounds, spacing them at least 2 inches/5 cm apart. Bake for 30 minutes, then brush with egg wash and bake for 3 to 4 minutes more.

SHRIMP SALAD PUFFS In a large bowl, whisk 77 g / ⅓ cup mayonnaise, 30 g / 2 tablespoons whole-grain mustard, 30 g / 2 tablespoons fresh lemon juice, 27 g / 3 tablespoons chopped fresh parsley, and 18 g / 2 tablespoons chopped fresh dill to combine. If desired, add up to 15 g / 1 tablespoon hot sauce, such as sriracha. Season the dressing with salt and pepper. Add 130 g / 1 cup minced red onion, 140 g / 1 cup minced celery, and 454 g / 1 pound chilled cooked shrimp (preferably small/51/60, or extra small/61/70). Split completely cool Large Gougères roughly in half, fill with the shrimp salad, and serve immediately.

Make Ahead and Storage
The gougères are best the same day they are baked. However, they can be made up to 24 hours ahead and stored in an airtight container (or frozen for up to 1 month) and refreshed in a 350°F/175°C oven until crisp, 10 to 12 minutes.

Piping Pastries

Pâte à choux batter can be piped into a variety of different shapes, for gougères (page 280), cream puffs, and éclairs, among other pastries. Piping is one of those things that may seem intimidating, but with practice, it's pure muscle memory!

To pipe a perfect round shape, hold the pastry tip (or the opening of the pastry bag) directly above where you want to pipe, with the bag perfectly straight up. Begin applying pressure to the bag: the batter will start to flow from the opening—at first, it will drop onto the parchment paper, and then it will start to flow over onto itself. Continue to apply pressure until you've achieved the size you want, then release the pressure.

Jalapeño Pastry Poppers

Makes 24 poppers

DIFFICULTY: **MEDIUM**

What's missing from the pub classic jalapeño poppers? In my opinion, a flaky, golden crust, and this recipe aims to right that wrong. These poppers parbake beautifully, which means you can assemble and partially bake them and then freeze them for long-term storage (see Make Ahead and Storage, below).

226 g / 8 ounces cream cheese, at room temperature

128 g / 1 bunch scallions, thinly sliced

100 g / 1 packed cup shredded cheddar cheese

9 g / 3 tablespoons chopped fresh cilantro

10 g / 2 cloves garlic, finely grated

3 g / ½ teaspoon kosher salt

Freshly ground black pepper

300 g / 12 large jalapeños

1 recipe Rough Puff Pastry (page 267), chilled as directed

Egg wash (see page 7) for finishing

Aleppo pepper for sprinkling (optional)

1. In the bowl of a stand mixer fitted with the whip attachment, whip the cream cheese until fluffy, 2 to 3 minutes; scrape the bowl well several times as it whips to ensure it is evenly aerated. Add the scallions, cheddar, cilantro, garlic, salt, and black pepper and mix well to combine. Transfer to a bowl and set aside.

2. Cut the jalapeños in half from stem to tip. Use a small spoon to carefully scoop out the seeds and ribs.

3. Use a small spoon to scoop the filling into the halved jalapeños, packing as much filling into each one as possible, about level with the cut edges of the pepper (or use a disposable piping bag with a ½-inch-/1 cm wide opening cut in the tip to pipe the filling into the peppers). Set the stuffed peppers aside.

4. Line two baking sheets with parchment paper. Divide the puff pastry into 2 equal pieces (about 300 g each) and wrap and refrigerate one piece while you work with the other.

5. On a lightly floured surface, roll out the puff pastry into a square slightly larger than 20 x 20 inches/51 x 51 cm. Use a pastry wheel to trim the rough edges, creating a 20 x 20-inch/ 51 x 51 cm square. Cut the dough into 12 equal strips (start by cutting it in half, then in half again, and so on, to help keep the pieces as even as possible).

6. Place the tip of a stuffed jalapeño at one end of one strip of dough and wrap the dough around it. Continue to wrap the dough in a tight spiral to encase the jalapeño. Use your finger to add a dab of water to seal the pastry well anywhere it seems likely to unravel. Transfer to one of the prepared baking sheets, with the final seam side down. Repeat with the remaining dough and peppers, rolling out the second piece of dough after you've made the first batch, staggering them on the baking sheets to leave at least 2 inches/5 cm between them. Refrigerate while the oven preheats.

7. Preheat the oven to 400°F/205°C with the racks in the upper and lower thirds.

(CONTINUES)

283

8. Egg-wash the chilled poppers and sprinkle Aleppo pepper on top, if using. Transfer to the oven and bake until the pastry is deeply golden brown, 30 to 34 minutes. Let cool for 5 minutes on the baking sheets before serving warm.

Make Ahead and Storage
The assembled poppers can be parbaked and frozen. Bake them for 20 to 25 minutes, until just starting to brown. Cool to room temperature, then freeze on parchment-lined baking sheets until firm. Transfer to airtight storage containers and freeze for up to 3 months. Bake at 350°/175°C (directly from frozen) on parchment-lined baking sheets until deeply golden and hot throughout, 15 to 18 minutes.

Cochons en Couverture

Makes 24 pastries

DIFFICULTY: **MEDIUM**

I never really liked the name "pigs in a blanket." It doesn't do justice to the bites of food that this wonderful recipe produces. I find that a lot of things sound sweeter in French, so we will take our puff pastry–wrapped pigs au français, s'il vous plaît. This recipe is good with either Rough Puff Pastry (simpler) or Yeasted Puff Pastry (more advanced). If you don't eat meat but don't want to be left out of the fun, try the Vegetarian Lentil Roll variation below.

COCHONS

1 recipe Rough Puff Pastry (page 267) or ½ recipe Yeasted Puff Pastry Dough (page 236), chilled as directed; see headnote

45 g / 3 tablespoons Dijon mustard

24 mini hot dogs, sausages, or cocktail weenies

Egg wash (see page 7) for finishing

SAUCY-SAUCE

80 g / ⅓ cup mayonnaise

80 g / ⅓ cup ketchup

15 to 30 g / 1 to 2 tablespoons sriracha, to taste

2 g / ½ teaspoon garlic powder

Kosher salt and freshly ground black pepper to taste

1. Make the cochons: Line two baking sheets with parchment paper. On a lightly floured surface, roll out the dough into a rectangle about 9 x 12 inches/23 x 30 cm and ¼ inch/6 mm thick. Spread the mustard evenly over the dough.

2. If necessary, turn the dough so that one of the longer sides is facing you. Cut the dough crosswise into strips ½ inch/1 cm wide (you will have 24 strips). Working with one piece of dough at a time, place a mini hot dog across one end of each dough strip, then roll up the dough around it. Place the pastries seam side down on the prepared baking sheets, staggering the rows to fit 12 cochons on each sheet.

IF YOU'RE USING THE ROUGH PUFF PASTRY, loosely cover the pastries with plastic wrap and refrigerate for 20 to 30 minutes before baking.

IF YOU'RE USING THE YEASTED PUFF PASTRY, cover the pastries with greased plastic wrap and let rise at room temperature until noticeably puffy, 1 to 1½ hours.

3. Preheat the oven to 375°F/190°C with the racks in the upper and lower thirds.

4. Egg-wash the surface of the pastries and transfer to the oven. Bake, switching the positions of the baking sheets halfway through, until the pastry is evenly golden brown: 26 to 30 minutes if using rough puff pastry, 30 to 35 minutes if using yeasted puff pastry.

5. Meanwhile, make the sauce: In a small bowl, whisk all the ingredients together until well combined.

6. Serve the warm piggies with the sauce.

(CONTINUES)

285

Variations

PULL-APART PIGS *If using Rough Puff Pastry*: Arrange the assembled pastries in two concentric circles on a parchment-lined baking sheet (see the photograph on page 264)—they should be touching one another. Egg-wash the surface of the dough and transfer to the oven. Bake for 25 to 30 minutes, or until the dough is deeply golden brown. Let cool slightly, then carefully transfer to a serving platter. If desired, place the sauce in a bowl in the center of the circle for serving.

If using Yeasted Puff Pastry: After assembling the pastries as directed above, let them rise, covered with greased plastic wrap, for 1 to 1½ hours, until noticeably puffy. Egg-wash and bake for 30 to 35 minutes, until the pastry is evenly golden brown.

VEGETARIAN LENTIL ROLLS Bring a medium pot of water to a boil. Add 200 g / 1 cup red lentils and simmer until tender, 15 to 18 minutes. Drain and transfer to a food processor or blender. Add 128 g / 1 bunch scallions, trimmed, 25 to 50 g / 1 to 2 canned chiles in adobo sauce (to taste), 10 g / 2 cloves garlic, chopped, 9 g / 1 tablespoon smoked paprika, and 3 g / 1 teaspoon garlic powder and process until smooth, then taste and season with salt and pepper. Add 90 g / 1⅓ cup panko bread crumbs and process until well combined. Turn the mixture out onto a work surface and divide into 4 equal portions. Form the lentil mixture into long logs about ¾ inch/2 cm in diameter, wrap tightly in plastic wrap, and refrigerate overnight. The next day, cut each log into 6 equal pieces (making 24 total). Use the lentil "sausages" in place of the mini hot dogs and proceed as directed. Bake for 30 to 34 minutes.

Brie Bites

Makes 15 bites

DIFFICULTY: **MEDIUM**

When I started seeing mini wheels of Brie in the store, I marveled at their cuteness. They also provide a lovely excuse to make individual puff pastry–wrapped Brie bites. I pair the cheese with a touch of hot pepper jelly, but it's also delicious with Caramelized Onions (page 26), Pickled Mustard Seeds (page 97), or just about any jam you like. If you can't find mini wheels, use 1-inch/ 2.5 cm cubes of Brie instead.

1 recipe Rough Puff Pastry (page 267), chilled as directed

105 g / ⅓ cup Pepper Jelly (page 136)

About 385 g / 15 mini Brie cheeses

Egg wash (see page 7) for finishing

Freshly ground black pepper for garnish

1. On a lightly floured surface, roll out the dough to a rectangle slightly larger than 9 x 15 inches/23 x 38 cm. Use a pastry wheel to trim the rough edges, making a 9 x 15-in/23 x 38 cm rectangle.

2. Cut the dough into 15 even squares: First cut it lengthwise into five 3-inch-/8 cm strips and then cut the strips crosswise into 3 x 3-inch-/ 8 x 8 cm squares.

3. Spoon 5 g / 1 teaspoon jelly onto the center of one square of dough and place a mini Brie on top of it. Pick up one of the corners of the dough and fold it over, pressing it down against the center of the Brie. Use your finger to dab a small amount of water onto the surface of the dough in the center, then fold another corner over onto the center as well. Continue this process, folding the corners over to encase the Brie and using water as needed to help seal the pastry. Press firmly with your fingers to smooth the dough where it overlaps to flatten it slightly and make sure the cheese is encased. Repeat with the remaining dough and cheese.

4. Line a baking sheet with parchment paper and transfer the pastries to it, seam side down, arranging them in staggered rows so they all fit on one baking sheet. Refrigerate while you preheat the oven.

5. Preheat the oven to 400°F/205°C with a rack in the center.

6. Egg-wash the surface of the pastries and garnish generously with black pepper. Transfer to the oven and bake until the pastries are deeply golden brown, 35 to 40 minutes. Cool for at least 10 minutes before serving warm.

Make Ahead and Storage
The bites are best the same day they are baked. They can be assembled ahead and refrigerated for up to 24 hours before baking.

Meatball Un-Sub

Makes 12 un-subs

DIFFICULTY: **MEDIUM**

I'm a big fan of hot sandwiches, and the meatball sub is high on my list of nearly perfect specimens. I say "nearly perfect," because there's no denying that the most delicious meatball sub is inherently a very messy one. But breaking it down into smaller pastries that can be eaten in a few bites does the trick for me. Fully wrapping the meatballs in dough can be trickier and lead to sogginess issues, so to keep this as simple as possible for bustling gatherings, I make these sort of open face. This makes them easier to eat too!

MEATBALLS

15 g / 1 tablespoon extra virgin olive oil, plus more for drizzling

230 g / 1 medium sweet onion, finely chopped

20 g / 4 cloves garlic, minced

10 g / ¼ cup chopped fresh parsley

56 g / 1 large egg, lightly whisked

15 g / 1 tablespoon Worcestershire sauce

15 g / 1 tablespoon Dijon mustard

3 g / 1 tablespoon chopped fresh oregano

1 g / 1 teaspoon chopped fresh thyme

6 g / 1 teaspoon kosher salt

Freshly ground black pepper

170 g / 6 ounces ground beef

170 g / 6 ounces ground pork

45 g / ⅔ cup bread crumbs, plus more as needed

UN-SUBS

½ recipe (about 475 g) pizza dough (page 181)

175 g / ¾ cup Roasted Garlic Tomato Sauce (page 155) or Spicy Creamy Tomato Sauce (page 155)

12 cooked meatballs (above)

240 g / 2 heaping cups shredded or finely chopped fresh mozzarella

1. Preheat the oven to 400°F/205°C with a rack in the center. Lightly grease a muffin pan with nonstick spray. Set a wire rack on a baking sheet.

2. Make the meatballs: In a medium skillet, heat the olive oil over medium heat. Add the onion and cook until tender, 4 to 5 minutes. Add the garlic and cook until fragrant, about 1 minute. Transfer the onion mixture to a medium bowl and allow to cool for 5 minutes.

3. Stir the parsley, egg, Worcestershire, mustard, oregano, thyme, salt, and pepper to taste into the onions. Add the meat and bread crumbs and mix just until uniformly combined.

4. Form the mixture into 12 equal portions and roll each one into a ball. Grease a baking sheet with olive oil, place the meatballs on it, and drizzle them with more oil.

5. Bake the meatballs until they are fully cooked, 22 to 24 minutes. When you remove the meatballs, place a baking steel or pizza stone on the oven rack, if desired (this will make a crispier bottom crust on the un-subs).

6. Make the un-subs: Divide the dough into 12 equal pieces (about 35 g each). Using oiled hands, gently stretch one piece of dough into a round, then place it in one of the cavities of the prepared muffin pan and press into an even layer that covers the base and sides of the cup. Repeat with the remaining dough.

7. Spoon 15 g / 1 scant tablespoon tomato sauce into the center of each muffin cup. Place a meatball in each one, spoon 5 g / 1 teaspoon tomato sauce on top of the meatball, and use the back of the spoon to spread it around to coat the surface.

8. Transfer to the oven and bake until the edges of the dough are lightly brown, 30 to 35 minutes. Use a small offset spatula and/or tongs to gently remove the unsubs from the muffin pan and transfer to the rack-lined baking sheet.

9. Divide the cheese among the un-subs, transfer the baking sheet to the oven, and bake until the sides of the crusts have browned more and the cheese has melted, 8 to 10 minutes. Serve warm.

Make Ahead and Storage
The un-subs are best the same day they are made. Store leftovers in an airtight container in the refrigerator and refresh by wrapping in foil and warming in a 350°F/175°C oven for 10 to 12 minutes.

Stuffed Mushroom Puffs

Makes 24 puffs

DIFFICULTY: **MEDIUM**

I was a picky kid, and mushrooms were on my list of least favorite foods. But when I started my pastry training, every instructor encouraged us to taste absolutely everything we could. I started by tackling foods I thought I didn't like, and soon I became a mushroom fanatic. Working with mushrooms is all about properly cooking them— roasting helps control the moisture and ensure nice color on the exterior (for more on this, see Roasted Mushrooms, page 295). This recipe combines the idea of a classic stuffed mushroom cap with a crisp, flaky crust. For a slightly less fussy version of the recipe, you can skip stuffing the mushrooms and instead just chop the roasted mushrooms; add them to the filling in step 6. That will allow you to use any kind of mushroom shape too, rather than white or cremini caps.

ROASTED MUSHROOM CAPS

About 360 g / 24 medium white or cremini mushroom caps

45 g / 3 tablespoons extra virgin olive oil

30 g / 2 tablespoons balsamic vinegar

Kosher salt and freshly ground black pepper

3 g / 1 teaspoon finely chopped fresh thyme (optional)

FILLING

28 g / 1 ounce / 2 tablespoons unsalted butter

15 g / 1 tablespoon extra virgin olive oil

650 g / 2 large sweet onions, thinly sliced

300 g / 2 large leeks, white and light green parts only, thinly sliced

30 g / 6 cloves garlic, minced

Kosher salt and freshly ground black pepper

115 g / ½ cup dry white wine

226 g / 8 ounces cream cheese, at room temperature

135 g / 1⅓ packed cups shredded Gruyère cheese

10 g / ¼ cup chopped fresh parsley

½ recipe Rough Puff Pastry (page 267), chilled as directed

1. Preheat the oven to 400°F/205°C with a rack in the center. Have two ungreased 12-cup mini muffin pans ready.

2. Roast the mushrooms: Arrange the mushroom caps in a single layer on a baking sheet, tops facing upward. Drizzle the olive oil and balsamic vinegar evenly over the mushrooms and toss well to coat. Season with salt, pepper, and the thyme, if using, and toss well again. Shake the tray to return the mushrooms into a fairly even layer.

3. Roast the mushrooms until they release their moisture and start to become tender, 15 to 22 minutes. Remove from the oven and cool to room temperature. Reduce the oven temperature to 350°F/175°C.

4. Meanwhile, prepare the filling: In a large pot, melt the butter over medium heat, then add the olive oil. Add the onions and cook until translucent, 4 to 5 minutes. Add the leeks and cook until they are wilted, 3 to 4 minutes. Reduce the heat to low and cook, stirring occasionally, until the onions and leeks are deeply caramelized, 30 to 35 minutes. Add the garlic

(CONTINUES)

293

and cook until fragrant, about 1 minute. Season with salt and pepper.

5. Raise the heat to high and add the white wine, stirring to deglaze the pot. Cook, stirring frequently, until the wine has almost completely evaporated. Remove from the heat and transfer the caramelized onions to a heatproof bowl.

6. Add the cream cheese to the bowl and stir well to thoroughly combine. Fold in the Gruyère and parsley.

7. Use a small spoon to scoop the filling into the cooled roasted mushroom caps, mounding it so it domes over the tops of the mushrooms and packing in as much as possible. Refrigerate while you prepare the pastry.

8. On a lightly floured surface, roll out the dough into a rough rectangle about ¼ inch/6 mm thick; don't worry about the exact dimensions of the dough, just try to keep it roughly square shaped and focus more on the thickness. Use a 2-inch/5 cm round cutter to cut out rounds of dough. You can press the dough scraps together and reroll them once or twice,

rolling and cutting until you have 24 rounds of pastry. If the dough gets warm or sticky as you roll it out, wrap and refrigerate it until it is firm before proceeding.

9. Dock each round of dough a few times with a fork. Place a piece of dough in each of the cavities of the mini muffin pans and press it evenly over the base and partway up the sides of the cavity. Refrigerate for 20 to 30 minutes.

10. Preheat the oven to 375°F/175°C with a rack in the center.

11. When the oven is preheated, place a stuffed mushroom in each cavity of the crust-lined muffin pans, pressing them down to the base of the cups if necessary. (It's nice if some of the pastry is visible around the edges of the mushroom caps, but with bigger mushrooms, it may not be.)

12. Transfer to the oven and bake until the pastry is deeply browned and crisp, 30 to 36 minutes. Let the pastries cool in the pan for 5 minutes, then run a small offset spatula around the edges of the puffs to release them from the pan. Serve immediately.

Make Ahead and Storage
The mushrooms can be roasted up to 2 days ahead, covered, and refrigerated. The filling can be prepared up to 2 days ahead and refrigerated in an airtight container. The baked puffs are best the same day they are baked. Store leftovers in an airtight container in the refrigerator (refresh as directed on page 120).

Roasted Mushrooms

Roasting mushrooms takes them from soft and spongy to a much more flavorful place, with a range of delightful crispness. While there are many ways to cook mushrooms, roasting is my go-to because I'm usually baking something, so my oven's already on. Roasting mushrooms is also a great way to concentrate their moisture content, which is helpful when using them in a filling or topping, or as an inclusion in a baked good.

To prepare mushrooms for roasting, wipe them clean with a dry cloth. If working with large mushrooms like oyster mushrooms, separate them into large chunks. Keep in mind that mushrooms shrink a lot as they cook, so if you want them to be bite-size after cooking, you can leave them a bit larger to start. Smaller mushrooms can be left whole or cut in half or into quarters. Some recipes call for removing the stems, but if they are clean and unbruised, I like to use the whole thing. You can trim off a small bit of the base stem, if desired. I often roast several pounds of mushrooms at a time, then enjoy them in various recipes or preparations.

Preheat the oven to 400°F/205°C with a rack in the center. Arrange 2 pounds mushrooms in a single layer on a baking sheet, drizzle with 60 g / ¼ cup extra virgin olive oil, and toss gently to coat. Season with salt and pepper and spread out on the baking sheet.

To partially roast the mushrooms, when they will be baked/cooked again (parcooking mushrooms this way is a great way to reduce their moisture for use in baking preparations), roast for 18 to 20 minutes, until tender and starting to brown but not crisp. To fully cook, roast until the mushrooms are lightly crisp and tender, 24 to 28 minutes. For super-crisp mushrooms, you can continue to roast until they are well browned, up to 15 minutes more.

Wee Quiches

Makes 12 mini quiches

DIFFICULTY: **MEDIUM**

While the word "mini" can sometimes mean fussy, mini quiches are simple to make. Because they are small, you can get away without parbaking the crust, as I would for a full-size quiche. They are perfect party fare since they can be served warm or at room temperature. My all-purpose crowd-pleasing combination of tomato, scallion, and cheddar can be replaced with any combo of veg, meat, or cheese that you wish. When I'm serving a really big group, I bake up multiple trays, each with a different filling. Looking for an even smaller (two-bite) treat? Try the Extra-Wee Quiches below.

2 recipes Pâte Brisée (page 321), prepared as a double batch, formed into a 1-inch-/2.5 cm thick disk, wrapped, and chilled

226 g / 4 large eggs

118 g / ½ cup heavy cream

115 g / ½ cup whole milk

4 g / ¾ teaspoon kosher salt

2 g / ¾ teaspoon freshly ground black pepper

20 g / 2 scallions, thinly sliced

125 g / 12 cherry tomatoes, quartered

75 g / ¾ cups shredded firm cheese, such as cheddar, Asiago, or Gruyère

1. Very lightly grease a 12-cavity muffin pan. On a lightly floured surface, roll out the dough into a large rectangle about ¼ inch/6 mm thick; don't worry about the exact dimensions of the dough, just try to keep it roughly rectangular in shape and focus more on the thickness. Use a 3¼-inch/8.25 cm round cookie cutter to cut 12 rounds from the dough. (You can press the dough scraps together and re-roll to cut out more rounds if necessary.)

2. Place one round of dough in each of the cavities of the prepared pan and press the dough firmly over the base and up the sides of the cups. Transfer the pan to the refrigerator and chill for 30 minutes.

3. Preheat the oven to 375°F/190°C with a rack in the center; place a baking steel or pizza stone on the rack, if you have one (this will ensure a crisper bottom crust when not parbaking).

4. In a medium bowl, whisk the eggs, cream, milk, salt, and pepper together to combine well. If you have a large liquid measuring cup or similar vessel with a pour spout, transfer the custard to it.

5. Remove the muffin pan from the fridge. Divide the scallions, tomatoes, and cheese evenly among the crusts. Carefully pour the custard over the vegetables/cheese, filling the crusts almost to the top.

6. Transfer the pan to the oven and bake until the edges of the crusts are deeply golden brown and the custard is set, 30 to 35 minutes. Cool for 5 minutes, then run a small offset spatula around the edges of each quiche and carefully remove them from the pan. Serve warm or at room temperature.

Variations

EXTRA-WEE QUICHES *Makes 24 two-bite quiches* Use a 2¼-inch/6 cm round cookie cutter to cut 24 rounds of dough, then press into the cavities of a greased 24-cavity mini muffin pan. Chill for 30 minutes. Divide the fillings and custard evenly among the chilled crusts—you'll probably have extra custard;

pour it into a lightly buttered ramekin and bake until set. Bake at 400°F/205°C (preferably on a baking steel or pizza stone) until the edges of the crusts are deeply golden brown and the custard is set, 20 to 25 minutes.

Make Ahead and Storage
The crusts can be prepared ahead and chilled for up to 24 hours (wrap tightly in plastic wrap). The quiches are best within 24 hours of baking. Store leftovers in an airtight container in the refrigerator.

Pork Lumpia

Makes 12 lumpia
DIFFICULTY: **HARD**

My brother Willie introduced me to crisp, juicy lumpia, and then fostered my sincere love of them. We sampled them first from a food cart on the streets of Amsterdam, and then he began hunting them down for regular consumption on his trips to visit me in New York City. I still think of him whenever I eat one, but now I express my own love for these bites of wonderfulness by making them as close to the traditional way as I can—beginning by making my own wrappers. The process reminds me of making a delicate pastry dough. I learned that the key to rolling out lumpia wrappers so beautifully thin comes from a special double-rolling technique. When you roll out each piece of dough on its own, it's difficult to get it much thinner than about ¼ inch/6 mm thick. But if you stack several pieces of rolled-out dough and roll again, they sort of cling to each other, enabling you to roll the whole stack out very thin. You briefly cook the stacks on the stovetop, and then you can peel the individual wrappers apart before you fill and fry the lumpia. It's a lovely process, as immensely satisfying as the freshly fried lumpia themselves.

WRAPPERS

180 g / 1½ cups all-purpose flour

2 g / ½ teaspoon fine sea salt

115 g / ½ cup room-temperature water (about 75°F/25°C)

Cornstarch for rolling

Neutral oil (such as canola or vegetable) for rolling

FILLING AND FINISHING

285 g / 10 ounces ground pork

110 g / ½ medium white onion, minced

75 g / 1 large carrot, peeled and finely shredded

40 g / 4 scallions, finely minced

15 g / 3 cloves garlic, minced

4 g / ¾ teaspoon kosher salt

2 g / ½ teaspoon freshly ground black pepper

56 g / 1 large egg

Egg wash (see page 7) for finishing

Neutral oil (such as canola or vegetable) for deep-frying

Sweet chile sauce for serving

1. Make the wrappers: In the bowl of a stand mixer fitted with the dough hook, mix the flour and salt on low speed to combine, about 15 seconds. Add the water and mix until the dough comes together around the dough hook, about 2 minutes. Raise the speed to medium and mix until the dough is smooth, 3 to 4 minutes more. (You can also mix the dough by hand—bring the dough together in a bowl, then knead until smooth, 5 to 6 minutes.)

2. Wrap the dough in plastic wrap and let rest for 30 minutes.

3. Place a small sifter over a bowl and fill it with cornstarch—you'll use this to sift over the dough and surface as you work. Divide the dough into 12 equal pieces (about 25 g each). Work with one piece of dough at a time, keeping the other pieces covered.

4. Dust a work surface and one piece of dough with cornstarch and use a rolling pin to roll the dough into a very thin round: Roll from

(CONTINUES)

the center outward and rotate the dough frequently to help prevent it from sticking. With this first rolling, you want to get the wrapper to about 5 inch/13 cm across. Brush the surface of the dough lightly with vegetable oil, sprinkle it with cornstarch, and set aside on your work surface. Roll out another piece of dough, brush lightly with vegetable oil, sprinkle with cornstarch, and stack on top of the first round. Continue until you've made a stack of 6 lumpia wrappers; cover loosely with plastic wrap. Repeat the process with the remaining dough to make a second stack of 6 lumpia wrappers.

5. Dust the work surface with cornstarch again, uncover one stack of the wrappers, and use the rolling pin to roll out each stack of wrappers even thinner—the rounds should be about 8 inches/20 cm wide. Repeat with the second stack of wrappers.

6. Heat a large nonstick skillet over medium heat. When it's hot, add one stack of lumpia wrappers and cook, turning once, for 10 to 15 seconds per side. Remove the stack from the pan, then gently pull the wrappers apart; set aside.

7. Make the filling: In a medium bowl, mix the pork, onion, carrot, scallions, garlic, salt, pepper, and egg together until well combined.

8. Scoop about 50 g/3 tablespoons of the filling toward the edge of a wrapper closest to you. Brush the far end of the dough lightly with egg wash. Fold the sides over the filling, then roll up the lumpia into a tight, skinny roll. Repeat with the remaining wrappers and filling.

9. Pour 2 to 3 inches/5 to 8 cm of oil into a heavy pot and attach a deep-fry thermometer to the side of the pot. Heat the oil over medium heat until it reaches about 325°F/165°C (you can also carefully check the temperature with an instant-read thermometer). Set a wire rack over a paper-towel–lined baking sheet.

10. Working in batches to avoid crowding, add the lumpia to the hot oil and fry until lightly golden brown and crisp, 6 to 8 minutes. Remove from the oil with a spider or slotted spoon and transfer to the rack to drain. When all the lumpia have been fried, heat the oil to 350°F/175°C and, again working in batches, fry the lumpia until deeply brown and very crisp, 4 to 5 minutes. Serve warm, with sweet chile sauce for dipping.

Make Ahead and Storage
The assembled lumpia can be frozen on a parchment-lined baking sheet until firm, then transferred to an airtight container and frozen for up to 3 months. Thaw the lumpia in the refrigerator for 2 hours before frying them. The fried lumpia are best immediately after cooking.

Dumpling Wrappers

Makes about 25 wrappers

DIFFICULTY: **MEDIUM**

As a lover of dough, I was happy to have the excuse to make my first dumpling wrappers. I was attempting to make a thicker, doughier style of dumpling and the store-bought wrappers available were too thin and delicate. This conundrum set me on a path I will follow the rest of my life: I love making dumplings. I find the process fun and even meditative—and the fruits of your labor are delicious to boot.

180 g / 1½ cups all-purpose flour

60 g / ½ cup cornstarch, plus more for dusting

2 g / ½ teaspoon fine sea salt

115 g / ½ cup water

1. Sift the flour, cornstarch, and salt into the bowl of a stand mixer. Attach the bowl to the mixer stand, fitted with the dough hook, and mix on low speed to combine, about 15 seconds. Add the water and mix on low speed until the dough comes together around the dough hook, about 2 minutes. Raise the speed to medium and mix until the dough is smooth, 3 to 4 minutes more.

If the dough appears dry, add more water 5 g / 1 teaspoon at a time until it comes together. (You can also mix the dough by hand—bring the dough together into a shaggy mass in a bowl, then knead on a clean work surface until smooth, 6 to 7 minutes.)

2. Gently round the dough (see page 104), transfer to a medium bowl, cover, and let rest for 45 minutes.

3. Divide the dough into 25 equal pieces (about 15 g each). Keep the dough you're not working with covered with plastic wrap. Lightly round each piece of dough, set aside on the work surface, cover, and let rest for 15 minutes.

4. Set a small sifter over a bowl and fill it with cornstarch—you'll use this to sift over the finished wrappers. Use a dry pastry brush to generously coat both sides of the wrapper with cornstarch—this will allow you to stack them without them sticking to one another. Stack in groups of 5 (to make it easier to separate the wrappers before using). The wrappers are ready to be used or wrapped and stored.

Make Ahead and Storage
The dumpling wrappers can be made ahead. Wrap the stacks of wrappers tightly in plastic wrap and place in a zip-top freezer bag. Refrigerate for up to 24 hours, or freeze for up to 2 months; defrost in the refrigerator overnight before using.

Steamed Pork and Chive Dumplings

Makes 25 dumplings

340 g / 12 ounces ground pork
40 g / 1 cup minced fresh chives
30 g / 3 scallions, finely minced
10 g / 2 cloves garlic, minced
5 g / 2 teaspoons cornstarch
56 g / 1 large egg, lightly beaten
45 g / 3 tablespoons soy sauce
10 g / 2 teaspoons sesame oil
Kosher salt and freshly ground black pepper (optional)
25 Dumpling Wrappers (page 301)

1. In a medium bowl, mix the pork, chives, scallions, garlic, cornstarch, egg, soy sauce, and sesame oil to combine. If desired, shape a little of this mixture into a small patty and cook in a small pan to test for seasoning before continuing, and season with salt and pepper if needed.

2. Spoon about 25 g / 1½ tablespoons of the filling into the center of one wrapper. Fold the dough over the filling to encase it and crimp the edges well to seal (see the photos on page 304). Repeat with the remaining wrappers and filling.

3. When you're ready to cook the dumplings, bring a large pot of water to a boil over medium heat. Working in batches to avoid crowding, add the dumplings to the water and use a spider or slotted spoon to gently move the dumplings around so they don't sink or stick to the bottom of the pot. If the water stops boiling, bring it back to a gentle simmer; if it's boiling rapidly, reduce the heat slightly. Cook the dumplings until they float to the surface and the filling is fully cooked, 8 or 9 minutes. Remove from the water with the spider or slotted spoon and serve immediately.

Panfried Mushroom Dumplings

Makes 25 dumplings

30 g / 2 tablespoons neutral oil (such as canola or vegetable), plus more for cooking the dumplings
140 g / 1 bunch scallions, thinly sliced
375 g / 4 cups finely chopped trimmed mushrooms (any variety; from about 1 pound)
7 g / 1 tablespoon finely grated peeled ginger
15 g / 3 cloves garlic, minced
30 g / 2 tablespoon rice vinegar
30 g / 2 tablespoons soy sauce
5 g / 1 teaspoon sesame oil
7 g / 1 tablespoons cornstarch
25 Dumpling Wrappers (page 301)

1. In a large skillet or wok, heat the oil over medium heat. Add the scallions, mushrooms, and ginger and stir-fry until the mushrooms have released their moisture and it has evaporated, 10 to 12 minutes.

2. Add the garlic and stir-fry until fragrant, about 1 minute. Add the vinegar, soy sauce, and sesame oil and stir well—the mushrooms should absorb the liquid almost immediately. Transfer to a heatproof bowl and cool to room temperature.

3. Stir the cornstarch into the filling, mixing well.

4. Spoon about 15 g / 1 heaping tablespoon of the filling into the center of one wrapper. Fold the dough over the filling to encase it and crimp the edges well to seal (see the photos on page 304). Repeat with the remaining wrappers and filling.

5. Pour ¼ inch / 6 mm of oil into a large nonstick skillet with a lid and heat until very hot but not

(CONTINUES)

smoking. You'll have to cook the dumplings in batches: Add only as many dumplings to the pan as fit comfortably (they shouldn't be touching) and sear until well browned on the bottom, 1 to 2 minutes (you can check them by gently lifting one up).

6. Add 60 g / ¼ cup water to the pan and immediately put the lid on (it will spatter!). Steam the dumplings until the water has completely evaporated and the filling is cooked through, 3 to 4 minutes. Remove the lid and cook for about 1 minute more to recrisp the bottoms of the dumpling. Remove from the pan, and repeat the process with the remaining dumplings.

7. Serve the dumplings hot.

Make Ahead and Storage
The filled dumplings can be prepared ahead and refrigerated or frozen. Place them on a parchment-lined baking sheet, cover with plastic wrap, and refrigerate for up to 6 hours before cooking. Or freeze the filled dumplings on the baking sheet until firm, then transfer to an airtight container and freeze for up to 3 months; add 2 to 3 minutes to the cooking time when cooking.

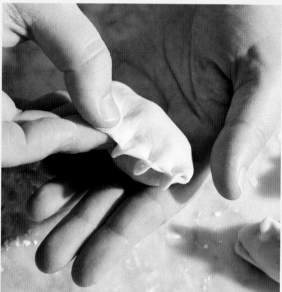

Potato, Onion, and Cheese Pierogi

Makes 18 pierogi

DIFFICULTY: **MEDIUM**

My dad has a rule: no starch on starch. But this baffles the rest of our family, who adore things like potatoes on pizza, or potato chips crumbled onto a sandwich. However, despite his firm starch stance, the rules do not apply to pierogi—soft, tender dough wrapped around an onion-spiked potato filling. The meatier chorizo, potato, and scallion variation below is an example of my perfect late-night, had-one-too-many-drinks sort of snacks.

DOUGH

280 g / 2⅓ cups all-purpose flour

3 g / ¾ teaspoon fine sea salt

75 g / ⅓ cup sour cream

56 g / 1 large egg, at room temperature

42 g / 1½ ounces / 3 tablespoons unsalted butter, melted

FILLING

42 g / 1½ ounces / 3 tablespoons unsalted butter

160 g / ½ large sweet onion, diced

226 g / 8 ounces potatoes, peeled and diced (about 1 large potato)

115 g / ½ cup sour cream

Kosher salt and freshly ground black pepper

100 g / 1 cup shredded sharp cheddar cheese

FINISHING

56 g / 2 ounces / 4 tablespoons unsalted butter

Freshly ground black pepper

Chopped fresh chives

1. Make the dough: In the bowl of a stand mixer fitted with the dough hook, mix the flour and salt on low speed to combine, about 15 seconds. Add the sour cream, egg, and melted butter and mix until a shaggy dough forms, about 3 minutes. If the dough seems dry or crumbly, add water 5 g / 1 teaspoon at a time until it comes together. Raise the speed to medium and mix until the dough is fairly smooth, about 2 minutes.

2. Turn the dough out and divide into 2 equal pieces (about 225 g each). Form each one into a disk about 1 inch/2.5 cm thick, wrap tightly in plastic wrap, and refrigerate for at least 1 hour (and up to 2 days).

3. Make the filling: In a large skillet, melt 28 g / 2 tablespoons of the butter over medium heat. Add the onions, reduce the heat to low, and cook, stirring occasionally, until they start to brown and caramelize, 25 to 30 minutes. Remove from the heat.

4. Meanwhile, place the potatoes in a medium saucepan, cover with water by 1 inch/2.5 cm, and bring to a boil over medium-high heat. Boil until the potatoes are tender, 12 to 15 minutes.

5. Drain the potatoes well and transfer to a medium bowl. Mash them with a potato masher, then fold in the sour cream, the remaining 14 g / 1 tablespoon butter, and salt and pepper to taste. Fold in the browned onions and cheese, cover, and set aside.

(CONTINUES)

6. On a lightly floured surface, roll out one disk of dough ⅛ inch/3 mm thick. Use a 3¼-inch/ 8 cm round cookie cutter to cut rounds from the dough. (Remove and reserve the scrap dough to re-roll as needed.) You should have 18 rounds.

7. Place about 25 g / 1 heaping tablespoon filling on one side of one round and gently fold the dough over the filling, taking care that there are no air pockets, to make a half-moon. If the dough is at all tacky, you can seal the pierogi without water. If the dough is dry or there is visible flour, use your fingertip to apply a little water to one side of the dough to help seal the edges. Use your fingers to firmly pinch the edges to seal, or press the tines of a small fork against them to seal, and place on a parchment-lined baking sheet. Repeat with the remaining rounds.

8. Repeat the process with the second disk of dough and the remaining filling.

9. Bring a large pot of water to a boil. Working in batches, add the pierogi a few at a time to the water—they will sink to the bottom, and if you add too many at once, they risk sticking to each other. Cook the pierogi until they float to the surface and the dough is cooked through, 4 to 5 minutes. Remove with a spider or slotted spoon, draining well, and transfer to a bowl or plate. Repeat with the remaining pierogi.

10. To finish the pierogi, in a large skillet, melt the butter over medium heat. Add the drained pierogi and cook, turning once, until lightly browned on both sides. Sprinkle with lots of pepper and finish with chives. Serve immediately.

Variation

CHORIZO, POTATO, AND SCALLION PIEROGI

Omit the onion and reduce the butter to 28 g / 1 ounce / 2 tablespoons. In a large skillet, melt 14 g / 1 tablespoon butter over medium heat. Crumble 140 g / 5 ounces ground chorizo into the pan and cook until well browned. Stir in 50 g / 5 scallions, thinly sliced, and cook until they wilt slightly, then remove from the heat. Prepare the potato filling as directed above and fold the chorizo/scallion mixture into the potatoes. You can use the cheddar cheese, or skip it (the chorizo adds a nice richness). Fill and cook the pierogi as directed.

Make Ahead and Storage

The dough can be made up to 2 days ahead and refrigerated, tightly wrapped, until ready to use. The assembled pierogi can be refrigerated on the lined baking sheet for up to 6 hours. Or freeze until firm, transfer to an airtight storage container, and freeze for up to 2 months. Cook the pierogi from frozen, but add 2 to 3 minutes to the cook time.

Swedish Sandwich Cake

Makes 6 to 8 servings

DIFFICULTY: **HARD**

One look, and I was in love with smörgåstårta—a stack of slices of bread and sandwich fillings that looks like a beautiful cake. The fillings can be just about anything, but I usually opt for my favorite egg salad, with layers of smoked salmon, sliced cucumbers, and mashed avocado. I recommend using herbs, edible flowers, fresh veggies, and microgreens to decorate the cake with the same abandon you'd normally use with sprinkles. This is the stuff of my fairy-tale tea party dreams—be sure your guests are standing nearby when you slice into it, because that's part of the fun.

HERBY EGG SALAD

226 g / 4 large eggs

60 g / ¼ cup mayonnaise

30 g / 2 tablespoons Dijon mustard

100 g / 2 stalks celery, minced

80 g / 8 scallions, thinly sliced

6 g / 2 tablespoons chopped fresh parsley

6 g / 2 tablespoons chopped fresh dill

6 g / 2 tablespoons chopped fresh chives

Kosher salt and freshly ground black pepper

SANDWICH CAKE

285 g / 10 ounces cream cheese, at room temperature

345 g / 1½ cups Greek yogurt

3 g / 1 teaspoon grated lemon zest

2 g / ½ teaspoon freshly ground black pepper

1 loaf Perfect White Sandwich Bread (page 130), cut into sixteen ½-inch-/1 cm thick slices

30 g / ¼ cup capers (optional)

226 g / 8 ounces thinly sliced smoked salmon

400 g / 2 avocados, halved, pitted, peeled, and thinly sliced

15 g / 1 tablespoon fresh lemon juice

300 g / 1 seedless cucumber, thinly sliced

About 35 g / 1 heaping cup sprouts (like radish or broccoli), rinsed and drained

GARNISH

Cherry tomatoes, halved, quartered, or whole

Seedless or Persian cucumbers, sliced

Radishes, trimmed and thinly sliced

Capers or caper berries

Snap peas, tender pea pods, and/or pea shoots

Microgreens, additional sprouts, or edible flowers

Everything Seasoning (page 177; optional)

1. Make the egg salad: Place the eggs in a small pot, cover with cool water by about 1 inch/ 2.5 cm, and bring to a boil over medium heat. Boil for 6 minutes. While the eggs cook, fill a bowl with ice water.

2. Drain the eggs, transfer to the ice water, and cool for 5 minutes. Drain, peel under cool running water, and finely chop.

3. In a medium bowl, whisk the mayonnaise, mustard, celery, scallions, parsley, dill, and chives to combine. Stir in the eggs and season with salt and pepper. Use the back of a fork to mash the mixture lightly—this will thicken it and make it easier to slice the "cake" later.

4. Assemble the cake: In the bowl of a stand mixer fitted with the paddle attachment, beat the cream cheese on medium speed until light and

fluffy, 3 to 4 minutes. Add the yogurt, lemon zest, and pepper and mix until well combined.

5. Place 4 slices of bread on a serving board or platter, arranging them to make a square shape. Spoon 100 g / ½ cup of the cream cheese mixture onto the bread and spread into an even layer, covering up the seams. If using, sprinkle the capers evenly over the top. Arrange the salmon in an even layer over the cream cheese. Place 4 more slices of bread on top of the salmon and press gently down to adhere slightly. Scoop the egg salad on top and spread in an even layer. Place 4 more slices of bread on top.

6. In a medium bowl, toss the avocado with the lemon juice, then use a fork to gently mash the avocado. Spread the mashed avocado in an even layer over the top layer of bread. Arrange the cucumber slices in an even layer on top, and then the sprouts. Finish the cake with the remaining 4 slices of bread.

7. Use the remaining cream cheese mixture to "frost" the top and sides of the cake. Chill the cake for at least 30 minutes (and up to 4 hours). Just before serving, decorate the sides and top of the cake with cherry tomatoes, cucumbers, radishes, capers, snap peas/pea shoots, and microgreens and sprinkle with everything seasoning, if desired.

Make Ahead and Storage
Once the cake is assembled, the bread will start to absorb moisture from the fillings (just like a regular sandwich), so it's best to assemble it no longer than 4 hours ahead.

CHAPTER 7

Pies and Tarts

TASTY STUFF ALL WRAPPED IN CRUSTS

It's no secret that I love pie, so much that I wrote a big, beautiful book on it: *The Book on Pie*. I adore anything in a crust—it gives the most amazing textural contrasts as you work your way through a slice. My grandma Jeanne (the dazzling woman I'm lucky enough to be named after) nurtured this love by spending a lot of time baking pies with me. Her kitchen became a creative space of sorts. We experimented more often than we followed recipes exactly, and we had some laughable failures. I've spent a huge chunk of my life trying to share the lessons I learned: pie can be *anything*.

This chapter was the hardest one in the book for me to write, because I am *never* at a loss for pie-deas. In *The Book on Pie* I talked about using leftovers to make great pies—I love to search through the depths of my fridge, see what bits and bobs I come up with, and turn them into a pie. But there were also a lot of other recipes that were ripe for pie-ifying, like the Tamale Pie-Pie on page 346, which uses corn tortilla dough (page 209) to create a press-in crust. The deep-dish mushroom potpie on page 324 enlists Buttermilk Biscuit dough (page 29) to make a woven topping. And the Croissant Breakfast Pie (page 241) uses Yeasted Puff Pastry Dough (page 236) for a crispy, golden crust. I hope you will find these recipes fun and satisfying to make. But more than that, I hope these pages spark some unique pie-deas of your own. And when it comes to pie techniques, the skills described below will serve you well even when your sweet tooth strikes. The pie-sabilities are truly endless.

Understanding Pie Dough

As someone who bakes a lot of pies, I think it's really all about muscle memory. Once you know what you're looking for, it's much easier to get to the desired result. Basic pie dough is a simple recipe, with very few ingredients: just flour, salt, fat, and water. But how you manipulate them can completely change the outcome. There are two major factors to keep in mind: fat size and hydration.

FAT SIZE

To make pie dough, chilled cubes of fat, such as butter or shortening, are mixed into the flour. The size the fat is reduced to at this stage is the main contributor to the final texture after baking.

FLAKY: Leaving the fat in larger pieces (the size of walnut halves) produces a lighter, flakier crust.

MEALY: Reducing the fat to smaller pieces (the size of peas) produces a denser but still-tender dough.

PÂTE BRISÉE: Dough made with this method is tender and lightly flaky, but it holds decorative details like crimping well. Mix the fat thoroughly into the flour until the mixture resembles cornmeal. I do this in the food processor, which makes quick work of it.

"EXTRA-FLAKY" (LAMINATING THE DOUGH): I enlist a simple form of lamination (see page 234) to add extra flakiness or create visible layers in my dough. This method is essentially a simpler version of the Rough Puff Pastry (page 267), with fewer folds—somewhere between a standard butter pie dough and rough puff in texture (I dare say . . . flaky AF). The fat is left in larger pieces than for flaky dough, slightly larger than walnut halves, but after mixing and chilling, the dough is rolled out ½ inch/1 cm thick and folded into quarters. This flattens out the pieces of butter in the dough, and then a second fold creates a layered, flaky dough. The dough should be chilled for at least 30 minutes before using.

HYDRATION

When a dough is properly hydrated, it will come together easily, although it may not appear smooth in texture—the flakier the dough, the craggier it may appear. When you place your clean, dry hand on the dough, it should come away with no visible stickiness or residue. The dough should be easy to roll out straight from the refrigerator.

TOO-WET DOUGH: A dough that's too wet will be sticky and difficult to handle without using a significant amount of flour for rolling it out. After baking, it will be tough and overly crisp, often unpleasantly so. If you see that your dough is too wet after mixing it, add more flour 7 g / 1 tablespoon at a time and gently knead a few times to incorporate it. And increase the chill time by 15 to 30 minutes to compensate for the additional handling. If the dough is still too wet after mixing and chilling, you can compensate by using more flour on your work surface and the dough as you roll it out. The dough will absorb this flour as you work, but be forewarned—it may still be tough/overly crisp after baking.

TOO-DRY DOUGH: A dough that's too dry will look crumbly and may even have visible dry patches of flour. It will be very difficult to work with, as it may be fall apart (very dry) or crack (slightly dry) when you roll it out or handle it. If you see that your dough is slightly too dry while you're still mixing, dip your fingers in ice water and gently flick a few drops onto the dough, then gently knead to incorporate. Continue if necessary until the dough is properly hydrated. If your dough is too dry after mixing and chilling, you can roll it out 1/2 inch/1 cm thick and gently flick a few drops of ice water over the surface as directed above, then gently fold the dough over onto itself and knead a few times to incorporate. Wrap and refrigerate for at least 30 minutes before using.

WHEN IN DOUBT, CHILL IT OUT

Chilling the dough is important. Many common pie problems can be alleviated or even prevented by thorough chilling. Cold dough is easier to work with, holds its shape better in the oven, and bakes better too! If you aren't sure whether or not you should give your dough another chill, it probably means you should: when in doubt, chill it out. The chart below shows the three most important times for chilling your dough.

	Minimum Chill	Recommended Chill	Maximum Chill
After Mixing	30 minutes	1 hour	2 days
Before Crimping	5 minutes	15 minutes	1 hour
Before Baking (optional)	15 minutes	30 minutes	1 hour

PREP SCHOOL

Lining the Pie Plate

After chilling, the dough is ready to be rolled out and transferred to the pie plate. Lightly flour the dough and work surface. Begin to roll out the dough by positioning the rolling pin in the center of the dough, then applying gentle pressure and push the pin away from you. Return it to the center and do the same, this time bringing the pin toward you. Rotate the dough frequently as you work, and even flip it over. This will help keep the dough from sticking and also allows you to feel the thickness to determine if there are thicker areas you haven't hit evenly with your pin yet. As the dough round (or rectangle) gets bigger, use the pin to help you move it around—roll it up around the pin, then unfurl in a new spot, rather than using your hands to move it. Instead of focusing on the diameter of the rolled-out dough, I often tell people to focus on the thickness. When the dough is rolled out evenly to the correct thickness (⅛ to ¼ inch/3 to 6 mm), it should be the correct size. Of course, you can always use your pan as a guide when you roll, placing it lightly on top of the dough to help see when you're getting close. I like to use the rolling pin to transfer the dough to the pie plate: place the rolling pin near the edge of the dough closest to you and roll up the dough around the pin. Gently unfurl the dough, centered, over the pie plate.

SINGLE-CRUST PIE: Once you've lined the pie plate with the dough, use scissors to trim away the excess dough, ideally ending up with ½ inch/1 cm of excess all around the edges. Tuck the excess dough under itself all around so the edges of the crust are flush with the edge of the pie plate. Press lightly to seal the dough all around. The crust is now ready to be crimped, if desired.

DOUBLE-CRUST PIE: Line the pie plate with the bottom crust as directed above, cover with plastic wrap, and refrigerate while you roll out the top crust. Roll out the top crust the same way you rolled out the bottom crust, then pour the prepared filling to the chilled bottom shell. Use the rolling pin to transfer the top crust to the pie, gently unfurling it over the filling. Pinch the top and bottom crusts together all around the edges. This both helps them adhere to each other and also thins out the part where they touch so it isn't too thick. Use scissors to trim away any excess dough, ideally ending up with ½ inch/1 cm excess all the way around the edges of the pie plate. Tuck the excess dough under itself all around so the edges of the crust are flush with the outer edge of the pie plate. The crust is now ready to be crimped, if desired.

CRIMPING AND FINISHING: There are lots of ways to add a little decorative flair to your piecrust edges. Here are a few of my favorites:

UTENSIL CRIMPS: Look around your kitchen, find a utensil, dip it in flour, and press it into the edges of your crust. Using the tines of a fork is the most common crimp, but the bowl of a spoon, the tip of tongs, or even a single pie weight can all make attractive impressions in the dough.

FINGER CRIMPS: There are as many styles of finger crimps as there are pie bakers in the world. I use my dominant hand to hold the outer edge of the crust. Then I use the pointer finger of my nondominant hand to press a V shape to create the crimp shape, while also pressing down to help seal the crust to the pie plate. Some people use their knuckles instead of their fingers—and there is no one right way!

CUTOUTS FROM THE TOP CRUST: Instead of cutting a vent in the top crust of a double-crust pie, use small cookie cutters to cut out decorative shapes instead.

SCRAP DOUGH: I use scrap dough to make decorative elements like cutouts, twists, or braids to decorate the crust edge or the top crust.

Whens and Whys of Pies

DOCK

"Docking" means to prick holes in the dough before baking. As the crust bakes, the steam can escape from these holes. Without docking, the dough is likely to puff up or form large air bubbles between the pan and dough, particularly during par- and blind-baking. For some doughs, like the Press-In Tart Dough on page 322, docking is all you need to prevent the dough from puffing up during baking. For most pie doughs, though, you usually need to use pie weights (see below).

EGG WASH

I usually egg-wash the surface of double-crust pies—not the edges, which tend to brown enough on their own. You can skip the egg wash when par- or blind-baking a bottom crust unless you want an added boost of shine around the edges—in which case, add the egg wash after removing the pie weights and returning the crust to the oven for its final bake.

CUT VENTS

Cutting a vent or a few vents in the top crust of a double-crust pie allows steam to escape as the pie bakes. Be sure to cut the vents after applying finishes like egg wash, which could close up the vents or pool in them.

PARBAKE

Parbaking means to partially bake a crust before filling it and then baking the pie. I recommend parbaking for all single-crust pies. It's difficult to sufficiently bake the bottom crust (especially when it's weighed down by filling) without giving it a head start. The docked pie crust should be well chilled. Cut a square of parchment paper that is slightly larger than your pie plate. Press the paper into the pie plate and fill with enough pie weights to come to the rim of the pan (I use ceramic pie weights, but you can also use dried beans or rice). Place on a parchment-lined baking sheet and bake at 425°F/220°C, preferably on a baking steel or stone, for 15 to 17 minutes, until the edges of the crust appear set and are just starting to lightly brown. Remove the pan from the oven and use the parchment paper to lift the pie weights out of the crust. Return the pan to the oven and bake until the base of the crust appears set, 2 to 3 minutes more. Let the crust cool completely.

BLIND-BAKE

Blind-baking refers to fully baking the bottom crust before filling it. It is usually done for single-crust pies with a cold-set filling. Follow the instructions for parbaking above, but after removing the pie weights, bake the crust for 10 to 12 minutes more, until it is evenly golden brown and fully baked.

Note: If your par- or blind-baked pie crust puffs up after you've removed the pie weights, even when you've docked the dough, dock it a few more times in those spots with a fork or the tip of a paring knife to deflate them before returning the crust to the oven.

Doneness Indicators

When it comes to pie crust, don't be afraid to get it *really* golden brown. A crust that appears browned in some places but still blond in others probably needs more oven time. Alternatively, to prevent overbrowning, you can tent the whole pie or a portion of it with foil for the remaining bake time if necessary.

PARBAKED CRUSTS: Look for lightly golden edges and a base that appears lighter in color, matte, and set.

BLIND-BAKING: Look for deeply golden edges and a lightly golden base.

DOUBLE-CRUST PIES: Look for even browning on the top crust. If it appears splotchy or blond, tent any darker portions with foil and keep baking.

FREE-FORM PIES: The pie should easily slide back and forth on the baking sheet if you shift the pan back and forth.

— FLAVOR BOOSTER —

Pie Dough

There are lots of ways to add other flavors to your pie dough. Dry ingredients are the easiest—adding dried spices or herbs, for example, to the flour, or subbing out some of the flour (as in the Spelt and Whole Wheat variations for the All-Buttah Pie Dough, page 320) is easy to do. Ingredients that contain a small amount of moisture, like fresh herbs, citrus zest, or firm cheeses, are usually stirred in after the fat is cut in (before adding the water). Or add flavor with a compound butter (see page 200). Compound butters may behave slightly differently than regular butter, depending on the moisture content and you may need to compensate for that by using less water.

PREP SCHOOL
Perfect Your Process

Deep-Dish Pie Plates

Regular pie plates are up to 1½ inches/4 cm deep, while deep-dish pie plates are typically between 1¾ and 2½ inches/4 and 6 cm deep. If you make a standard pie recipe in a deep-dish pie plate, the filling may seem skimpy. In that case, you might want to add another layer of filling for a layered pie (like the Hominy and Greens Pie on page 326). But if you try to make a deep-dish pie recipe in a standard pie plate, the filling may mound over the top edges of the pie plate or be at risk of overflowing. A cast-iron skillet makes a good substitute for a deep-dish pie plate if you don't have one. I also use other large pans, like springforms or casserole dishes up to 3 inches/8 cm deep, for some of the recipes in this book.

Pie Weights

Pie weights are used to weight down the base and sides of the crust during par- or blind-baking. I have a large collection of ceramic pie weights, but dried beans or rice work just fine, and you can reuse them many times (they will no longer be edible). About 1.36 kg / 3 pounds dried beans or rice will be enough to fill a standard or deep-dish pie plate.

Baking Steels and Baking Stones

Baking steels and baking stones (also known as pizza stones) retain heat, helping promote even browning of the bottom crust. They also help the oven temperature stay regulated and come back to temperature faster after opening the oven door. I like to use a baking steel when parbaking a crust, but keep in mind that with longer total bake times (around 1 hour or more), there can be too much browning. In those cases, I place the oven racks in the upper and lower thirds of the oven, with the baking steel or stone on the bottom rack. I bake the pie on the bottom rack for up to 50 minutes, then move the pie to the upper rack for the remainder of baking, so it is no longer in direct contact with the stone.

Easiest Crusts Ever

Scared of pie dough? Never fear! There are many delicious crust alternatives. Here are a few of my favorites:

Crumb Crust

Crumb crusts can be made of just about anything. They are more commonly thought of for sweet pies and other applications, like graham cracker crust, but in the savory world, you can make them with just about anything crispy, like crackers or pretzels. Grind them into crumbs, coarse or fine, depending on the recipe. Add melted butter to the crumbs and mix to combine—the crumbs should hold together when you squeeze them between your fingers. Greasier ingredients, like potato chips, will probably not make ideal crumb crusts.

Cooked-Grain Crust

Leftover cooked grains can be combined with egg whites to produce an easy press-in crust; see the Spicy Eggplant Pie on page 355, which is made with a cooked-rice crust. Cooked-grain crusts are also delicious made with quinoa or bulgur, or even leftover small pasta shapes like orzo.

Tortilla Crust

Flour tortillas are one of my favorite unusual crust alternatives. An XL Flour Tortilla (page 212) perfectly lines a standard pie plate—just coat the pan with nonstick spray, warm the tortilla, and press it in. Small tortillas (flour or corn) can be used to line individual baking dishes (or can be baked free-form on a baking sheet). You can also overlap several tortillas to line a larger baking vessel, or stack tortillas to create a sliceable end result; see the Enchilada Pie on page 363.

Phyllo Crust

I use homemade Phyllo Dough (page 224) for the Root Vegetable Pastilla on page 226. You can also stack up to 8 buttered sheets of thawed frozen store-bought phyllo dough to make an easy crust that bakes up golden and very crisp. Because they are so thin, phyllo crusts don't usually require parbaking.

All-Buttah Pie Dough

Makes one 9-inch/23 cm crust (see Note)
DIFFICULTY: **MEDIUM**

This is my go-to pie dough recipe: all buttah, all the time. Butter can be harder for beginners to work with than other fats, like shortening, because it has a lower melting point, but the flavor can't be beat. Once you know how to handle it, it's easy. The key? When in doubt, toss everything (the ingredients, the bowl, even the half-mixed dough) into the fridge before continuing. Colder is always better when pie dough is involved. Once you've tried your hand at the classic version here, try the golden cheese variation or the nutty-tasting variations made with spelt or whole wheat flour below.

151 g / 1¼ cups all-purpose flour

1 g / ¼ teaspoon fine sea salt

113 g / 4 ounces / 8 tablespoons cold unsalted butter, cut into ½-inch / 13 mm cubes

57 g / ¼ cup ice water, plus more if needed

1. In a medium bowl, whisk the flour and salt to combine. Add the cold butter cubes and toss well, separating the cubes and ensuring that they are fully coated in flour. Use your hands or a pastry cutter to cut the butter into the flour by pressing the pieces between your fingers, flattening the cubes into big shards (you can also do this by gently pulsing the ingredients in the food processor). As you work, continue to toss the butter with the flour, recoating the shingled pieces. Continue to mix in the fat to the desired level, depending on the final texture you want (see page 312).

2. Make a well in the center of the flour mixture (if using a food processor, transfer the flour mixture to a medium bowl at this point). Add the ice water to the well and toss with your hands to mix the flour and water together (this will start to combine them without creating too much gluten). As the flour begins to become hydrated, you can switch to more of a gentle kneading motion. Then continue lightly kneading the dough, adding more water, about 15 g / 1 tablespoon at a time as necessary, until it is properly hydrated: It should be uniformly combined and hold together easily, but it won't look totally smooth. Dough that is too dry may have sort of a "dusty" appearance or pockets of flour; it will be crumbly and won't hold together. Dough that is too wet will feel sticky or tacky.

3. Turn the dough out and form it into an even disk (if you are multiplying the recipe to make several crusts, divide the dough appropriately). Wrap tightly in plastic wrap and refrigerate for at least 30 minutes (and up to 2 days) before using.

4. This dough is best baked at 400 to 425°F/ 205 to 220°C. Roll out as directed on page 314 and transfer to a 9-inch/23 cm pie plate (this makes enough for a standard pie plate, with some excess dough to be trimmed away, or a deep-dish pie plate, with little to no scrap dough). Parbake (see page 315), blind-bake (see page 316), or fill and bake as directed.

Note: This recipe can be increased by up to 4 times. More than that, the dough becomes difficult to mix effectively.

(CONTINUES)

Variations

GOLDEN CHEESE PIE DOUGH **After cutting in the butter in step 1, stir in 113 g / 4 ounces shredded firm or semi-firm cheese, such as cheddar, Gruyère, Manchego, or Parmesan, and proceed as directed.**

SPELT PIE DOUGH **Reduce the all-purpose flour to 60 g / ½ cup and add 100 g / 1 cup spelt flour.**

WHOLE WHEAT PIE DOUGH **Reduce the all-purpose flour to 90 g / ¾ cup and add 90 g / ¾ cup whole wheat pastry flour (preferred) or whole wheat flour. This dough will require more water to come together—I usually start with 75 g / ⅓ cup.**

Make Ahead and Storage
The tightly wrapped dough can be refrigerated for up to 3 days. Wrapped in plastic wrap and then aluminum foil, it can be frozen for up to 3 months. Thaw overnight in the fridge before using.

When to Cheese, Please

There's a lot of cheese in this book, and you'll notice that in different recipes it's added at different times. Here's a guide to achieving the perfect cheese texture on top of your baked good using shredded, grated, or thinly sliced cheese.

Before Baking	The cheese is likely to brown and become very crisp. This is especially important to note for long bake times, like pies.
Mid-Bake	The cheese is added partway through baking so that it melts but stays gooey and doesn't brown much.
After Baking	Slices or shredded cheese can be added after baking. It will melt in the residual heat of the baked good (think: the cheese on top of a burger). Cheese can also be used as a finishing/garnishing element once the baked good has cooled.

Pâte Brisée

Makes one 9-inch/23 cm crust

DIFFICULTY: **EASY**

Pâte brisée, a classic French pastry dough, is easy to make and reliably tender and flaky. I often recommend it as a great place to start for anyone who has struggled with pie dough in the past. While you can mix the dough by hand, the food processor makes quick work of it. This is the best crust when I want to get from zero to pie as quickly as possible. The result is versatile enough for many pie preparations, and it also works beautifully for décor work.

151 g / 1¼ cups all-purpose flour

2 g / ½ teaspoon fine sea salt

113 g / 4 ounces / 8 tablespoons cold unsalted butter, cut into ½-inch / 13 mm cubes

45 g / 3 tablespoons ice water, plus more as needed

1. In the bowl of a food processor, pulse the flour and salt to combine. Add the butter and pulse until the mixture resembles coarse meal. Drizzle the water over the flour and pulse to incorporate, stopping before the dough comes together into a ball. If the dough is dry or crumbly, add more water 15 g / 1 tablespoon at a time, pulsing until it comes together.

2. Turn the dough out, form into a disk, and wrap tightly in plastic wrap. Refrigerate for at least 30 minutes (and up to 2 days) before using.

3. This dough is best baked at 400°F/205°C. Par-bake (see page 315), blind-bake (see page 316), or fill and bake as directed.

Make Ahead and Storage
The tightly wrapped disk of dough can be refrigerated for up to 2 days. Wrapped in plastic wrap and then aluminum foil, it can be frozen for up to 3 months. Thaw overnight in the fridge before using.

Press-In Tart Dough

Makes one 9- to 10-inch/23 to 25 cm tart crust

DIFFICULTY: **EASY**

This dough is so easy it doesn't even require a rolling pin—just press the dough evenly into the pan. Amanda Hesser, one of the founders of Food52, taught me the wonderful trick of lining the sides of the pan first—it makes it easier to keep the crust even. Then crumble the rest of the dough over the base of the pan and press it into an even layer.

180 g / 1½ cups all-purpose flour

12 g / 1 tablespoon granulated sugar

3 g / ¾ teaspoon fine sea salt

113 g / 4 ounces / 8 tablespoons cold unsalted butter, cut into ½-inch/1 cm cubes

30 g / 2 tablespoons ice water, plus more if needed

1. In the bowl of a food processor, pulse the flour, sugar, and salt to combine. Add the butter and pulse until the butter is fully incorporated—the mixture will look a bit like cornmeal. Drizzle the water over the flour and pulse to incorporate, stopping before the dough comes together into a ball. If the dough is dry or crumbly, add more water 5 g / 1 teaspoon at a time, pulsing until it comes together.

2. Transfer the dough to a 9- to 10-inch/23 to 25 cm tart pan and press some of it evenly up the sides of the pan to line them. Then press the rest of the dough over the base in an even layer. Dock it a few times with a fork and refrigerate for 30 minutes before using.

3. This dough is best baked at 375°F/190°C. Fill and bake as directed, or parbake (see page 315) or blind-bake (see page 316) without pie weights: Parbake for 18 to 22 minutes, or blind-bake for 28 to 32 minutes. If the crust puffs up during baking, use the tip of a paring knife to dock it again, or gently press the crust against the base of the pan using a small offset spatula to deflate it.

Variations

OLIVE OIL PRESS-IN TART DOUGH **Replace the butter with 115 g / ½ cup extra virgin olive oil. Pulse to combine as directed in step 1, then add water 15 g / 1 tablespoon at a time and pulse until the mixture comes together around the blade.**

HERB PRESS-IN TART DOUGH **Add up to 9 g / 3 tablespoons fresh herbs along with the salt in step 1.**

PARMESAN PRESS-IN TART DOUGH **Add 50 g / ½ cup finely grated Parmesan cheese along with the salt in step 1.**

Make Ahead and Storage
This dough is best used the day it's made.

Double-Crust Mushroom Potpie

Makes one 9-inch/23 cm deep-dish pie

DIFFICULTY: **MEDIUM**

A potpie usually has just a top crust, but I unapologetically choose to go the double-crust route. I bake it in a springform pan so I can get plenty of filling inside, for an ideal flakiness-to-creamy-filling ratio. Sometimes I stir in some peas or corn at the end of cooking this filling. Be sure to check out my classic chicken and turkey potpie subs in the Variations below.

1360 g / 3 pounds mushrooms (any variety, or a combination), cut into bite-size pieces

30 g / 2 tablespoons extra virgin olive oil

85 g / 3 ounces / 6 tablespoons unsalted butter

440 g / 2 medium sweet onions, diced

220 g / 4 medium carrots, peeled and diced

200 g / 4 stalks celery, diced

25 g / 5 cloves garlic, minced

Kosher salt and freshly ground black pepper

115 g / ½ cup dry Madeira or sherry

40 g / ⅓ cup all-purpose flour

690 g / 3 cups vegetable broth

118 g / ½ cup heavy cream

6 g / 2 teaspoons chopped fresh rosemary

3 g / 1 teaspoon chopped fresh thyme

3 recipes All-Buttah Pie Dough (page 319; I like to use the Extra-Flaky method here—see page 312), prepared as one large batch and chilled

1. Make the filling: Preheat the oven to 375°F/190°C with a rack in the center.

2. Spread the mushrooms into an even layer on a baking sheet. Drizzle with the olive oil and toss gently to coat. Transfer to the oven and roast until the mushrooms are lightly browned, 20 to 25 minutes. For even cooking, remove the pan from the oven halfway through roasting and toss the mushrooms, then spread out again in an even layer and return to the oven.

3. While the mushrooms roast, in a large pot, melt 28 g / 1 ounce / 2 tablespoons of the butter over medium heat. Add the onions, carrots, and celery and cook, stirring occasionally, until tender, 7 to 9 minutes.

4. Use a slotted spoon to transfer the roasted mushrooms to the pot (leaving any liquid in the pan behind—you can add it later along with the vegetable broth, if you like) and cook, stirring occasionally, for 2 minutes. Add the garlic and cook until fragrant, about 1 minute. Season the mixture with salt and pepper to taste.

5. Add the Madeira or sherry to the pot and cook, stirring frequently, until most of the liquid has evaporated, 8 to 10 minutes.

6. Add the remaining 56 g / 2 ounces / 4 tablespoons butter to the pot, stirring until melted. Sprinkle the flour evenly over the mushrooms and immediately stir to combine. Cook, stirring constantly, for 1 minute. Add the broth, stirring well, and bring the to a simmer over medium-low heat, stirring constantly. Continue to simmer, stirring occasionally, until the sauce has thickened, 4 to 5 minutes.

7. Stir in the cream, rosemary, and thyme and simmer for 1 to 2 minutes more. Season with salt and pepper to taste again. Remove from the heat and cool completely. You can do this

(CONTINUES)

more quickly by pouring the mixture onto a baking sheet and spreading it into an even layer.

8. Assemble the potpie: Divide the pie dough into 2 pieces, one twice as large as the other (you'll use two-thirds of the dough for the bottom crust and one-third for the top crust). Wrap and refrigerate the smaller portion while you roll out the bottom crust.

9. Place a 9-inch/23 cm springform pan on a parchment-lined baking sheet. On a lightly floured surface, roll out the dough to a round about ¼ inch/6 mm thick; it should be about 17 inches/43 cm across. Use the rolling pin to carefully transfer it to the springform pan and gently unfurl it into the pan. Gently lift the edges of the dough and press it evenly over the base and up the sides of the pan. If necessary, use scissors to trim away excess dough, leaving just a 1-inch/2.5 cm overhang. Dock the base and sides of the crust all over with fork. Cover loosely with plastic wrap and refrigerate for 30 minutes. Toward the end of chill time, preheat the oven to 425°F/220°C with a rack in the center; if you have a baking steel or pizza stone, place it on the rack.

10. Uncover the crust. Cut a piece of parchment paper that is slightly larger than the pan, press it into the pan, and fill with enough pie weights to come to the rim of the pan. Transfer the baking sheet with the pan to the oven and bake for 18 to 20 minutes, until the crust is lightly golden at the edges.

11. Remove the paper and pie weights, return the crust to the oven, and bake until the base appears evenly baked and set, 5 to 6 minutes more. Remove from the oven and immediately use scissors to trim away the edges of the crust. Discard (aka: snack on) the trimmings and cool the crust to room temperature. (Leave the oven on.)

12. Spoon the filling into the cooled crust, spreading it into an even layer. On a lightly floured surface, roll out the second piece of dough to ¼-inch-/6 mm thick round about 10 inches/25 cm wide. Use the rolling pin to transfer the dough to the pie, unfurling it over the filling. Trim the excess dough away with scissors, leaving only about ½ inch/1 cm all around the edges. Gently tuck the excess dough between the bottom crust and the sides of the pan. Use a fork to crimp the edges, firmly pressing the top crust against the bottom crust.

13. Egg-wash the top of the pie (no need to egg-wash the crimped edges—they will brown enough on their own). Use the tip of a paring knife to cut a few vents in the top crust. Transfer the pie to the oven and bake until the crust is deeply golden brown; the filling should be bubbling up through the vents (or there should be lots of steam puffing out of the vents), 45 to 55 minutes.

14. Cool the potpie for at least 15 minutes before slicing and serving warm.

Variations

CHICKEN OR TURKEY POTPIE **Omit the mushrooms and olive oil and start with step 3. In step 7, stir in 575 g / 4 heaping cups diced cooked chicken or turkey along with the cream and herbs. Proceed as directed.**

DEEP-DISH POTPIE WITH WOVEN BISCUIT TOPPING **Make a double recipe of dough (you'll only be making a bottom crust). Make 1 recipe Buttermilk Biscuit dough (page 29), form it into a disk 1 inch/2.5 cm thick, wrap tightly in plastic wrap, and refrigerate for 1 hour. In step 12, spoon the filling evenly into the bottom crust.**

On a lightly floured surface, roll out the biscuit dough ½ inch/1 cm thick. Cut into

strips and weave into a lattice on the top of the pie. Trim away the excess dough so that the edges of the lattice are flush with the edges of the bottom crust. Use a fork to crimp the edges of the biscuit lattice against the bottom crust to seal. If the biscuit dough feels sticky at this point, refrigerate the pie for 15 minutes before continuing. Egg-wash the top of the pie (no need to egg-wash the crimped edges), then bake at 350°F/175°C until the biscuit topping is evenly browned and baked through, 50 minutes to 1 hour. Cool for at least 15 minutes before serving warm. Note: You will have some extra biscuit dough—smoosh it back together, chill it, and then roll/cut/bake as classic biscuits (see page 29) or freeze to bake later.

Make Ahead and Storage
The filling can be made up to 3 days ahead and refrigerated in an airtight container. The bottom crust can be parbaked up to 24 hours ahead. This pie is best eaten the same day it's made. Store leftovers, covered, in the refrigerator and refresh as directed on page 365.

Hominy and Greens Pie

Makes one 9-inch/23 cm deep-dish pie

DIFFICULTY: **MEDIUM**

This pie contains two fillings that are each delicious on their own but together are a real delight. One is braised greens; the second is a creamy, cheesy "stew" made with hominy, dried maize (corn) kernels that are soaked in an alkaline solution (nixtamalized) that gives them their puffed appearance and appealing texture. This is a hearty comfort food—one that you'll want to bake when the weather first turns chilly, and then keep making until spring comes.

BRAISED GREENS FILLING

30 g / 2 tablespoons extra virgin olive oil

320 g / 1 large sweet onion, minced

About 20 g / 2 serrano chiles or 1 large jalapeño, minced (optional)

680 g / 1½ pounds greens (collards, mustard greens, chard, or kale), tender stems finely chopped, leaves roughly torn

20 g / 4 cloves garlic, minced

60 g / ¼ cup dry white wine

Kosher salt and freshly ground black pepper

HOMINY FILLING

One 795 g / 28 ounce can hominy, well drained

15 g / 1 tablespoon extra virgin olive oil

43 g / 1½ ounces / 3 tablespoons unsalted butter

140 g / 1 bunch scallions, thinly sliced

14 g / 2 tablespoons all-purpose flour

305 g / 1⅓ cups whole milk

50 g / ½ cup shredded cheddar cheese

50 g / ½ cup shredded Monterey Jack cheese

Kosher salt and freshly ground black pepper

One 9-inch/23 cm pie crust made with All-Buttah Pie Dough (page 319), parbaked (see page 315) and cooled completely

Smoked paprika for finishing

1. Make the greens: In a large pot, heat the olive oil over medium heat. Add the onion and chile(s) and cook until starting to become tender, 4 to 5 minutes. Add the greens a few handfuls at a time, letting each addition wilt, 30 seconds to 1 minute, before adding more.

2. Add the garlic and toss to combine. Add the wine, season with salt and pepper, cover the pot, and cook until the greens are tender, 6 to 8 minutes. Remove the lid and continue to cook, stirring occasionally, until any remaining moisture has evaporated, 2 to 4 minutes more. Remove from the heat and cool to room temperature.

3. Make the hominy: Preheat the oven to 375°F/190°C with a rack in the center.

4. Spread the hominy in an even layer on a baking sheet. Drizzle the oil over the top and toss gently to coat. Transfer the hominy to the oven and toast until fragrant and lightly browned, 8 to 10 minutes. Set aside.

5. In a medium pot, melt the butter over medium heat. Add the scallions and cook for 1 minute, stirring constantly, or until wilted. Sprinkle the flour over the scallions and stir to combine, then add the milk, stirring frequently while you bring the mixture to a simmer.

6. Add the toasted hominy and cook, stirring frequently, until the sauce is thick and coats the hominy. Turn off the heat and fold in the

cheeses. Season with salt and pepper. Let cool for at least 10 minutes.

7. Scoop the cooled greens into the pie crust and pack into an even layer. Scoop the hominy mixture on top and sprinkle with smoked paprika.

8. Place the pie on a parchment-lined baking sheet, transfer to the oven, and bake until the filling is deeply browned on top and set, 40 to 45 minutes. Cool the pie for at least 15 minutes before slicing and serving warm, or cool completely and serve at room temperature.

Make Ahead and Storage
The two fillings can be made up to 2 days ahead and stored in airtight containers in the refrigerator until ready to use. The crust can be parbaked up to 24 hours ahead. The baked pie is best the same day it's made.

Roasted Tomato Pie

Makes one 9-inch/23 cm deep-dish pie

DIFFICULTY: **EASY**

After a complicated start to my relationship with tomatoes early in life, I eventually "got it"—and fell hard. One of my favorite ways to enjoy them is in a classic Southern-style tomato pie. Layers of sliced tomatoes are piled into a crust and topped with a mixture of mayonnaise and shredded cheese. The oil in the mayonnaise melts in the oven, slowly coating the tomatoes resting underneath it and surrounding them as the two bake into the most delicious filling. The egg in the mayonnaise combines with the cheese to form a delectable, crisp top "crust." There's only one thing I do that breaks from the classic: I roast the tomatoes ahead to concentrate their moisture. This means I can pack more tomatoes into the crust without it threatening to become a soggy mess midbake, and it also ensures that it's sliceable post-bake and doesn't drastically sink as it cools.

About 1050 g / 6 large heirloom tomatoes, sliced ½ inch/1 cm thick

30 g / 2 tablespoons extra virgin olive oil

Kosher salt and freshly ground black pepper

One 9-inch/23 cm deep-dish pie crust made with Pâte Brisée (page 321), parbaked (see page 315) and cooled completely

45 g / 3 tablespoons Dijon mustard

50 g / ½ cup finely grated Parmesan cheese

20 g / ½ cup finely minced fresh chives

115 g / ½ cup mayonnaise

50 g / ½ cup shredded sharp cheddar cheese

Chopped fresh herbs for garnish (optional)

Thinly sliced tomatoes for garnish (optional)

1. Preheat the oven to 400°F/205°C with the racks in the upper and lower thirds.

2. Arrange the tomato slices in a single layer on two baking sheets. Drizzle the olive oil evenly over them and season with salt and pepper. Roast the tomatoes until they've released some juices and start to appear slightly dry on the surface, 20 to 25 minutes; rotate the sheets between the racks halfway through roasting.

3. Use an offset spatula to gently loosen each tomato slice from the baking sheets—they will have softened but should still be intact. Set aside to cool slightly. Reduce the oven temperature to 375°F/190°C.

4. Place the parbaked pie crust (still in the pie plate) on a parchment-lined baking sheet. Use a pastry brush to brush the mustard evenly over the base and up the sides of the crust. Sprinkle the cheese evenly over the base (you can shake the crust a little to help coat the sides of the crust with cheese the same way you would coat a cake pan with flour).

5. Arrange a layer of the roasted tomatoes, overlapping slightly, in the crust, packing them in tightly. Scatter some of the chives over the tomatoes and sprinkle with pepper. Continue layering the remaining tomatoes, sprinkling chives and pepper over each layer, finishing with the remaining chives and a little more black pepper.

6. In a small bowl, stir the mayonnaise and cheese together. Spoon this mixture over the surface of the pie and spread into a fairly even layer.

7. Transfer the pie to the oven and bake until the topping is deeply golden brown and crisp and

(CONTINUES)

the tomatoes are bubbly, 30 to 35 minutes. Remove from the oven and cool the pie to room temperature before slicing and serving. Garnish with fresh herbs and thin slices of fresh tomato, if desired, just before serving.

Variations

ROASTED TOMATO GALETTE: Reduce the amount of tomatoes to 680 g / 4 large heirloom tomatoes and roast and cool as directed in steps 1 and 2. Omit the pie crust. Instead, prepare a batch of Rough Puff Pastry (page 267). On a lightly floured surface, roll out the pastry into a round about 15 inches/38 cm wide and ¼ inch/6 mm thick. Use a rolling pin to gently transfer the dough to a parchment-lined baking sheet (it will hang over the edges of the pan for now, which is okay). Spread the mustard evenly over the crust, leaving a 1½-inch/4 cm border of dough uncovered all the way around. Sprinkle about half of the Parmesan evenly over the mustard. Arrange the roasted tomatoes, tightly overlapping the slices, in a spiral shape on top of the mustard/Parmesan. Sprinkle the chives over the tomatoes and season with black pepper. Dollop the mayonnaise and cheddar mixture over the surface and carefully spread into a fairly even layer. Fold the uncovered border of dough over, partially covering the tomatoes, letting the dough naturally pleat as you fold it over. Egg-wash the exposed dough and garnish with the remaining Parmesan. Bake at 400°F/205°C until the tomatoes are bubbly, the top and exposed crust are deeply golden brown, and the galette slides back and forth on the parchment when you gently shake the baking sheet, 40 to 45 minutes. If the crust or topping begins to brown too quickly, reduce the oven temperature to 375°F/190°C for the remainder of the bake time. Cool for at least 15 minutes before slicing and serving warm, or cool completely and serve at room temperature.

Make Ahead and Storage

The tomatoes can be roasted up to 2 days ahead and stored in an airtight container in the refrigerator. The crust can be parbaked up to 24 hours ahead. The pie is best the same day it's baked. Store leftovers at room temperature for up to 24 hours.

Preparing Tomatoes for Baking

When tomatoes are in season, they are exceptionally (and unpredictably!) juicy. Precooking them allows you the most flexibility, boosts the flavor, and helps ensure a less soggy end result in baked goods that feature tomatoes.

ROASTING: Roasting concentrates the moisture—and the flavor too. It's great for ripe summer tomatoes, heirloom varieties, and cherry tomatoes. Small and medium tomatoes can be roasted whole, larger tomatoes should be sliced or chopped. Leave slices thicker and chopped tomatoes a bit larger than you ultimately want them, as they will shrink as they cook. Put the tomatoes on a baking sheet (or sheets), toss or drizzle them with extra virgin olive oil, season with salt and pepper, if desired, and roast at 400°F/205°C. Roast whole tomatoes until the skin is blistered and the tomatoes collapse slightly; roast sliced or chopped tomatoes until they release some juices and the surface appears slightly dry (it's okay if they turn dark or even black at the edges). Cool before using.

BLANCHING, PEELING, AND SEEDING: Add the tomatoes to the water and blanch for 30 seconds to 1 minute, then transfer with a slotted spoon or spider to an ice water bath. Remove the skins, halve the tomatoes, and remove the seeds and stem ends. Blot the tomatoes dry and cool before using.

Quiche Any Way!

Just about anything is delicious enveloped in an eggy custard. See the basic ratios for different pan sizes below. I enjoy my quiche with a decent amount of vegetables, bacon, and/or cheese. If you prefer a plain custard, you may want to increase the amounts below by 56 to 113 g / 1 or 2 more eggs and another splash of dairy.

MINI (FOR 12 MUFFIN PAN–SIZED QUICHES OR ABOUT 24 MINI MUFFIN PAN–SIZED QUICHES): 226 g / 4 large eggs + 230 g / 1 cup milk, cream, or half-and-half

STANDARD PIE PLATE (9 INCHES/23 CM WIDE AND UP TO 1½ INCHES/4 CM DEEP): 340 g / 6 large eggs + 230 g / 1 cup milk, cream, or half-and-half

DEEP-DISH PIE PLATE (9 INCHES/23 CM WIDE AND 1½ INCHES/4 CM OR MORE DEEP): 454 g / 8 large eggs + 290 g / 1¼ cups milk, cream, or half-and-half

SKILLET (ABOUT 9 INCHES/23 CM ACROSS AT THE BASE AND AT LEAST 2 INCHES/5 CM DEEP): 510 g / 9 large eggs + 1½ cups milk, cream, or half-and-half

Now, what about those inclusions? I pile them into a parbaked crust and pour the custard over them. That way, I can ensure an even distribution throughout the custard. Here are a few of my favorite quiche combos:

- Asparagus, peas, and ricotta cheese
- Chopped bacon, spinach, and dollops of Tomato Jam (page 135)
- Crumbled cooked sausage, sautéed mushrooms and peppers, and grated provolone cheese
- Grilled vegetables with dollops of Pesto (page 96)
- Caramelized Onions (page 26), chopped fresh herbs, and grated Swiss cheese
- Diced ham, raw or leftover cooked greens, and sliced red onion

Cobb Quiche

Makes one 9-inch/23 cm quiche

DIFFICULTY: **MEDIUM**

My mom always says she is shocked at how many eggs I go through. It's not just the constant stream of cookies and cakes that are always being baked up in my kitchen—it's also the fact that I love to eat eggs. In the morning, I poach, boil, or fry myself an egg or two to get the day started. On busy days, my husband sometimes makes me an omelet or a scramble for lunch. I often make us quiche for dinner (or at almost any time of day), with a simple salad alongside. This quiche was designed to be an all-in-one situation, with the crisp salad served right on top of it. For even more quiche, check out the Wee Quiches on page 296, Croissant Breakfast Pie (page 241), and my ideas for creating your own variations on quiche on page 331.

QUICHE

One 9-inch/23 cm pie crust made with All-Buttah Pie Dough (page 319) or Pâte Brisée (page 321), parbaked (see page 315) and cooled completely

112 g / 1 cup (not packed) finely grated Parmesan cheese

215 g / 1½ cups diced cooked chicken

100 g / 1 cup finely chopped cooked bacon

140 g / 5 ounces blue cheese, crumbled

40 g / 4 scallions, thinly sliced

340 g / 6 large eggs

230 g / 1 cup whole milk

2 g / ½ teaspoon kosher salt

2 g / ½ teaspoon freshly ground black pepper

SALAD

45 g / 3 tablespoons extra virgin olive oil

15 g / 1 tablespoon red wine vinegar

5 g / 1 teaspoon Dijon mustard

Kosher salt and freshly ground black pepper

215 g / 1 large avocado, halved, pitted, peeled, and diced

Fresh lemon juice for the avocado

226 g / 1½ cups quartered cherry tomatoes

10 g / ¼ cup finely minced fresh chives

226 g / 8 ounces romaine lettuce, chopped (about 1 medium head)

1. Preheat the oven to 375°F/190°C with a rack in the bottom; if you have a baking steel or pizza stone, place it on the rack.

2. Place the cooled pie crust (still in the pan) on a parchment-lined baking sheet. Spread 56 g / ½ cup of the grated Parmesan evenly over the base of the crust. Arrange the chicken and bacon in an even layer on top of the Parmesan. Crumble the blue cheese over the top and sprinkle the scallions evenly over the cheese.

3. In a medium bowl, whisk the eggs, milk, salt, and pepper until well combined. Carefully pour the custard over the filling ingredients in the crust. Sprinkle the remaining 56 g / ½ cup Parmesan evenly over the top.

4. Transfer the pie to the oven and bake until the custard appears set around the edges but is still slightly jiggly in the center, 30 to 35 minutes. If you'd like, turn on the broiler and broil the quiche for 1 to 3 minutes, to brown the top. Cool for at least 15 minutes before slicing and serving warm, or cool completely before serving.

5. Just before serving, make the salad: In a jar, combine the oil, vinegar, and mustard. Seal the jar and shake the mixture well until thick and combined. Season with salt and pepper to taste.

6. In a large bowl, toss the avocado with a little lemon juice to coat. Add the tomatoes and chives and toss to combine. Add the romaine. Shake the dressing again, drizzle it over the salad, and toss well.

7. Serve slices of the quiche with the salad alongside, or pile the salad on top of the quiche before slicing (messy, but fun).

Make Ahead and Storage
The crust can be parbaked up to 24 hours ahead. The quiche is best eaten the same day it's made, but it can be held for up to 24 hours refrigerated (once cool). Refresh as directed on page 365. Store leftovers in the refrigerator, wrapped in plastic wrap.

Scrambled-Egg Tartlets with Peas

"Something light and romantic to start with—something that will go wonderful with champagne. Truffles go wonderful with champagne. AND scrambled eggs!"

Makes four 4-inch/10 cm tartlets

DIFFICULTY: **EASY**

So sayeth Sookie St. James of Gilmore Girls, *and so say I. For most of my life, I kept a mental checklist of traits my eventual life partner would have. My husband doesn't know it, but he checked one of these boxes very early on, long before we were married, when he made me a plate of scrambled eggs. One particularly romantic night, he piled the eggs into the center of a single plate, with buttered toast arranged neatly around it, for us to share. Eggs, toast, and champagne is the date night that sums up our life together—and to me, it's the sweetest. For anyone not convinced that scrambled eggs are romantic, I created these tartlets. They are both simple and beautiful—but if you've got an occasion to make them Sookie-level special, you can shave a few slices of fresh truffle on top.*

1 recipe Press-In Tart Dough (page 322), prepared through step 1

145 g / 1 cup fresh or frozen peas

115 g / ½ cup ricotta cheese

454 g / 8 large eggs

Kosher salt and freshly ground black pepper

56 g / 2 ounces / 4 tablespoons unsalted butter

30 g / 2 tablespoons heavy cream

10 g / ¼ cup minced fresh chives

1. Divide the dough into 4 equal pieces (about 75 g each). Put each piece into a 4-inch/10 cm tartlet pan and press some of the dough up the sides to line it, then pressing the rest of the dough evenly over the base of the pan. Dock each crust all over with the tines of a fork and refrigerate for 30 minutes. Toward the end of the chill time, preheat the oven to 375°F/190°C with a rack in the center.

2. Place the chilled tart shells on a baking sheet and transfer to the oven. Bake until the crust is evenly brown and appears set, 22 to 25 minutes. Cool completely.

3. Bring a medium pot of salted water to a boil. Set up a medium bowl of ice water. Add the peas to the boiling water and blanch until tender, 2 to 3 minutes. Drain the peas in a colander and transfer them to the ice water to stop the cooking, then drain and set aside.

4. Unmold the tartlet shells and place on individual plates or a serving platter. Spoon 30 g / 2 tablespoons ricotta into each shell and spread in an even layer.

5. In a medium bowl, whisk the eggs well to combine. Season with salt and pepper and whisk vigorously for 30 seconds to 1 minute.

6. Heat a large nonstick skillet over medium heat. When it's very hot, add the butter and swirl/tilt the pan so the butter evenly coats the base of the pan. Add the eggs to the pan and cook, stirring the eggs constantly with a silicone spatula, until they are almost set, 4 to 5 minutes. (Derek also swirls the pan as he cooks the eggs.)

7. Just before the eggs are set, remove the pan from the heat, add the cream, peas, and chives, and stir well to combine and heat throughout.

8. Immediately spoon the scrambled eggs into the tart shells and serve.

Note: This recipe is really adaptable because the blind-baked crust can be filled with just about anything. And if you don't have mini tartlet pans, you can divide the crust into 12 equal pieces (about 25 g each), press them into the cavities of a muffin pan, and blind-bake as directed on page 316. I sometimes use the rings of wide-mouth Mason jar lids as makeshift tart pans; the recipe will make 6 tartlets in the rings.

Make Ahead and Storage
The crusts can be blind-baked up to 24 hours ahead (if desired, refresh in a 350°F/175°C oven for 5 to 10 minutes to recrisp slightly). The assembled tarts are best served immediately.

Caramelized Onion Custard Tart

Makes one 9-inch/23 cm tart

DIFFICULTY: **EASY**

For lovers of all things onion, this tart is the stuff of dreams. My favorite part about it is that the very soft, caramelized onions and the thin layer of custard almost become one in the oven. Instead of a filling studded with onions, it eats like a creamy, oniony custard filling. I keep things simple here with a press-in tart crust, but this custard (and the one in the leek variation below) is also delicious in Pâte Brisée (page 321)—use it to line the tart pan and parbake as directed on page 315.

CARAMELIZED ONIONS

28 g / 1 ounce / 2 tablespoons unsalted butter

30 g / 2 tablespoons extra virgin olive oil

1280 g / 4 large sweet onions, halved lengthwise and thinly sliced

Kosher salt and freshly ground black pepper

45 g / 3 tablespoons apple brandy or apple cider

6 g / 2 teaspoons chopped fresh thyme

3 g / 4 large fresh sage leaves

TART

One 9-inch/23 cm crust made with Press-In Tart Dough (page 322), parbaked (see page 315) and cooled completely

113 g / 2 large eggs

80 g / ⅓ cup crème fraîche

6 g / 1 teaspoon kosher salt

1 g / ¼ teaspoon freshly ground white pepper

1 g / ¼ teaspoon freshly grated nutmeg

100 g / 1 cup shredded Gruyère cheese

1. Make the onions: In a large pot, heat the butter and olive oil over medium heat. When the butter is melted, add the onions and cook, stirring frequently, until they wilt and start to soften, 6 to 8 minutes. Reduce the heat to low, season with salt and pepper, and cook, stirring frequently, until the onions are deeply golden brown and caramelized, 40 to 50 minutes.

2. When the onions are caramelized, add the brandy or cider to the pan, stirring to deglaze it, then stir in the thyme and sage leaves. Cook, stirring frequently, until the liquid has entirely evaporated, then remove from the heat and cool to room temperature. When the onions are cool, remove and discard the sage leaves.

3. Preheat the oven to 375°F/190°C with a rack in the center.

4. Place the parbaked crust (still in its pan) on a parchment-lined baking sheet. Spoon the caramelized onions into the tart shell, spreading them evenly.

5. In a medium bowl, whisk the eggs well. Add the crème fraîche, salt, pepper, and nutmeg and whisk well to combine. Whisk in 75 g / ¾ cup of the cheese. Pour the custard over the onions in an even layer. Sprinkle the remaining cheese over the top.

6. Bake the tart until the custard is just set, 30 to 35 minutes. Cool for at least 15 minutes before slicing and serving warm, or cool completely and serve at room temperature.

Make Ahead and Storage
The caramelized onions (or leeks) can be made up to 2 days in advance and stored in an airtight container at room temperature. The tart is best within 24 hours of baking.

Broccoli Rabe, Sausage, and Ricotta Galette

Makes one 12-inch/30 cm galette

DIFFICULTY: **MEDIUM**

Early in my career, I scored a regular food-styling gig with a produce supplier who educated people about the wonder that is broccoli rabe, aiming to make it a more popular veg in the States. I spent four years cooking it in dozens of different ways, using recipes from cooks and recipe developers all over the country. I adore the bitterness of broccoli rabe in all its various forms. In this recipe, it's blanched and pureed with chives and Parmesan, baked in a rough puff pastry crust, and topped with a layer of juicy sausage and creamy ricotta: a perfect demonstration of what's to love about rabe.

BROCCOLI RABE PUREE

285 g / 1 bunch broccoli rabe (broccolini makes a fine, less bitter substitute), ends trimmed and coarsely chopped

140 g / 1 bunch fresh chives

50 g / ½ cup finely ground Parmesan cheese

60 g / ¼ cup extra virgin olive oil

15 g / 3 cloves garlic

Kosher salt and freshly ground black pepper

GALETTE

340 g / 12 ounces ground sausage (or about 4 sausages, casings removed and crumbled)

170 g / 1 small red onion, diced

1 recipe Rough Puff Pastry (page 267), chilled as directed

226 g / 1 cup ricotta cheese

Egg wash (see page 7) for finishing

Sesame seeds for garnish (optional)

1. Make the puree: Bring a large pot of water to a boil. Set up a medium bowl filled with ice water. Add the broccoli rabe to the boiling water and blanch for 2 minutes, stirring once or twice. Drain the broccoli rabe in a colander and transfer to the ice water to cool completely, then drain well.

2. Transfer the broccoli rabe to the bowl of a food processor, along with the chives, Parmesan, olive oil, and garlic. Process to a fairly smooth puree. Season with salt and pepper to taste and set aside.

3. Make the galette: Heat a large skillet over medium heat. Crumble the sausage into the hot pan and cook, stirring occasionally, until well browned, 5 to 7 minutes. Add the onions and cook just until wilted and softening, 2 to 3 minutes. Set aside to cool while you prepare the pastry.

4. Line a baking sheet with parchment paper. On a lightly floured surface, roll out the dough into a round about 15 inches/38 cm wide and ¼ inch/6 mm thick. Use the rolling pin to transfer the dough to the prepared baking sheet, unfurling it roughly into the center (it will hang over the edges of the pan at this point).

5. Spoon the broccoli rabe puree onto the center of the dough and spread into an even layer, leaving the outer 2 inches/5 cm of dough uncovered all the way around. Spoon the sausage and onion mixture evenly on top of the puree. Add the ricotta in heaping dollops over the surface of the filling. Gently fold the uncovered edges of the dough up and over to cover the edges of the filling, letting the dough naturally pleat as you go. Transfer the galette to the refrigerator.

6. Preheat the oven to 400°F/205°C with a rack in the center.

7. Remove the galette from the refrigerator and egg-wash the exposed dough. Sprinkle the sesame seeds, if using, over the exposed dough. Transfer to the oven and bake until the crust is deeply golden brown, 40 to 45 minutes; the galette should easily shift back and forth on the pan when you shake it lightly.

8. Cool the galette for at least 20 minutes on the baking sheet before serving warm, or cool completely and serve at room temperature.

Make Ahead and Storage
The broccoli rabe puree can be made up to 2 days ahead, as can the sausage and onion mixture. Store separately in airtight containers in the refrigerator. The baked pie is best the same day it's made.

Crispy Kale Skillet Galette

Makes one 12-inch/30 cm galette

DIFFICULTY: **EASY**

I always have a bunch—or a few bunches—of kale on hand in my refrigerator. It's hearty, has a long shelf life, and can be cooked in so many ways. One of my favorite ways to cook it is in a gratin, and this galette is like a greens gratin inside a crust. The kale is tossed with creamy béchamel before it is piled high into the crust, and then in the oven, the kale in the filling becomes soft while the top turns beautifully crisp.

2 recipes All-Buttah Pie Dough (page 319), made as one large batch and chilled

14 g / 1 tablespoon unsalted butter

75 g / 3 shallots, thinly sliced

1 recipe Béchamel Sauce (page 56), rewarmed until fluid and cooled slightly (not piping hot)

< 1 g / ¼ teaspoon freshly grated nutmeg

3 medium bunches lacinato kale, stems removed and leaves roughly torn

Kosher salt and freshly ground black pepper

140 g / 5 ounces sharp white cheddar cheese, shredded

Egg wash (see page 7) for finishing

1. On a lightly floured surface, roll out the dough into a round about 15 inches/38 cm wide and ¼ inch/6 mm thick. Use the rolling pin to transfer the dough to a 12-inch/30 cm cast-iron or other ovenproof skillet and unfurl it into the pan. Gently lift up the dough at the edges and use your hands to nudge it into the base of the pan, leaving an overhang all around. Cover with plastic wrap and refrigerate.

2. Preheat the oven to 375°F/190°C with a rack in the center; if you have a baking steel or baking stone, place it on the rack.

3. In a small skillet, melt the butter over medium heat. Add the shallots and cook until translucent, 3 to 4 minutes. Transfer to a large bowl and stir in the béchamel and nutmeg until well combined. Add the kale and toss until evenly coated. Season with salt and pepper.

4. Pile the kale into the pastry-lined skillet—it will be mounded quite high. Sprinkle the cheese all over the top. Fold the excess dough over the outer edges of the filling, letting it pleat naturally as you go. Egg-wash the surface of the dough.

5. Bake the galette until the crust is deeply golden brown and the surface of the kale is browned and crisp, 50 minutes to 1 hour.

6. Cool for 10 minutes before slicing and serving warm, or cool completely and serve at room temperature.

Make Ahead and Storage
This galette is best the same day it's baked.

Mini Beet Wellingtons

Makes 4 individual Wellingtons

DIFFICULTY: **MEDIUM**

I love the idea of beef Wellington, but I understand why it falls into the category of intimidating bakes. Subbing whole vegetables, like roasted beets, for the meat takes away one of the trickiest parts of the equation—getting the meat cooked just right. I also replaced the traditional mushroom mixture that's pressed onto the outside of the beef with a flavorful blend of tangy cheeses, chives, and smoked almonds. Then the whole thing is wrapped tightly in puff pastry for beautiful individual pie-packets that are just as impressive to slice into as their meatier cousin.

ROASTED BEETS

About 600 g / 4 large beets, peeled

30 g / 1 ounce / 2 tablespoons unsalted butter, melted

Kosher salt and freshly ground black pepper

WELLINGTONS

340 g / 12 ounces goat cheese

113 g / 4 ounces Gorgonzola dulce

60 g / ½ cup bread crumbs

10 g / ¼ cup minced fresh chives

8 ounces smoked almonds (or roasted almonds), very finely chopped (you can do this in the food processor)

1 recipe Rough Puff Pastry (page 267), chilled as directed

Egg wash (see page 7) for finishing

Freshly ground black pepper for garnish

1. Roast the beets: Preheat the oven to 400°F/205°C with a rack in the center. Have a baking sheet ready, along with four pieces of aluminum foil large enough to wrap up the beets.

2. In a large bowl, toss the beets with the melted butter until well coated. Place one beet on top of each piece of foil. Season with salt and pepper and drizzle any remaining butter over the beets, then wrap each one in foil and arrange on the baking sheet.

3. Transfer the baking sheet to the oven and roast until the beets are just fork-tender, 40 to 45 minutes. Carefully unwrap the beets and let cool completely. (Leave the oven on.)

4. Prepare the Wellingtons: In a medium bowl, mix the goat cheese, Gorgonzola, bread crumbs, and chives together until well combined. Place the nuts in a shallow bowl.

5. Divide the cheese mixture into 4 equal portions (about 130 g each). Use your hands to firmly press one portion in an even layer around one of the beets. Roll the beet in the ground nuts to coat thoroughly. Transfer to a plate and repeat with the remaining beets, cheese mixture, and nuts. Refrigerate while you roll out the dough.

6. On a lightly floured surface, roll out the dough to a square about ¼ inch/6 mm thick. Cut the dough into 4 circles large enough to wrap around the beets; since every beet is a little different, I usually place one of the beets in the center and use a paring knife to trace a circle around it, allowing plenty of excess so the beet will be fully encased (about 6 to 6 ½ inches/15 to 16 cm wide).

7. Wrap each beet completely in a round of pastry. Use a small amount of egg wash to help

seal the pastry seam on the bottom of the beets. Transfer the beets, seam side down, to a parchment-lined baking sheet. If the dough feels at all sticky or soft, refrigerate for 30 minutes before baking.

8. Egg-wash the surface of the pastry and sprinkle with black pepper. Transfer to the oven and bake until the crust is deeply golden brown, 35 to 40 minutes. Check the pastries about halfway through the bake time—if the crust has browned sufficiently, tent the Wellingtons with foil for the remainder of the bake time. Let rest for 10 minutes before serving warm.

Make Ahead and Storage
The beets can be prepared through step 7, wrapped well, and refrigerated for up to 24 hours before baking. The baked Wellingtons are best within a few hours of baking.

Moules Frites Tart

Makes one 10-inch/25 cm tart
DIFFICULTY: **HARD**

The first time I went to Paris, I was just a kid, and I fell in love as much as anyone who walks those lovely streets does. But it was a few more years until I fell in love with food, and in that sense, I didn't really experience Paris until my second trip. I visited bakery after bakery in the morning hours, and then somewhere around midday, my husband and I would sit down at a café and share some mussels and fries. I loved the tender mussels, and dunking my fries in their flavorful broth. While this may be an unusual combination for a tart, it's so much fun to make and serve. And, just like Paris, it's romantic, sharp, and a showstopper.

STEAMED MUSSELS

14 g / 1 tablespoon unsalted butter

50 g / 2 shallots, minced

15 g / 3 cloves garlic, minced

1020 g / 2¼ pounds fresh mussels, rinsed, cleaned, and debearded

290 g / 1¼ cups dry white wine

1 bay leaf

FRITES

Neutral oil (such as canola or vegetable) for deep-frying

570 g / 1¼ pounds russet potatoes, peeled

Kosher salt and freshly ground black pepper

FILLING

28 g / 1 ounce / 2 tablespoons unsalted butter

100 g / 4 shallots, minced

225 g / 3 cups diced mushrooms (from about 8 ounces mushrooms; any variety you like)

Reserved white wine broth (from above)

60 g / ¼ cup heavy cream

10 g / ¼ cup chopped fresh parsley

One 10-inch/23 cm tart crust made from Press-In Tart Dough (page 322), blind-baked (see page 316) and cooled completely

1. Make the mussels: In a large sauté pan, melt the butter over medium heat. Add the shallots and garlic and cook, stirring, until fragrant, about 1 minute. Add the mussels and toss to combine. Add the white wine and bay leaf and bring to a simmer over medium-high heat. Cover the pan and steam the mussels until they open, 4 to 6 minutes. Drain the mussels in a colander set over a bowl; reserve the broth. Discard the bay leaf.

2. Allow the mussels to cool until they are easy to handle, then remove them from the shells, discarding the shells, and transfer to a bowl. Cover and refrigerate.

3. Make the frites: Pour 2 inch/5 cm of oil into a medium pot. Attach a deep-fry thermometer to the side of the pot and heat the oil to 360°F/180°C (you can also carefully check the temperature with an instant-read thermometer). Line a baking sheet with a few layers of paper towels.

4. While the oil heats, cut the potatoes: You can cut them by hand or use a mandoline, which makes easier work of this—the ultimate goal is matchstick size. If using a knife, first cut the potatoes into very thin (⅛-inch-/3 mm thick) slices, then cut the slices into very thin strips.

5. Working in batches to avoid crowding the potatoes, add them to the hot oil by the handful and

fry, stirring them occasionally and monitoring them closely—they are thin and will cook quickly!—until they are evenly golden brown. Use a spider or slotted spoon to remove them from the hot oil and drain on the paper towels. Season immediately with salt and pepper, tossing to evenly distribute.

6. Make the filling: In a medium pot, melt the butter over medium heat. Add the shallots and cook until translucent, 4 to 5 minutes. Add the mushrooms and cook until they are tender and have browned slightly, 7 to 9 minutes.

7. Add the reserved mussel broth to the pot, bring to a simmer over medium-high heat, and cook until the liquid has almost entirely reduced (there should only be about 60 g / ¼ cup remaining), 6 to 9 minutes. Add the cream, bring to a simmer, and cook until the sauce thickens slightly, 2 to 3 minutes.

8. Remove the pot from the heat and stir in the reserved mussels. Fold in the parsley. Let cool for 10 minutes.

9. To serve: If desired, unmold the tart shell, then place it on a serving board or platter. Spoon the filling into the crust in an even layer and top with the frites. Serve immediately.

Make Ahead and Storage
The tart should be served as soon as it is assembled.

Tamale Pie-Pie

Makes one 9-inch/23 cm deep-dish pie

DIFFICULTY: MEDIUM

I love the concept of tamale pie: a base chili mixture topped with cornbread batter, then baked to casserole-level perfection. But as with most things called pie, I want it to have a yummy bottom crust too. Enter the tamale pie-pie. It's got both a delicious masa crust and a delicious cornbread topper, with plenty of the juicy meat filling inside. (This is also delicious made in a parbaked version of my Cornmeal Pie Crust in The Book on Pie.*)*

½ recipe (350 g) Corn Tortilla dough (page 209; you can make the rest of the dough into tortillas), prepared through step 3

FILLING

15 g / 1 tablespoon extra virgin olive oil

325 g / 1 large white onion

15 g / 3 cloves garlic, minced

454 g / 1 pound ground beef

6 g / 2 teaspoons chili powder

5 g / 1½ teaspoons ground cumin

3 g / 1 teaspoon onion powder

3 g / 1 teaspoon ground coriander

3 g / 1 teaspoon garlic powder

2 g / ½ teaspoon smoked paprika

Kosher salt and freshly ground black pepper

395 g / 1¾ cups prepared enchilada sauce

100 g / 1 cup shredded cheddar cheese

CORNBREAD TOPPER

80 g / ⅔ cup all-purpose flour

35 g / ¼ cup yellow cornmeal

13 g / 1 tablespoon light brown sugar

7 g / 1½ teaspoons baking powder

2 g / ½ teaspoon fine sea salt

75 g / ⅓ cup buttermilk, at room temperature

56 g / 1 large egg, at room temperature

14 g / 1 tablespoon unsalted butter, melted

One 113 g / 4-ounce can diced green chiles (optional)

100 g / 1 cup shredded cheddar cheese

1. Preheat the oven to 400°F/205°C with a rack in the center. Lightly grease a 9-inch/23 cm cast-iron skillet with nonstick spray.

2. Press the tortilla dough evenly over the base and up the sides of the prepared pan. Dock the base and sides a few times with a fork. Transfer to the oven and bake until the dough is starting to lightly darken at the edges, 18 to 20 minutes. Remove from the oven and set aside to cool.

3. Make the filling: In a large skillet, heat the oil over medium heat. Add the onion and cook until translucent, 4 to 5 minutes. Add the garlic and cook until fragrant, about 1 minute.

4. Add the beef, stirring to break up the meat, and cook, stirring occasionally, until well browned, 7 to 9 minutes. If there is a lot of fat in the pan, you can drain some of it off before proceeding.

5. Stir in the spices and enchilada sauce and bring to a simmer. Simmer, stirring occasionally, for about 5 minutes, until the mixture thickens slightly. Remove from the heat and cool for at least 30 minutes before using.

6. Pour the filling into the cooled crust and spread into an even layer. Scatter the cheese

evenly over the top. Set aside while you pre-heat the oven to 350°F/175°C.

7. Make the cornbread topper: In a medium bowl, whisk the flour, cornmeal, brown sugar, baking powder, and salt to combine. Add the buttermilk, egg, and melted butter and mix to combine. Fold in the chiles, if using.

8. Spoon the batter on top of the filling and top with the cheese. Transfer the pie to the oven and bake until the cornbread topper is baked through (a toothpick inserted into the center should come out clean) and the filling is bubbling, 30 to 35 minutes.

9. Cool for 10 to 15 minutes before slicing and serving.

Make Ahead and Storage
The filling can be made up to 2 days ahead and refrigerated in an airtight container. The pie is best the same day it is made.

347

Shepherd's Potpie

Makes one 9 x 13-inch/23 x 33 cm pie

DIFFICULTY: **EASY**

I've long struggled with shepherd's pie—which is to say, I actually love it, but as much as I love potatoes, I miss the pastry crust I associate with the word "pie." So my version includes both: a creamy mashed potato base and a crispy, flaky crust on top. It's the best of both worlds in one comforting casserole.

MASHED POTATO BASE

680 g / 1½ pounds russet potatoes, peeled and diced

170 g / 6 ounces cream cheese, at room temperature

57 g / ¼ cup sour cream

28 g / 1 ounce / 2 tablespoons unsalted butter

Kosher salt and freshly ground black pepper

FILLING

28 g / 1 ounce / 2 tablespoons unsalted butter

220 g / 1 large sweet onion, diced

220 g / 4 medium carrots, peeled and diced

200 g / 4 large stalks celery, diced

20 g / 4 cloves garlic, minced

40 g / 2 tablespoons tomato paste

680 g / 1½ pounds ground lamb

23 g / 3 tablespoons all-purpose flour

226 g / 1 cup beef broth

1 bay leaf

10 g / ¼ cup chopped fresh parsley

5 g / 1 tablespoon chopped fresh thyme

4 g / 2 teaspoons chopped fresh sage

200 g / 1⅓ cups fresh or frozen peas

Kosher salt and freshly ground black pepper

ASSEMBLY

½ recipe Rough Puff Pastry (page 267), chilled as directed

Egg wash (see page 7) for finishing

Flaky sea salt and freshly ground black pepper

1. Make the mashed potatoes: Place the potatoes in a medium pot and cover with water by at least 2 inches/5 cm. Bring to a boil over high heat, reduce the heat, and simmer until a fork easily pierces the flesh, 12 to 15 minutes. Drain the potatoes well and transfer to a medium bowl.

2. Add the cream cheese, sour cream, and butter to the potatoes and mash with a potato masher until relatively smooth. Season with salt and pepper.

3. Lightly grease a 9 x 13-inch/23 x 33 cm casserole dish, spoon the potatoes into it, and spread into an even layer. Set aside.

4. Make the filling: In a large pot, melt the butter over medium heat. Add the onions, carrots, and celery and cook until the onions begin to turn translucent, 4 to 5 minutes. Add the garlic and cook until fragrant, about 1 minute.

5. Add the tomato paste and cook for 1 minute, then add the lamb and cook until lightly browned, 5 to 6 minutes. Sprinkle the flour evenly over the lamb, stir well, and cook, stirring constantly, for 1 minute. Add the beef broth and bay leaf and cook over medium-low heat, stirring occasionally, until the liquid comes to a simmer and thickens, 3 to 5 minutes. Remove the bay leaf and stir in the parsley, thyme, sage, and peas. Season with

salt and pepper, remove from the heat, and set aside to cool.

6. While the lamb cools, prepare the dough: On a lightly floured surface, roll out the dough to a rectangle about 10 x 14 inches/25 x 36 cm and ¼ in/6 mm thick. Use the rolling pin to transfer the dough to a parchment-lined baking sheet. Cover with plastic wrap and refrigerate while you preheat the oven.

7. Preheat the oven to 400°F/205°C with a rack in the center.

8. Spoon the cooled lamb filling over the mashed potato base and spread into an even layer.

Uncover the pastry and use a pastry wheel or paring knife to cut it into random shapes (or use a cutter, or just unfurl the entire sheet of pastry on top of the filling. If you do this, be sure to use a paring knife to cut a few vents into the surface of the crust).

9. Arrange the pastry shapes on top of the filling, overlapping them as necessary to fully cover it. Egg-wash the dough and sprinkle with flaky salt and black pepper.

10. Transfer to the oven and bake until the crust is deeply golden brown and the filling is bubbly, 45 to 50 minutes. Cool for at least 10 minutes before scooping and serving warm.

Make Ahead and Storage
The mashed potato base and lamb filling can be made up to 24 hours ahead and refrigerated, covered. The pie is best the same day it's made. Store leftovers in the refrigerator in an airtight container.

Nearly-Full English Pies

Makes 8 individual pies

DIFFICULTY: **MEDIUM**

As a morning person, I'm a big fan of a good break-fast. Naturally, I am happy traveling in the UK, where huge, hearty "full" breakfasts are some-times the only thing on the morning menu. These pies boast all my favorite components of that classic—baked beans, bacon, sausage, mush-rooms, tomatoes, and eggs, atop a flaky, golden crust. Even if you're not a morning person, the smell of these little pies as they bake might make you into one.

BAKED BEANS

About 120 g / 4 strips thick-cut bacon, cut in half

170 g / 1 small sweet onion, minced

10 g / 2 cloves garlic, minced

One 425 g / 15-ounce can navy or white beans, drained well

60 g / ¼ cup ketchup

40 g / 3 tablespoons light or dark brown sugar

42 g / 2 tablespoons molasses

15 g / 1 tablespoon Worcestershire sauce

2 g / ½ teaspoon mustard powder

Kosher salt and freshly ground black pepper

PIES

140 g / 5 ounces ground breakfast sausage (or 4 to 5 sausages, casings removed)

75 g / 1 cup sliced mushrooms

250 g / 2 medium tomatoes, cut into 4 thick slices each

1 recipe Rough Puff Pastry (page 267), chilled as directed

8 fried eggs, jammy eggs, or scrambled eggs (see page 45) for serving

Minced fresh chives for garnish

Freshly ground black pepper for garnish

1. Make the baked beans: Heat a medium skillet over medium heat. Add the bacon and cook until the fat has rendered and the bacon is very crisp, 5 to 7 minutes. Using a slotted spoon, remove the bacon from the pan and reserve.

2. Add the onions to the fat remaining in the pan and cook until translucent, 4 to 5 minutes. Add the garlic and cook until fragrant, about 1 minute.

3. Stir in the beans, ketchup, brown sugar, molas-ses, Worcestershire, and mustard and cook, stirring frequently, until the sugar has dis-solved and the mixture is thoroughly com-bined. Season with salt and pepper, remove from the heat, and set aside.

4. Preheat the oven to 325°F/160°C with a rack in the center.

5. Lightly grease an 8 x 8-inch/20 x 20 cm square baking pan (or small casserole dish) with non-stick spray and pour the beans into it, spread-ing them in an even layer. Cover the pan tightly with aluminum foil, transfer to the oven, and bake until the sauce has thickened and the beans are very soft, 1½ to 2 hours. Set aside to cool completely.

6. Heat a medium skillet over medium heat. Crumble the sausage into the pan and cook, breaking it up into small bite-size crumbles, until well browned, 4 to 5 minutes. Transfer the sausage to a medium bowl and set aside.

(CONTINUES)

7. Add the mushrooms to the fat remaining in the pan and cook until they begin to soften, 3 to 4 minutes. Remove from the pan and set aside.

8. Crank the heat under the pan up to medium-high. When the pan is nice and hot, add the tomato slices and cook, turning once, until the surface appears slightly dry, 1 to 2 minutes per side. Remove from the pan and set aside.

9. Prepare the dough: Line two baking sheets with parchment paper. On a lightly floured surface, roll out the dough into a rectangle slightly larger than 12 x 24 inches/30 x 60 cm and about ¼ in/6 mm thick. Use a pastry wheel, bench knife, or knife to trim the dough to 12 x 24 inches/30 x 60 cm. Cut the dough into 8 equal squares (6 x 6 inches/15 x 15 cm) and place on the prepared baking sheets. Carefully fold about ½ inch/1 cm of two opposite sides of one square over to create a thicker "wall" of dough along those edges. Repeat on the two other sides, so the square has walls all around. Dock the bottom of the square (not the walls). Repeat with the remaining pieces of dough. Refrigerate, uncovered, while you preheat the oven.

10. Preheat the oven to 400°F/205°C with the racks in the upper and lower thirds.

11. Scoop about 55 g / scant ¼ cup beans into the center of each pastry. Place a half strip of the reserved bacon on top of each one on a diagonal. Divide the mushroom/sausage mixture evenly among the pastries, piling it on top. Finally, place a tomato slice on top of each one.

12. Egg-wash the edges of the crusts and transfer to the oven. Bake until the crust is deeply golden brown, 30 to 35 minutes.

13. Serve immediately, topping each pastry with a fried egg, jammy egg, or a scoop of scrambled eggs. Garnish with chives and pepper.

Make Ahead and Storage
The baked beans can be made up to 2 days ahead and refrigerated in an airtight container. The pies are best the same day they are baked.

Melon, Prosciutto, and Ricotta Tart

Makes 1 large tart (about 8 servings)

DIFFICULTY: **EASY**

This is one of my favorite ways to pie in the summer. A slab of crust is blind-baked, cooled, and then topped with fresh ingredients. The crust bakes quickly, which means less time with the oven on (a must, come summer). But the thing I love most? This produces incredibly beautiful tarts— you can really have fun arranging the ingredients on top. It's endlessly adaptable too; be sure to check out the Variations below. I like to finish the crust with a hefty sprinkling of Parmesan for extra saltiness and texture, but you can always leave it out to let the flavor of your toppings shine.

2 recipes All-Buttah Pie Dough (page 319), prepared as one large batch and chilled, or 1 recipe Rough Puff Pastry (page 267), chilled as directed

Egg wash (see page 7) as needed

Freshly grated Parmesan cheese for sprinkling (optional)

226 g / 1 cup whole-milk ricotta cheese

Freshly ground black pepper

255 g / 9 ounces thinly sliced honeydew or cantaloupe (about ¼ medium melon)

140 g / 5 ounces thinly sliced prosciutto

Torn fresh basil leaves for garnish

1. Preheat the oven to 400°F/205°C with a rack in the center; if you have a baking steel or baking stone, place it on the rack. Line a baking sheet with parchment paper, and have a second baking sheet and another piece of parchment at hand.

2. On a lightly floured surface, roll out the dough into a rough rectangle a little larger than 10 x 15 inches/25 x 38 cm and about ¼ inch / 3 mm thick. Use the rolling pin to gently transfer the pastry to the parchment-lined baking sheet. Use a pastry wheel or knife to trim the rectangle to 10 x 15 inches/25 x 38 cm. (Note: This doesn't really need to be precise, and you can opt not to trim the edges at all, although they may just brown a bit more.) If the dough feels at all sticky or warm, refrigerate it for 15 to 20 minutes before proceeding.

3. Cover the dough with the second piece of parchment paper and place the other baking sheet on top (this will help keep the pastry flat as it bakes). Transfer to the oven and bake until the dough has puffed up slightly and is starting to turn a pale golden color, 20 to 22 minutes. Remove from the oven and carefully lift off the top baking sheet and parchment paper.

4. Egg-wash the surface of the crust. If desired, sprinkle Parmesan cheese over the crust. Return the baking sheet to the oven and bake until the crust is deeply golden brown, 12 to 15 minutes more. Let the crust cool completely on the pan, then transfer it to a cutting board or serving platter.

5. Just before you're ready to serve, spread the ricotta cheese evenly over the crust. Sprinkle with pepper. Arrange the slices of melon and prosciutto over the cheese—you can do this in a more even, thinner layer with the ingredients overlapping slightly, or you can make it more rustic and voluminous. Sprinkle the basil over the top and serve immediately.

(CONTINUES)

Variations

MORTADELLA, PEACH, AND FETA TART
Replace the melon with an equal amount of thinly sliced peaches (about 2 medium peaches) and the prosciutto with sliced mortadella. After assembling, crumble 28 g / 1 ounce feta cheese over the surface of the tart.

BEET, ONION, HERB, AND GOAT CHEESE TART **Replace the melon and prosciutto with 340 g / 12 ounces cooked beets (about 4 medium beets), thinly sliced, and 85 g / ¾ cup thinly sliced rounds red onion (about 1 small onion). After assembling, crumble 28 g / 1 ounce goat cheese over the surface of the tart.**

SMOKED FISH, TOMATO, CUCUMBER, AND RICOTTA TART **Replace the melon with 170 g / 6 ounces ripe tomatoes (about 1 large or 2 to 3 medium tomatoes), thinly sliced, and 170 g / 6 ounces European (seedless) cucumber (about ½ cucumber), thinly sliced, and the prosciutto with an equal quantity of the smoked fish of your choice. Replace the basil with small dill sprigs. After assembling, sprinkle 20 g / 2 scallions, thinly sliced, and the dill over the surface of the tart.**

Spicy Eggplant Pie in Leftover-Rice Crust

Makes one 9-inch/23 cm pie

DIFFICULTY: **EASY**

I often say that you can turn just about anything into a pie—and that includes leftovers. I use leftover cooked rice to make this easy press-in crust. It's naturally gluten-free (see the Note if you want to make it vegan too), and this same technique can be used with just about any other kind of cooked grain, such as quinoa or bulgur, and small pastas like orzo also work. This is an excellent picnic or lunch-box pie because the rice keeps the filling packed tightly inside each slice, so it's easy to wrap a slice or two to carry with you.

CRUST

550 g / 3 packed cups cooked rice (any kind)

28 g / 1 ounce / 2 tablespoons unsalted butter, melted

28 g / ¼ cup white or black sesame seeds (optional)

4 g / 1 teaspoon fine sea salt

2 g / ½ teaspoon freshly ground black pepper

70 g / 2 large egg whites, lightly whisked

FILLING

906 g / 2 pounds eggplant, sliced into 1-inch-/ 2.5 cm thick rounds

Extra virgin olive oil for drizzling

60 g / ¼ cup white miso paste

21 g / 1 tablespoon honey

15 g / 1 tablespoon rice vinegar

15 g / 1 tablespoon soy sauce

10 g / 2 teaspoons sesame oil

30 to 45 g / 2 to 3 tablespoons sambal oelek

15 g / 1 serrano chile, minced

14 g / 2 tablespoons sesame seeds

300 g / 1 cup canned crushed tomatoes

140 g / 1 bunch scallions, thinly sliced

10 g / ¼ cup chopped fresh cilantro

1. Make the crust: Preheat the oven to 375°F/190°C with a rack in the center. Grease a 9-inch/23 cm springform pan lightly with nonstick spray and place on a baking sheet.

2. In a medium bowl, toss the rice and melted butter together. Add the sesame seeds, if using, salt, and pepper and toss well. Add the egg whites and mix until the rice is evenly coated. Scoop the rice mixture into the prepared springform pan and press it evenly over the base and about halfway up the sides.

3. Transfer to the oven and bake the crust until the edges are starting to lightly brown, 25 to 28 minutes. Remove from the oven and cool to room temperature. Raise the oven temperature to 425°F/220°C.

4. Make the filling: Arrange the eggplant in an even layer on a lightly greased baking sheet. Drizzle or brush a little olive oil over each slice of eggplant, then turn them over and drizzle or brush the other side. Transfer to the oven and roast until the bottom of the slices is lightly browned, 8 to 10 minutes.

5. Meanwhile, in a small bowl, whisk the miso, honey, vinegar, soy sauce, sesame oil, sambal oelek, serrano, and sesame seeds together.

6. Remove the eggplant from the oven and gently flip each slice over. Spoon a dollop of the miso

(CONTINUES)

mixture onto the center of each slice of eggplant, then use the back of the spoon to spread it fairly evenly across the eggplant. Return to the oven and roast until the miso mixture is browned and the eggplant is very tender, 10 to 15 minutes more. Remove from the oven and let cool until easy to handle. Reduce the oven temperature to 375°F/190°C.

7. Coarsely chop the eggplant into bite-size pieces and transfer to a large bowl. Add the tomatoes, scallions, and cilantro and stir to combine. Scoop the filling into the parbaked crust and pack tightly into an even layer.

8. Transfer the pie to the oven and bake until the top crust is browned and crisp, 20 to 25 minutes.

9. Cool the pie for 5 minutes before removing the ring of the springform pan. Slice and serve warm, or let cool and serve at room temperature.

Note: For a vegan replacement for the egg in the crust, whisk 12 g / 2 tablespoons flaxseed meal with 70 g / ⅓ cup warm water. Let sit for 5 minutes before using.

Make Ahead and Storage
The filling can be made up to 2 days ahead and refrigerated in an airtight container. The pie is best within 24 hours of baking.

Meat 'n' Potatoes Pie

Makes one 9-inch/23 cm deep-dish pie

DIFFICULTY: **MEDIUM**

Growing up in the Midwest meant that dinner was very often some kind of meat and potatoes. The combination also happens to make an excellent dinner pie—which is how this beauty found its way to my oven and table one blustery winter day. The filling is my go-to beef stew, made a bit thicker for pie so it's sliceable. Topped with a version of Duchess potatoes, this pie is perfect comfort food, but it's also equally worthy of an occasion.

FILLING

30 g / 2 tablespoons neutral oil (such as canola or vegetable)

906 g / 2 pounds beef stew meat, cut into 1-inch/2.5 cm cubes

Kosher salt and freshly ground black pepper

220 g / 1 medium sweet onion, diced

100 g / 2 stalks celery, diced

160 g / 3 medium carrots, peeled and diced

14 g / 1 tablespoon unsalted butter

40 g / ⅓ cup all-purpose flour

301 g / 1 cup beer

452 g / 2 cups beef broth

30 g / 2 tablespoons tomato paste

1 bay leaf

2 g / 1 tablespoon chopped fresh thyme

DUCHESS POTATOES

906 g / 2 pounds russet potatoes, peeled and diced

70 g / 2.5 ounces / 5 tablespoons unsalted butter, melted

60 g / ¼ cup heavy cream

65 g / 3 large egg yolks, at room temperature

25 g / ¼ cup freshly grated Parmesan cheese

Kosher salt and freshly ground black pepper

One 9-inch deep-dish pie crust made with All-Buttah Pie Dough (page 319), parbaked (see page 315) and cooled completely

1. Make the filling: In a large pot, heat the oil over medium heat. Season the beef with salt and pepper. Working in batches if necessary to avoid crowing the pot, add the beef to the pot and sear until well browned on all sides, 1 to 2 minutes per side. Transfer the beef to a plate and set aside.

2. Add the onion, celery, and carrots to the pot and cook until just starting to become tender, 4 to 5 minutes.

3. Add the butter to the pot and stir until melted. Sprinkle the flour over the vegetables and cook, stirring constantly, for 1 minute. Add the beer and stir well to deglaze the pot. Add the beef broth, tomato paste, and bay leaf and bring to a simmer, stirring occasionally.

4. Return the beef to the pot and simmer, uncovered, until tender, 40 to 50 minutes. Stir in the thyme and season the filling with salt and pepper. Remove from the heat and let cool completely.

5. While the filling is cooling, make the mashed potatoes: Place the potatoes into a medium pot and cover with water by at least 1 inch/ 2.5 cm. Bring to a boil over medium heat and cook until the potatoes are very tender, 18 to 20 minutes. Drain well.

6. Transfer the potatoes to a medium bowl and mash with a potato masher or large fork until very smooth. In a small bowl, whisk 56 g /

4 tablespoons of the melted butter, the cream, egg yolks, and Parmesan to combine. Fold this mixture into the mashed potatoes and mix until evenly combined. Season the mashed potatoes with salt and pepper and transfer to a pastry bag fitted with a large (½-inch/1 cm) star tip (or cut a ½-inch/1 cm opening in the bag).

7. Preheat the oven to 400°F/205°C with a rack in the center. Place the pie crust (still in the pan) on a parchment-lined baking sheet.

8. Scoop the cooled filling into the crust and spread in an even layer. Pipe the mashed potatoes in small spirals (the same way you might top a cupcake) all over the surface of the filling. Brush or drizzle the remaining 14 g / 1 tablespoon melted butter over the potatoes.

9. Transfer to the oven and bake until the potatoes are golden brown, the filling is bubbling up, and the crust is deeply golden brown. Cool for at least 15 minutes before slicing and serving warm.

Make Ahead and Storage
The beef filling can be made up to 3 days ahead and refrigerated in an airtight container. The pie is best eaten the same day it's made. Store leftovers in the refrigerator in an airtight container and serve at room temperature or slightly warmed.

Manchego Chess Pie

Makes one 9-inch/23 cm pie

DIFFICULTY: **EASY**

Chess pie is a classic custard pie, thickened with eggs and cornmeal. Cutting the sugar that's usually used and adding some shredded Manchego takes it to a deliciously salty place. For even bolder flavor, try the Yellow Curry and Garlic Chess Pie variation below. Both versions are delicious with a big salad (like the Always Salad, page 94).

One 9-inch/23 cm pie crust made with All-Buttah Pie Dough (page 319) or Pâte Brisée (page 321), parbaked (see page 315) and cooled completely

226 g / 4 large eggs

230 g / 1 cup buttermilk

5 g / 1 teaspoon apple cider vinegar

50 g / 3 tablespoons fine yellow cornmeal

28 g / 1 ounce / 2 tablespoons unsalted butter, melted

2 g / ½ teaspoon fine sea salt

2 g / ½ teaspoon freshly ground black pepper

1 g / ¼ teaspoon smoked paprika

125 g / 1¼ cups finely grated Manchego cheese

1. Preheat the oven to 375°F/190°C with a rack in the center. Place the pie crust (still in the pie plate) on a parchment-lined baking sheet.

2. In a medium bowl, whisk the eggs, buttermilk, vinegar, and cornmeal until well combined. Add the melted butter and whisk well to combine. Whisk in the salt, pepper, and paprika, then add the cheese and mix to combine.

3. Pour the custard into the prepared crust and transfer to the oven. Bake until the custard appears set around the edges but is still slightly jiggly in the center, 35 to 40 minutes.

4. The pie is delicious slightly warm, but I usually serve it at room temperature, letting it cool completely on a wire rack. You can also chill the pie for up to 24 hours and slice and serve cold.

Note: This pie is delicious paired with something fruity. Try spreading a thin layer of fig preserves over the surface of the fully cooled pie, or serve with thin slices of quince paste alongside.

Variation

YELLOW CURRY AND GARLIC CHESS PIE

Omit the smoked paprika and Manchego. Squeeze the cloves from 1 head Roasted Garlic (page 159) into a small bowl. Add 30 g / 2 tablespoons yellow curry paste and mash together with a fork until well combined. Whisk the melted butter into the bowl, then add to the cornmeal mixture at the point where the butter is added in step 2.

Make Ahead and Storage
The pie can be made up to 24 hours ahead and stored, loosely covered, in the refrigerator until ready to serve.

Enchilada Pie

Makes one 9-inch/23 cm deep-dish pie

DIFFICULTY: **EASY**

My mom loved the freezer-friendliness of enchiladas when I was growing up, often assembling multiple trays of them to keep on hand for big family suppers. My enchilada pie is similarly freezer-friendly (see Make Ahead and Storage, below) and just as craveably delicious. It's an all-in-one sort of dinner; I usually serve it with an array of toppings, like salsa, sour cream, and chopped tomatoes and jalapeños, so everyone can customize their own serving.

FILLING

15 g / 1 tablespoon neutral oil (such as canola or vegetable)

220 g / 1 medium white onion, diced

140 g / 1 bunch scallions, sliced into ½-inch/1 cm pieces

15 g / 3 cloves garlic, minced

About 560 g / 4 packed cups shredded cooked chicken

One 425 g / 15-ounce can black or pinto beans, drained

9 g / 1 tablespoon chili powder

6 g / 2 teaspoons ground cumin

3 g / 1 teaspoon ground coriander

3 g / 1 teaspoon onion powder

3 g / 1 teaspoon garlic powder

2 g / ½ teaspoon dried oregano, preferably Mexican

115 g / ½ cup prepared enchilada sauce

Kosher salt and freshly ground black pepper

100 g / 1 cup shredded Monterey Jack cheese

ASSEMBLY

Four XL Flour Tortillas (page 212), or store-bought 10-inch / 25 cm flour tortillas

135 g / 1⅓ cups prepared enchilada sauce

150 g / 1½ cups shredded Monterey Jack or cheddar cheese

SERVING (OPTIONAL)

Sour cream

Sliced jalapeños

Minced red onion

Chopped tomatoes

Chopped fresh cilantro

1. Preheat the oven to 350°F/165°C with a rack in the lower third. Lightly grease a 9-inch/23 cm springform pan with nonstick spray.

2. Make the filling: In a large pot, heat the oil over medium heat. Add the onions and cook until they start to become translucent, 4 to 5 minutes. Add the scallions and garlic and cook until fragrant, about 1 minute.

3. Add the chicken and beans and stir well to combine. Add the chili powder, cumin, coriander, onion powder, garlic powder, oregano, and enchilada sauce and heat, stirring occasionally, until the filling is hot throughout. Season with salt and pepper, stir in the cheese, and remove from the heat.

4. Assemble the pie: Heat a medium skillet over medium heat until it's nice and hot. Add one

(CONTINUES)

363

tortilla to the pan and heat it, turning once, to make it more pliable (but not to toast it), 10 to 15 seconds per side. Transfer it to the prepared springform pan, placing it so it covers the base and the edges come very slightly up the sides.

5. Spoon one-third of the filling into the springform pan. Heat another tortilla as directed above and place it on top of the filling, pressing down lightly. Pour ⅓ cup / 33 g of the enchilada sauce evenly over the tortilla, then top with one quarter of the cheese. Repeat this process, layering tortillas, filling, sauce, and cheese, finishing the stack with the final tortilla. Drizzle the remaining sauce on top, and sprinkle with the remaining cheese.

6. Transfer the pie to the oven and bake until the cheese is melty and bubbly and the edges of the crust are crisp, 30 to 35 minutes.

7. Remove from the oven and let cool for 10 minutes, then remove the springform ring. Slice the pie and serve immediately, garnished with sour cream, jalapeños, onion, tomatoes, and/or cilantro, if desired.

Variation

BEEF ENCHILADA PIE Substitute the ground beef filling from Frybread Tacos (page 191) for the chicken filling (you can stir in the beans and cheese from the chicken filling, if you like).

Make Ahead and Storage
The pie can be assembled up to 24 hours ahead and refrigerated, covered with plastic wrap. It can also be frozen, wrapped tightly in plastic wrap and then foil, for up to 1 month; thaw overnight in the refrigerator before baking. The baked pie is best served the same day it's made. Store leftovers tightly wrapped in the refrigerator; for best results, reheat in the microwave.

Rewarming Pastries

Since a lot of savory pastries are especially delicious served warm, it's great to know how to rewarm leftovers. Here's some guidance for some of the ways I reheat, in order of how much time they take/ how hungry you might be.

IN THE OVEN: Wrap the pastry in foil and place it in a 350°F/190°C oven for 8 to 10 minutes. The foil helps prevent the pastry from drying out and over-browning.

IN THE TOASTER OVEN: Wrap the pastry in foil and place it in a toaster oven on either the "toast" or "bake" setting for 3 to 4 minutes.

IN THE MICROWAVE: Okay, okay—some people will hate on me for this. But a lot of pastries heat well in the microwave, primarily because it doesn't take long. If the pastry has become stale, I wrap it in a lightly damp towel, which helps to steam it as it warms. Microwave for 15 to 20 seconds.

Resources

Bake It Up a Notch with Food52
food52.com/tags/bake-it-up-a-notch
Video tutorials on baking techniques.

Baking Steel
bakingsteel.com
My preferred brand, ideal for baking breads, pizzas, and pies.

Despaña
despanabrandfoods.com
Specialty ingredients, including vinegars, pickled peppers, and Spanish ham.

Field Company
fieldcompany.com
Cast-iron skillets and Dutch ovens.

Food52
food52.com/shop
Beeswax wrap, dough/bowl covers, rolling pins, and more.

IGourmet
igourmet.com
Spices and specialty ingredients.

Kerekes Baking Supply
bakedeco.com
Baking equipment, including springform pans, tart pans, and pie weights.

King Arthur Baking
kingarthurbaking.com
Baking equipment, bread-baking supplies, and specialty ingredients.

Masienda
masienda.com
Tortilla presses, comals, and masa.

Milk Street Store
store.177milkstreet.com
Equipment and specialty ingredients, including Calabrian chiles and balsamic pearls.

Tillamook
tillamook.com
Butter, cream cheese, and cheese.

Weee!
sayweee.com
Asian ingredients, including bao flour and chile crisp.

Acknowledgments

Baking up a book is a huge task, and I'm so grateful for all the people who ensured I didn't have to do it alone!

Thank you to my agent, Doe Coover, for helping bring this idea to fruition. Thank you to my editor, Sarah Kwak, for her wise advice and for letting me be myself. Thank you to Allison Chi, Tai Blanche, and Mumtaz Mustafa for thoughtful, beautiful ideas and for letting me be involved in the process. Thank you to Judith Sutton for your thoughtful copyediting. Thank you to Rachel Meyers, Katie Tull, Hannah Dirgins, and the entire team at HarperCollins Publishers for supporting this project.

Thank you to Alahna Blakeman for helping me keep my eye on the ball and my head in the game.

Thank you to the many wonderful recipe testers who lent a hand for this savory creation: Evan Coben, Kelly Dumke, Derek Laughren, Kathy McDowell, Steve McDowell, Kaitlin Wayne, and Stephanie Whitten. Thanks to the friends and family who provided all kinds of support: Liliana Cabrera, Chris Hurte, Theresa Katan, Rose Levy Beranbaum, Abby McDowell, Sarah McDowell, Willie McDowell, Rachel Oliver, Mercedes Spanoudakis, Martha Velásquez, and Maggie Wheeler.

Thank you to everyone who helped on the photo shoot: To Mark Weinberg—I'm so grateful to get to be in the same room as you when you do your magic! Thanks for making this project such a special one. To Kaitlin Wayne—thank you for your skills, enthusiasm, and support in and out of the kitchen. I couldn't have done this year without you! Thank you to Stephanie Loo, Stephanie Whitten, and Shilpa Uskokovic for all your hard work and thoughtful insights. I'm so grateful to have had your brilliant hands and brains in my kitchen for a few magical days!

Thank you to Amanda Hesser and the staff of Food52 for their support—and a shout-out to Gabriella Mangino and the video and creative teams for their help in times of need.

Thank you to my friends at Tillamook for providing enough butter for all my wildest dreams.

Thank you to ButcherBox for keeping us in perfect proteins.

To Cafasso's Fairway Market in Fort Lee, New Jersey: You're very special, and I love you.

Thank you to my niblings who always inspire me: Tim, Arlo, Jocelyn, and Lucy.

To my incredible mom and dad for always going above and beyond.

And to my husband, Derek Laughren. There aren't enough words to thank you for all you did to help me make this book. I truly, madly, deeply . . . couldn't have done it without you. Thank you.

Index

31192022458473